LUTHER'S WORKS

LUTHER'S WORKS

WORKS

VOLUME 28

COMMENTARIES ON
1 CORINTHIANS 7
1 CORINTHIANS 15

LECTURES ON
1 TIMOTHY

HILTON C. OSWALD
Editor

CONCORDIA PUBLISHING HOUSE · SAINT LOUIS

Contents

General Introduction	vii
Introduction to Volume 28	ix
COMMENTARY ON 1 CORINTHIANS 7	1
COMMENTARY ON 1 CORINTHIANS 15	57
LECTURES ON 1 TIMOTHY	215
CHAPTER ONE	217
CHAPTER TWO	256
CHAPTER THREE	281
CHAPTER FOUR	308
CHAPTER FIVE	332
CHAPTER SIX	361
Indexes	385

General Introduction

THE first editions of Luther's collected works appeared in the sixteenth century, and so did the first efforts to make him "speak English." In America serious attempts in these directions were made for the first time in the nineteenth century. The Saint Louis edition of Luther was the first endeavor on American soil to publish a collected edition of his works, and the Henkel Press in Newmarket, Virginia, was the first to publish some of Luther's writings in an English translation. During the first decade of the twentieth century, J. N. Lenker produced translations of Luther's sermons and commentaries in thirteen volumes. A few years later the first of the six volumes in the Philadelphia (or Holman) edition of the *Works of Martin Luther* appeared. Miscellaneous other works were published at one time or another. But a growing recognition of the need for more of Luther's works in English has resulted in this American edition of Luther's works.

The edition is intended primarily for the reader whose knowledge of late medieval Latin and sixteenth-century German is too small to permit him to work with Luther in the original languages. Those who can, will continue to read Luther in his original words as these have been assembled in the monumental Weimar edition (*D. Martin Luthers Werke*. Kritische Gesamtausgabe; Weimar, 1883 ff.). Its texts and helps have formed a basis for this edition, though in certain places we have felt constrained to depart from its readings and findings. We have tried throughout to translate Luther as he thought translating should be done. That is, we have striven for faithfulness on the basis of the best lexicographical materials available. But where literal accuracy and clarity have conflicted, it is clarity that we have preferred, so that sometimes paraphrase seemed more faithful than literal fidelity. We have proceeded in a similar way in the matter of Bible versions, translating Luther's translations. Where this could be done by the use of an existing English version — King James, Douay, or Revised Standard — we have done so. Where it could not, we have supplied our own. To indicate this in each specific instance would have been pedantic; to adopt a uniform procedure would have been artificial — especially in view of Luther's own inconsistency in this regard. In each volume the translator will be responsible primarily for matters of text and language, while the responsibility of the editor will extend principally to the historical and theological matters reflected in the introductions and notes.

Although the edition as planned will include fifty-five volumes, Luther's writings are not being translated in their entirety. Nor should they be. As he was the first to insist, much of what he wrote and said was not that important. Thus the edition is a selection of works that have proved their importance for the faith, life, and history of the Christian Church. The first thirty volumes contain Luther's expositions of various Biblical books, while the remaining volumes include what are usually called his "Reformation writings" and other occasional pieces. The final volume of the set will be an index volume; in addition to an index of quotations, proper names, and topics, and a list of corrections and changes, it will contain a glossary of many of the technical terms that recur in Luther's works and that cannot be defined each time they appear. Obviously Luther cannot be forced into any neat set of rubrics. He can provide his reader with bits of autobiography or with political observations as he expounds a psalm, and he can speak tenderly about the meaning of the faith in the midst of polemics against his opponents. It is the hope of publishers, editors, and translators that through this edition the message of Luther's faith will speak more clearly to the modern church.

JAROSLAV PELIKAN
HELMUT LEHMANN

Introduction to Volume 28

I N this volume we have brought together three shorter commentaries on Pauline epistles by Dr. Martin Luther: a 1523 commentary on 1 Corinthians 7 in the form of "wedding present" for a friend, a 1534 commentary on 1 Corinthians 15 in the form of a series of sermons, and the 1527–28 lectures on 1 Timothy.

The first of these is an exposition of 1 Cor. 7 with special emphasis on the blessings of Christian marriage and on the freedom to marry or not to marry.

Luther had not himself deigned to write a specific answer to John Faber's 1521 *Opus adversus nova quaedam et a christiana religione prorsus aliena dogmata Martini Lutheri,* newly reprinted in Leipzig in April 1523, after it had already drawn from Erasmus the comment: "Faber is bold to utter whatever comes into his mouth, but eventually he will meet an avenger, and the dagger will be put to the whetstone." It fell to Justus Jonas to take up the gauntlet, for as a newlywed he was particularly touched by detailed defense of the celibacy of the priesthood in Faber's book. Faber had set out to write a refutation of Luther's defense for his thesis concerning the authority of the pope and the jurisdiction of the church of Rome, but it was the treatment of celibacy in Faber's book that aroused special interest. It was at this point, too, that the reply to Faber scored best. The coarse directness of the Jonas style was felt to be refreshing over against the class-conscious, sophisticated, learned diatribe of the cleric. Faber, who admitted that he was anxiously awaiting Luther's own reply to his book, must have been especially chagrined to have Jonas taunt him with the statement that he had accomplished what neither pope nor schoolmen nor ecclesiastical orders had been able to do so far, to silence Luther — but only because Luther's friends had begged him to spare the poor man.

But even though Luther did not reply to Faber but contented himself with appending a letter of encouragement to the reply of Justus Jonas, he probably was moved more than ordinarily by the effusions of Faber to study particularly 1 Cor. 7, the chapter on which, ever since

Jerome, the church had confidently based its views concerning the preeminence of the celibate life. Melanchthon had already given a commentary on this chapter in 1522, had criticized Jerome as "superstitiously extolling celibacy," and had emphasized that "neither celibacy nor marriage is prescribed" but that "either one is to be chosen without sin."[1] But his commentary was too brief to provide convincing exegetical proof, and so Luther felt obliged, in spite of a busy schedule, to supply what was needed — an exegetical study of the whole chapter. He completed his work in August 1523 and dedicated it to Hans von Löser as "a Christian epithalamium" for Löser's wedding, which took place the following year and at which Luther performed the ceremony. There was a Catholic answer, though not until 1527, when Conrad Kollin, the prior of the Dominican monastery at Cologne issued his *Refutation of the Lutheran Wedding Song*.[2] Luther apparently never took note of it.

Our second item is a series of sermons on the Christian view of death. These sermons form a running commentary on 1 Corinthians 15. Luther's activities as a preacher in 1532 suffered many interruptions on account of recurring poor health. For weeks at a time he was not able to do any work, so that he complained, "I eat, drink, and sleep, but I cannot read, write, or preach. I am nothing but a bother to the world." For a while his preaching was confined to his own house, but eventually he was able to resume his full schedule of sermons. The death of Elector John the Steadfast on August 16 and the presence in Wittenberg of his son and successor, John Frederick I, occasioned an additional special series of sermons in the castle church from August 18 to September 6, especially the funeral sermon on Sunday, August 18, on 1 Thess. 4:13 ff., and a continued exposition of this text the following Thursday.

The first of this series of 17 sermons on 1 Cor. 15 was preached August 11, in the afternoon, and the series continued, mostly Sunday afternoons, with some interruptions, until April 27, 1533. George Rörer preserved both the dates and the sermons themselves. Caspar Cruciger freely edited and published the set of sermons in German and dedicated the collection to Elector John Frederick, saying in his dedicatory preface: "May it please your Grace to lend the association of your name to these sermons . . . for it is of the utmost importance

---

[1] Cf. *Corpus Reformatorum*, XV, 441.
[2] *Eversio Lutherani epithalamii.*

to promote the Word of God in every way before the ungrateful world to attract and draw insolent hearts to it."

The lectures on 1 Timothy complete the series of shorter lectures (together with lectures on Titus, Philemon, and 1 John [*Luther's Works*, Vols. 29 and 30]), which Luther held at Wittenberg during the period August 1527 to March 1528, when the university was officially in residence at Jena, having left Wittenberg on account of a plague. Among the few who chose to remain in Wittenberg with Luther and Bugenhagen throughout these trying months was George Rörer, that faithful auditor and recorder of Luther's lectures and sermons. He incidentally provided our only external witness concerning time and place of these lectures when in a letter of February 26, 1528, he writes to Stephan Roth that in spite of the well-meant advice of Roth and also of Bugenhagen that he should seek a "change of air" because of recent delicate health he cannot see his way clear now to leave Wittenberg "before Dr. Martin puts the finishing touch on the First Epistle to Timothy," but that he is thinking of leaving right after Easter (April 12). Thus the return of the university to Wittenberg would approximately coincide with the conclusion of these lectures.

Rörer's persistence provides us with a full transcript (but also the only one) of these lectures. His characteristic interest also provides notations of the dates on which the lectures were held, except that Rörer apparently neglected to enter one date between March 9 and 12, for the material assigned to March 9 is approximately twice the volume of a normal lecture. The lectures began January 13 and ended March 31. The week of January 27 no lectures were held because Luther was away at Torgau, and between March 16 and 30 there were no lectures because of trips to Altenburg and Torgau.

But Rörer obviously did not have opportunity to revise and prepare this transcript for publication. The manuscript reveals problems similar to those encountered in the commentaries on Titus and Philemon of about the same time (cf. *Luther's Works*, 29, p. x). Most bothersome are those sentences which end abruptly with "etc." What Rörer did not supply (either because of Luther's fast dictation or because of Luther's abrupt style) is not always self-evident, as the "etc." would suggest. We have either indicated as conjectures such additions as seemed reasonable or transmitted the original without additions when more than one solution to the problem seemed possible.

H. O.

COMMENTARY ON
1 CORINTHIANS 7

Translated by
EDWARD SITTLER

TO THE AUGUST AND HONORABLE HANS LOSER OF PRETZSCH, HEREDITARY MARSHAL OF SAXONY, MY GRACIOUS LORD AND FRIEND[1]

GRACE and peace in Christ! August and honorable sir, my dear Lord and friend: I am keeping my promise to you according to my capacities and am most hopeful that you, too, according to your noble inclinations, will do as you said and no longer postpone your marriage. But that you may approach this in as Christian a way as possible, I have taken it upon myself to interpret the seventh chapter of the First Epistle of St. Paul to the Corinthians — this I do as a service to you and as an aid to all those who take a liking to it. My reason for this choice is that this very chapter, more than all the other writings of the entire Bible, has been twisted back and forth to condemn the married state and at the same time to give a strong appearance of sanctity to the dangerous and peculiar state of celibacy. And to tell the truth, none have given themselves such airs with this chapter as the very people who have been least chaste. I, too, once considered chastity as ordinary as they pretend it to be. But, thank God, the last three years have taught me how little chastity there is in the world outside marriage, both in convents and monasteries.

But God has laid it upon me to preach about marriage and to tear the veil from the chastity which is of the devil, so that there may be less fornication and our poor youth may not be so pitiably and dangerously misled by falsely glorified chastity. Therefore I must take particular care that this chapter, which is their principal defense, no longer remain to cover their shame but be understood according to the true meaning of St. Paul. And so I should like to give you this on the occasion of your wedding;[2] thus I, too, shall once have sung a Christian epithalamium, or wedding song, as they used to do in the

---

[1] In 1531 Luther dedicated his exposition of Ps. 147 to the marshal of the elector of Saxony. In 1533 Löser, together with Melanchthon and Jonas, was a sponsor at the baptism of Luther's son Paul. Cf. *Luther's Works,* 14, p. 110; 54, p. 184.

[2] Not until December 1524 did Löser marry Ursula von Portzig. Luther performed the ceremony at Pretzsch in the presence of Amsdorf, Melanchthon, and Jonas.

olden days, so that your plans may be carried out to the honor of God and for the promotion and fulfillment of your own blessedness. With this I commend you and your dear bride to the mercy of God. Amen.

Wittenberg, in the year 1523

Martin Luther

PREFACE[1]

"WHAT a fool is he who takes a wife," says the world, and it is certainly true. And many learned scholars have decided that a wise
man should not take a wife, even if she were wisdom personified. This,
too, is true and well said, for those who believe that there is no life
after this one (as such people do) act almost wisely in falling back on
free fornication and not tying themselves to the labor of married life.
In this way they have at least fewer evil days in this life. Our clergy
have also grasped this point and have neatly committed themselves to
chastity, that is, to free fornication, as Dan. 11:37 [2] prophesied of them
when he said: "They will neither regard nor desire women."

But on the other hand the Spirit says: "He is a wise man who takes
a wife." This, too, is certainly true, and this truth leads to the conclusion that a wise man should take a wife, even though she were foolishness personified. This, too, is right and well said, for since a Christian
man is waiting for another life after this one, it is a matter of wisdom
that he should have fewer good days on earth so that in eternal life
he might enjoy only happy ones; and this seemed good to God when
He created man and woman and brought them together.

In other words, there are two different views of matrimony: one
derives from the smart alecks and sophisticates, that is, the principal
fools and blind men in the sight of God. These fellows view the state
of marriage as a superfluous, presumptuous human thing that one
could dispense with and do without, just as I can do without an extra
jacket or coat. Then they fill the world with their foolish and blasphemous scribbling and screeching against the married state, advising all
men against it, although they themselves feel — and abundantly demonstrate by their actions — that they cannot do without women, these
being created specifically for marriage; instead they run after and
plague themselves with whores day and night.

Of this kind is that arch-fool, Johann Schmid of Constance,[3] that

<hr>

[1] Only the Latin translation of 1525 has this heading.

[2] The Weimar text has Dan. 8, but the Erlangen edition, following the
Wittenberg edition, has Dan. 12.

[3] Johann Heigerlin of Leutkirch, the son of a smith and therefore also called
Fabri, Faber, or Schmid, had been rewarded with the canonicate of Constance
for his defense of the papacy against Luther. His *Opus adversus nova quaedam
et a christiana religione prorsus aliena dogmata Martini Lutheri,* originally pub-

renowned whoremonger, who has written an immense book, recently
printed in Leipzig, against the state of matrimony. He tries to talk
everyone out of it but says nothing more than that there is much effort
and labor connected with it, as though this were not sufficiently known
throughout the world and as if this ass must first teach us what every
village peasant knows. If I were chastity herself, I could think of no
greater and more unbearable shame and disgrace than to be praised
by such rascals, whoremongers, and enemies of chastity. They rail
against us, charging that we are enemies of chastity and promoters of
marriage who prefer to see men married; and we are to consider them
extremely wise, though they cannot but devote themselves to incessant
fornication and though they praise chastity with their pens only and
defame the married state.

They are rascals, not only on the surface but in the bottom of their
hearts, and they are unworthy of an answer. And what matter if the
whole world were to complain about the state of matrimony? We see
right before our eyes that God daily creates not only men but also
women and maintains their lives; and yet it is certain that he does not
create any woman for the purpose of fornication. But since God's work
and Word stare us in the face, declaring that women must be used
either for marriage or for fornication, these heathenish pretenders
should shut their blasphemous mouths and leave God's Word and
work uncriticized and unhampered; unless perhaps they would like to
teach us according to their own famed sagacity and contrary to God
that all women should be strangled or banished. This would make
a fine fool of God: what He does is no good; what we do is well done.

Now therefore since God created woman that she should and must
be with man, it should suffice us that God is on our side, and we should
honor the married state as a divine and noble institution. And if the
wiseacres do not want to enter it, then let them continue in their
heathenish blindness to practice rascality and fornication so long as
God may allow it. We have God's Word on our side; that will remain
and not be moved by such blundering Smiths,[4] though they were more

lished in Rome in 1522 and then reprinted in Leipzig in 1523 under the auspices
of Duke George of Saxony, was a sellout. The answer to this attack on Luther,
though impatiently awaited even by Faber himself, did not come until later in
1523, and then from the pen of Justus Jonas, a more suitable protagonist on the
subject of marriage since he had married already in February 1522, whereas
Luther was still single. Luther contented himself with the incidental defense
contained in the present essay.

4 See n. 3 above.

numerous than the sands of the sea. Still it is a great sin and shame that we Christians have become such great fools that we first have to ponder and decide whether women ought to be married or not, just as though someone should ask whether he ought to eat and drink in this life. Now let us hear the words of St. Paul.[5]

[5] The Weimar edition quotes the full text of Luther's German translation of 1 Cor. 7 at this point. Since that text is repeated as commented upon, we have omitted it here.

The Seventh Chapter
of the First Epistle of St. Paul
to the Corinthians

THE occasion of the writing of this chapter was this: Those people of Corinth who became Christians, especially those converted from Judaism, held to the law of Moses in addition to the Gospel. But Moses had commanded every person to marry: every man was to have a woman, every woman was to have a man, for celibacy was condemned as an unproductive state. This all happened because Christ had been foretold as coming from the seed of Abraham, and since nobody knew which person that was to be, all Jews had to marry in honor of this seed and submit until He came.

So the Corinthians asked whether they still had to keep this law of Moses or had authority to remain unmarried, saying that they had a desire and love for chastity and had been freed from many other laws of Moses through the Gospel. Those of weak conscience found it difficult to abandon the law of Moses, to which they were accustomed. Here St. Paul answers them and says that to remain chaste is not only free but also good for those who have the will and desire for it. But he speaks rather shyly and carefully about this and persists in bringing in the state of matrimony, saying:

1. *It is well for a man not to touch a woman.*

2. *But because of the temptation to immorality, each man should have his own wife, and each woman her own husband.*

Consider how quickly he breaks off in this statement, saying that it is well not to touch a woman, but he neither commands nor advises anybody to follow this but quickly goes over to talk of marriage as though he were afraid that such a fine thing would become rare and degenerate into general fornication, and so he orders that each should have his own spouse to avoid fornication. This, then, would be the first conclusion: that whoever does not feel that he has that precious quality but rather is inclined to fornication, he is commanded to marry. And this commandment is to be received as coming not from a human being but from God. From this it follows that nobody can vow to be chaste, nor should he keep such a vow but rather break it if he finds or feels that he does not have that precious quality but is inclined to fornication; for such a vow is really made contrary to God's command. But one cannot vow anything against God's command, and even if the vow were made, still he is condemned who keeps it.

This touching of a woman has been interpreted so narrowly by some that they do not even want to touch the hands or the skin of a woman. For this purpose they have made many laws and regulations in order to keep themselves so far removed from women that they could neither see nor hear them, thinking that by so doing they had promoted chastity in a masterly fashion. This kind of thinking is typical of those who conceived of and founded monasteries and nunneries, or thought to preserve chastity by keeping the boys away from the girls and the girls from the boys. How this turned out and how they made room for the devil in so doing — this would be awful to hear and tell.

Such poor blinded people thought chastity could be put into people from without, whereas it is a gift from heaven and must come from within. Although it is true that there is attraction and temptation wherever men and women are together, the matter is not helped by separating them. For how does it help me if I do not see, hear, or touch a woman and still my heart is full of women and my thoughts are taken up with them day and night, thinking of the shameless things that one might do? And of what help is it to a girl to shut her up so that she neither sees nor hears a man, when her heart still sighs day and night, without ceasing, for a young man?

One has to have the heart for chastity, otherwise all such things are worse than hell and purgatory. Therefore these words of St. Paul must be understood in a spiritual sense and for the heart, in this way: he is spoken of as not touching a woman who because of his own heart's desire and love keeps his body away from women, but not the one who outwardly remains chaste with women yet inwardly and in his heart is full of desire and love for women. The latter is a hypocrite whose chastity is a pretense before others but lost before God, yes, a double unchastity. The words of St. Paul are spoken in the freedom of the spirit, demand a free spirit, and must be understood with a free spirit. But hypocrites are unwilling to understand them so. They make a dead letter and cowardly law of them, a law that applies force and makes their lost false chastity difficult with outward abstinence from women.

Just consider for a moment what reprehensible murderers of souls they are who want to force this outward chastity upon young people, forcing them to bear this secret suffering (as they call it) without ever considering whether they have the inner will and desire for it. They think that the bitterer chastity is for someone and the harder to endure, the more precious it will be to God, just like any other bodily suffering or accident. They cannot see that the difference between such suffering and bodily suffering is greater than that between heaven and earth, for one can bear other sufferings in good conscience without sin, and the suffering is only physical pain. But this suffering is a sinful suffering that one cannot bear in good conscience, for in itself it is sin and wrong. Therefore there is no help or counsel for it except to escape it and get rid of it. This can be achieved through marriage and in no other way. But in the other suffering we should counsel them to patience, even if they cannot rid themselves of their suffering.

In the same way St. Paul wants us to understand his words spiritually also when he says, "It is well for a man not to touch a woman," namely, what is well here is not to be thought of as virtue before God, as though a celibate were better in the sight of God than a married man, as the text has also been interpreted so far by St. Jerome.[1] Such an effect belongs only to faith and not to works. Rather these words speak of the temporal security and rest that a celibate has in this life as compared with a married man. For whoever lives unmarried and a celibate is relieved of all the labor and disgust which are a part of the married state. In short: It is a beautiful, delightful, and noble gift for him to whom it is given to have the will and desire for celibacy, and St. Paul will later explain in detail what he means by this gift. He did not want to leave those uncomforted who desired to remain celibates. Still one must not deny that before God a married woman is better than a virgin, although the married woman has much labor and trouble here on earth, and the virgin much happiness, ease, and comfort.

Here then is St. Paul's meaning: It is well for a man not to touch a woman, and in the New Testament — unlike the Old — it is not a sin for a man to be without wife and child. In other words, whoever has the grace by choice and desire to live the life of a celibate can look forward to happy days, as the proverb says: "Fool, take a wife, and that will end your joy," or again: "Marriage is brief joy and long disgust," and many similar proverbs concerning the married state, all of them agreeing with St. Paul's statement here that it is well for a man

---

[1] Jerome, *Adversus Iovinianum*, I, 3 ff., *Patrologia, Series Latina*, XXIII, 213 ff.

not to touch a woman. That is why the law of Moses decreed that one should leave the newly married man free for one whole year to be happy with his wife and not draft him into the army or charge him with any office,[2] as though Moses wanted to say: "The joy will last for a year; after that we shall see."

Wherever there is not present this grace to live a celibate life by choice and desire, there it is better to marry. There is no other means to help there except marriage. Therefore if one cannot have the happy days of celibacy, then one must accept the evil days of marriage, for it is better to suffer evil days without sin in marriage than happy days without marriage in sin and unchastity. But no one likes to subject himself to such evil days, therefore everyone avoids marriage. This explains the saying "It takes a brave man to take a wife"; truly, he must be brave, and no one is so capable of this as a devout Christian, who lives by faith — he can adapt himself to these evil days and not complain, cry out, and blaspheme God and His works, as do the foolish, blind smart alecks.

And this is the meaning of St. Paul in moving so quickly from the praise of chastity to marriage and to say: "But because of the temptation to immorality, each man should have his own wife, and each woman her own husband." What does he mean, "because of the temptation to immorality"? Obviously this: When one cannot have the happiness which comes from chastity by choice and desire, then certainly unchastity and fornication will be present. But to avoid this, it is surely better to live a godly and blessed life, to deny oneself the happy days of those who do not touch a woman, and to submit to evil days in order to avoid sin. For it is better to be unhappy without sin than to sin without unhappiness, or even to sin *with* unhappiness.

Notice in the words of St. Paul that he does not expect much chastity from the Corinthians, for he says: "To be sure, it is a delicate matter concerning chastity; yes, if unchastity would only disappear; therefore let each man have his own wife, etc." He did not take that elevated view of chastity that we have had until now and still have, but wanted to see all men bound in marriage. And being full of the Holy Spirit, he certainly knew human nature and capacities far better than all the bishops who followed him, who have rejected and perverted the divine order so that St. Paul's words are no longer binding, "each man should have his own wife," but rather they preach: "Some may

2 Cf. Deut. 24:5.

have wives, some should not have wives," thus making "some" out of "each." But more of this later. St. Paul goes on to say:

3. *The husband should give to his wife her conjugal rights, and likewise the wife to her husband.*

4. *For the wife does not rule over her own body, but the husband does; likewise the husband does not rule over his own body, but the wife does.*

Here St. Paul instructs married people in their conduct toward one another with respect to marital duty and speaks of "conjugal rights." It is a right, yet it should occur voluntarily. This right arises out of God's permission of the marriage state and His forgiveness of what otherwise He punishes and condemns. For thus the state of matrimony is constituted in the law of love so that no one rules over his own body but must serve his partner, as is the way of love. Such is not the way of fornication, where none rules over the other or owes his partner anything, rather each seeks only his own in the other. Therefore it is against the law of love and also against God. Truly it is a profound saying that no one rules over his own body, that where fornication tempts, one should be subservient to the other and can give himself to no other. Thus we see that adultery is the greatest thievery and robbery on earth, for it gives away the living body, which is not ours, and takes another living body, which is also not ours.

Now the words of St. Paul are clear enough and do not need much commentary, so I do not wish to beat them out too thinly and write confusingly of marital obligations. A Christian person will, of himself, know how to conduct himself in such matters so as to live moderately. It is of no significance here, how wildly or cruelly an unchristian person conducts himself in this area. Some of the older teachers used to quote the pagan saying: "He who is too violent in love commits adultery with his own wife." [3] But it was spoken by a heathen, therefore I ignore it and say it is not true. Certainly no one can commit adultery with his own wife unless he did not think of her as his wife or did not touch her as his wife.

I do not think that this matter can be better dealt with than St. Paul here deals with it when he says that marriage is there as a help and means against unchastity. Therefore whoever uses it to avoid fornication has, as I see it, St. Paul as an advocate and patron. And by the

---

[3] *Adulter est in suam uxorem omnis impudicus vel amator ardentior* was cited by Jerome, *Adversus Jovinianum*, I, 49, *Patrologia, Series Latina*, XXIII, 281.

same token it is not proper that in some places they separate the bride and bridegroom until the third night and instruct them to contain themselves until the third night, according to the example of Tobias (Tob. 8:4). My own view is that everyone should do as he sees fit, for I have seen what misfortune has resulted when the evil spirit constantly wants to meddle. If the example of Tobias is so binding, why is not the example of the patriarch Jacob much more so, who in the first night touched and knew his Leah? It should be a matter of freedom, and they are fools who lay snares and laws in such matters. The bride is the bridegroom's and not the ruler over her own body, and furthermore one should let the matter rest there and not try to do everything better.

In the same way these people have excluded certain days, such as Christmas Eve,[4] or during pregnancy, etc.[5] Of course, it is very well and good to be moderate in all things, but one should not set up absolute laws in these matters but let stand the words of St. Paul, who points out to us that no one rules his own body. May it be on this day or that, according as God disposes. His concern is that fornication be prevented and not given cause or opportunity. Oh, how many laws this little saying of St. Paul repeals: "No one rules over his own body"! It can brook no laws. How can someone forbid me the body given to me by God's law and power? God's permission is greater than mankind's prohibition; what He grants to me, St. Peter shall not deny me. Then follows:

5. *Do not refuse one another except perhaps by agreement for a season, that you may devote yourselves to prayer; but then come together again, lest Satan tempt you through lack of self-control.*

St. Paul has very little confidence in their chastity because he well knows the devil and his tricks and the weakness of the flesh too. Here you see that married people are so bound up in one another that one cannot withdraw from the other even to fast or pray without the agreement of the partner; St. Paul would rather see prayer and fasting be relaxed than that one should so rule his body as to deny it to the marriage partner. Yet prayer is indeed a precious good work, and that it must give way before what seems to be such a trivial work, this is all the result of the law of love in which they are bound.

[4] Ambrosiaster, on 1 Cor. 7, *Patrologia, Series Latina*, XVII, 217.

[5] Jerome, *Adversus Jovinianum*, I, 49, *Patrologia, Series Latina*, XXIII, 281.

The fasting and prayer referred to here is a specially arranged exercise, as when a man and wife agree to fast and pray three, four, or six days, or a week or two, as anyone may freely take such a period of fasting upon himself to chastise the body and may do this as long as he wishes without any law or persuasion on the part of the authorities. Apart from this, married people are obligated like all other Christians to pray and fast in an evangelical way. For Christ has said to all Christians that "they ought always to pray" (Luke 18:1). This fasting means to eat and drink in moderation; and praying is to groan and cry from the heart, etc.

What refusing one another consists of between married people and what the reasons for it are, this I leave to married people themselves; I can well believe that there are many reasons, as is to be expected in a state created and instituted for evil and not for happy days, and anger and dissension will occasionally also play a role. Excessive "spirituality" also tends to get the upper hand. St. Paul allows only one reason, and neither I nor anyone else should prescribe more: that is, when both agree on a number of days during which they will chastise themselves more completely in a particular way through severe fasting and equally energetic prayer, particularly when there is some necessity for it. For strong prayer should be accompanied by strong fasting. Still St. Paul leaves it up to the individual and makes no law concerning it, leaving it rather to be agreed upon by both. Therefore no one can be compelled by order to such fasting and prayer, as has been done hitherto.

So much for that. Next St. Paul turns his attention to the three states of chastity: widowhood, matrimony, and virginity. He teaches us what we need to know of each.

I

WIDOWHOOD

6. *I say this by way of concession, not of command.*

7. *I wish that all were as I myself am. But each has his own special gift from God, one of one kind and one of another.*

If above he already said in the way of command: "But because of the temptation to immorality, each man should have his own wife," and enjoined "conjugal rights" in the married state, why does he in this passage say that he speaks "by way of concession, not of command"?

Doubtless he wants to say that marriage should be a free choice and not required of everyone, as in the Old Testament; therefore he commands no one to marry but leaves it to the individual. But once having married, the individual is commanded to maintain the conjugal rights. But where the grace to be free to marry or not marry is not present, there marriage is commanded, yes, even more than commanded.

Why, furthermore, does he say: "I wish that all were as I myself am"? Is this not spoken against matrimony, as though he wanted no one to marry? True, Paul wishes that everyone might have the great gift of chastity so that he would be relieved of the labor and cares of marriage and might be concerned only with God and His Word, as he himself was. And who wouldn't wish this for everyone, especially since Christian love desires all good things, both temporal and eternal, for everyone? Love knows no limits of the good it can do and desire, even though it be something impossible, as when Paul in Rom. 9:3 wishes himself cut off from Christ for the salvation of the Jews.

"But," he says, "each has his own special gift from God, one of one kind and one of another." Here he confesses that his wish cannot be fulfilled and that it is not God's will to grant everyone this great gift. Note this passage well, for there is much in it, and it praises marriage no less than celibacy. For when one compares marriage and virginity, then of course chastity is a nobler gift than marriage. Nevertheless, marriage is just as much a gift of God, St. Paul says here, as chastity is. A man is nobler than a woman, yet woman is just as much a creation of God as is man. For God all things are equal which yet among themselves are unequal. Everything He has created calls Him Creator and Lord, and none of it calls Him so more or better than another, whether it be small or large. Therefore marriage and virginity are equal before Him, for both are His divine gift, even though, when compared, one is better than the other.

From this it is clear how grievously in error are those who glorify nuns, claiming that their state is more glorious and better in the sight of God than matrimony. They contrive fictitious crowns for them and all kinds of virtues and honors, and thus they produce vainglorious, unchristian, and even ungodly people who rely more on their station and work than on faith in Christ and on God's grace, despising marriage as something much inferior — even before God — to their own status and calling themselves "brides of Christ." They are rather the brides of the devil, because they do not use chastity as it should be used, namely, not to pretend to be better in the eyes of God but to make people here on earth freer and more capable to give attention to God's Word rather than to marriage.

Now since both are a gift from God and marriage is given as a common gift to all but chastity is reserved for the few as a very special gift, it is clear that each must consider carefully whether he finds in himself the common or the special gift. And since St. Paul here freely concludes that it is a gift, we must admit that it is not our doing, possession, or capacity. Therefore no one can either vow it or keep such a vow. For I cannot bind in promise that which is His or is His gift unless He has already given it to me or I am certain of His promise to give it to me, as was Jeremiah (Jer. 16:2). And that is why there is no example of vows in the Scriptures except of things that have already been given to us or are to be given to us, as for instance in Num. 30,[6] where we read of houses, fields, money, cattle, the chastisement of the body with fasting or other discipline, etc.

Now that we are at the place where Paul praises matrimony so highly, calling it a divine gift, let us look a bit further and show that matrimony is the most religious state of all, and that it is unjust and wrong to refer to certain others as "religious orders" while calling marriage a "secular order." It should be just the reverse, that marriage should be called the real religious order, as in truth it is, and these other orders should be called the real secular orders, which in truth they are. They have introduced a complete misuse of words into society, buttering the mouths of all of us and misleading us to call religious things secular and secular things religious.

In the first place, nothing should be called religious except that inner life of faith in the heart, where the Spirit rules. But since that also is termed religious which happens outwardly to the body through the spirit of faith, let us be very just and precise in our differentiation and understand that the state of marriage in all fairness should be termed religious and the religious orders secular. I speak here of the orders and the religious who have let people call and describe them thus. Those that act in true faith and are genuinely religious, they certainly belong to the right religious order of chastity.

In the second place it cannot be denied that the doings and life of the religious are just as outward, temporal, and carnal as those of mar-

---

[6] The Weimar editor suggests that Lev. 27:9 ff., 14 ff., 17 ff. are appropriate for the first section of the series of vows here mentioned, and Num. 30:13 for the second section.

ried people, for they are performed just as much by the body and its members as those of married people are. But whatever is performed by the body and its members must be a bodily and outward function, and even the intentions and thoughts at the heart of such outward bodily works must also be of the body and be called such. Now if any order is to be termed a religious one, then something more and different must be in it than such outward doings and life, namely, the faith of the heart, which is spirit and makes everything in man religious, both inwardly and outwardly.

Now consider the religious orders so famous up to our time. The first thing you notice is that they are most securely provided with all the necessities of the body. A guaranteed income, food, clothing, shelter, and all sorts of other things they have in superfluity, earned by the work and care of others and given to them, so that they are not endangered in any way nor wish to be. Furthermore, no one enters the religious orders, or wants to enter, unless he is assured that he will receive lifelong care for his body; and the majority in the monastic and clerical orders are on the lookout that their stomachs and bodies get their due.

What else is this but to seek and have a position where one need not look to heaven and expect his daily bread from God or trust that God will provide? In short, in such estates faith has no place, no room, no time, no work, no exercise, for they sit prepared with everything, and that close at hand. Here is no *substantia rerum sperandarum,* no "conviction of things not seen," as is characteristic of faith, but rather *certitudo rerum possessarum,* "the certainty of things at hand." [7]

But if you take a wife and are married, this is the first shock: How are you going to support yourself, your wife, and child? And this will go on for your whole life. Therefore the state of marriage is by nature of a kind to teach and compel us to trust in God's hand and grace, and in the same way it forces us to believe. For we can see that where there is no faith in marriage, there it is a most miserable institution, full of worry, fear, and hard work. On the other hand, the less faith these famous religious orders have, the better they get along, for their stomachs are filled gratis, and they need not look to God's hand nor await His goodness.

Tell me, then, which of these orders could justly be termed a reli-

---

[7] Luther contrasts the definition of faith in Heb. 11:1 with the philosophy of the "bird in hand."

gious order, if not the one in which faith is a necessity and has its own work to do, having daily cause to exercise trust in the Lord and living according to these words of Ps. 145:15-16: [8] "The eyes of all look to Thee, and Thou givest them their food in due season. Thou openest Thy hand, Thou satisfiest the desire of every living thing"? Only the order of marriage has such a reason for and exercise in faith toward God. But no religious order has this, and none of them wants it, for they were founded and endowed precisely so that they should have need for no such a reason. And thus they have cast out faith and stopped up all the holes, lest it come back in.

Is this not indeed a perverse outrage, that they boast of their spirituality and boast of their orders as religious, when by their very nature and kind these orders cannot contain even a droplet of faith? When the Spirit and such religious orders are about as compatible as Christ and Belial, day and night, spirit and flesh, believing and feeling? For where there is no faith nor room nor cause for it, there can be no Spirit, and such a thing must of necessity be wholly carnal, worldly, physical, and external, as our experience with the members of these orders does indeed teach us. Furthermore, they attack marriage as worldly and carnal and don't see that it has been instituted by God, that it drives and helps along toward the Spirit and faith, and that it must consist almost entirely of faith if it is to prosper. For whatever is God's work and business is so arranged that it must practice and exercise faith. Where this is not done, it becomes a burdensome and unbearable thing. But whatever men contrive, that will flourish best without faith, for it wants to be sure of things and certain of its supply.

Consider this, then, as the first point, that marriage by nature is of such a kind that it drives, impels, and forces men to the most inward, highest spiritual state, to faith. And there is no higher or more inward state than faith, for it depends solely on God's Word and is naked and divested of all that is not God's Word. And there is nothing higher or more inward, either in heaven or on earth, than God's Word, which is even God Himself. The religious orders, on the other hand, are by nature of a kind to tempt men to scatter themselves in temporal and outward things so that they have enough for their bodies, so that they finally do not even want to be religious orders unless first they have enough for outward needs and are sure of their supplies and don't

[8] The Weimar text has "Ps. 103," but the editor suggests Ps. 145:15-16 and also the parallel statement of Ps. 104:27-28.

have to have faith and trust in God. Surely one must say that such religious orders are by nature very earthly, worldly, and heathenish compared with the order of marriage. And by the same token the order of marriage is a heavenly, spiritual, and godly order compared with the religious orders.

I say "by nature" deliberately, for it is true that many do not make the right use of marriage in faith, turning the good in it to evil through their lack of faith. On the other hand, it is not impossible that someone may make good use of a religious order through his faith, turning what is bad in it to something good for himself by means of his faith. But because of such good or bad usage one cannot say that therefore marriage is bad or the religious orders are good. For faith makes all things good, even death and all misfortune. Lack of faith makes all things bad and destructive, even life and God Himself. But at present we are not speaking of the use or misuse of orders, but of the nature and kind of these orders in themselves; and we conclude that marriage is gold and the religious orders are dirt, because the one promotes faith and the other unbelief.

In the second place, marriage strengthens not only the heart and the inmost nature through faith in God but also the body outwardly through works; so that marriage promotes both faith and works and helps, supplies, and guides both body and soul. For marriage is by nature such that it must work and support itself by means of its hands, precisely according to God's Word in Gen. 3:19: "In the sweat of your face you shall eat bread." It must risk it that all its labor may fail and suffer much damage, that it may suffer the many things that can happen to wife, child, and servants, and who can detail the whole picture of the "sweat of the face"? Certainly in the matrimonial order the body has its share of work, cares, and troubles, just as the heart has its troubles with faith; yet nothing is more certain than that all this is of God and pleases Him well.

But the religious orders are not supported by their labor. They are like a lazy rogue who does not exert himself bodily but lets others work for him, filling his belly through the sweat and blood of others. Nor does he anticipate the slightest danger or damage to his possessions, so that, in short, there is in that situation very little "sweat of the face." His way of life follows the pattern of Ps. 73:5-6:[9] "They are

---

[9] The Weimar text has "Ps. 13," but the editor points out that Luther, quoting from memory, confused Ps. 14 (13) with Ps. 73, both of which contain descriptions of the ungodly.

not in trouble as other men are; they are not stricken like other men. Therefore pride is their necklace, etc." And although they pray and sing and pursue their spiritual occupations, this in no way contributes to the exercise of the body. Furthermore, even though these things are done in the finest way, it is still not certain that they are pleasing to God. Such things, because they are done without His command, cannot please Him.

Here you might say: "If that's the way you look at it, then the best thing would be for no one to remain chaste and everyone to get married; but that would certainly contradict this text of St. Paul." Answer: I am speaking here of the religious orders over against the matrimonial order, and not about the state of chastity. Religious orders are good for nothing, and it were better that nobody were a religious but that everyone were married. But the state of chastity is quite different from a religious order, and St. Paul is not speaking of religious orders but of the true state of chastity. There is no more unchaste state than the religious orders, as we find confirmed daily. And even though some within them live chastely, still they do not use this state as St. Paul wants to see it used, so that it is not at all the same chastity concerning which St. Paul here instructs us. For they make of their chastity merit, credit, and glory before God and the world, and they place their reliance on it, which is against faith. But St. Paul makes of it a technique and service for God's Word and faith. He goes on to say:

8. *I say therefore to widowers and widows, It is good for them if they abide even as I.*

From this text it follows that St. Paul had had a wife, for he considers himself a widower.[10] Later he speaks of virginity in particular, which he does not ascribe to himself. Although many think that he remained a virgin, because he says in 1 Cor. 9:5-6: "Do we not have the right to be accompanied by a sister as a wife, as the other apostles and the brothers of the Lord and Cephas? Or is it only Barnabas and

---

[10] The text on which Luther comments here in 1523 is from his German translation of 1522. It reads: *Ich sage zwar den widwehern und witwynnen.* The 1530 edition, described by V. Dietrich as *denuo emendatum summa diligentia* (W, *Deutsche Bibel,* VI, xxv), reads: *Ich sage zwar den ledigen und witwin* (W, *Deutsche Bibel,* VII, 102). The last edition for which Luther could accept responsibility, that of 1546, has *Ich sage zwar den Ledigen und Widwen* (W, *Deutsche Bibel,* VII, 103). But as late as 1538 Luther is quoted as saying: "It is likely that he (Paul) had been a husband, for the Jews were accustomed to marry early and yet live a life of chastity (W, *Tischreden,* IV, 162).

I who have no right to do this?" But this does not prove anything, rather it gives further evidence that he did have a wife but didn't want to take her with him, as the other apostles did with their wives; or else he indicates that he does not now have a wife, like the other widowers, but would certainly like to have one.

It is certainly conceivable that he did have a wife. For in Jewry everyone had to marry, and celibacy was not allowable unless by special permission and as an exception made by God. This is supported by the passage in Phil. 4:3, where he says: "And I ask you also, true yokefellow, help these women, for they have labored side by side with me in the Gospel." This true yokefellow many people take to be Saint Paul's wife, because he does not mention her name and otherwise never uses the address "true yokefellow," which in Greek means someone who pulls with us in the same yoke and has a special relation to us different from others, as married people have. Furthermore, he commands this yokefellow to help women.[11]

His speaking in this way must indicate either that St. Paul's wife had died when he wrote this epistle and indicated that he was a widower or else that he must have put her from him with her consent and did not take her with him and therefore lived chastely with her in the state of matrimony, as stated in chapter 9. Whatever the case may be, whether his wife was dead or had consented to live separately from him for the sake of the Gospel, one thing is certain: that he was living as a widower at that time and had been a married man. Now let us consider what this text shows us.

There are some who have advanced to the point where they are forced to admit that priests and bishops may marry and that married men may become priests and bishops, because the Scriptures convince them that almost all the apostles were married and many bishops after them. But they cast about for a way out, saying: "Yes, of course, we read that men who were first married became apostles and bishops. But there were those who became apostles, bishops, and priests before marriage, and we do not read that at any later date they were married; therefore now, too, priests may not marry." Let us now answer these people.

[11] Erasmus' *Novum Instrumentum* (1526), his Greek New Testament with notes and a Latin translation, commented on Phil. 4:3: "They are called yokefellows, as if they bore the yoke together. . . . Some people apply this to Paul's wife. . . . There are important authorities among the Greeks who think Paul had a wife. And it makes sense here for women to be commended to women."

First, if you admit at the very start that married men became bishops and priests and that they can be and become such — as the example of the apostles teaches and confirms — who are you to forbid that any married man should become a priest? You are driving away from the priesthood not only those who want to marry but also those who are already married, which is against Christ and all the apostles and also against the teaching of St. Paul (even though he remained unmarried) [12] when he says that one should choose for a bishop a man with only one wife and well-behaved, obedient children. Now tell me, whom should we believe to be wiser and more holy — Christ or you? Christ takes married men as priests and confirms this in His apostles, but you condemn them. In this either Christ is a fool and in the wrong, or you are necessarily antichrists and deceivers.

My friends, if you had only not meddled with this one little principle, that according to the example of the apostles and the teaching of Christ married men may become priests, and if you had not persisted in forbidding priests to marry, there would not have been so much trouble. For then many married men would have become priests, and many would first have tried marriage, and there would have been far fewer whoremongers. Now you pretend that you have not read that priests have been married, and in so doing you thrust the whole married state out of the priesthood in contradiction to God, nature, reason, and justice, from sheer insolence, and without reason; and you have filled the world with fornication.

Second, why have you not read this text and given it due consideration? Does it not say here clearly that a priest may marry? For even if I concede that St. Paul was a virgin or a widower, still he says that he has the right to be accompanied by a wife. Tell me, was St. Paul at that time not an apostle, a bishop, and a priest? How dare he presume to have the right and authority to marry? And since the high order of the apostles permitted a person to marry or stay married, why should not the lesser order of priests permit both remaining married and being married?

Since St. Paul is a widower here and still presumes to have the right to take a wife, he is certainly a bigamist under papal law, although he is apparently not too concerned about that. A bigamist is so evil, in canon law, that even if he were without a wife at the moment, still he could not be a priest. A bigamist, however, is one who

---

[12] This statement should no doubt be understood in the light of p. 22 above.

has had two wives. In the Old Testament it was a man who had two wives at one and the same time. But canon law has interpreted these sayings differently and has invented three kinds of bigamy: first, if one marries two wives, one after the other, even if they were both virgins; second, if one marries only once but marries a widow; third, if one marries a woman who is defiled, even if he did not know this before and took her to be a virgin.[13]

For the pope these are all "bigamists," or "men with two wives," and none of them may become priests after the death of such wives. But even though one were to defile a hundred married women, corrupt a hundred virgins, and keep a hundred whores at one time, still this man can be a priest, become or remain a priest — so remarkably holy is this priesthood! No sin or shame is so great or so widespread in the whole world as to prevent a man from being or becoming a priest, except the state of holy matrimony, which they themselves name and confess a sacrament and work of God. This one work of God has no place in the priesthood.

Please explain to me how such vicious sacrilege can be harmonized with the teaching of St. Paul, who was a widower and assumed the right to marry, giving all widowers and widows the right to marry, excluding no one, neither priest nor layman. What can we answer except to say that such human restrictions are so obviously and scandalously opposed to God's Word, that we are taken to be no better than sticks and stones, and that we are expected to believe that whoring is better than marriage? And what do they expect to achieve by this, if not to defame the divine institution of marriage and pave the way for fornication throughout the world? And this is what is happening before our very eyes, as Daniel prophesied of the rule of the Antichrist, saying: "He shall give no heed to women" (Dan. 11:37),[14] as though he were saying: "Only to whores will he give heed."

Third, since they have to admit that the apostles remained married although they were already in the office of apostles, I should like to know why marriage is not permissible in the priesthood or after taking the priestly office? Is the poor little state of marriage such a devilish thing when it is entered into after the priesthood? Or is it so eminently divine when it precedes it? Are we to suppose that it suffers such a

---

[13] Luther had already ridiculed these artificial definitions of bigamy in his treatise *The Babylonian Captivity of the Church* (1520). Cf. *Luther's Works*, 36, p. 114. See also *Luther's Works*, 41, pp. 156—158.

[14] Cf. *Luther's Works*, 41, p. 163.

great change merely because of the going before or coming after? Truly all reason must admit and anyone can understand that whatever remains divine during and after the entry into the priesthood, this can also certainly be accepted during the priesthood itself or entered into before the priesthood.

Furthermore, it is a shameful pretense to confess marriage a godly thing and a holy sacrament and then not permit such a godly thing and holy sacrament to stand beside the holiness of priests. How does it come about that here God must oppose Himself, that one of His works cannot suffer the other, that one holiness persecutes the other, and that one sacrament damns another? O insolent, blind outrage, that such unholy bunk has not only been fed to the people, but that they have been taught to think it the best, and still do! How could it ever have come to this end, if God's anger had not punished and blinded the world?

But let us stick to St. Paul, who will not mislead us. He tells us that widowers may marry, God willing, whether they be priests or not. They may also take wives, virgins or widows, and the priest will not lose standing if he marries a widow nor gain it if he takes a virgin. All such things should be open to Christians, for St. Paul wrote this epistle not only to laymen but also to bishops and all Christians in Corinth together. And since he did not make an exception of any person or estate, it is not for us to interpret or stretch his words to cover laymen or any other persons or conditions.

St. Paul well knew that by his teaching and conduct Christ did not want to obstruct or break any of God's creatures or works. Now man is the creature and work of God, created to be fruitful and multiply according to Gen. 1:28. Through His Gospel and priesthood He therefore does not want to make of man a stick or a stone nor hinder him in his natural function, which God implanted in him. As for forbidding priests to marry, what is that but to say that a man is not to be a man but is to cease being God's creature and work in favor of human presumption and legalism? Only God, who created us, may effect such a transformation through His gifts and power; human law or free will or effort are here all wasted and in vain. St. Paul now says:

To the unmarried and the widows I say that it is well for them to remain as I do.

9. *But if they cannot exercise self-control, they should marry. For it is better to marry than to be aflame with passion.*

Indeed, it is well to remain like St. Paul. But he goes right on to say why it is not well to remain so and better to marry again than to remain a widow. Here St. Paul has piled all the reasons for marrying in one heap and set the goal for all the glory of chastity when he says: "But if they cannot exercise self-control, they should marry." This is as much as to say: Necessity orders that you marry. Much as chastity is praised, and no matter how noble a gift it is, nevertheless necessity prevails so that few can attain it, for they cannot control themselves. For although we are Christians and have the spirit of God in faith, still we do not cease to be God's creatures, you a woman, and I a man. And the spirit permits the body its ways and natural functions, so that it eats, drinks, sleeps, and eliminates like any other human body.

Therefore mankind is not deprived of its male or female form, members, seed, and fruit, so that the body of a Christian must fructify and multiply just like that of other human beings, birds, and all the animals, as it was created by God to do according to Gen. 1:28. So it is by necessity that the man is attracted to the woman and the woman to the man, except where God performs a miracle by means of a special gift and withholds His creatures from one another. When St. Paul says, "But if they cannot exercise self-control, they should marry," it is as though he were to say: "Those to whom God has not given a special gift but lets their bodies retain their way and nature, for them it is better, yes, necessary, to marry and not to remain virgin or widow. For it is not God's intention to make this special grace a general one; rather marriage is to be general according to God's original institution and creation in both bodies. He will not cancel and deny His creation in everyone.

Furthermore, a Christian is spirit and flesh. According to the spirit he has no need of marriage. But because his flesh is the common flesh, corrupted in Adam and Eve and filled with evil desires, therefore because of this very disease, marriage is a necessity for him and it is not in his power to get along without it. For his flesh rages, burns, and fructifies just like that of any other man, unless he helps and controls it with the proper medicine, which is marriage. God suffers this raging passion for the sake of marriage and its fruits. In Gen. 3:16 He indicated what He would suffer from man in that He did not take away the blessing of procreation but rather confirmed it, knowing full well that man's nature was corrupted, full of evil desires, and unable to carry out this blessing without sinning.

It is useless and futile, yes, a very foolish and evil thing, that the attempt is now being made to despise matrimony and to lure people away from it to celibacy because marriage is full of misery and disgust. For things are not at all helped by this, but grim necessity always lies in our path and says: It cannot be, it will not be, one cannot cling to heaven. As St. Paul says here: "If they cannot exercise self-control, they should marry." On the other hand, extreme praise of marriage, though it is a godly institution, full of all spiritual good, also does not help matters, for none — or very few at any rate — are going to be induced to enter it because of such qualities. Human nature is afraid of trouble and labor.

There are many other reasons why people marry. Some marry for money and property. Many people marry because of sheer immaturity, to seek sensual pleasure and satisfy it. Some marry to beget heirs. But St. Paul gives but this one reason, and I know of none fundamentally stronger and better, namely, need. Need commands it. Nature will express itself, fructify, and multiply, and God does not want this outside marriage, and so everyone because of this need must enter into marriage if he wants to live with a good conscience and in favor with God. If this need were not there, all the other reasons taken together would make very poor marriages. This is particularly true of that smart immaturity which leads fools to take lightly such a serious, needful, godly estate; but it is not long until they realize what they have done to themselves.

But what do these words mean: "For it is better to marry than to be aflame with passion." I have no doubt that everyone who wants to live chastely, though unmarried and without special grace for it, will understand these words and what they convey. For St. Paul is not speaking of secret matters, but of the common, known feeling of all those who live chastely outside of marriage but do not have the grace to accomplish it. For he ascribes this flaming with passion to all who live chastely but without the necessary grace, and prescribes no other medicine than marriage. If it were not so common or if there were some other advice to be given, he would not have recommended marriage. This thing is known in German as "the secret disease," but this expression would not be so common either if the ailment were truly rare.

There can also be no doubt that those who have the grace of chastity still at times feel evil desires and are tempted. But it is transitory, therefore their problem is not this burning. In short, "aflame with passion" is the heat of the flesh, which rages without ceasing, and daily attraction to woman or to man; we find this wherever there is not desire and love for chastity. People without this heat are just as few and far between as are those who have God's grace for chastity. Now such heat is stronger in some, and weaker in others. Some among them suffer so severely that they masturbate. All these ought to be in the married estate. Truly it can be said: for every chaste person there should be more than a hundred thousand married people.

It will be best to give you an example. St. Jerome, who glorifies chastity and praises it most solemnly, confesses that he was unable to subdue his flesh with fasts or wakes,[15] so that his chastity became for him an unimaginable plague. Oh, how much precious time he must have wasted with carnal thoughts! But he insists that chastity is something that we can achieve and a common possession. You see, this man lay in heat and should have taken a wife. There you see what "aflame with passion" means. For he was of the number who belong in marriage, and he wronged himself and caused himself much trouble by not marrying. We can read of many more such incidents in the lives of the fathers.

So this is St. Paul's conclusion: Where there is not a special gift of God, one must either be aflame with passion or marry. Now it is better to marry, says St. Paul, than to burn. Why? Because this burning, even if no act were to result from it, is still lost chastity, because it is held to not from desire and love, but with great dislike, unwillingness, and pressure. Before God this will be counted as unchastity, because the heart is unchaste and the body simply was not permitted to be unchaste. What use is it that you hold with such enormous, sour, unwilling effort to a lost and unchaste chastity? It were better to marry and rise above such unhappiness. For although in marriage there is also much trouble and unhappiness, still one can enter into it with good will and at times have peace and happiness. But outside marriage, where there is no grace, it is impossible to have good will toward chastity and live happily in it.

Consider how foolish are those teachers and administrators who drive young people to chastity in monasteries and nunneries, claiming that the harder it is for them and the more unwilling they are, the better their chastity is. They should play around with other things

[15] E. g., Jerome, Letter XXII, To Eustochium, 7, *Patrologia, Series Latina,* XXII, 398 f.

and take something besides chastity, for it cannot be voluntary without a special grace. Everything else can be voluntary, if only faith is present. They act like the Jews who burned their children in honor of the god Molech (Jer. 32:35), so that I sometimes think St. Paul used the word "aflame" because he wanted to touch upon and refer to this abomination. For what is it to allow a young person to suffocate in such heat in a monastery or elsewhere his whole life but to burn a child to death in honor of the devil by making it observe a miserable, lost chastity?

In honor of such teachers and administrators I must tell you what I once heard from a brave man. Perhaps these blind boneheads will then see just how wisely they are proceeding. There once was one of those preachers who cried out that one really had to do something big and almost inflict harm on oneself if one wanted to serve God. He cited the incident from the *Lives of the Saints* in which Simeon stood on one leg atop a high pillar for a whole year and prayed constantly, neither eating nor drinking, until the maggots grew in his foot; and these turned to jewels as they fell off.[16] "This is the way you must torture yourselves," the preacher shouted, "if you want to serve God." It is only fitting that such lies be preached by such preachers; doubtless they were in ancient times fabricated by the devil through his evil minions to make fun of the Christians and counteract the miracles which they performed in such large numbers in those days, making them seem like so much trickery.

But this fool of a preacher found another fool as a pupil, according to the proverb: "One fool makes ten more." This fool wanted to serve God by hurting himself and no longer urinating. After he had held off for four days and became very sick, and nobody could talk him out of it, and he wished for death; finally God inspired someone with the idea that he should praise and support this fellow in his undertaking (the way one must humor idiots in what they do, as Solomon tells us [17]). "But," he said to him, "the story is that you are doing this solely for the glory in it, and if that is true, then it is all useless." When he heard this, the fool left off his foolishness and said: "If that's what they're going to think, then I won't hold it any longer." [18]

[16] Cf. *Patrologia, Series Latina*, LXXIII, 328 f.

[17] Cf. Prov. 26:5.

[18] Luther had used these stories also in his *Lectures on Romans* (*Luther's Works*, 25, pp. 410—411), and they are included in the Cordatus collection of Table Talk (W, *Tischreden*, III, 51—54).

Well, that is a pretty crude piece of foolishness, but it should not be despised. God has shown by means of it, so I say at any rate, the damage done by such teachers and administrators. So let us forget all about this incident. The truth is, as the Scriptures and all experience teach us, that this life on earth is a miserable life, full of misery and suffering regardless of what estate you choose for yourself (provided it is godly). Still there is none so miserable who, if he were ordered to hold his urine or excrement, would not rather choose the state he was in rather than accept such an impossible order; but since nobody is bound to such an order, nobody pays any attention to the benefits and delight of elimination. Meanwhile he looks at and complains about the miseries of the state he is in, which are not one tenth what such a misery would be.

It is the same with this burning. Those who are married, they are rid of this; they can extinguish what burns them and pay no more attention to such torment (just as a woman after a birth sees things quite differently than before and in the birth), but instead they see nothing but the trouble and unhappiness of their married estate. When good is present, it goes unobserved; when the bad is over, it is forgotten. But those who are still caught in passion and have no hope, must they not make fun of those fools who are married and yet still complain about marriage? For the former must hold what cannot be held, and do it all for nothing and waste all the bitter effort — that is indeed a terrible pity! Would they not much rather bear all the unhappiness of marriage than such burning? That is what St. Paul is speaking about when he says: "It is better to marry than to burn," as though he were saying: "Marriage is a bad thing, but burning is still worse." In short: Better an unhappy marriage than unhappy chastity. Better a sour and difficult marriage than a sour and difficult chastity. Why? The latter is a sure loss; the former can be of use.

I say this only of that burning which those suffer who control themselves — of whom there are few; for the majority do not suffer such heat, neither do they control themselves, but they do as they please and relieve themselves; of this I shall not write at present. But if they relieve themselves outside of marriage, then the pangs of conscience are soon there, and this is the most unbearable torment and the most miserable of earthly estates. This is the unavoidable result, that most of those who live without marriage and without grace in celibacy are forced to sin bodily in unchastity, and the others are forced to outward chastity and inward unchastity. The former must needs lead a damnable life, the latter an unholy useless one. And where are the spiritual and secular rulers who consider the plight of these poor souls? Every day they are helping the devil to increase this misery with their pressures and compulsion.

II

MATRIMONY

10. *To the married I give charge, not I but the Lord, that the wife should not separate from her husband.*

11. *But if she does, let her remain single or else be reconciled to her husband, and that the husband should not divorce his wife.*

In the foregoing the apostle has spoken of widowers [19] and widows, among whom a man may take a wife or — in fact, it is good, if they have the grace — stay single. But this cannot be conceded for married people. For them there is God's command that compels them to stay together. That widowers and widows stay single, however, is neither a command nor prohibition from God but simply the apostle's own good advice; they are left free before God in good conscience either to marry again or to stay as they are.

But here the apostle concedes that man and wife may separate, provided that they do not marry again. In so doing he repeals the law of Moses according to which the man could send away his wife if he were displeased with her or tired of her and take another. And she, too, could take another, according to Deut. 24:1 ff. Now although Moses gave such a law to the Jews, to people who were hardheaded and heathenish, still such actions are not fitting for a Christian, and therefore Christ himself revoked it in Matt. 19:8-9. For in the Old Testament there were laws governing not only the spiritual realm but also the secular order, because God ruled over the same people both in the spiritual and the secular realm. In the same way we still have in the imperial code many laws for the secular realm which would be most unfitting for Christian use, as, for instance, the use of force against force, litigation in the courts, etc.

For many different kinds of laws are necessary to ward off and control evil, and many other kinds are required to teach and govern the good. This law therefore was made to repress and control the evil,

[19] Cf. p. 21, n. 10, above.

so that they would not kill their wives or do even worse things. But Christians should be benevolent in their hearts and not need such laws but keep their wives as long as they live. Where there are no Christians, or only crude, false Christians, there even today it would be good to hold to this law and allow them, like heathen, to divorce their wives and marry others, so that they would not set up two hells in their disunited lives, one here and one there; but they should know that by separating they are no longer Christians but heathen and in a damnable condition.

The apostle refers to one cause of divorce: anger — when a man and his wife cannot live together in harmony but only in hatred and dispute, so that they can neither pray nor do any other good work. The text clearly states this by admonishing them either to be reconciled and not separate or to live without marriage if they cannot be reconciled and wish to separate. Where reconciliation is recommended, there anger and disharmony are indicated. The apostle certainly permits such separations by being lenient over against the weaknesses of Christians when two people simply cannot get along together. In all other cases everyone is obligated to carry the burden of the other and not to separate from him. That is also the reason why he does not permit divorced persons to change their status, that they may have the opportunity to come together again; yes, he may even thereby urge and force them together, for they may not have the grace of chastity.

But what if one party did not want to be reconciled with the other but remained quite separate and the other could not control himself and needed a mate? What should that party do? May he change his status? Answer: Yes, without doubt. For since he is not commanded to live in chastity and he does not have the grace to do so, and his spouse will not return to him, taking away the body he cannot do without, therefore God will not demand the impossible because of the disobedience of the other, and he should then act as though his spouse were dead. This is particularly true because it is not his fault that they cannot be reconciled. But the one who does not want reconciliation must remain unmarried, as St. Paul points out here. He goes on to say:

12. *To the rest I say, not the Lord, that if any brother has a wife who is an unbeliever, and she consents to live with him, he should not divorce her.*

13. *If any woman has a husband who is an unbeliever, and he con-*
    sents to live with her, she should not divorce him.

Because St. Paul here bears witness that these words are not from
the Lord but from himself, he indicates that these things are not commanded by God but are left to the individual to choose in one way or
another. For he distinguishes his own words from the Word of the
Lord, that the Lord's Word is to be a commandment, but his own
words advice. And he wishes to say this: "To the rest," that is, where
there is no problem of anger between married people, as when there
are two married people of whom the one is a Christian and the other
non-Christian (as so often happened when the faith was newly
preached among the heathen, so that one was converted and the other
not), even though the Christian may divorce the non-Christian, the
apostle's advice is that he do not do so, provided the non-Christian
accepts and is satisfied with the choice of the partner to be Christian
and does not object to or prevent his living a Christian life or force
the mate to deny Christ or live in an unchristian way.

This is what St. Paul means when he says, "and she consents to
live with him, etc.," that is, if the non-Christian is content and willing
to stay with the Christian spouse and allows him to do all things
proper to a Christian. For marriage is an outward, physical thing
that neither promotes nor hinders faith, and the one partner may well
be a Christian and the other non-Christian, just as a Christian may
eat with a heathen, Jew, or Turk, or drink, buy from him, and have
all ordinary commerce with him.[20] In the same way one marriage
partner may now be a true devout Christian and the other an evil,
false Christian; still it is not necessary to dissolve the marriage because
of piety or malice.

But if the non-Christian should not let his spouse be a Christian
and live a Christian life and should hinder and persecute him, then it
would be time to keep these words of Christ also physically: "He who
loves wife or child [21] more than Me is not worthy of Me" (Matt. 10:37).
Then divorce is in order; but once the divorce is effected, then there

[20] Luther had already previously denounced the impediments to marriage
due to "spiritual affinity," "legal affinity," and "disparity of religion" in *The
Babylonian Captivity of the Church* (1520) and *The Estate of Marriage* (1522).
Cf. *Luther's Works,* 36, pp. 99—101; 45, pp. 24—25.

[21] Luther provides an extension of the meaning of the passage by substituting
"wife or child" for "father or mother" and "son or daughter."

must either be reconciliation, or that partner must remain unmarried who will not be reconciled, while the other is permitted to change his status, as explained above.[22] For one must honor Christ, the spouse of the soul, more than the spouse of one's body; and where the one will not tolerate the other, one must stay with the spouse of the soul, who is eternal, and let the physical one go and take another who will tolerate the eternal spouse alongside himself.

And the same procedure is to be followed when a man encourages or forces his wife to commit theft, adultery, or any other wrong against God; here we have the same cause for divorce — and if they are not reconciled — the one may change his status. This explains why adultery brings on divorce and permits a change of status. For in the Old Testament, in Deut. 13:6-10, it is commanded that a man should kill his wife, brother, or best friend if they should advise or induce him to commit anything contrary to God. But in the New Testament, where one does not kill in the body, it is sufficient to divorce and separate from such persons.

From this it follows that those cases were wrong where we read how certain wives, with the consent of their husbands, committed adultery in order to save their husbands from death or prison. For one should keep God's commandments, even though it may cost us husband or wife, life or property. And no one has the right, for any reason whatever, to permit his wife to commit adultery. St. Paul says further:

14. *For the unbelieving husband is consecrated through his wife, and the unbelieving wife is consecrated through her husband. Otherwise your children would be unclean, but as it is, they are holy.*

This is spoken in the Hebrew way and according to the manner of St. Paul, to the effect that all things are holy to him who is holy. Thus he says in Titus 1:15: "To the pure all things are pure"; or in Romans 8:28: "We know that in everything God works for good with those who love Him," which is to say: A Christian spouse may not be divorced but can live with a non-Christian mate and even conceive and raise non-Christian children. The reason is this: if the non-Christian spouse does not prevent the Christian mate from leading a Christian life, then faith is such a mighty thing that no hurt will come from living with a non-Christian; it will make no difference whether he

22 Cf. p. 32.

associates with religious or irreligious people, for even death, that most terrible thing of all, is still a holy thing for a Christian.

Faith can use all things for its purpose, whether good or bad, except unbelief and its fruits. For these are directly contrary to faith and do not permit faith to remain; those things that do permit faith to remain are themselves rendered harmless by faith, are made pure, holy, useful, and salutary, so that the believer may live with them and keep them without danger. If this were not so, no Christian could live, for he is forced to live among evil and non-Christian people. But if he does not follow them but puts them to good use, he may live with or among them to the end that they may gain piety and become Christians.

To a Christian, therefore, the entire world is holiness, purity, utility, and piety. Contrariwise, to a non-Christian the whole world is unholiness, impurity, uselessness, and destruction — even God with all His goodness, as Ps. 18:26-27 says to God: "With the pure Thou dost show Thyself pure; and with the crooked Thou dost show Thyself perverse." Why is this? Because the pure, that is, the believers, can use all things in a holy and blessed way to sanctify and purify themselves. But the unholy and the unbelievers sin, profane, and pollute themselves incessantly in all things. For they cannot use anything in a right, godly, and blessed way, so that it might serve their own salvation.

In the same way children are also holy, even though they are neither baptized nor Christians. They are not holy in themselves (St. Paul is not discussing *this* holiness here) but are holy to you, so that your own holiness may associate with them and raise them without profaning you, just as though they were holy things. St. Paul also wants to convey this: If a Christian spouse should have grown children with a non-Christian mate (as often happened in those days) and the children should not want to be baptized or become Christians, then, inasmuch as no one should be forced to believe but only willingly be drawn by God through His Gospel, the father and mother should not abandon the children or withdraw or fail in their motherly or fatherly duties, as though they could thereby sin and pollute themselves in unbelieving children; rather they should guide and care bodily for these children as though they were the holiest of Christians. For they are not impure or unholy, Paul says; that is, your faith can demonstrate itself in them and thus remain pure and holy.

So it should be done now and at all times. Where children do not want to accept the Gospel, one should not therefore leave them or send them away but care for them and support them like the best of all Christians, commending their faith to God, so long as they are obedient and upright in all other things having to do with outward living. For parents can and should resist and punish outward evil acts and works. But nobody can resist and punish unbelief and an inwardly evil nature except God alone. Thus this text of St. Paul's also concerns us and strengthens us, making all things holy and pure to the believer.

15. *But if the unbelieving partner desires to separate, let it be so; in such a case the brother or sister is not bound. For God has called us to peace.*

Here the apostle releases the Christian spouse, once the non-Christian partner has separated himself or will not permit his mate to lead a Christian life, giving the former the right and authority to marry another partner. What St. Paul says here concerning a non-Christian spouse is also applicable to a false Christian; so that if such a one wanted to traduce his spouse to his unchristian ways and not permit the Christian way of life or would separate himself, then that Christian spouse would be free to marry another. If this were not permitted, the Christian spouse would have to follow after the non-Christian mate or live a life of chastity without the will and capability to do so, and he would thus be the prisoner of another's caprice and live in danger of his soul.

St. Paul denies this and says that in such cases the brother or sister is not bound. It is as if he wanted to say: "In other cases where married people remain together, as in the marriage bond and similar things, one is bound to the other and not entirely his own, so that neither can change from the other; but in this matter, where one partner holds the other to an unchristian life or separates from him, the Christian is not bound or compelled to stay with such a mate. But if someone is not bound, he is free and released. If he is free and released, he may change his status, just as though his spouse were dead.

But what would happen if the next spouse also went astray and tried to force his mate into a heathen or unchristian way of life or separated from him, and so on until the third and fourth mate, as often as the case may occur — could a man then have ten or more wives who were still living, all of whom had run away from him? Or on the other hand, could a woman have ten or more husbands, all of whom had run away from her? Answer: We can't tell St. Paul to shut up; likewise we can't prevent those who are so inclined from using his teachings as often as they please. His words are clear: a brother or sister is not bound but free if the partner separates and will not consent to live with his mate. He does not say that this should happen only once but lets it work itself out as often as necessary, for he does not want to bind anyone to the danger of unchastity because of the frivolity and malice of another.

But shouldn't the Christian mate wait until his non-Christian spouse comes back or dies, as has been the custom and canon law until now? Answer: If he wants to wait for his mate, that is up to his good will. For since the apostle proclaims him free and unbound, he is not obliged to wait for his mate but may change his status in the name of God. I wish to God that people had made use of this teaching of St. Paul or would begin to make use of it in cases where man and wife run away from each other or one leaves the other sitting, for much whoring and sin have resulted from them. This has been increased by the senseless laws of the pope, which, in direct contradiction to this text of St. Paul, compel and force the one mate not to change his status on pain of losing his soul's salvation, but to wait for the runaway spouse or the death of the same. This means that the brother or sister in such cases is truly bound in irons, because of the wantonness and wickedness of another, and for no cause is driven into the danger of unchastity.

Now, what if the runaway mate should return and wanted to make amends, should one permit him to do this and accept him? Answer: When the one who has remained behind has not changed his status, he may accept the returning mate, and it is advisable that they again sit down together. But where the one has already changed his status, he should let the other one go and not receive the returning spouse. Here we may profit from what is written of the rejected wife in Deut. 24:3-4, that the first man cannot take her back again, even though she is separated from the second by death or a bill of divorce. One should do the same today, so that the runaway is punished. And if one were to do so, there would doubtless be less running away. But now that the pope has opened the door to the runaways and given their wickedness and foolishness the right and authority to return, it is no wonder that the world is full of torn and broken marriages, yes, is full of fornication, which is just what the devil intended with such laws.

But when both are guilty and both run away, it is fitting that they both cancel their wrongs, become reconciled, and sit together again. And this teaching of St. Paul should be stretched to cover all sorts of divorces, such as when a man and wife run away from one another not because of his or her Christian faith but because of some other matter, be it anger or any other dissatisfaction; nor should it be asked that the guilty party reconcile himself or remain unmarried, or that the innocent mate be free and have authority to remarry if the other will not be reconciled. For this is all unchristian and heathen, that a spouse runs away from his mate out of momentary anger or any other dissatisfaction, refusing to share fortune and misfortune, the sweet and the sour, with his partner — as he is obligated to. Such a spouse is truly a heathen and unchristian.

"God has called us to peace," Paul says; that is, we should live peaceably with one another. Therefore a Christian spouse should not quarrel with his non-Christian mate concerning belief or unbelief nor separate from his mate if that non-Christian mate permits him to lead a Christian life. Each one should leave the other to his faith and commend the whole matter to God. For no one can be driven or forced to believe; instead, God must draw him in grace, and we should teach, admonish, and supplicate, not force. And so a Christian spouse should conduct the outward forms of the married state peaceably with his non-Christian mate and not threaten or defy his partner either with running away or turning him away. For God is not a God of dissension but a God of peace, Rom. 15:33.[23] Therefore He does not teach us dissension but calls us to peace. St. Paul next says:

16. *Wife, how do you know whether you will save your husband? Husband, how do you know whether you will save your wife?*

Only, let everyone lead the life which the Lord has assigned to him.

This means that you should live peaceably with one another in marriage, even with a non-Christian spouse, so long as he does not interfere with your Christian life, and not defy him, nor drive or force him to believe. For it is not your work or within your power that

23 Cf. 1 Cor. 14:33.

anyone should believe, but that is solely in God's power. But since you do not know whether you are worthy that God should save your spouses through you, you should live in peace with them; and no husband should put pressure on his non-Christian wife or quarrel with her concerning faith, nor should any wife do so with a non-Christian husband. If God wants to convert them through you, He will help you to achieve this and distribute among you the grace and gifts for that purpose. This seems to me to be the proper understanding of St. Paul in this passage, that he wants nobody to be forced into faith or piety but that we should live in peace with all men until God with His grace converts through us those whom He wants converted, as St. Peter also teaches in 1 Peter 3:1 f.[24]

One should also treat a spouse who is falsely Christian in the same way; that is, one should tolerate in peace his evil life and not defy him or force him toward the good, but instead, one should in peace and friendliness help him toward it. For you are perhaps not worthy to bring anyone to piety. If you should be worthy, however, God will assign and lend you the grace for it according to His will. Meanwhile you may be certain that you should live with your non-Christian or evil mate, so long as you do not follow or approve of his unbelief or evil life, and he on his part does not force or hold you to it; and you should tolerate such unbelief and injustice from your partner just as one has to tolerate them from the rest of the world and from devils, and you should use kind words to him and live in peace until God grants His grace, so that he, too, may be converted. We continue:

17. *Only, let everyone lead the life which the Lord has assigned to him, and in which God has called him. This is my rule in all the churches.*

This verse concludes the part dealing with the state of matrimony. Its meaning is this: Faith and the Christian life are so free in essence that they are bound to no particular order or estate of society, but they are to be found in and throughout all orders and estates. Therefore you need not accept or give up any particular estate in order to be saved. On the contrary, the estate in which faith and the Gospel find you, there you may stay and find your salvation. Therefore it is not necessary that you give up marriage and leave your non-Christian spouse for the sake of your faith or salvation. On the

---

[24] The text has "1 Peter 2," but we have followed the Weimar editor's suggestion.

other hand, it is not necessary for you to be married, either to a Christian or a non-Christian spouse, for the sake of faith or salvation. And finally, if you are married, whether to a Christian or non-Christian, a virtuous or an evil mate, you are not on that account either saved or condemned. If you are unmarried, you are also on that account neither saved nor condemned. All this is free, free. But if you are a Christian and remain one, then you will be saved; and if you remain unchristian, then you will be condemned.

"This is my rule in all the churches" means "among all Christians to whom I preach. For I do not teach them to leave their present estate and cause dissension, but to stay as they are and live in peace." You see from this that St. Paul considers no single estate blessed except this one — the estate of being Christian; the others are free in the sense that they cannot in themselves further our salvation or damnation. All of them, however, can become blessed through faith or damnable through unbelief, even though in themselves they be well maintained. What is to become of all the monks and nuns and other religious orders that they have elevated to orders of blessedness equal to or even greater than this one true order of salvation? All of them together are lost unless they set them free, so that their consciences are no longer bound and their bodies are restrained not for salvation's sake, but solely as a temporal discipline, as I have often said before.

18. *Was anyone at the time of his call already circumcised? Let him not seek to remove the marks of circumcision. Was anyone at the time of his call uncircumcised? Let him not seek circumcision.*

19. *For neither circumcision counts for anything nor uncircumcision, but keeping the commandments of God.*

Here he gives us several examples for his conclusion that everyone should lead the life to which God has called him. The first part concerns the Jews and heathen, and it means: It makes no difference whether you are a Jew or heathen. If you are circumcised and under the Jewish law, do not imagine therefore that that is a sin or a wrong and you must free yourself of it. For faith is more than circumcision and all law, so that you may be circumcised or uncircumcised and neither is necessary for salvation; rather you are free to remain in either condition. In the same way it is not necessary to marry or remain unmarried, but you are free to do either. Likewise, if you are a heathen, uncircumcised and outside the Jewish law, you should not think that this is wrong and that you must be circumcised; this is optional. Faith alone justifies you, and it alone fulfills the commandment of God.

These two sentences, "Let him not seek to remove the marks of circumcision" and "Let him not seek circumcision," are not to be understood as though St. Paul forbids circumcision or having a foreskin. For who could follow both admonitions at the same time, since they are contrary to one another — circumcision and uncircumcision? He himself says here, "Circumcision counts for nothing," and this contradicts the words "Let him not seek to remove the marks of circumcision." For if he is not to seek to remove the marks of circumcision, then he must be circumcised, and how could circumcision then count for nothing? Therefore when he says, "Uncircumcision counts for nothing," he contradicts the words "Let him not seek circumcision." For if he is not to seek circumcision, he must have a foreskin, and how could uncircumcision then count for nothing? St. Paul simply forbids that these things become matters of necessity and conscience. In short, these things are to be optional in themselves, neither right nor wrong. And so one is not to seek to remove the marks of circumcision, as though it were necessary to be uncircumcised, and on the other hand one should not seek circumcision, as though it were necessary to be circumcised. For both are of no value for salvation, and both may be accepted without qualms of conscience. Therefore neither Jewish nor heathen birth or customs can of themselves hinder or advance us in God's sight, but only faith.

In the same way one should also say to our people: Marriage is nothing, and celibacy is also nothing. To have a heathen spouse is nothing, and to have a Christian spouse is also nothing. Those who are married should stay married. Those who are unmarried should not marry — that is, they should not be disturbed in their consciences as to whether they should marry or not. Here is another example. To be a monk is nothing, and to be a layman is also nothing; to be a priest is nothing, and to be a nun is also nothing. The layman should not become a monk, and the monk should not become a layman; all of which is to say that it should not be a matter of necessity or conscience whether one is a monk or a layman. Rather each should remain as he is, provided that faith is pure and unshaken. For where faith cannot be maintained, there the monk should abandon his order just as a married person should leave an unchristian spouse who drives or keeps him away from the Christian faith.

But here the Jews might say to Paul: "You say that circumcision
is nothing, but only keeping God's commandments. Now, circumcision has been strictly commanded to us by God; how could it then
be nothing?" It would take too long to speak on this point here;
I have done so adequately in other places.[25] Briefly, all the laws in
the book of Moses were given until Christ should come; when He
came, He was to teach and bring faith and love. Where these are,
there all the commandments are fulfilled and annulled and set free,
so that after the coming of Christ no more commandments are needed,
except those of faith and love. If love commands it, then I should be
circumcised; if not, then I should let it be. When love demands anger,
then I should get angry; when it does not, I should forget it. When
love demands an oath, then I should swear an oath; when it does not,
then I should not. And so one is to deal with regard to all the commandments of God and men. But what love is — how it gives attention
only to the desire and need of the neighbor — and what faith is I have
spoken of sufficiently in another place.[26]

20. *Everyone should remain in the state in which he was called.*

21. *Were you a slave when called? Never mind. But if you can gain
your freedom, avail yourself of the opportunity.*

Here he again repeats his final conclusion and gives another example: the slave and the freeman. For at that time there were many
bondsmen, as there still are in many places, now termed serfs, whom
St. Paul calls slaves. Now, just as a marriage partner is to conduct
himself toward his mate, to whom he is bound in body, so a slave
should conduct himself toward his master, whose bodily possession
he is. That is to say, his being a serf does not hinder him in his Christian belief, and he dare not run away from his master for that reason
but should remain with him, regardless of whether the master is a
believer or an unbeliever, righteous or evil; unless, of course, his
master were to hold or force him away from his faith or compel him
to associate himself with his evil life. In that case it is time to leave
him and run away. And all that was said above [27] concerning a Christian marriage partner and how he should conduct himself toward his

[25] Luther had taken up this point in the 1519 *Lectures on Galatians.* Cf. *Luther's Works,* 27, pp. 333—336.

[26] E. g., in the 1520 pamphlet *The Freedom of a Christian.* Cf. *Luther's
Works,* 31, pp. 367 f.

[27] Cf. pp. 36—38.

mate, the same is to be said here of the relations of a Christian serf toward his non-Christian master.

And what Paul here says concerning a slave, the same is to be said of all paid servants, maids, day laborers, workmen, and domestics in their relations to their masters and mistresses. It should also be said of all vows, associations, corporations, or of any tie by which one person is related or obligated to another: in all these matters service, loyalty, and duty are to be maintained, regardless of whether the one party is Christian or non-Christian, good or bad, so long as they do not hinder faith and justice and allow you to live your Christian life. For all such estates are free and no impediment to the Christian faith; and if the king of Poland or Hungary allies himself with the Turks, he should hold to it and say, as St. Paul here teaches us, "God calls us to peace."

"But," St. Paul says, "if you can gain your freedom, avail yourself of the opportunity." This does not mean that you should rob your master of your person and run away without his knowledge and consent, but it means you are not to interpret the words of St. Paul, when he says that everyone should remain in the estate in which he was called, to mean that you must remain a serf, even though you could gain your freedom with the knowledge and consent of your master. St. Paul wants only to instruct your conscience, so that you know that before God both estates are free, whether you are a bondsman or a freedman. He does not wish to hold you back from gaining your freedom, if you can do so with the consent of your master. Therefore it should be the same to your conscience whether you gain your freedom or remain a serf, provided it is done in God and with honor. For the Christian faith does not teach us to take from another what is his but instead to fulfill all duties, even toward those to whom one is not obligated and who have no claim to us.

22. *For he who was called in the Lord as a slave is a freedman of the Lord. Likewise he who was free when called is a slave of Christ.*

This means: It is the same for God whether you are free or in bondage, just as circumcision and uncircumcision are the same; neither hinders faith and salvation. It is the same as when I say: It makes no difference to faith whether you are poor or rich, young or old, beautiful or ugly, learned or ignorant, layman or priest. For he who is called in poverty is rich before God. He who is called in riches is poor before God. He who is called in youth is old before God. He who is called in age is young before God. He who is called in ugliness is beautiful before God. And again: He who is called in ignorance is learned before God. He who is called as a layman is a priest before God. All this is true because faith makes us all equal before God and no difference of person or status will count.

The same is true here: "He who was called as a slave is a freedman of the Lord." This means that before God he counts as much as though he were free and not a slave. Again: "Likewise he who was free when called is a slave of Christ." This means that he is no better than one who is a slave. For things will be as St. Paul says in Gal. 3:28:[28] "There is neither Jew nor Greek, there is neither slave nor free, there is neither male nor female; for you are all one in Christ Jesus." There we have the same faith, the same possessions, the same inheritance — everything is equal. One could even say: He who is called as a man is a woman before God. And she who was called as a woman is a man before God. Therefore the words "a slave of Christ" cannot refer to the service one renders Christ but means rather that one is a slave among men on earth because one's self belongs to Christ and is subservient to Him, so that the slave is equal to a freedman, and the freedman is equal to the slave; but one is still the property of Christ, whose slave one is.

23. *You were bought with a price; do not become slaves of men.*

What is the meaning of these words? Paul has just taught us that one should remain a slave and that this does not stand in the way of Christian faith; but here he forbids us to become slaves. Doubtless he says this as a general rule to contradict those teachings of men which destroy the freedom and equality of belief and place the individual conscience in a vise. For instance, when someone teaches that a Christian may not marry a non-Christian and remain with her — as the rules of the church do — he obstructs the freedom that St. Paul teaches us here and forces people to obey these rules more than God's Word. He calls this "serving men," for these people think they are slaves of God and serving Him, when in reality it is but the teaching of men they serve, and they thereby become the slaves of men. The same is true of those who preached that Christians must be circum-

---

[28] The Weimar editor has corrected the reference from the text's "Gal. 5."

cised and thereby canceled this same freedom. At all points we find
Paul caring and fighting for true Christian freedom against the snare
and dungeon of human regulations.

That this is his true meaning is demonstrated in his words: "You
were bought with a price." By this he means Christ, who with His
own blood bought us and set us free from all sin and law, as we see
in Gal. 5:1. But this purchase does not work itself out according to
the way of the world and does not affect the relations men have with
one another, such as that of a servant toward his master or that of a
wife toward her husband. These relationships are all left intact, and
God wants them maintained. The effect of this purchase is spiritual
and takes place in our conscience. Therefore before God no law any
longer binds or imprisons us. We are all free from all things. Before
we were bound in sin, but now we are rid of all sin. Whatever outwardly remains of relationship or freedom is neither sin nor virtue
but only outward tranquillity or trouble, joy or suffering, as is all
other bodily good and ill, in both of which we can live free and without sin.

24. *So, brethren, in whatever state each was called, there let him remain with God.*

Here Paul repeats this conclusion concerning Christian freedom
for the third time: that all outward things are optional or free before
God and that a Christian may make use of them as he will; he may
accept them or let them go. But here the apostle adds the words
"with God." This means, to the extent that it is of importance between
you and God. For you are doing no service for God if you marry,
remain unmarried, whether you are in bondage or free, become this
or that, eat this or that; on the other hand, you do not displease Him
or sin if you put off or reject one or the other. Finally, you owe God
nothing but to believe and confess; He releases you from all other
things so that you can do as you please without endangering your
conscience. This is so thoroughly true that He does not inquire on
His own behalf whether you have let your wife go, have run away
from your master, or have not kept your agreement, for what does He
profit whether you do these things or don't do them?

But because in this relationship you are bound up with your neighbor and have become his servant, it is God's will that no one be deprived of what is his by means of His freedom but rather that those

things of your neighbor be protected. For although God pays no attention to these things on His own account, He pays attention to them on
account of your neighbor. This is what he means with the words
"with God," as though He were admonishing us: "I did not make you
free among men or with your neighbor, for I do not wish that which
is his taken from him until he gives you permission. But you are entirely free with Me and cannot ruin yourself in My sight by keeping
to or refraining from outward things." Therefore notice this and differentiate between the freedom existing in your relation to God and
the freedom existing in your relation to your neighbor. In the former
this freedom is present, in the latter it is not, and for this reason: God
gives you this freedom only in the things that are yours, not in what
is your neighbor's. There differentiate between what is yours and
what is your neighbor's. That is why no man can leave his wife, for his
body is not his own but his wife's, and vice versa. Likewise the servant
and his body do not belong to him himself but to his master. It would
be of no importance to God if the husband were to leave his wife, for
the body is not bound to God but made free by Him for all outward
things and is only God's by virtue of inward faith. But among men
these promises are to be kept. In sum: We owe nobody anything but
to love (Rom. 13:8) and to serve our neighbor through love. Where
love is present, there it is accomplished that no eating, drinking, clothing, or living in a particular way endangers the conscience or is a sin
before God, except when it is detrimental to one's neighbor. In such
things one cannot sin against God but only against one's neighbor.

And it should be emphasized that this little word "call" does not
in this context mean the social status to which one is called, as when
one says, "Your status is 'married,'" or, "His status is 'priest,'" and
so on, as everyone has his calling from God. Here St. Paul is not
speaking of this calling. He speaks instead of the evangelical call,
which is as much as to say: "Remain in that calling to which you
were called, that is, where you receive the Gospel; and remain as you
were when you were called. If the call comes to you in the married
state, then remain in that wherein you were found. If you are called
in slavery, then remain in the slavery in which you were called."

But what if the Gospel calls me in a state of sin, should I remain
in that? Answer: If you have entered into faith and love, that is, if
you are in the call of the Gospel, then sin as much as you please. But
how can you sin if you have faith and love? Since God is satisfied

with your faith and your neighbor with your love, it is impossible that you should be called and still remain in a state of sin. If, however, you remain in that state, then either you were not called as yet, or you did not comprehend the call. For this call brings you from the state of sin to a state of virtue, making you unable to sin as long as you are in that state. All things are free to you with God through faith; but with men you are the servant of everyman through love.

From this you will see that monasticizing and making of spiritual regulations is all wrong in our time. For these people bind themselves before God to outward things from which God has made them free, thus working against the freedom of faith and God's order. On the other hand, where these people should be bound, namely, in their relations with other men and in serving everyman in love, there they make themselves free, serving no one and being of no use to anyone but themselves, thus working against love. Therefore they are a perverse people, perverting all the laws of God. They want to be free where they are bound and bound where they are free, and yet they hope to be seated much higher in heaven than ordinary Christian people. But they who make such a hellish prison out of heavenly freedom and such a hostile freedom out of loving service shall sit in the deepest hell.

III

THE UNMARRIED STATE

25. *Now concerning the unmarried, I have no command of the Lord, but I give my opinion as one who by the Lord's mercy is trustworthy.*

26. *I think that in view of the present distress it is well for a person to remain as he is.*

We have now heard enough praise of the married state, and it is time to preach of its troubles and do honor to the unmarried state. If it were not St. Paul, I should truly be vexed that he gives such miserly praise and small honor to the noble state of celibacy. First he says that it is not commanded by God, as little as marriage is; that is, it should be free for everyone. But he thus robs it of all the honor that great preachers have up to the present ascribed to it. For where there is no command, there is also no virtue or reward before God; the thing is then in itself absolutely independent. It will be immaterial to God whether you are unmarried or not. And as he says above (v. 22),

"For he who was called in the Lord as a slave is a freedman of the Lord," so here, too, one could say: "She who is called as a virgin is a wife before God," and, "She who is called as a wife in the Lord is a virgin before the Lord." For all is equal before God, and there is no difference between persons nor achievement through works, but solely this one same faith, in all and through all.

The Holy Spirit has therefore told us through St. Paul that celibacy is a very precious thing and highly to be respected on earth so that nobody, because of the greatness and dignity of this estate, should think himself better than another poor Christian but should rather remain in that simplicity of faith that makes us all one before God. For our poisonous nature simply cannot tolerate that it should not preen itself before God in works; and the better the work, the more credit it wants for it. Therefore it is also blinded by the pure radiance of virginity that it considers no estate higher before God than virginity, because nothing that we do on earth is greater or more beautiful. And so it concludes that just as a virgin counts for more on earth, so it will also be in heaven.

This is the source of all those nonsensical teachings of the devil which prepare special little crowns [29] in heaven for all virgins and make them brides of Christ, as though other Christians were not brides of Christ. Then all the poor misguided young people go wild, each one striving toward this little crown and wanting to fill heaven with virgins and brides of Christ. In the meantime the Christian faith is despised and forgotten and finally extinguished, although it alone can win the crown and make us brides of Christ. Know this, however, and remain certain of it, that such becrowned virgins who rely on such teachings and pretend virginity in this fashion instead of the way St. Paul teaches, not one of them is a pure virgin or can remain one, and at the last they will be found to be neither virgins nor brides of Christ.

Second, St. Paul says that in his opinion the unmarried state is good "in view of the present distress." This is the first praise St. Paul has given to virginity. And from this you will see what kind of bless-

---

[29] What Luther here calls *Krönlein* refers to a term originally borrowed from the description of the golden border (*corona aureola*) of the table for the bread of the Presence (Ex. 25:25). In the Middle Ages the *aureola sanctorum* was a distinction awarded to virgins, martyrs, and teachers of the church for their victories over flesh, death, and the devil. It was variously represented in the arts by styles called aureole, nimbus, halo, glory, or mandorla.

ing St. Paul meant when he said above (v. 1), "It is well for a man not to touch a woman," for he said nothing about the virtue of it or its reward in heaven. St. Jerome, too, erred on this point,[30] for he misunderstood and misinterpreted Paul. Paul speaks only of the blessing in this temporal life, as I shall continue to show. This is indeed a good reason to remain unmarried and avoid the troubles of marriage — that a Christian is always under the threat of persecution for the sake of the Gospel, living in constant danger of losing his goods, his friends, and his life, and facing exile or execution. This is what St. Paul terms "the present distress."

Now tell me, where will you find a virgin in any nunnery, as far as the might of the pope reaches, who has remained a virgin for this reason? How are their goods, bodies, or lives endangered? They are so firmly assured of their goods, lives, and friendships, through both papal and imperial power, that no more secure people ever lived on earth. Accordingly, everyone will have to admit that they do not remain virgins because of distress and danger but because of security and in order not to have distress, which is just the opposite of the reason given here by St. Paul. For if the people in the monasteries ever were in such danger or distress, you would see that where there are now thousands upon thousands of monasteries not a wall would be left standing. But why do I waste all these words? You can see well enough for yourself how much need and danger these monastic institutions together with the whole papacy are suffering with regard to their bodies and property: they are all fattened swine, the whole lot of them.

But you say: "But married people have to suffer the same distress and danger for the sake of the Gospel as do the unmarried, for as the Gospel is common to all Christians, so is the cross and persecution. Didn't Abraham, in just such distress, have to take Sarah and leave his father, his goods, and risk his life with her at all times?" Answer: St. Paul does not say that because of such distress one should or must remain unmarried. He says that it is good and useful to remain so. Distress is common to all, but the unmarried have an easier time of it than the married ones. For if Abraham had not had his Sarah, he would have been spared much trouble and pain and would have got along much easier. An unmarried person is only one body and need care for nobody else; a married person is dependent on the partner,

[30] Cf. p. 11, n. 1, above.

much care and effort is required, and quite a variety of incidents are involved, as experience teaches us only too well.

Many will make a wry face at this and be very peeved that they have preserved their virginity for nothing, especially since God will not regard them any more highly than other Christians. But by this very sign one will know that they are the foolish virgins (Matt. 25:3 ff.) who have spilled their oil in that they have remained virgins not from simple Christian belief but for the sake of reward, reputation, honor, and glory. They did not consider that it is well to remain so, as St. Paul tells us here, but wanted to gain something good by it in the life to come. Thus they have made a trade out of their virginity, hoping to gain something with it before God, not being satisfied with the temporal advantage of chastity and the eternal gain of faith. Therefore they cannot help but be downcast, for all this has been difficult for them and yet they have preserved a lost chastity.

27. *Are you bound to a wife? Do not seek to be free. Are you free from a wife? Do not seek marriage.*

28. *But if you marry, you do not sin, and if a girl marries, she does not sin. Yet those who marry will have worldly troubles, and I would spare you that.*

Here you have a statement on both, that neither one is a sin, neither marrying nor not marrying. The apostle's prime concern is to instruct the conscience and secondly to say what is most proper here on earth and for the best. And he emphasizes with very sober words why it is well not to marry and says: "Those who marry will have worldly troubles." This is the song that the whole world sings, recites, and writes about married life: that nobody should marry if he wants peaceful days, and there is much effort and many evil days in that estate which the unmarried are spared. I shall not try to relate the sorrows of married life, for I am told that I know nothing about it and have not experienced it.

Very well, then, but I believe St. Paul in this matter. Furthermore, I know of these sorrows from the Scriptures. The first evidence is when God says to Adam in Gen. 3:19, 17: "In the sweat of your face you shall eat bread" and "In toil you shall eat of it all the days of your life." Here the curse is laid upon man that he must feed himself and his wife, and his faith is put to the test, for "poverty is pain." In this same category belong misfortune with servants, danger to cattle and property, and finally the cunning and deceptions of those with whom he must live and associate. For often one must practice concealment and hold one's tongue and put up with some very evil tricks, because one is bound to one's wife, all of which he would not suffer if he were free. For her part the wife has her own troubles, what with conceiving and bearing children, giving birth to them in pain, not sleeping at night, wearing herself out, and hurting what she most prizes, all of which she would not have to suffer if she would remain a virgin; and God said to her in Gen. 3:16: "In pain you shall bring forth children."

The second evidence of sorrow, which St. Peter mentions is that a woman is a weak vessel and fragile,[31] so that a man must endure much on her account if they are to stay united. It is for this reason that one seldom finds a good marriage where love and peace are at home. Furthermore, according to Gen. 3:16, God made woman subject to man, so that she must travel and stay where he travels and stays, and her spirit must be broken often. If there are more vexations connected with this estate and if you want to know them, just take a wife yourself; but I think these are the most serious ones, for they cover many things indeed. But all this is neither sin nor evil in the sight of God but only a temporal, outward unpleasantness in this life which all of us must consider when we want to, or must, marry. Doubtless it has been mentioned by the apostle so that nobody should despise the married state because of its difficulties, as though it were displeasing to God for that reason, or, as the false teachers have said, as though it were impossible to serve God in that state, for they have placed and praised all good works and service to God outside this estate.

For this reason St. Paul tempers his words and speaks of "worldly troubles" and not of "spiritual troubles." For the trouble of the spirit is sin and an evil conscience, but the world's troubles are outward unpleasantness, strain, and boredom. And that which St. Paul terms "worldly" in the Hebrew manner we term "bodily," so that troubles of the flesh are the same as troubles of the body, not that they are of the body like a sickness, but that they are troubles in the things with which we must bodily associate, or troubles that concern the body, such as wife and child, servants, house and land, cattle and property, and all such things among people in general in this false and evil world.

[31] Cf. 1 Peter 3:7.

Now he who has the grace to remain chaste should restrain his curiosity, stay away from marriage, and not deliberately call forth such misfortunes unless forced by necessity, as St. Paul faithfully advises him here and as he should be advised. For it is a great and noble freedom to be unmarried, and it saves one much worry, unpleasantness, and suffering, which St. Paul wishes for everyone when he says, "and I would spare you that." This is the proper praise of the unmarried estate: not to mention its merit and virtue before God but to praise its peace and pleasure in this life. There are always those who rush into marriage from curiosity and without any need to, who might otherwise remain chaste, and thus they unnecessarily seek evil days. And if they find them, it serves them right.

29. *I mean, brethren, the appointed time has grown very short; from now on, let those who have wives live as though they had none,*

30. *and those who mourn as though they were not mourning, and those who rejoice as though they were not rejoicing, and those who buy as though they had no goods,*

31. *and those who deal with the world as though they had no dealings with it. For the form of this world is passing away.*

This is a general teaching for all Christians, that they should treasure that eternal blessing which is theirs in the faith, despising this life so that they do not sink too deeply into it either with love and desire or suffering and boredom, but should rather behave like guests on earth, using everything for a short time because of need and not for pleasure. This would mean having a wife as though I did not have one, when in my heart I would rather remain unmarried but in order to avoid sin have found it necessary to have one. But he who seeks not necessity but also desire, he does not have a wife but is himself possessed by a wife. A Christian should hold to this principle also in all other things. He should only serve necessity and not be a slave to his lust and nurture his old Adam.

32. *I want you to be free from anxieties. The unmarried man is anxious about the affairs of the Lord, how to please the Lord;*

33. *but the married man is anxious about worldly affairs, how to please his wife,*

34. *and his interests are divided. And the unmarried girl or woman is anxious about the affairs of the Lord, how to be holy in body*

and spirit; but the married woman is anxious about worldly affairs, how to please her husband.

Here we see another fruit and use of chastity on earth: that one may better please the Lord. Not in the way that the monastics now say, however, with their singing and readings, for with them it is no longer a divine service. Instead one should, in a blameless way, attend to the Word of God, read daily, pray, act, and preach as Paul admonishes Timothy.[32] For a married man cannot give himself up entirely to reading and praying but is, as St. Paul here says, "divided"; that is, he must devote much of his time to making life agreeable for his wife, and like Martha, he is bound up in the multitude of concerns demanded by married life. An unmarried person is undivided by such concerns and can give himself entirely to God.

But the apostle does not want to condemn the married estate on this account. For he does not say that a married man is anxious only about the affairs of this world, or is separated from God. He says only that he is divided and is anxious about many affairs and cannot constantly pray or attend to the Word of God; although his work and care is good, still it is much better to be free to pray and attend to God's Word. In so doing the unmarried person is of much use and comfort to many people, yes, to all of Christendom, and this reason is great and noble enough to keep everyone from marrying who has the grace to remain single. But our monastics, who neither pray nor learn God's Word but torture themselves with the regulations of men and murmur and howl in the choir, they would do better to tend pigs as married people.

35. *I say this for your own benefit, not to lay any restraint upon you, but to promote good order and to secure your undivided devotion to the Lord.*

Paul says here: "I do not command chastity but leave it to your choosing; furthermore I do not advise it for you, as though you had to be ashamed if you did not remain chaste but would rather marry, for I want no one to be ensnared or bound in this. All I say is that the unmarried state is a free and fine thing. He who wants to and can do so, let him accept it." Here you see that no snare is to be laid in these matters, nor is anyone to be forced to chastity by commands or vows.

[32] Cf. 1 Tim. 4:13.

It is also certain that Paul addressed these words to all Christians in Corinth and not only to the laity. He ascribes no virtue to the unmarried state in the sight of God but commends it for its good and utility in this life, as he also did above.

36. *If anyone thinks that he is not in good repute because of his unmarried daughters, because they are over marriageable age, and it has to be, let him do as he wishes: let them be married — it is no sin.*

This is a strange text, that one may give a young woman in marriage solely because one has been made fun of on account of his daughters being over the usual marriageable age. But even in this case St. Paul wants everyone to feel free to do what he thinks is good and useful. "If it has to be," he says, that is, if it cannot be otherwise, and if it is the custom in your city and among your associates that one is ashamed to have his daughters become old maids, one should do as he wishes: he should marry them off, or refuse to be shamed. Truly this shows no great opinion of the unmarried estate, that the apostle would sacrifice it solely because of a little shame or derision. He must not have known about the little virgin crowns.[33]

37. *Nevertheless, he who standeth steadfast in his heart, having no necessity, but has power over his own will and has so decreed in his heart that he will keep his virgin, does well.*

In the immediately preceding passage he says, "If anyone thinks . . . because of his unmarried daughters," and here he says, "he who . . . will keep his virgin," both of these referring to the father, mother, brother, or whoever the guardians are. Thus it is indicated that children should not marry or remain unmarried from their own whim, but those under whose authority they are should give them in marriage or keep them from it. But where they have no such guardians or they refuse to accept the responsibility for them, they should do as they can. What Paul says about the "power over his own will" is to be understood to mean that no guardian may restrain an unmarried woman against her will, for where her will opposes his, there he has no power over his own will. This would also be true in other cases where he might be forced by others to give her in marriage, such as his being shamed because of his old maids or being put under pressure by his friends or those in authority.

[33] Cf. p. 48, n. 29, above.

38. *So then he who gives her in marriage does well; but he who does not give her in marriage does better.*

Here we find expressed the authority of the parents over their children: the children may not marry or remain unmarried without parental consent, as I have often stated.[34] Concerning the words "well" and "better" I have already said enough above; [35] "it is well" should be understood to mean that on earth the married state is good, that is, without sin and pleasing to God and optional for everybody. But the unmarried state is more peaceful and freer.

39. *A wife is bound to her husband as long as he lives. If the husband dies, she is free to be married to whom she wishes, only in the Lord.*

40. *But in my judgment she is happier if she remains as she is. And I think that I have the Spirit of God.*

Paul says the same thing in Rom. 7:2 ff., using a spiritual metaphor that he states here and elaborates on there. But it is the conclusion of this chapter that marriage is a bound thing in this world but free before God, just as he says above that a slave is a freedman before the Lord, even though he be a slave in this world. Those who live without marriage are free and unbound, both before God and in this world. Therefore he terms their estate more blessed than the married estate, not in the sense of eternal blessedness, in which only faith will be greater or count for more according to its quality, but in the sense of this life, in which that state has less trouble, worry, danger, and work.

Now we may summarize this chapter thus: It is well not to marry unless it is necessary. It becomes necessary when God has not given us the rare gift of chastity, for no one is created for chastity, but we are all born to beget children and carry the burdens of married life, according to Gen. 1, 2, and 3. Now, if someone should not suffer from this necessity, he would be the exception solely by the grace and the miraculous hand of God, not because of command, vow, or intent. Where God does not effect this, it may be attempted, but it will come to no good end. Therefore they are nothing but abominable murderers of souls who put young people into monasteries and nunneries and keep them there by force, as though chastity were something that

---

[34] E. g., in *A Sermon on the Estate of Marriage*, 1519 (*Luther's Works*, 44, pp. 11 f.) and in the sermon on Matt. 2:1-12 for Epiphany in *Kirchenpostille*, 1522 (W, X-i-1, 642—645).

[35] E. g., p. 49 above.

could be put on and off like a shoe and something that is in our hand. Meanwhile they themselves take quite a different view and drive others to attempt what they have never even raised their little finger to attempt or would not be able to. It is easy to say: "Be chaste," but why are you not chaste? It is great for you to eat like a pig and drink like a horse while telling me to fast! But enough said for those who are willing to listen. And what more can one say to those who will not listen? May God enlighten them or prevent them from strangling souls in this fashion! Amen.

In conclusion I herewith bring to the attention of all that everything published with my consent and knowledge has first been inspected by the proper people, not only according to the imperial order but also in keeping with the authority of our university. Things published elsewhere and behind my back should in all fairness not be ascribed to me.[36]

36 About a month before the completion of this treatise on 1 Cor. 7, Luther had released an answer to a mandate of the Diet of Nürnberg entitled *Against the Perverters and Falsifiers of the Imperial Mandate.* Regarding Article III of the mandate, "That nothing new should be printed or be put up for sale unless it has first been approved by responsible people in the government," Luther wrote: "This article has long been overdue, and I will of course comply with it, for we at the university have adopted a similar code in the past year. But this is not to be taken to mean that it is forbidden to print and to sell the Holy Scriptures or that the stricture applies to things already in print. . . . The Word of God must remain unrestricted" (W, XII, 65).

COMMENTARY ON
1 CORINTHIANS 15

Translated by
MARTIN H. BERTRAM

The Fifteenth Chapter of St. Paul's First Letter
to the Corinthians

PREFACE

Tʜɪs chapter deals throughout with our article of faith concerning the resurrection of the dead. This theme was occasioned by the fact that a number of factious spirits had arisen among the Corinthians who were ruining their faith and teaching that the resurrection of the dead is nothing. And there were others, as St. Paul states elsewhere, who tried to be clever and subtle and alleged that the resurrection had taken place a long time ago. As they interpreted it, we arose from sin through Baptism and entered into a new spiritual life, etc. Matters finally came to such a pass that people believed (as in the case of the Sadducees in the days of Christ) that man's years did not extend beyond this life, that man's life was comparable to that of a cow or of other animals, and that man was created for no other purpose than to live blamelessly here on earth. And thus this doctrine gave birth to many impertinent fellows who believed absolutely nothing regarding the resurrection or a future life, who only ridiculed this doctrine and mocked the Christians in every way. They acted like real heathen. St. Paul quotes their own words, as they said: "What kind of bodies will we have if we all rise again? Where will we all find room? If we all live at the same time, how can we find sufficient food and drink? How can we all have wives and beget children and perform other natural functions of this body and this life? etc." And thus others too now began to affect wisdom. They made bold to figure out with their own reason and cleverness how it would be possible if all who had ever been born were to rise again at the same time and forgather again in a life such as we now lead, etc. With such inane babble they weakened the Christians' faith in this article and perverted this article into tomfoolery. And unfortunately today we have again arrived at the point where many, both peasants and townspeople, and particularly Junker Hans of the nobility, prate so absurdly, shamelessly, and heathenishly about this when they presume to be so smart and stick their nose into the Scriptures. For now they have become so learned through us that they are all our teachers and each one claims to know everything.

Paul had to appear on the scene against such base wiseacres, who also aspired to be acclaimed as excellent teachers, and he had to prevent this poison from spreading. He had to compose a whole long chapter in strong and solid proof of this article of faith and in refutation of their injurious prattle. Thereby he also served us in the future, so that we might be safeguarded the more strongly and be equipped to preserve this article — for the latter is so vigorously, mightily, and clearly substantiated here — especially since the apostles themselves prophesied that in these latter days many mockers would arise in Christianity who would ridicule our belief and the article pertaining to the Last Day, the resurrection, and the future life, and who would surely deride us as the biggest fools still to hope for this and to suffer every peril and privation because of it, such as we already see come to pass.

It is truly a sin and a shame, indeed a miserable plague, that the time should come in Christendom, not only in these days of the world's last dregs but even already in the time of the apostles, yes, even among those whom they had shortly before visited and taught, even where they had shortly before planted and founded Christianity, that such a calamity should befall so soon, that some of them dared to arise, such as the apostles' disciples, and publicly proclaim that there was no resurrection and no future life, and that those who professed to be Christians should deny and ridicule this article, although they were baptized on it and had become Christians by reason of this, the article on which also all their hope and consolation should be based. Thus they had forfeited everything with this and had believed, acted, and suffered in vain. For where this article is surrendered, all the others are gone too; and the chief article and the entire Christ are lost or preached entirely in vain.

For after all, that is the goal of our faith in Christ, of Baptism, of sermon, and of Sacrament, that we hope for a new life, that we come to Christ, that we rule eternally with Him, delivered from sin, devil, death, and every evil. Whoever does not think accordingly, or who even denies and derides this, will surely also have a low regard for Christ and for all that He did as well as for all that He gave us and instituted for us. For what would it amount to if we had received nothing better from Him than this wretched life and if we relied on Him in vain and suffered all that devil and world can inflict on us, and if

He proved a liar with His great promises to us? As St. Paul himself says later (v. 19): "If in this life only we have hoped in Christ, we are of all men most to be pitied." But what more shameful thing might be said of Christians than that such is being preached among them and that they still have no higher regard for their Christ? And yet it happened that the dear apostle had to experience this from his pupils. He had to see and hear this in his own parish or diocese. It must have pained him that he was unable to fend this off, and that he could only strengthen and preserve the assailed faith of a small and faithful group through this epistle.

But this has been recorded as our warning and admonition, that we, having the precious Word in its purity, be concerned and intent on being guided by it, apprehend it well and firmly, adhere to it, and do not become slothful, secure, and weary of it, lest factious spirits and wiseacres arise also among us to destroy these articles of faith and deprive us of them (on which our entire salvation and happiness are founded). For since the Corinthians, St. Paul's own disciples, to whom he had also preached and imparted the unadulterated Word, fell so miserably, a striking example has been placed before our very noses, bringing home to us the statement of St. Paul in 1. Cor. 10:12: "Therefore let anyone who thinks that he stands take heed lest he fall," being too sure of himself. This prompts us, when seeing or hearing someone who has become such a sow and heathen, to say apprehensively and prayerfully: "Dear Lord, do not let me fall thus." For this happens so easily when we feel secure and careless. For the devil surely presses us hard and assails us and also great men with the temptation to disbelieve this article or to doubt it. Pope, cardinals, and other great men, especially in Italy, are also fine, wise, intelligent, and learned people; yet if three could be found who believed this article, we should say that these were many. Therefore we may well take a lesson from the fact that the foremost and almost the first congregation among the Gentiles, in whose midst St. Paul had preached the longest, was split into such factions the moment he turned his back. It deteriorated to such an extent that it is terrible to recall. What might we who are preaching now expect when the holy and exalted apostle, compared to whom we are nothing, experienced this at the hands of his disciples? Moreover, this happened during his own lifetime, obliging him to resist this with writings and in every other way possible.

It is, God be praised, more tolerable when this error is confined to the mad rabble, such as the peasant in the village, the citizen in the towns, the nobility in the country, who lead such an infamous life, with no regard for God and God's Word. For these die as they lived, that is, like sows and cows. Thus a peasant said to his pastor, who visited him when he was about to die and asked him whether he desired extreme unction, "No, dear sir, a peasant dies very well without unction." But it is the very devil when this finds its way into the pulpit and the article of faith is assailed by those who are preachers and, following Paul, ascend the pulpit and govern Christendom in his stead. When such men open their despicable mouth and instill this in the people, they above all others work this murderous damage, especially if they are learned and very intelligent. For if only the pastors remain faithful and preserve the doctrine, God will bestow His grace that there will always be a number to accept it; for where the Word is pure and unadulterated, there will, of course, be fruit.

Therefore I have exhorted so often, and still exhort, that all who wish to be saved pray diligently, as Christ Himself commands us to pray (Matt. 9:38), that God may grant us faithful laborers and pastors who are sincere and adhere to the Word. Then if God be willing, there will be no danger. For the pulpit can and must alone preserve Baptism, Sacrament, doctrine, articles of faith, and all estates in their purity.

However, if we neglect to pray and if we anger God with our security, weariness, and ingratitude, He will send us, instead of St. Paul and all upright pastors, stupid asses who will snatch away both Sacrament and Word, and we lose everything, both in the doctrine and the office. Thus we can observe today that this has already befallen several countries and cities, which have not only lost the Word through such men but have also been led into every sort of misery. Through his lies and deceit the devil always leads to murder and ruin. But if faithful pastors had remained in those places, the pure doctrine would surely also have remained, and other misery would have been spared them, even though the rabble had espoused the error enthusiastically. For it does not dismay me so much to have a lout or a dolt blaspheme or to have a plebeian, insolent nobleman rave and rant, or to have some other wiseacre jeer. For all of these, Christendom and the pulpit will remain intact. But the damage is wrought when they who teach become factious spirits themselves and the people are obliged to preserve themselves, and not only to preserve themselves, but also to be on guard and defend themselves against their own pastors. That is done only with great difficulty. For even without this the poor multitude is soon mislead; it cannot govern and lead itself.

Therefore, I say, we are to think of this as put before our eyes as a terrible example which serves to startle and to warn us; and if such spirits were to arise in our midst, we must not permit this article to be taken from us or to be perverted. For I regret to say that I am worried that our great ingratitude merits that some men will arise also among us and publicly deny this article. Therefore it is indeed necessary that we pray earnestly, sincerely, and incessantly to have the pulpit remain pure, so that such affliction may be prevented or checked. For the pulpit can still staunchly resist all sorts of error and endure the whole world's malice. Let whoever will be converted, be converted; and whoever does not wish to be, let him be gone. At least some will be saved. But where darkness encompasses the whole world and Christians are few in number and, moreover, when the pulpits are occupied by worthless, pernicious pastors, the time will not be far distant when thunder, lightning, and every plague of false doctrine will burst in upon us unexpectedly and before we are aware of it, which believes neither this nor any other article of faith. And we will have to tolerate pastors who mislead us with such loose prattle of reason, yes, even of the vulgar, beastly understanding which sows also have, such as those people in Corinth also shared, as we shall see. Therefore Paul takes this matter very seriously in order to preserve his people in the faith in this article against such abominable factions. And he substantiates this article so mightily that even the gates of hell cannot undo matters wherever the Word is adhered to and one does not give way to let blind, foolish reason indulge in subtle arguments; for reason knows nothing and can comprehend nothing of such sublime matters. And thus St. Paul begins:

1-2. *Now I would remind you, brethren, in what terms I preached to you the Gospel, which you received, in which you stand, by which you are saved, if you hold it fast — unless you believed in vain.*

That is spoken as it were by way of preface. Thereby he wants to draw them away in the very beginning of his discourse from their subtle disputations over this article and bring them back to the Word which he had preached to them. He wishes to exhort them to remember and to abide by what they had heard, that they might not be diverted from it nor give heed to other instruction. Here he gives them a gentle dig, although clothed in fine and proper words, because they had permitted themselves to be carried so far adrift and had arrived at a point where it became necessary to admonish them not to forget this and where the necessity of this reminder really marked a disgrace for them. But thus it goes, as I said before, when false teachers are given an opening and gain entry somewhere; people first become sated with the true doctrine and no longer have any regard for it, and thus they become ever more estranged from it until it is finally forgotten entirely.

Therefore St. Paul introduces his remarks with these words: "Now I would remind you, etc.," as if to say: "I perceive clearly that it will be necessary always to admonish you to be mindful of what I preached to you, lest you lose sight of it or let it be supplanted in your heart by a different message and doctrine." For wherever this is not constantly pursued and recalled, and where the heart does not occupy itself with it, there doors and windows stand wide ajar for all sorts of seduction to enter and for the extinction and removal of pure doctrine.

"But I remind you," St. Paul says, "of the precious Gospel which I, Paul, proclaimed to you. For I behold that others, too, wish to enjoy the repute of preaching the Gospel. In that way they would suppress my doctrine, so that whatever Paul proclaims would be accounted nothing. Instead they want to be regarded as the true apostles and teachers of the Gospel, and they alone want to have the glory and the function to preach it correctly. To counteract this, I must remind you and arouse you to recall and to behold what you received from me. For you originally received it and learned it from no other than from me. It is from me that you learned what the Gospel, what Christ, what faith, and what everything is. If you ponder this, you will, I am sure, cling to it and not be misled so easily to something different by their boasting and prating. For if you wish to heed the Gospel properly and adhere to it, you must reasonably heed what was first proclaimed to you, what was implanted by me and believed by you. For I was, as you know, the first to bring you the message of Jesus Christ. Next to God, you are indebted to none but me for arriving at this knowledge and for being incorporated into Christendom. Therefore you must not esteem this so lightly and be turned away from it by people who boast of the Gospel at my expense, as though they would teach it to you differently or better than I did. Actually you would know of no Gospel if it had not been for me; indeed, these other people, one and all, would not know a letter of the Gospel if they had not heard and learned it from me. But now they use it against me and also divert you, under its very name, from it."

You see, St. Paul had the same experience that we have today at the hands of our factions. Now that the Gospel has again been brought into the light of day by us and they themselves have learned it from us, they encroach upon our work and force themselves into places where the Gospel has begun to take hold and where we cleared a way for it. What we planted and what we taught correctly they now spoil by presuming to be our teachers and to improve everything we did, although without us they would never have learned as much as a word about it. Thus Paul, too, had to endure that a number of his pupils, who regarded themselves much smarter and more learned, arose as soon as he had departed and presumed to reform and correct everything as though his Gospel were nothing. And yet they, under the name of the Gospel, perverted and ruined everything and did nothing but mislead the people.

"Furthermore," Paul continues, "you know that the Gospel was not only first proclaimed to you by me but also that its coming to you and its stay with you was not without fruit. For by the grace of God you accepted it as the true Gospel and recognized it as the real truth. And through it you obtained God's Spirit and God's grace and a sincere faith in Christ. And as many of you as are Christians today still stand solely by virtue of that same Gospel which you received from me. And not only that, but by the same Gospel you are also saved. Therefore you should hold fast to it by all means. You should not be persuaded to gape openmouthed at a different Gospel proclaimed to you by others, who make my message contemptible among you, as though it were nothing and as though they could preach a loftier Gospel.

"For even if you had nothing else, you must note the fruits produced among you by my Gospel. Compare this with what they teach you. See whether they are able to give you anything better. Then you will have to understand that you became Christians through my Gospel, that you were baptized in this, that you believed in it, and that you must still remain in that faith to be saved. That the others did not accomplish with their preaching, nor can they do this now, for they cannot present a different and better Gospel which produces more than mine produced and still produces. And if you wish to follow a preacher of the Gospel, you should much rather follow me, who first proclaimed it to you and from whom they, too, first had to learn it. You yourselves must bear witness that I proclaimed it to you correctly and that you thereby received the Spirit and much fruit; that, even though they boast much and make me appear contemptible to you, they cannot do better than I — if only they could do as well as I, but unfortunately they are unable to do this. Instead they spoil and undo everything, so that you again lose both the Gospel and its fruits. Why, then, would you permit yourselves to be duped and fooled and deceived so abominably by their loose talk?"

But when Paul and other true pastors boast thus — as indeed they must boast of their Gospel — and declare that they alone proclaim the truth, and when the factious spirits hear this, they become foolish and silly and make such an ado and say: "Well, is he not proud and presumptuous! He can do nothing but praise himself, just as though he alone were everything, as though he could not err, and as though others did not also have the Spirit, etc." And amid such an outcry they pretend to have unusual humility and profound devotion and nothing but the Spirit. And then the mob rallies to them, believing that this must surely be true. And as it is, the factious spirits enjoy two great advantages with the rabble: the one is curiosity, the other, satiety. Those are two large gates through which the devil can pass with a wagon of hay, indeed, with all of hell, prompting them to say: "Oh, this man can preach about nothing but Baptism, the Ten Commandments, the Lord's Prayer, and the Creed, with which even the children are conversant. What's the idea, that he constantly harangues us with the same message? Who is not able to do that? After all, one must not always stick with the same thing, but develop and progress, etc." That signifies satiety with and weariness of the message. Junker Curiosity joins himself to this and says: "Oh, we must also hear this fellow. He is a fine, learned, and pious man, etc." Thus they lend a hand and humor this curiosity to hear whatever their ears itch to hear, saying: "Dear people, all this while you have been hearing the selfsame thing. You must progress beyond that and hear and examine not only one but also others." And thus a person follows these people, lets himself be coaxed and wheedled, stands there gaping and staring and gives ear to all that is told him.

And that demonstrates the truth of what Moses says in Deut. 29:19: *absumit ebrius sitientem*,[1] "a drunkard leads the thirsty, and both are

[1] Luther has adapted the Vulgate's *absumat ebria sitientem*.

lost." For the teacher is drunk and full of the vile devil, belching and vomiting forth. And they are so curious, allowing themselves to be led and taught as anyone chooses to lead and teach them, as people "who will listen to anybody and can never arrive at a knowledge of the truth," as St. Paul says (2 Tim. 3:7). That will also come to pass when we are gone. Everywhere such drunkards will spew out to the poor people: "Do you suppose that these men knew everything, or that you understood them correctly? You have much to learn." With such talk such a preacher can lead a multitude to its destruction.

Whoever wants to be proof against that and be safe must take this admonition to heart and be warned to retain and cling to this Word which Paul proclaimed and to ignore whatever objections others might raise to it, even though these may boast of their side of the story and lend it a good appearance. For here you hear what fruit this Gospel of St. Paul produced among them and what fruit it still produces, namely, that all became Christians through it and were saved and that people must still be saved by it. And since this fruit is ours by virtue of the Gospel, why should we search further or permit ourselves to be diverted from this and be directed and led to other things? For whatever directs us otherwise can surely not be as good, but it must be false and sheer seduction, since it pretends to have something which we already have by means of this Gospel; and thereby it denies all this or disdains it utterly. Therefore Paul addresses the Corinthians as though it were unnecessary to admonish them beyond asking them to recall and observe what they received and how they became Christians. "For if you note that," he wants to say, "you will surely adhere to it and remain safe from all sorts of error. For you can easily differentiate between my doctrine and theirs and judge in accordance with what you gain from each, observing whether they are able to submit something better than my Gospel, by which you are saved." And let us note here that Paul is speaking of the oral presentation of the Gospel preached by him and that he assigns to it such a claim and such praise, that they "stand in it and are saved by it" alone. This is done in contrast to our blind spirits who disdain the external Word and Sacrament, and in their stead adduce their own imaginary spiritism.

However, Paul appends a warning by way of precaution, saying: "If you hold it fast — unless you believed in vain." Those are hard and sharp words, and yet they are spoken in a friendly and winning tone, so that they might see how faithfully and fatherly he is disposed toward them and how concerned he is about them. He wishes to say: "You know, of course, what I proclaim to you, if you but recall that and hold to it and not let yourselves be misled by others. You also perceive what others are proclaiming as you compare the two, unless it be that you did not hold to it but already forsook it and believed in vain, which I hope is surely not the case."

For Paul is speaking as a faithful pastor, who must do both, hope for the best regarding them and simultaneously be concerned about them. Thus he wants to comfort them lest they despair and to admonish them to return and cling to this firmly when they are tempted to fall away. And again he wants to warn them not to be unconcerned but to remember the danger and harm which failure to remain staunchly with what they heard from him entails, as if to say: "I assure you, if you do not adhere to the Gospel and, instead, give ear to others, then my preaching was in vain and you believed in vain. Then all that was yours till now was futile and is lost, both Baptism and Christ. Then you can no longer hope for salvation, and all that you did hitherto is destroyed and ineffectual. That will be the result if you want to listen to those who boastfully allege to have something different and something more precious. Therefore I want to have done my duty and have a clear conscience, having warned you faithfully against incurring your own harm and ruin. Now the fault is not mine but yours if the Gospel is preached in vain and fails to produce what it should. For, as you know, I did not stint preaching to you but I gave richly of what I received [as he will state later]. No, the fault is yours because you did not remain true to it. But if you did retain it, you know how and in what form I preached it to you. For I did not preach it, as they claim and say, in a human form, in accord with reason and understanding. For to proclaim it in such a worldly form, or to judge in accordance with it, surely is to destroy and surrender the Gospel entirely. And if you surrendered such a form as I preached to you, you have also surrendered the faith and with it lost everything pertaining to your salvation." Both to say that and to hear that would be terrible; and this should be sufficient warning to hold assiduously and diligently to the Gospel preached by the apostle Paul.

Behold, thus the apostle at the very outset wants to lead us away from all disputation and tutelage of reason and direct us solely to the Word, which he had received from Christ and had proclaimed to them. And thereby he wishes to show us how to conduct ourselves and act over against all articles of faith. With regard to this I always say that faith must have absolutely nothing but the Word on its side and must permit no subtle argumentation or human ideas in addition. Otherwise it is impossible for faith to be retained and preserved. For human wisdom and reason cannot progress beyond judging and concluding in accordance with what it sees and feels or with what it comprehends with the senses. But faith must transcend such feeling and understanding or make its decision contrary to these and cling to whatever the Word submits. Reason and human competence do not enable faith to do that, but this is the work of the Holy Spirit on the heart of man. Otherwise, if man could comprehend this with his reason, or if he were to resolve this in accordance with what is and what is not consonant with his reason, he would not need faith or the Holy Spirit.

For instance, in this article we are asked to believe in the resurrection of the dead, to believe that all men will be revived again on one day, that our body and soul will be united as they are united today. To believe that is surely not man's competence and power. For reason does no more than merely to observe the facts as they appear to the eye, namely, that the world has stood so long, that one person dies after another, remains dead, decomposes, and crumbles to dust in the grave, from which no one has ever returned; in addition, that man dies and perishes so miserably, worse and more wretchedly than any beast or carcass; also, that he is burned to ashes or turns to dust, with a leg resting in England, an arm in Germany, the skull in France, and is thus dismembered into a thousand pieces, as the bones of the saints are usually shown. When reason approaches this article of faith and reflects on it, it is entirely at a loss. Here so many odd, peculiar, and absurd ideas present themselves that reason must necessarily judge that there is nothing to it. It judges in the same manner as in everything else; for instance, when misfortune strikes and we permit reason to cogitate and to measure what it finds in God's Word with its own understanding. Or when man feels his sin and his conscience and fails to hold exclusively to the words of grace and forgiveness through Christ but only surveys his sin and reflects on the Law and on works and tries to scourge and torment himself with these, he surely removes himself from forgiveness and has lost the grace which he should apprehend through faith.

That has been the experience of all heretics with the exalted article of Christ. And this still happens to our factions today with regard to

Baptism and the Sacrament, because they do not simply believe the Word but in addition speculate and brood with their reason. And reason cannot but say that bread is bread and that water is water. How can bread be Christ's body, or how can water be a washing of the soul? Reason cannot and will not remain within the Word or be captive to it, but it must also give its cleverness a voice, and this insists on understanding and mastering everything, etc. And because reason sees this running directly counter to its understanding and to all senses and feeling, and contrary to all experience too, it departs from it and even denies it. Or when it cannot get around the Word, it twists it and it trims it with glosses, forcing the Word into agreement with reason. Then faith no longer has any room but must give way to reason and perish.

But over against all that reason suggests or tries to fathom and explore, yes, against everything that all senses feel and comprehend, we must learn to adhere to the Word and simply to judge according to it, even though our eyes behold how man is interred, furthermore, that he decays and is consumed by worms and finally crumbles into dust. Likewise, even though I feel sin oppressing me so sorely and my conscience smiting me, so that I cannot ignore these, yet faith must conclude the opposite and hold firmly to the Word in both these instances. For if you want to judge according to what you see and feel, and if you, when God's Word is held before you, hold your feeling against that, saying: "You are indeed telling me much, however, my heart is telling me far differently, and if you felt what I feel, you, too, would talk differently, etc.," then you do not have God's Word in your heart; this has been suppressed and extinguished by your own ideas, reason, and reflections. In short, when you no longer accord the Word greater validity than your every feeling, your eyes, your senses, and your heart, you are doomed, and you can no longer be helped. For this is called an article of faith, not one of your reason or wisdom, nor of human power or ability. Therefore here, too, you must judge solely by the Word, regardless of what you feel or see. I, too, feel my sin and the Law and the devil on my neck. I feel myself oppressed under these as under heavy burdens. But what am I to do? If I were to judge according to my feeling and my ability, I, together with all other men, should have to perish and despair. However, if I wish to be helped, I must surely turn about and look to the Word and say accordingly: "Indeed, I feel God's wrath, the devil, death, and hell; but the Word conveys a different message, namely, that I have a gracious God through Christ, who is my Lord over the devil and all creatures. To be sure, I feel and see that I and all other men must rot in the ground; but the Word informs me differently, namely, that I shall rise in great glory and live eternally.

That is the knowledge and the wisdom of faith. It renders the wisdom of the world, which regards this a stupid message, foolishness. The world's wisdom gives itself great airs and says: "Well, all the Gospel can talk about is that we are to be lords over death, sin, and all things; and yet we observe only the opposite in us and the whole world, namely, that death, sin, and devil prevail, and not life." Worldly wisdom is based and founded on such observations. It says: "Preach as you may and say what you will, but I see things differently." Therefore these two facts must stand side by side, that we are lords over devil and death and that we at the same time lie prostrate at their feet. The one must be believed, the other is felt. The devil must be lord over the world and whatever is part of it. He holds us with all his might. He is far stronger than we are. For we are his guests, residing as strangers in an inn. Therefore, whatever dwells in us, in our flesh and blood, of the world and this life must be subject to the devil, enabling him to deal with us as he wishes.

Now you will say: "What are you preaching and what, after all, do you believe? Since you yourself confess that we do not feel or perceive this, your message is necessarily vain and a mere dream. For if there were some basis to your message, this would have to be demonstrated also by experience." I reply: "That is exactly what I am saying, namely, that we must first believe contrary to our experience what cannot be believed humanly, and that we must feel what we do not feel." Accordingly, in the very thing in which the devil, with respect to feeling, is my lord, he must be my servant. And when I lie prostrate and the whole world lies on top of me, I am still lying on top. How is that? If it is to be true, you say, experience must come along, and this must be perceived. You are right; however, perception must follow later, and faith must precede it, working without and beyond perception. Thus my conscience must, as it feels sin and as it fears and trembles, become lord and victor over sin; not through feeling and thinking but through faith in the Word. And thereby it is comforted and sustained against and over sin until sin is banished entirely and is no longer felt. Thus death, too, lies prostrate under us, so that it cannot devour or hold us. And yet it attaches itself to our neck with pestilence, sword, and all sorts of troubles and hurls us under itself into the grave, where we have to rot. And yet we do not remain there permanently but break away and come forth more gloriously than the heaven with sun and stars. That is what Christ also experienced. When He died and was buried, there was no perception or expectation of life. And it was so very hard for the disciples to believe that the Christ lying in the grave behind a sealed rock was the Lord over death and grave. They themselves said (Luke 24:21): "We had hoped that he was the one to redeem Israel."

Therefore it is all-important to heed St. Paul's admonition here, to adhere firmly to the Word which we received, to call this to mind constantly, and with it to fend off all questioning, subtle arguing, and disputing, and not to give way to the devil's suggestions, whether these be from without by his factions or from within by our own heart. And in that way we must learn to know the power and might of God in this same Word, namely, that we are saved thereby and solely by it resist the devil's power and all errors. For to believe firmly that I am a Christian, a child of God, and that I am saved, when I feel sin and a bad conscience; to believe that I will live eternally, endowed with a beautiful, glorious body, although I lie under the sod — that requires a divine and heavenly power and a wisdom which is not governed by any feeling or perceiving, but which can look beyond that, convinced that this is not human prattle or phantasy but that it is the Word of God, "who is able to do far more abundantly than all that we ask or think" (Eph. 3:20). For He has already resurrected our Lord Jesus Christ. Although no one else was executed so ignominiously and shamefully nor died such a vile and (according to the Law) accursed death, etc., so that His name was in much worse odor than that of any other person on earth, yet He proved that Scripture is more than the feeling, the thinking, and the experiencing of all men.

For no one could ever have understood or thought that Christ would be alive on the third day. Within all the world's wisdom there was not an iota of knowledge regarding this. And yet we have the Word which declared Him alive while He was still lying in the grave. And as this Word declared, so it had to happen, even though all the world's senses and reason and everything else contradict it. Thus it also happens to us. The dead repose under the ground, long decomposed or devoured by maggots and all sorts of other vermin, or they are turned to dust, or they lie dispersed everywhere; but in the Word which we believe and profess they are assuredly alive and risen. The world does not have this power and is unable to do this; but the Word has it and is able to do it. And thus it must come about, for it is God's own power and might.

This must strengthen and comfort us, even though our faith is not so firm as it should be and even though we do not feel this as clearly as we should like. Yet we should hold to it, constantly pursue it, and never dismiss it from our heart. Thus we also believe but feebly that we through Christ are lords over world and devil; we feel the direct opposite much more. But we console ourselves as much as we can with the fact that we have the Word, which excels all might and wisdom.

Likewise, although I feel my sin and cannot have as confident and cheerful a heart as I should like, still I must permit the Word to have sway and say accordingly: "I am lord over sin, and I don't want to know of any sin." "Indeed," you will say, "let your own conscience say that; it feels and experiences something far different." That is surely true; if things followed the rule of feeling, I would surely be lost. But the Word must be valid over and beyond all of the world's feeling and mine. It must remain true no matter how insignificant it may appear and how feebly it may be believed by me; for we all see and experience the fact that sin condemns us straightway and consigns us to hell, that death consumes us and all the world, and that no one can escape it. And you venture to speak to me of life and of righteousness, of which I cannot behold as much as a small spark! To be sure, that must be but a feeble life. Yes, indeed, but a feeble life by reason of our faith. But no matter how feeble it is, as long as the Word and a small spark of faith remain in the heart, it shall develop into a fire of life which fills heaven and earth and quenches both death and every other misfortune like a little drop of water. And the feeble faith shall tear these asunder so that neither death nor sin will be seen or felt any longer. However, to adhere to faith in the face of seeing and feeling calls for an arduous battle.

Therefore faith is not such a slight object as one assumes but a valiant hero who is to hold to the Word; this appears so insignificant and as nothing, so that all the world would not give a penny for it. And yet it is so active and so mighty that it tears heaven and earth apart and opens all graves in the twinkling of an eye. And if you but remain with it, you shall live eternally by it and become lord over all things, even though your faith is feeble and your feeling strong. You will live henceforth, no matter how feebly you may live, so long as you do not live according to your ideas and reason but according to Scripture. For the devil has contended against Scripture and the Word until now, but he has never been able to detract from it or to invalidate it. Indeed, he slinks around us on all sides [2] in order to lure us away from it; but he does not attack the Word itself. And so long as you have it in your heart, he does not face you squarely. He may make you writhe, but he will not overcome you.

Thus Scripture reports of the patriarch Jacob (Wisd. of Sol. 10:12): *Certamen forte dedit ei.* "He [3] let him wage a strong and gallant battle, so that he might learn to know the power of the Word from battle and victory." For we never perceive what power inheres in the letter until we become engaged in battle. Then we discover that it can stand its ground against all errors, against sin, death, and devil. The world does not believe that, nor do all who insist on judging according to their own feeling and who torment themselves with oppressive thoughts of sin and death, until they rid themselves of these and entertain other thoughts. But nothing comes of this, there is no other consolation than that found in holding to the Word, which says: "You hear clearly that Christ rose for you and extinguished your sin and your death, etc." In brief, we cannot prevail against sin, death, and hell otherwise than through the Gospel; of this Gospel Paul declares that we stand in it and are saved by it. If he had been acquainted with anything else with which to comfort and preserve them, he would undoubtedly have apprised them of it too. Here he shows us the easiest method with which to achieve this goal; it requires no expense and no trouble. It costs no more than a word with which we are to withstand death and all our other foes. We may feel differently and be weak; that does not matter, so long as we cling to the Word. A mother will not cast her child out because it is frail and scabby. It is weak, to be sure, and cannot help itself, but so long as it rests on its mother's lap and in her arms, it need not worry. But if it strays away from its mother's care, it is lost. Emulate that example if you

---

[2] Cf. 1 Peter 5:8.

[3] The subject in this sentence from the Apocrypha is "wisdom." Luther supplies the masculine pronoun *Er* instead, perhaps to remind the reader of the personification of wisdom in God.

want to be saved. See to it that you remain in the Word. By it God wants to bear you up and sustain you, so that you will not be lost.

3-7. *For I delivered to you as of first importance what I also received, that Christ died for our sins in accordance with the Scriptures, that He was buried, that He was raised on the third day in accordance with the Scriptures, and that He appeared to Cephas, then to the Twelve. Then He appeared to more than five hundred brethren at one time, most of whom are still alive, though some have fallen asleep. Then He appeared to James, then to all the apostles.*

With these words St. Paul explains and repeats the essence of His Gospel, which he preached to them, the Gospel in which they stand and by which they must be saved. Thus he composes a whole sermon on the resurrection of Christ, which might well be read and discussed on the Day of Easter. For from this flow the basis and the reason of this article on the resurrection of the dead which he is elaborating. And his sermon substantiates this doctrine most forcefully, both by proof from Scripture and by the witness of many living people, etc. He wishes to say: "I gave you nothing but what I myself received, nor do I know anything else to proclaim as the basis of our salvation than the Lord Jesus Christ, as He most certainly both truly died and also rose again from the dead. That is the content and the sum and substance of my Gospel, on which you and I were baptized and in which we stand. Thus I did not steal anything, nor did I spin a yarn, nor did I dream this up; no, I received it from Christ Himself." With this he pricks those false teachers. It is as though he were to say: "If they proclaim something different, they cannot have received it from Christ. It must represent their own dreams and phantasy. For they obviously did not receive it from us nor from other apostles (since we all agree and are in accord with our message), much less from Christ. Therefore it must be sheer seduction and deception. Thus Paul also boasts in Gal. 1:11, 12, 17 [4] over against the false apostles that he did not receive this doctrine from man nor from the apostles themselves, and that his proclamation was not derived from human reason or wisdom, that no man had invented it or contrived it of himself, but that it was a message which he had to receive through divine revelation. That was something those people could not boast of or

---

[4] The Weimar text has "Gal. 2."

maintain. Indeed, his own reason had contributed absolutely nothing to this, nor had he striven to obtain it. In fact, he had once persecuted it and raged against it like a raving, silly dog. God's Word is so far beyond all reason, also beyond the apostles' own knowledge or wisdom, that no one can attain it by his own power or understanding, to say nothing of contriving or devising anything better, as those people among the Corinthians alleged to be able to do.

Paul adduces two kinds of proof (in refutation of their false teaching) in support of his message, or Gospel, which he has preached concerning Christ's resurrection. First, he points out that he took this from Scripture and that he proves this with Scripture. In the second place, he cites his own experience and that of many others who saw the resurrected Christ. For it is the mark of a fair man to prove and attest what he proclaims and says, not only with words but also with deed and example both of himself and others. And thus Paul enumerates the eyewitnesses of Christ's resurrection; first, Cephas, or Peter, then the Twelve, to whom Christ showed Himself alive, so that they heard and saw Him and associated with Him in His external, physical essence. Later He was seen by more than five hundred brethren who were assembled together, then separately by James, and finally by all the apostles. Here Paul calls all those apostles (different from the Twelve) who were sent out by Christ to preach. For He selected the Twelve especially (as something more than plain apostles, or messengers) to be His witnesses not only of the resurrection but also of His entire life, of His words and deeds heard and seen by them, so that they might disseminate the Gospel after Christ. "All of these are, in addition to me, reliable witnesses of what we saw and experienced, carried out as foretold in Scripture."

And note how Paul again extols and exalts the testimony of Scripture and the external Word as he emphasizes and repeats the phrase "in accordance with the Scripture." To be sure, he does not do this without reason. He does this in the first place to resist the mad spirits who disdain Scripture and the external message and in place of this seek other secret revelation. And today every place is also teeming with such spirits, confused by the devil, who regard Scripture a dead letter and boast of nothing but the Spirit, although these people retain neither Word nor Spirit. But here you notice how Paul adduces Scripture as his strongest proof, for there is no other enduring way of preserving our doctrine and our faith than the physical or written Word, poured into letters and preached orally by him or others; for here we find it stated clearly: "Scripture! Scripture!" But Scripture is not all spirit, about which they drivel, saying that the Spirit alone must do it and that Scripture is a dead letter which cannot impart life. But the fact of the matter is that, although the letter by itself does not impart life, yet it must be present, and it must be heard or received. And the Holy Spirit must work through this in the heart, and the heart must be preserved in the faith through and in the Word against the devil and every trial. Otherwise, where this is surrendered, Christ and the Spirit will soon be lost. Therefore do not boast so much of the Spirit if you do not have the revealed external Word; for this is surely not a good spirit but the vile devil from hell. The Holy Spirit, as you know, has deposited His wisdom and counsel and all mysteries into the Word and revealed these in Scripture, so that no one can excuse himself. Nor must anyone seek or search for something else or learn or acquire something better or more sublime than what Scripture teaches of Jesus Christ, God's Son, our Savior, who died and rose for us.

In the second place, Paul does this in order to resist (as I stated before)[5] the temptation to take counsel with reason in this and other articles of faith, or to listen how the world with its wisdom presumes subtly to argue and to speculate about this. For if we consult these and permit them to teach us in this, faith will be crowded out, and this will be regarded as a foolish message and be made sheer mockery. That is what happened among the Corinthians, as we shall hear later. However, we who want to be Christians and men of faith must not look for or ask to see what human reason says here, or how this agrees with reason, but what Scripture teaches us, by which this was proclaimed in advance and is now confirmed by public testimony and experience. We let him who does not want to believe that go his way, for he will surely have or believe nothing at all of Christ or of the Gospel.

Such a Gospel no factious spirit will ever produce, no matter how clever or learned he may be. He will never be able to prove his story irrefutably both with Scripture, or God's Word, and then also with people who witnessed and experienced it. You may cheerfully defy them and challenge them to step forth and produce one of these. The first thing that all factions are sure to do is to come

[5] Cf. pp. 68—69 above.

trotting along with their own ideas, concocted by reason, and even though they do use Scripture, they have first conceived their own thoughts, brought these in and mixed them in so that Scripture must now agree with them and permit itself to be interpreted and stretched accordingly. That is exactly what we notice today in our people with regard to Baptism and the Sacrament. With their head they observed, first of all, that Baptism is nothing but water, similar to any other water. And after they have comprehended that and cannot see anything beyond that, they run to the Scriptures, where they have found the statement that we should not repose our trust in any creature, that external things cannot help the soul, etc. And thus they contrive their doctrine: "Water is water; and one must not put any trust in it, because it is creatural. Therefore Baptism cannot be a washing of the soul and wash away sin." Such passages of Scripture, that one must not believe in any creature, etc., must serve them for their trumpery and attest their fantasy and notions. Now, that Scripture is true and certain; but, behold, how shamefully they strain the passage and apply it to Baptism, making nothing but a creature of it. That is not correct; for God Himself together with Christ, His dear Son, and the Holy Spirit are in Baptism.

They do the same thing with the holy Sacrament. To them what we receive can be nothing but bread and wine. They do the same with the spoken Word and with other divine ordinances, as, for instance, with secular government and also with the state of matrimony. There they drivel and say: "Oh, married life is worldly and sinful, for it is associated with the creature, with wife and children, with house and home, etc. But he who wants to serve God must keep himself free of all creatures." When the common people hear that, they immediately concur as though this were something precious; and they disdain married life, government, and all other estates ordained by God. This seems a beautiful thought, and they apply verses of Scripture in proof, saying that one must love God above all things, that one must forsake house and home and all things for God's sake, etc.[6] In reality this is no more than what their fantasy introduced in the first place, that matrimony is something carnal from which one must keep away and remain pure. That is how reason views this in its blind delusion, although Scripture praises and exalts it as the order and creation of God, etc. Yet their story seems excellent to the rabble,

---

6 Cf. Matt. 22:37; 19:29.

especially since Scripture is stretched to fit the case, so that the people cannot defend themselves against this.

But we say, no matter how man and woman be constituted with regard to their external appearance and as viewed by reason, they are at all events adorned with the jewel called God's Word. God created them for the estate of matrimony, joined them together, and blessed them. That is the bond which unites them, namely, God's command and commandment, enjoining them not to separate but to remain together. And thus this estate is based on God's Word; thereby it is sanctified and pure, so that it must not be reviled as carnal or sinful. But to judge it solely by veil and hat, as the mad saints do with their reason — well, a sow could do that as well; for it, too, would be smart enough to say that it sees nothing holy in that. But he who regards God's Word, which instituted this estate and sanctified it, will not be led astray by such fantasies and by such misinterpretation of Scripture. For the Word will clearly teach him that this estate is not reprehensible but pleasing to God and holy, as far as it itself is concerned, if one but uses it properly. And therefore we may well conclude that, since it has God's Word and command, we must not abandon it. But you may say: "Does that verse [7] not tell us that we must forsake everything?" Indeed, you are right. However, under what circumstances are we to forsake all? Surely not in the manner in which God joined husband and wife together. Otherwise, why should He have joined them together and added His commandment? No, this applies to leaving either Christ and God's Word or wife and child, etc., as Christ clearly says in this context (Mark 10:29): "For My sake and for the Gospel, etc."

I am citing this example to illustrate that they do not teach Scripture correctly, and that they themselves do not understand how Paul lauds his doctrine and proves it mightily with Scripture. And I also do this as a warning to be on guard and not to raise many questions as to what reason has to say about this, nor to listen to the Enthusiasts and factious spirits, but to look solely to Scripture. For if you fail to cling to this, both the factious spirits and your reason will soon mislead you. I myself am also a doctor and have read Scripture, and yet I experience this daily. If I am not properly clad in my armor, such thoughts come to me, and I stand in danger of losing Christ and the Gospel. If I am to stand my ground, I must constantly adhere to Scrip-

[7] Matt. 19:29.

ture. How, then, will a person fare who is without Scripture and proceeds equipped with nothing but reason? For what might I believe regarding this article, which teaches that another life follows the present one, if I were to listen to reason when it comes gushing along with its notions and says: "What becomes of him whom the ravens devour or of him who remains in the water and is eaten by the fish and is completely consumed? Where do the people remain who are burned to ashes, who crumble into dust, who are scattered over the whole earth and vanish? Yes, what becomes of every person who is buried in the ground and is consumed by worms?" I may entertain similar thoughts with regard to all the other articles of faith if I follow my reason, also those which seem very insignificant. I might, for instance, ask concerning the Virgin Mary how it was possible for her to become pregnant without a man, etc. But this is the rule: These articles of faith which we preach are not based on human reason and understanding, but on Scripture; it follows that they must not be sought anywhere but in Scripture or explained otherwise than with Scripture.

That is one way in which Paul refutes the factious spirits, saying that they advance their own ideas without Scripture and that they can submit nothing to support these. The other point is that none of them is able to present witnesses to attest their story, men who might prove it with their own experience. And he also describes such persons nicely in Col. 2:18, where he says that they "insist on self-abasement and worship of angels, taking their stand on visions, puffed up without reason by their sensuous minds." It is as though he were to say: "It is surely the manner of all factions to present things which none of them has seen or experienced, so that they lack the testimony of experience as they lack the testimony of Scripture and the Word." But "we speak," says Christ (John 3:11), "of what we know, and bear witness to what we have seen." And in 1 John 1:1-3 we read: "That which we have heard, which we have seen with our eyes, which we have looked upon and touched with our hands, concerning the word of life . . . that we proclaim to you." "And thus we, too," says Paul, "proclaim to you in this article that which I and all the apostles, in conjunction with five hundred brethren, have seen and in which we all concur unanimously."

These are, of course, despicable spirits who shamelessly dare to teach things of which they themselves are ignorant and for which they can adduce neither Scripture nor examples, for which they present proof neither of doctrine nor of deed. This makes their story a two-fold lie, both as regards doctrine and deed. What they say amounts to less than nothing. They make a great noise as they boast and persuade people with fine and great words. Indeed, they even support this with an oath, so that one might think it the unalloyed truth. That is just what our people did, and still do, with the Sacrament. The pope's crowd, monks and priests, did the same with their doctrine of works. They all preach that if a pious monk lives in conformity with his monastic rules, he is saved, if God wills. Likewise, if a person gives many alms and establishes religious offices, he may rest quite assured that God will reward him with heaven for this, etc. Thus all that they preach and teach is based on untrustworthy delusion, something that no one has ever experienced. Nor can they present anybody who might testify and say: "Indeed, I experienced it." I, too, was such a pious monk for all of 15 years. Yet with all my Masses, with prayers, fasts, vigils, and chastity I never advanced to the point where I could say: "Now I am certain that God is gracious to me," or: "Now I have tried and experienced that my order and my austere life have helped me and have promoted me heavenward." Is this not an odious doctrine and a vexatious plague to hoax and fool people with such prattle, for which they have no basis at all in Scripture and no reliable testimony? They merely prate and blind the people with an airy, delusive vision. So the devil blinds and charms people's eyes physically with a phantom that does not exist in reality.

Therefore we must accept these words of St. Paul as an admonition to adhere firmly to this doctrine and proclamation, for which we have both reliable Scripture and also reliable experience. These are to be two proofs, just like two touchstones of the true doctrine. Now, whoever refuses to believe these two and still looks for something else or, finding nothing of the kind, clings to still others, deserves to be deceived. And yet this was all of no avail, nor does it avail today, with the multitude. They want to be deceived and misled.[8] They pay heed only when someone presents something novel and embellishes this prettily. But he who will be taught and not err must watch for these two points: who can adduce testimony for his doctrine from Scripture and from reliable experience. We are able to prove our doctrine and proclamation. I, too — praise God — can proclaim from experience that no works are able to help or comfort me against sin

8 Cf. *Luther's Works,* 20, p. 238, n. 6.

and God's judgment but that Christ alone can still and console my heart and my conscience. For this I have the testimony of all of Scripture and the example of many pious people, who say the same and have experienced it. In contrast, all the factions can prove or attest nothing from their own experience or from that of others. Finally we must also note here how St. Paul describes and defines his Gospel, namely, as a proclamation from which we learn that Christ died for our sin and that He rose again. And he proves both from Scripture. There you have everything in a nutshell, and yet it is stated clearly. Accordingly, you may judge all doctrine and life and know that whoever presents anything else as the doctrine of the Gospel and adds some of our own deeds and holiness surely misleads the people. You hear no mention of any works here, and nothing is said of what I must do or not do to atone for, or to remove, sin and to be justified before God, etc., but only what Christ did to that end, namely, that He died and rose again. After all, those are not my works or those of a saint or of all the people on earth. But how do I bring it about that this helps me and avails for me? Not otherwise than by faith. Paul declares that the Corinthians received this by faith, that they stand in it, and that they are saved by it. And a little later (v. 11) he will say again: "So we preach and so you believed." Thus he impresses these two points everywhere as the chief article and the epitome of the Gospel, by which we become Christians and are saved, if we retain it and adhere to it firmly and not let it be preached in vain, as I have said often and in much greater detail.[9]

8-11. *Last of all, as to one untimely born, He appeared also to me. For I am the least of the apostles, unfit to be called an apostle, because I persecuted the church of God. But by the grace of God I am what I am, and His grace toward me was not in vain. On the contrary, I worked harder than any of them, though it was not I, but the grace of God which is with me. Whether then it was I or they, so we preach and so you believed.*

He wants to say: "I did not receive this from others who were apostles before me and who saw and heard Christ and also ate and drank with Him; no, I beheld Him myself like all the others. I was appointed an apostle by Him, so that I may well boast and must boast that I am an apostle." For that he is sent and commissioned directly

---

[9] The first sermon on 1 Cor. 15, preached in the afternoon of August 11, 1532, the Eleventh Sunday After Trinity, ends here.

by his Lord Himself is indeed a true apostolic condition, or quality, of which every apostle may surely boast legitimately. Thus Paul always glories that he was not invested with his apostolate as a fief "from men or through man" (Gal. 1:1) but by Christ and through Christ Himself, who appeared to him particularly after the other apostles and gave him a special command to preach the Gospel among the Gentiles, as he testifies Acts 26:20 and also 1 Cor. 9:21 and 2 Cor. 12:11.

Using figurative language, Paul calls himself "one untimely born," that is, a child born prematurely, before it is fully matured, and, as we say, remains unbaptized. Paul wants to say: "I was just like a child that comes into the world before its due time, that cannot survive and 'never sees the sun,' as Ps. 58:8 puts it, that cannot enjoy this life. I came from my mother virtually as an immature or untimely, aborted fruit. This mother was the synagog, or Jewry, in which I lived and had my being, which was to give me spiritual life and bring me into the kingdom of God, so that I might live to God and bear fruit and also beget spiritual children from the Jewish nation, as the other apostles did. But I came to be an immature and dead child that persecuted Christ and His Christendom. Things went awry with me for my mother, and I did not develop normally; for she did not bear me as the people under the Law should be born, preserved under the Law and encompassed there as in a mother's womb, that I might be prepared for Christ and might learn to know and accept Him, etc." Thus Paul rejects all his previous holiness with these words. It is as though he would say: "To be sure, I was a pious Jew and conducted myself blamelessly in the Law like no other in my generation, etc.[10] And yet I regard all of that as an unripe and decayed fruit, without purpose and never beholding the sun until I was reborn by Christ. Just as such a child is cast forth from its mother's womb and is buried forthwith and thus passes from one place of darkness to another, so all my righteousness in the Law is also nothing but a rejected thing which serves no purpose in the sight of God and is assigned to damnation. Now I am ashamed of it and must condemn it myself. Yet I formerly esteemed it highly and supposed that I merited much with it before God. Similarly the Jews and all the Jewish saints are still an immature fruit that does not see the sun; this sun is our Lord Jesus Christ. They remain in darkness and pass from one death to another.

[10] Cf. Gal. 1:14; Phil. 3:6.

Therefore I cannot boast that my holiness and merits persuaded Christ to reveal Himself to me, to accept me in grace, and to appoint me an apostle. No, I would have remained just such dead, rejected fruit like the others who remained in their Judaism. But if I was to become good fruit and fit for life, I had to be born in Christ through Baptism, being brought to this and reared and trained by the Gospel."

Now Paul undertakes a long digression and excursus, as he enlarges on his office before he again reverts to the article of faith under discussion, the resurrection. He says: "I am, admittedly, the least of the apostles; but by the grace of God I am what I am, etc." Thereby he wishes to shield his apostolate from contempt, even though he was the least and was by reason of his person unworthy, having persecuted the Christians. But God had wrought far more by him than by any of the other apostles, even of the most exalted ones. For the factious spirits contemned him, as they always do, and adopted as their maxim and chief wisdom: "Is the Holy Spirit such a poor beggar that He can find no one but this one Paul?" Just so they say today: "Are the people in Wittenberg the only smart ones? Could no one else know something too? And might the Spirit not also dwell among us? What more do they know than we do?" And aping them, vulgar louts come strutting along and boast: "After all, I , too, am a Christian and have the Spirit just as well as my pastor or doctor, etc. Should I not be able to preach and to judge as well as he?" Thus they come prating about nothing but spirit in their great zealotry.

It is vexatious for a true apostle and a faithful, called pastor to see and to hear that people despise the precious office and the Word, that they show little appreciation for these and superciliously criticize them. What is to be done in this matter? Nothing can be done. It cannot be prevented; Christ Himself was not exempt from it. As He says in Matt. 11:19, He had to complain that wisdom is constrained to justify itself and that it must be taken to school by its children. Solomon, too, laments that there is no end to the criticism of true teachers and to the writing of books.[11] And it must always be thus. Where God grants His grace and someone begins a work and succeeds in it, a whole nest of vermin immediately comes along. Everyone presumes to be smart and able to do it better. So nothing is accomplished, and the net result is that the world is filled with wiseacres. That was also the experience to date on the part of schoolmen when the *Book of*

[11] Cf. Eccl. 12:12.

Sentences had appeared and one or two had written about it.[12] Soon every place was teeming with authors. No one regarded himself a doctor without parading his knowledge and writing a book about it. That is the way it happens also in all the other professions, indeed, in every trade. The real masters must put up with such botchers and bunglers who poke their noses into everything, who, although they know nothing, always ape everything and try to improve on it.

St. Paul, too, accomplished no more with his Gospel among such people when he preached so faithfully than to have them open their worthless mouths for no other purpose than to despise and criticize him and to boast: "Dear friends, we did not issue from a stone.[13] Indeed, we are baptized and are Christians as well as Paul is. What was he other than a persecutor of Christians, as he himself must admit? Furthermore, he is not an imposing figure, but is small and skinny." They also reproached him for his voice and his pronunciation. They, on the other hand, were great shouters, such as the rabble is fond of hearing and as could fill the people's ears. With their ridicule they destroyed everything they could find in him, and in that way they extolled themselves and gave themselves a reputation. That is also what people do to us and what many who are now not worthy of unlatching our shoestrings will do to us after we are gone. They will criticize us severely and disparage us, as though we were less than nothing.

It is because of these people that Paul is constrained to say this of himself. It is as though he were to say: "I am well aware that they besmirch my name and sully my reputation and that they boast over against this that they are good and qualified people and of good repute. They criticize and revile me as the least and the most unworthy of the apostles, yes, they say that I should not be regarded an apostle. But what am I to do in this matter? I have to commend it to Him to whom Baptism, Gospel, and everything belong. If He does not wish to protect and preserve these Himself, any action of mine will be unavailing here. I can do no more than to declare what is the true Gospel and Word of God and, together with this, to admonish

[12] Peter Lombard's *Sentences* were much commented on, perhaps most notably by Thomas Aquinas.

[13] In Homer, *Odyssey,* XIX, 163, Penelope asks her returned husband Ulysses (unrecognized in the role of a needy beggar) to reveal his identity, saying: "You must have had a father and a mother of some sort; you cannot be the son of an oak or a rock." The phrase has become proverbial for legitimacy. Cf. *Luther's Works,* 40, p. 236, where a reference to the *Iliad* is cited.

and to warn. Let him who does not care to give heed and to follow me launch out on his own adventure." That is what we have to do also with our people. We can do no more than to warn them faithfully and diligently. In that way we can at least keep the doctrine pure. We must let him who refuses to accept that go his own way and see what he gains thereby. If he does not want the true doctrine and the apostles, he will find a plenitude of factious spirits and the devil in the bargain. Meanwhile God will surely provide for the preservation of His Christendom despite this. He will see to it that it will avail them nothing to shout so vociferously, that they are learned and are disciples of the apostles, and that I, on the other hand, am but a vagrant and apostate apostle.

St. Paul is saying: "I suppose that it behooves me more than others to say of myself that I was a persecutor and murderer of Christians, that I contemplated the extermination of all of Christendom, and that I am not worthy of being called an apostle, etc." Similarly I and many pious people with me confess that we were despairing and condemned people under the papacy and that we led shameful lives in monasticism, daily blaspheming and disgracing God and His dear Son with our Masses and idolatrous worship, etc. And still God had compassion with us and graciously received us and called us through His Holy Spirit to proclaim Christ. And He granted us many greater gifts than were given to others. And we can glory with Paul that God brought the Gospel into the light of day through us and disseminated this so widely. They have to grant us the boast that we preceded them in the preaching of the Gospel and that they would probably know nothing about it if we had not first publicized it. In brief, no matter what we were, they still have to receive the Gospel, absolution, and the Sacrament from their pastors and called preachers and not disdain such a divine order, if they cherish their salvation. For if God had chosen to do otherwise, I suppose He would have assigned them precedence and had them preach prior to others, so that we should have to remain silent and listen to them.

But God follows this method and chooses poor sinners, such as St. Paul and we were, to fend off the arrogance and conceit of such wiseacres. For He does not wish to use such self-assured and presumptuous spirits for this work, but people who have been through the mill, have been tested, and crushed, and who know and must confess that they were as vile as St. Paul had been, and who, burdened with real and grave sins before God, know that they are God's and Christ's enemies. Thus they remain humble and can neither presume nor boast, as those untried spirits do, that God had chosen them because of their piety, holiness, and erudition. No, God must always retain the honor and the boast for Himself, so that He can say to them when they are tempted to pride: "My dear people, what do you have to boast of? Or, over against whom do you want to raise your boast? Do you not know what kind of people you were and what you did both against Me and against Christendom, spotting yourselves with the blood of many people? Or, do you propose to forget the mercy and compassion I showed you?" In this way he ties the stick to the dog's neck.[14] Everybody must look behind himself and see in what filth and stench he was mired. Then such people will, I suppose, soon forget any pride and arrogance.

Therefore St. Paul now declares: "Even though you thoroughly despise me and disparage me, saying that I was a persecutor of Christians and a blasphemer and that I am even now nothing but an untimely birth and the least among the apostles, how do you like to hear me say this, that I am an apostle nonetheless, and that this man who was so vile surpassed the other apostles in his work and in doing good? Although this does not justify me before God, I may glory over against my noisy critics and defamers and in defiance of them say: 'Still I did more than you and others, even more than the great apostles, although you presume to be better and more learned than I.' You may say: 'Indeed, I have the Spirit as well as you do.' I reply: 'No, that does not suffice for this.' And that you may know it, I tell you that you do not have the Spirit for this. For, as I said, if God had ordained you to be an apostle or pastor, I should be obliged to hear you and I myself would have to remain silent. But now that He ordained me to that office, it is incumbent on you to listen to me and regard me as your apostle or doctor. However, if you are endowed with special gifts, with the Spirit, with understanding, and with the ability to expound Scripture, use these (as St. Paul declares in 1 Cor. 14:16 ff.) properly and in season and in the place to which you were called, and not with such pride and boasting as you are now displaying against your true and called apostle. For thereby you betray that your spirit is not the Holy Spirit but the vile devil and that you have

---

[14] *Den Knüttel dem Hund an den Hals binden* refers to the practice of tying a stick to a dog's neck to prevent his running freely and damaging private hunting grounds. See also *Luther's Works*, 46, p. 112.

as yet not savored or smelled anything of God's Spirit. For that is not what a pious person does. No, even when he hears an error preached, he proceeds with humility and admonishes the preacher in a friendly and fraternal way; he refrains from such defiant and arrogant talk.

"Therefore it is not a question whether those people are of greater renown and can shout more. No, the question is who administers his office faithfully and accomplishes much in it. Thus," says St. Paul, "you must mark whether this person is called and whether the doctrine which he introduces agrees with mine, for I was sent by God to be your pastor. Pay no regard to my insignificance. You cannot vilify or ridicule me so severely in view of my past life that I will not admit and confirm it. And yet that same Paul who once was a blasphemer is now an apostle and wants to be accounted an apostle. For I must not be appraised now according to the person I once was but in accordance with the office that is mine now. As to my person I can indeed bear to be criticized and belittled; indeed, it may be said truthfully that I am the least of the apostles and not worthy of being called an apostle, not even a Christian, as one who persecuted Christendom and God's children and helped to slaughter innocent people. However, with regard to the office to preach, to baptize, etc., to which I was commissioned, I want no one to judge me and to despise me. The devil shall not interfere here, nor shall he have any thanks for it.[15]

"Even if my person was as evil as a human being can be, I am now forgiven, and by God's grace I am now what I am. And that I want to be. My boast will be that as far as I am concerned I am converted and that the blasphemer and persecutor has become a Christian and an apostle who has established and planted the belief in Christ among the Gentiles. I am not boasting of this in view of any doing and worthiness of my own, as though I had this of myself. This is neither natural nor within the power of man, but it is nothing other than the boundless mercy of God, who accepted me into His grace without any cooperation or any thoughts of my own, who absolved me from murder and bloodshed and endowed me with the knowledge of Christ and the gifts of the Spirit, and who, in addition, placed me into the most sublime office. Therefore I do not want to see this office despised. If it derived from my working or doing, I should be glad to see it trampled underfoot together with my former life and Jewish sanctity.

[15] *Und kein' Dank dazu haben,* as in stanza 4 of *Ein feste Burg.*

But since it is nought but God's work and mercy, I want to praise it and have it praised by everybody in defiance of the devil and the whole world. Or him who despises it I will condemn to the abyss of hell. In brief, whatever criticism is leveled against our person we should endure and will endure, but whatever is mercy, particularly this office, which has and dispenses sheer mercy, we want to see honored by everyone who claims to be a Christian."

And here you see that St. Paul calls a good and true pastor grace of God, saying that it is not within man's doing or ability to be or to make a pastor, and that it is also not man's doing to be a Christian and to hear the Word or a sermon gladly, but that this is a divine matter and nothing but a heavenly gift and present, without and beyond, yes, against, nature, which God alone effects in us, without any help or ideas of ours. "Such a man," says Paul, "am I, who by the grace of God brought you the Gospel, as I also received it by that grace, I who was presented to you by God as a rich and precious gem. As such you must regard and honor me, so that no one may rebuke me or upbraid me, as if this were my own doing or that I had come by my own decision. For I am not like those who set themselves up as pastors and who force themselves in, as those sneaks of the factions do or as self-styled scholars and preachers do. No, whatever I am and can do, whatever I have and present, is and shall be nought but the grace of God." That is the way Christians must boast, if they boast at all, not of their spirit, as the arrogant spirits do, nor of their great knowledge or their own wisdom, nor of their sanctity, nor of whatever we ourselves are or can do.

St. Paul speaks at some length of his boast, saying: "And His grace toward me was not in vain. On the contrary, I worked harder than any of them, etc." That is displaying still more defiance over against their contempt for his poor and insignificant person, which, they say, is as nothing in comparison with the other apostles. Here he not only makes bold to call himself the equal of the others, but he declares that he may well go beyond that and glory in the fact that God has done great things through him, that He accomplished more through him than He did through the others. He enlarges on this elsewhere. He uses these words, "God's grace was not in vain toward me," against his factions and against all types of factions which, although they have and occupy such an office of grace, nevertheless fail to remain in this grace but fall from it and become loose and idle prattlers and zealots.

They indeed do shout and bluster much, but they do nothing, nor do they accomplish what their office demands of them. Thus the grace of God is in vain toward them. But "toward me," Paul says, "it was not in vain, for by it I carried the Gospel throughout the world of the Gentiles and converted many people." Elsewhere he says (Rom. 15: 19) that from Asia to Italy he filled every place with the Gospel. "Indeed, I can defy those who despise and belittle me because of my person," he says, "and I can challenge them to match these accomplishments. For when it comes to boasting, as they like to boast against me, I can say that I did more than they all. And this I may do with God and in all honor. I shall willingly concede to them and yield to them if they are able to boast not of grace but of their own knowledge or great gifts. But they shall not venture to say that they preached as much and bore as much fruit as I did by the grace of God."

One might apply the words "I worked harder than any of them" to all the apostles. That is the usual way, too, implying that Paul is exalting himself over the other apostles. But since Paul is speaking so generally here and addresses "all" without distinction, I think that he is not referring to the true apostles but that he is defying the factious spirits. It is as though he were to say: "Even if they had done much to boast of, still the whole lot of them did not do as much as I did, and yet I am only one individual and regarded as the least of the apostles." Thus it remains *in materia subjecta* [16] of whom he is speaking here. For with these words he does not wish to belittle the true apostles, among whom he also numbers himself, but he is attacking the others, the false apostles, who are criticizing him and finding fault with him.

But if someone wishes to apply these words, "I worked harder than any of them," to all the apostles, he may interpret them to mean that Paul's work was more extensive than that of all the others. For the latter had to remain in Jerusalem and in the land of the Jews; they were not sent to any nation other than their own. But Paul and Barnabas were set apart, as we read in Acts 13:2, as two special preachers who were to journey out into the whole world of the Gentiles. Thus Paul penetrated the entire Roman empire with the Word, and this empire is, I suppose, twelve times as large as the Jewish realm. Therefore Paul may well boast that he worked harder than

[16] I. e., on the basis of considerations not absolute.

they all, that is, that he traveled farther in his apostolate or that he got in touch with and covered more countries and people with his preaching than the others. In view of this he often calls himself an apostle and teacher of the Gentiles, so that we may well regard him as our father and apostle and regard ourselves as the heirs of his pulpit. And yet, the apostle's chief meaning is directed against his factions, and he wants to say: "A curse on their boasting, blustering, and raging, for I can truly boast and say that I am not only an apostle, but also a productive apostle and that I was of greater benefit to Christendom and wrought more fruit there than all of them together did during their whole lifetime or than they ever will do."

And lest some one find reason to suppose that he is arrogant with his boasting and that he wants to exalt himself over all the other apostles when he says that he alone accomplished the best, he is quick to add "though it was not I, but the grace of God which is with me, etc." He brushes all of this away from his person and attributes it to sheer grace, so that these remarks cannot be prompted by arrogance. No, they reflect true Christian humility, for he confesses that he is nothing at all. And yet there is a blessed arrogance in him, which does not boast presumptuously of himself or of any other man, but of God's work and grace. And all of this Paul does for the good and salvation of the people, lest they be misled by the factions' shouting and boasting and that they may be advised what they have in him. For it is needful and necessary for the people to be warned and deterred from following the factious spirits and enabled to differentiate thus among pastors: "This is our pastor, whom God has given us and who first preached God's Word correctly, who wrought and effected much good, and who proved himself through the grace of God. The other, however, comes sneaking in here, or he has broken in here without a commission, ridiculing the first pastor. And no one knows who this man is or if he may be trusted. Therefore we will give ear to the former, whom God gave us, and remain with him."

Behold, thus the true doctrine may be retained in the hearts of the people, so that they remain with what God gave them and with what they recognized. This is recorded to serve as an example for us. For we, too, must boast over against the papacy and all factions that God gave us His Word and true preachers of the same. And although they despise us and condemn us as heretics, we are for all that true pastors and servants of Christ. Moreover, we have been called and ordained to teach by the pope himself. They shall not disdain such our defiant boast. It is not that we thus claim to be better before God, but thus our doctrine becomes more firmly rooted in the people and is not shaken and doubted. For if we ourselves were to falter and to doubt that we are true pastors, all the people would follow us and also doubt and become uncertain about the matter.

After all, every person must be able to boast thus in his vocation and his life and be convinced that he is pleasing God. For instance, every father may boast over against his child that he is a father and that he is privileged to deal with his son as a father, even though he may not be a Christian and even though he does not believe in the Gospel. He should not let others despise him, even though he may be poor, decrepit, and ill, as though this disqualified him as a father. No, he should say to his son: "No matter what my condition otherwise may be, I am still your father, and you are my son, and you cannot deprive me of my paternal position nor withdraw from obedience to me, etc. For I did not make myself your father by my own design and volition, but God created you thus and gave you to me." Similarly, every master of a household should boast over against his servant, a government or a prince over against their subjects, and say: "Although I may be inept, frail, etc., I am nonetheless your master, and you are my servant or subject. And you must also regard and honor me as such, no matter how proud you may be, and not be thanked for it either.[17] This you must not do for my sake but for God's, for He wants it that way. If I am frail, so that my person does not appeal to you, that makes no difference. For all of that you shall not say that I am not your master; for that is not my arrangement, but God's work and order.

Since such boasting is necessary in the secular realm, it must far more be in place in the spiritual office, which is entirely God's work and rule. And yet everybody presumes to criticize and despise it at will. We must boldly defy such insolent spirits with God's Word and order and say: "Disapprove of me and contemn me with regard to my person whoever will, but on the other hand, with regard to my office you must honor and laud me, as you love Christ and your soul's salvation. For you are not my pastor or preacher, but God ordained me to be your pastor, in order that you might receive the Gospel from me and come into the kingdom of God through my office."

[17] Cf. p. 88, n. 15, above.

See, that is how the apostle first digresses from his theme and talks of his office. He does this to frighten the people and to turn them away from their factious spirits, who attacked the article of the resurrection. He makes mention of this also to strengthen his proclamation, saying that he is called to this office by God and that he has shown himself as one who preached and worked by grace alone. In that way he adduces a triple testimony for his proclamation. In the first place, Scripture, or God's Word; in the second, the experience of many people; in the third, his office and its fruits. May God supply those who refuse to accept or respect that with a plenitude of factious spirits who will pour their spirit into them with large dippers. Therefore Paul concludes with the words of verse 11: "Whether then it was I or they, so we preach, and so you believe." It is as though he would say: "Now you heard what I am and what I have preached and done, what my office and my doctrine are as a true apostle. I proclaimed what the other apostles proclaimed, who witnessed of this with me. In fact, I carried this message farther than they did, out into the world. And in that way you, too, accepted it, believed it, and recognized that it is the doctrine and the Gospel from which this article is derived and on which it is based. Therefore you must remain faithful to it and not be diverted from it by other preachers." Thus he sums up his work or office and its fruit, showing that his proclamation was in the final analysis about nothing other than the article of the resurrection, according to Scripture and the reliable testimony of many people. And now he takes the article itself in hand, to put it on a firm foundation, to prove it, and mightily to refute the error of those who had sowed the poison among Christians that there is no resurrection.[18]

12-15. *Now if Christ is preached as raised from the dead, how can some of you say that there is no resurrection of the dead? But if there is no resurrection of the dead, then Christ has not been raised; if Christ has not been raised, then our preaching is in vain and your faith is in vain. We are even found to be misrepresenting God, because we testified of God that He raised Christ, whom He did not raise if it is true that the dead are not raised.*

There you can see first of all what pious little children these tender

[18] The second sermon in the series, preached September 8, 1532, the Fifteenth Sunday After Trinity, ends here.

factious spirits were who reviled Paul and ventured to reproach him
with his ordinary person and with his past life, as though they themselves were so spiritual and the most excellent saints. And still they
presume to say this about themselves and to preach that there is
nothing to the resurrection, despite the proclamation and testimony
of all true apostles and its basis in Scripture and their experience.
Is this not a disgrace and an abomination on the part of those who
desire to be called Christians and who boast of great spirituality as
the first pastors after the apostles, some of them even consecrated and
inducted into office by Paul himself? And they proclaim this among
his disciples, to whom he himself had preached and on whom he had
impressed this article so long!

Paul stakes everything on the basic factor with which he began,
namely, that Christ arose from the dead. This is the chief article of
the Christian doctrine. No one who at all claims to be a Christian or
a preacher of the Gospel may deny that. With this he wants to confront them and force them to the conclusion that their denial of the
resurrection of the dead denies even more definitely that Christ rose
from the dead; for if the former is not true, the latter must be fabricated also. And since every Christian must believe and confess that
Christ has risen from the dead, it is easy to persuade him to accept
also the resurrection of the dead; or he must deny in a lump the Gospel
and everything that is proclaimed of Christ and of God. For all of
this is linked together like a chain, and if one article of faith stands,
they all stand. Therefore Paul also makes all things interdependent
here, and he always deduces one thing from the other.

But among the heathen and the unbelievers, who deny not only
the article which Paul undertakes to prove but also everything that
he cites in proof, this appears to be weak dialectics or proof. They
call this *probare negatum per negatum* and *petere principium*.[19] Thus
someone may accuse another person in court and say: "You are a
rascal, etc.," and when he is asked to prove this, he may constantly
repeat the same and cry: "It is true, you are a rascal, and you remain
a rascal, being born a rascal." That would not be proving it, but
would be empty, idle talk. If the person were to prove this, he would
have to proceed to present witnesses and produce other reliable proof
against the other. Thus it also seems here when Paul says: "If there

[19] "Proving what has been denied by what has been denied" and "begging
the question."

is nothing to the resurrection of the dead, then Christ, too, has not risen from the dead." For if we tell a heathen that, he has as little regard for the one as he has for the other; he believes that Christ rose from the dead just as little as that we rise from the dead. Therefore such an argument does not convince him at all. And even if it were a strong argument, it would after all be no more than an *a particulari ad universale*.[20] It would not be a true deduction to conclude: "Since this one Christ arose, it follows that everyone must arise from the dead." It would be just as illogical to say: "This judge is a rascal, therefore all judges are rascals. One pastor is a factious spirit, therefore all pastors are heretics." It does not reflect masterly learning to make a whole summer out of a single day or to call the whole world rascally because of one rascal, in brief, to generalize from one factor. So this seems a rather weak proof: "If the dead do not arise, then Christ, too, has not risen." For even if we grant that the one person, Christ, God's Son, has arisen, we cannot infer from this that we must all rise.

But I stated that this is primarily a sermon for Christians, who believe the article regarding Christ's resurrection and know its power and understand why He arose, namely, to overcome death and to rescue us from death and enable us to live with Him eternally. For since He is our Head and we are His body and members, He must through His resurrection also resurrect us and transplant us into a new life, etc., as He often declares elsewhere. However, lest someone find fault with his argumentation, Paul continues and strengthens his viewpoint. He intertwines and interlaces his argumentation to make it cogently conclusive. He makes proper use of that device of dialectics which is known as *reducere per impossible*.[21] He wants to say: "Whoever denies this article must simultaneously deny far more, namely, first of all, that you believe properly; in the second place, that the Word which you believe has been true; in the third place, that we apostles preach correctly and that we are God's apostles; in the fourth place, that God is truthful; in brief, that God is God.

For all of this must follow, one from the other: If my belief is not correct, the Word, too, must be false. If the Word is incorrect, the preacher, too, must be incorrect. Therefore God, too, who sends the

---

[20] An argument "from the particular to the universal," a generalization.

[21] A contraction for *reducere per deductionem ad impossibile,* the same as *reducere ad absurdum,* a device that disproves by arguing to an impossible or false conclusion.

preachers, must be a false god. But if He is false, He is not God. And may he who ventures to say that God is not God be gone. For we have nothing to do with him who believes nothing at all, who denies everything that is said about God and God's Word. Therefore this is also taught in the schools: *Contra negantem prima principia non est disputandum,* "one must not dispute with him who dares to deny what nature teaches everybody and what everybody's reason and understanding must concede." Such a person must be advised to see a physician to have his brain purged. For that is tantamount to saying that white is not white but black and that two are not two but one. But we are addressing people who regard God as a true God, who is truthful and does not lie, people who regard the apostles as His ambassadors and witnesses, as men who proclaim His Word and who must be heard as He Himself is heard. As Christ says (Luke 10:16): "'He who hears you hears Me,' and he who hears Me hears My Father." Those are our *principia,* the bases and the chief article on which the entire Christian doctrine is founded. For all of Scripture asserts solely of that God and of His Son and apostles that their proclamation constitutes the right Word of God and that whoever believes this will be saved. If you deny all of that, I shall have nothing to do with you. For whoever denies God and His Word, His Baptism and Gospel, will not find it hard to deny the resurrection of the dead as well. If you dare to say that God is not God and that the apostles and Christendom do not teach and believe correctly, it is easy for you — and nothing seems better — to knock the whole bottom out of the barrel and say that there is no resurrection, neither heaven nor hell, neither devil nor death nor sin, etc. For what will you believe if you do not believe that God is something?

But if you choose to be numbered among those who regard God and His apostles, His Word and Christendom, as truthful, we shall indeed convince and constrain you to believe also this article. For what Christendom believes and the apostles proclaim cannot be a lie. Thus it is also impossible for the apostles to be false witnesses of God; otherwise God would not be truthful and could not be God. Now that these *principia* stand, it follows logically and necessarily that you have to believe the resurrection of the dead, as surely as God is God. For He revealed the resurrection through His Son in Scripture and had it proclaimed through the apostles; and it was accepted and believed by Christendom. In view of all of this, it must be correct and true.

So all of this ties together, the apostles' Word and Christ's Word, the belief and the profession of Christendom, and God's truth and majesty, so that one cannot give one the lie without involving the other. And because that is and remains certain and true, it must also be certain that the dead will arise, since this is comprehended in God's Word and in the Christian faith. In that way it forms a chain, with everything linked together and with everything falling apart together, so that we have to declare: "As surely as it is true that God lives and that Christ lives and that Christendom's faith and proclamation are correct and true, this article is also true." But, if someone dares to contradict this, we let him go to the devil as one who shall not have fellowship with us who believe and have accepted the Word and who, furthermore, have learned from experience that God confirms His Word and that He gathers His Christendom and has preserved it to date, that many saintly people have confessed this with their blood, that they have been tested and sustained in their faith through all sorts of opposition and temptation and have died believing in this article. And because we stand on that foundation and hold to these parts, this article will surely also be preserved for us and will not topple.

Behold, thus this text contends mightily in defense of our faith. This is the right way to defend our doctrine, for we cannot prove our faith and all the articles in any other way. Whoever refuses to believe that God, Christendom, faith, and the Word are really something will not give ear to instruction or persuasion. All that may be said to him is futile and lost. It is the same as trying to convince a Turk with our faith. He will concede nothing and will reject all your reasons.

This is what we tell him: "If you come to the point where you no longer accept Christ and His apostles and Scripture, let Satan himself thank you. For after all, we do not proclaim ourselves or anything invented or contrived by man, but the very Word which is founded on Scripture from the beginning, the Word of Christ, God's Son, which was promised by God Himself to our first father, Adam, and to Christendom. Whoever does not want to have that, may seek out a different one. We, however, want to adhere to what Adam began, what all holy fathers and pious Christians have believed, and what has to date maintained itself against all power, wisdom, and might of the world and against the gates of hell, and what will endure as long as the world stands. And whoever accepts that will surely also believe and retain this article with us. For with such people I can reason and I can convince them when I say: "If you believe in Christ and believe that He rose from the dead, how can you deny that the dead will arise, etc.? For you must be mad and stupid to believe in Christ and to disbelieve His Word and His apostles." In brief, we know that Adam, our very first father, already believed this article when he was told that the woman's Seed should bruise the serpent's head (Gen. 3:15). From him this was transmitted to us all; just as he comprehended it, so it was passed from one to the other. It was preached and treated with ever growing clarity, from Adam to Abraham, from Abraham to Moses, David, etc., and thus to Christ and the apostles, from whom it came down to us.

In this way St. Paul contended for and achieved this article from the true and strongest *principiis,* so that he who denies the resurrection of the dead must also deny that Christ rose from the dead. But whoever denies that, denies everything. He regards God and Christ in all His words and works as a liar, indeed, as absolutely nil. Such a person must be considered an infamous, godless heathen, whom neither God nor the world can counsel, and with whom no one should have anything to do. I am unable to proclaim or to support this more strongly and powerfully. Therefore we must hold firmly to such a foundation, be sure of our ground, and not build on a hollow delusion. For as surely as you believe other articles of faith, you must also believe this one. Thus if you can believe that God is God, you must also not doubt that you will rise from the dead after this life; for if you were to stay under the ground, God would first have to become a liar and not be God. But if it is true that God cannot lie or deny or abandon His deity, this article, too, must become true. It is as certain before God as if the resurrection had already taken place, even though present appearances would belie this, with man lying under the ground, stinking like a rotting carcass, and consumed by maggots and worms.

For he who wants to believe must ignore what his five senses comprehend and demonstrate. God, too, does not regard these, nor is He governed by them. On the contrary, His concern is to make His words come true: "Death, I will be your death" (Hos. 13:14), "I will devour you and will revive him whom you devoured, or I will no longer be God." And just as God pays no attention to the conditions confronting our senses, such as those of one lying ten fathoms in or under the ground, or of another burned to ashes and scattered in all four directions or consumed by beasts, birds, and worms — in His eyes all is nothing but life; for He will create a new and eternal life from this temporal death and corruption — so we, too, must view this. We must judge contrary to our feelings and in accordance with what God says, as convinced as though this had already come to pass. We must zealously guard against doubting this at all.

For ponder this yourself and see what a sin it is to entertain any doubt regarding this article, since Paul states that this is the same as denying God and Christ, as renouncing your faith, Baptism, and the Gospel, giving these the lie and saying: "I believe that there is no God, no Christ, and that all that is said about faith is an abominable lie." You would graft happiness and a strong faith into your heart if you vividly pictured this to yourself and reflected: "Oh, it would be terrible and awful and the gravest blasphemy to disbelieve this article; for as St. Paul says, then I would simultaneously have denied that Christ arose from the dead and that God is truthful. May God protect me from saying that and from admitting such horrible blasphemy into my heart. Therefore I shall harbor no doubt regarding this article but regard it as more certain than my own life and boldly depart this life trusting in it and convinced that after I am dead and decayed, I shall come forth again, more beautiful and brighter than the sun."

Thus this text serves both to strengthen the believers and to frighten the others, that they may know what a great blasphemy those who deny this article are committing. It is as though Paul were saying: "Dear Corinthians, this is not a matter for jest or ridicule; for if you deny this article, you are not denying anything trivial, nor for that matter a single article, but you are actually giving God the lie to His face, saying: 'God is not God, Christ is nothing, etc.' But if you have any regard for God and Christ — as you surely must have if you want to be Christians and have us preach to you — you cannot deny this article. For the inference will constrain you to say: 'In truth, if Christ has His apostles proclaim this and, in addition, has proved this by deeds, there can be no doubt regarding it.' Therefore, venture forth and depart this life boldly in faith in this article, convinced that after we are long in our graves and are decomposed, and the beautiful trumpet will sound and say, as Christ did to Lazarus: 'Peter, Paul, come forth!' — that we will then come forth in a moment like a spark, more resplen-

dent than the entire heaven, with our whole body and all our members
again completely intact, even though we may now be burned to ashes,
consumed in the water, torn to bits by wolves, or eaten by ravens.[22]

16-19. *For if the dead are not raised, then Christ has not been raised.*
If Christ has not been raised, your faith is futile and you are
still in your sins. Then those also who have fallen asleep in
Christ have perished. If for this life only we have hoped in
Christ, we are of all men most to be pitied.

Here St. Paul affirms the foregoing argument. He carries it even
further and supports it and sums up all that would follow if one were
not sure of this article in Christendom. He pursues this point to insure
that his Corinthians adhere to this staunchly and surely over against
their false teachers. We can gather from this that they did not take
this article seriously and that St. Paul was vexed to see them treat it
so coldly and indifferently, moreover, put it in doubt, indeed, that some
spoke of it so carelessly and even heathenishly, as though it were nothing at all. There are still many who do not believe this in their hearts
and secretly regard this as a big laugh, especially those who claim to
be smart and very intelligent and who measure and judge God's Word
with their reason. They are like the Sadducees and their disciples in
the days of Christ, who spread that poison among God's people. This
had already been disseminated widely. It necessarily follows, especially where factious spirits arise, who agitate this and spew it out
among the people, that the majority remain steeped in such shameful
unbelief, live riotously, and care neither about God nor about the life
beyond, just as though there were neither hell nor heaven; and yet they
are called Christians and are baptized. And no matter how much
they are preached to, all is preached to deaf ears. Later on they make
sport of it, and St. Paul will later mention their mocking.

St. Paul here names the parts one after the other and arrays them
per impossible,[23] as I said. In the first place, if the dead do not arise,
it follows that Christ, too, did not arise. Reasoning: Christ is, as we
know, also one of the dead, indeed, He is the Head of us all and, as
he says later, "the Firstfruits," who was to rise. And if this article is
not true in Him, it is true in no one. In the second place, it would also
follow that our preaching is in vain. For why should we bestow such

---

[22] The third sermon in the series, preached in the afternoon of September 22,
1532, the Seventeenth Sunday After Trinity, ends here.

[23] Cf. p. 95, n. 21, above.

pains, why hazard to preach, to encumber ourselves with so much toil, and all of this at the risk of life and limb and all sorts of danger, if this were naught but an empty, worthless, and useless bauble? Indeed, then we should hold our tongue and forsake pulpit with Baptism, Sacrament, and Scripture. For do you suppose that this was introduced to subdue the peasants, to govern land and people, and to learn how to husband resources and to farm? The heathen were conversant with all of that even before anyone had heard of Christ; this was taught them by reason, yes, necessity also forced them into this. For that you need no Scripture or pulpit, no Gospel, indeed, no knowledge of God.

Therefore, if we knew of no other life, we should also hold our peace and let the people live like cows and pigs, which probably also know very well what is good for them. We should let it rest at that and neglect pulpit and all. We should not devote so much attention to it as to create such a stir over it in the world, if it were but effort lost and if it would serve and help neither this nor that life. Therefore, if you desire no other life nor believe in it, just disregard preaching. If you do not care to have a God, you also do not need to hear us, nor need we preach to you. For, God be praised, we are not so stupid that we should wish to propagate this doctrine in vain, or only to regulate this body and this life with it. No, we find that ordered very well already by the heathen and by reason. Our only concern is to teach how — after our Baptism — we may get from this to yonder life. To that end we have to preach and to admonish daily. But if there were nothing to the resurrection, all of that would be entirely in vain and futile.

In the third place, Paul said, your faith would be futile and nothing but an empty and worthless idea. For if the resurrection is nothing and yet I believe in it, what is that but a mere dream with sequel? Then all of Christendom from the beginning of the world would have followed a false belief, and all would be poor, bewitched people who permitted themselves to be fooled and mislead by an empty dream and phantom, one for which people had to endure every persecution, distress, and torture. And after hoping for and relying on this for a long time, they would have had to depart this life and die in that confidence and then find themselves deceived shamefully. If it were true, as some people declare, that this article is false and that there is nothing to a life beyond, this would constitute the greatest deception ever perpetrated on earth. Thus many people regard also what we say about heaven and hell as mere fable and fiction, contrived solely for the purpose of terrifying the common people, who presumably could not be tamed or restrained except by painting the devil black and making hell hot for them.

But nothing is accomplished by that either. For if people are not better instructed than to believe this empty delusion, they will still remain as they are and both live and die like pigs. They will believe just as much as a certain village mayor. When he was about to die, he told his pastor, who had debated a long time with him about the resurrection in an effort to convince him of its reality: "To be sure, I am ready to believe this; but you will see that nothing comes of it." The majority of the people in the world still think that. But whoever is a Christian must not be so uncertain in his belief; he must be sure of it, knowing how he will fare and paying no heed to the supposing and wavering or the mocking of other people. He must be able to reply: "If you do not want to believe, go your way and learn from experience. Your boasting to us will end soon. There is One who can take your conceit out of you. And even if you don't believe, He will still find people who do. In the meantime, let us see who has deceived whom."

In the fourth place, St. Paul says, we, too, would be false witnesses, we who say and teach that Christ has arisen, if the dead do not arise. And as that belief would be false, we, too, would be nothing but the devil's buffoons and liars, who speak of themselves and babble of things of which they know nothing. As base liars and rascals they invent things, cheating people out of their lives and out of all they have. We are, however, Christ's apostles and faithful witnesses. We can prove that we were called and commissioned by God and that we proclaim the truth, so that many people, mightily persuaded, join us of themselves and because of this suffer all that befalls us. This demonstrates that we are in earnest about this and do not joke or engage in trickery, as though we were vagrants or charlatans.

The fifth part follows. If there is nothing to the resurrection, Saint Paul says, "you are still in your sins," both you and all those "who have fallen asleep in Christ." Then Christ would be of no avail at all to you. For what good would you derive from the fact that you proclaim and believe you were redeemed from sin and were justified by His resurrection, if there is nothing to that resurrection and if you were not also redeemed from death and would not rise and live again? That you and all other Christians from the beginning were baptized on this, heard the Gospel, and lived as Christians who had remission of sin from their Lord would all be in vain. Believing that all ends with death, you would die like the cattle and have no more than the heathen and unbelievers. It would be disgraceful indeed to declare that Christ is nothing and that He does not help either the living or the dead.

The sixth and final point with which St. Paul concludes is: "If in this life only we have hoped in Christ, we are of all men most to be pitied." That is tantamount to saying: "If it were true that there is no life after the present one, I should gladly forgo Baptism, pulpit, and all of Christianity." For observe a Christian and compare him with people who do not believe. The latter live in a whirl of pleasure; they have and they do what they please, and when they have lived their life, "they perish forever without any regarding it," as Job 4:20 says. They never experience what real suffering or sadness, misery and grief are. In contrast to them, we who want to be Christians endure all kinds of troubles and misfortunes, so that people despise and vilify, revile and slander us. The world is so hostile to us; it begrudges us our very life on earth. Daily we must be prepared for the worst that devil and world can inflict on us. In the face of this, who would be stupid enough to be a Christian if there were nothing to a future life? Who would not say: I, too, want to have good times and revel as those people do? With what wrongdoing do I charge myself that I let myself be tormented so and endure such sorrow, spite, hatred, and envy from the world? In addition to this, a Christian must suffer so much inward grief and heartache, such fear and terror of death, of sin, and of God's wrath. These are real blows indeed.

For that external suffering is only child's play, it is only the ABC of a Christian's misery and trouble with which the world persecutes him, exiles him, and displays all sorts of malice. But this fear and woe caused by God's wrath really pierces his heart: the fear of eternal death, of becoming partners of the devil in the abyss of hell. This haunts him day and night. Against this the Christian has to contend, well-nigh sweating blood. I should much rather lie in jail for a year, suffer hunger and thirst, than to endure such mortal fright with which the devil afflicts Christians, who, after all, believe and are certain of the future resurrection and of eternal life awaiting them and, on the other hand, of judgment and eternal fire awaiting the evildoers. And

just because they know that, they have no rest until they are rescued
from this vale of tears. For here the two paths lie before them; in addition, the devil and their own conscience attack them, telling them
that they are not pious and calling Scripture to witness that we are
all sinners and guilty of damnation. The devil knows how to turn that
to account and to torment a person so that he breaks out in cold sweat.
Therefore it is necessary for a person to struggle and contend, lest he
be engulfed in sadness and fear, but that he may instead remain confident that God is gracious to him and wants to take him unto Himself
in heaven. The others, the great multitude, know nothing of this. They
fear neither God's wrath and judgment nor devil or death. They think
that their own death is not unlike the death of a cow. In the meantime,
they are secure and happy and experience nothing at all of such
a heartache. Therefore a Christian is an especially wretched person,
suffering more of whatever may be termed misery than others. His
heart is daily roasted on the fire. He must always be terrified, fearful,
and trembling when the thought of death and God's severe judgment
occurs to him. He must always worry that he has angered God and
merited hell, although he may be pious and well practiced in faith.
For such thoughts will not cease; rather, they are felt more and more
and always become stronger than the good thoughts. Therefore we
behold some people who are so depressed and so beaten and so assailed and wretched in their hearts that they can impart this to no one.
They are bereft of all joy and happiness and do not care to live.

Therefore, St. Paul says, we would be mad and foolish to subject
ourselves to such misery, fear, sadness, and distress and never be safe
from death and devil for a moment, if we had nothing but this life.
What could we possess on this earth, even though we might acquire
all the goods of the world, to compensate for being Christians and
cumbering ourselves with such suffering? Who would want to bear
that and spend his life thus in nothing but misery and distress and not
get anything but this life in return?

The heathen said very wisely: *Qui mortem metuit, quod vivit, perdit id ipsum*,[24] "he who fears death is a fool, for thereby he loses his
own life." It would indeed be well spoken, if anyone could do it. For
everybody is well aware that he accomplishes no more with this fear
than to spoil this life itself, so that he derives no benefit and no joy
from it. This can be observed in those who are so steeped in sadness

[24] The quotation has not been identified.

that they could find neither consolation nor joy, even if we decked them out with every golden ornament, filled them with the best meat and drink, and entertained them with all sorts of pastime and music. They feel nothing of life, but harbor only thoughts of death and find themselves in death already. Therefore they advise that there is nothing better than simply to cast all such fears aside, to force them from your mind, and think: "Why should we worry about this? After we are dead, we are dead." Just as the Corinthians said, as St. Paul indicates later (v. 32): "Let us eat and drink, for tomorrow we die, etc." That is making short shrift of it and extinguishing God's wrath, hell, and damnation completely.

However, Christians cannot do that. They cannot dismiss this so from hearts which would gladly believe. On the contrary, the more faith struggles and would strengthen itself, the more this is felt. Thus it is not sure of life for a moment, and God's judgment and the pit of hell always stare it in the face. Such people must be comforted with this message: "My dear man, you may feel this very much, and it may pain you uninterruptedly to live thus, and, admittedly, you are a poor, miserable person; but be patient and be assured that this must be because you are a Christian. Otherwise you would not be so tormented. However, you must fend this off and cling with a firm faith to the fact that your Christ has risen from the dead. He, too, suffered such anguish and fear of hell, but through His resurrection He has overcome all. Therefore, even though I am a sinner and deserving of death and hell, this shall nonetheless be my consolation and my victory that my Lord Jesus lives and has risen so that He, in the end, might rescue me from sin, death, and hell.

With such faith Christians must soothe and assuage their suffering and check their unhappiness. Otherwise it would be impossible to comfort a saddened and frightened heart or to divert the thoughts with any earthly joy. This, however, is effected when the Man Christ declares that He is the God and Savior of the wretched. Not those who live in security, in a whirl of pleasures, and free of all fear, but those who fear the devil and hell must occupy themselves with Baptism, the pulpit, and the Gospel and conclude thus: "The fact that I feel this fear of hell and of God's judgment is a reliable sign that I am also a Christian and have some faith; for whoever is terrified by this must surely believe that there is a heaven and a hell. On the other hand, whoever does not fear these does not believe anything.

For that reason I must comfort myself in such terror and fear, pull myself together by faith, and say to the devil and to my heart: 'You frighten me with sin and hell, but Christ tells me of heaven, righteousness, life, and eternal bliss. He must have greater weight with me than all my feelings and ideas.'" And thus we must ever struggle and resist, firmly holding and clinging to this article. This will be necessary both in life and in death.

So you see that St. Paul spoke the truth when he said: "If for this life only we have hoped in Christ, we are of all men most to be pitied," and we are also the greatest fools, for we alone renounce all goods and comforts, all joy and happiness of this life and of all creatures, we expose ourselves to every peril of life and limb in vain and for nothing and to the terrible and unspeakable terror of hell, so that we have to live in contempt and in misery before the world and in eternal fear before God. After all, there is no trouble or misfortune, no fire, no rope, no sword on earth comparable to this plague. And should we go into this or remain in it voluntarily? We should rather imitate the world or our rabble today and say: "Why do you make such a great ado about the Gospel and faith? If I but had enough money to count out, etc." "But be off, dear brother, with your crowd. Be of good cheer as long as it lasts. Because you are no Christian and believe nothing regarding God or devil, it is easy for you to revel. Nobody is there to assail you. But if you, too, want to be a Christian and strive earnestly for the life to come, you will surely feel the devil pressing you and all Christians hard with every creature which he can use for that purpose. He will terrify you, aggrieve you, he will choke you that you will find rest neither by day nor by night. And your own experience will constrain you to profess that there is no life or existence on earth more wretched than that of a Christian. For all of this misery and grief arises because of Christ. It is due to the fact that the devil is hostile to Him and to His Word and to His rule, to Baptism, and to all of Christendom. We have to suffer for that now; and we must not imagine that we will have happiness and peace here on earth.

But to the others he can grant good times and peace, although in the end he will also reward them as the hangman rewards his servant. In the meantime we must constantly be his target as his sworn enemy. Daily we must run into his spears and illustrate the saying: The greater one's piety, the earlier one's death. For if God is to preserve a pious person to grant him a long life, a special power and might will be required, a power surpassing that of both man and devil. Otherwise the devil in his great malice and anger will butcher and slaughter them all in one heap, just like poor sacrificial sheep.[25]

20-21. *But in fact Christ has been raised from the dead, the Firstfruits of those who have fallen asleep. For as by a man came death, by a Man has come also the resurrection of the dead.*

Here St. Paul draws the conclusion from the foregoing statements and comments that it is not true, as reason might lead one to assume, that there is nothing to the Christians' faith and proclamation and that we are nothing but the most wretched people on earth. Here he presents the only true consolation against such external appearances and feelings. For, as I said, Christians have to have a stronger consolation than gold and silver, singing and dancing, and all that the world possesses. A miser can be consoled with money, a sick person with medicine, a beggar or a hungry person with a piece of bread; but none of these can help a Christian. For because he believes and knows that God has both a heaven and a hell, he is immediately terrified by God's wrath; he becomes a timid and dejected person. Therefore he finds joy and solace only in the promise of the life to come as he hears this article which informs him that Christ has risen from the dead, that He will also awaken him and transport him from death and every misfortune to joy eternal.

We easily perceive that St. Paul was very much in earnest and that he was particularly fond of emphasizing this article. In fact, he stresses no other as much as this one. He does this like a person made wise and instructed by his own experience, which tells him that he must absolutely cling to this alone by faith and disregard whatever reason together with all five senses wants to add. He must also refuse to see and feel whatever is seen and felt. Otherwise Christians will have nothing but misery, lamenting and weeping, and one misfortune after the other. Therefore we must, of course, have something else to fortify and hearten us and enable us to look elsewhere than at this miserable, wretched existence. That is accomplished solely by this message. For we are not baptized and called, and we do not hear the Gospel, to discover how to become rich, how to acquire and retain goods and honor. That the jurists must teach and deal with. Nor are we to do

[25] The fourth sermon, preached October 6, 1532, the Nineteenth Sunday After Trinity, ends here.

this to find out how we are going to obtain meat and drink. It is the duty of our parents to procure that. Nor how to govern and to protect country and people. That devolves on lords and princes. No, we hear the Gospel that we may direct our hearts to another life and existence, which is not yet present and yet will surely appear.

Therefore Paul now declares: "Though we may be more wretched than any other people on earth, though we may be frightened by whatever will frighten and aggrieve us, death, hell, and every misfortune, and though these may become as severe as they can; now Christ has arisen, not from sleep," he says, "but from death; for He died and was buried the same as other people. But He came forth alive from the grave in which He lay and destroyed and consumed both devil and death, who had devoured Him. He tore the devil's belly and hell's jaws asunder and ascended into heaven, where He is now seated in eternal life and glory." This is to be comfort and defiance. For on His name we are baptized, and we hear and profess His Word. After Him we are called Christians, and for His sake we suffer every misfortune and grief from the hand of the devil. For this is not aimed at us but at Him and His kingdom, whose enemy the devil is. He tries to destroy it, and he treats us so roughly and wearies us with pursuit, harassment, and death so that we might forsake Christ.

But we will confront him confidently and say: "No, you despicable, vile devil, you will not bring matters to such a pass that I surrender Baptism and the name of my Lord for your sake. If you can defiantly rely on and make an uproar with your death, fire, water, pestilence, and hell, we can defiantly rely on this Lord Jesus Christ, who has vanquished you. He can again destroy you and cast you into hell eternally — as He in fact will do — and wrest us alive from your jaws. Therefore devour us if you can, or hurl us into the jaws of death, you will soon see and feel what you have done. We, in turn, will cause such a great disturbance in your belly and make an egress through your ribs that you wish you had rather devoured a tower, yes, an entire forest. For you previously consumed a Person and put Him under the ground, but He was too strong for you. To your great disgrace you had to return Him although you blasphemed defiantly: 'He saved others; He cannot save Himself, etc.' (Matt. 27:42). But now He defies you in return; He has become your death and hell. And soon He will overthrow you completely through us on the Day of Judgment."

You, of course, will say: "It is easy for Christ to defy the devil and death, for He is enthroned on high where no one can harm Him. But what do I gain thereby? Or, how will I obtain that? As you can see, I remain behind." St. Paul replies with one short statement, saying: "Christ has been raised from the dead, the Firstfruits of those who have fallen asleep." For with the word "Firstfruits" he implies that Christ is not the only one to arise but that others will follow later. You must not regard this Man as one who arose for Himself alone. We would be but poorly comforted if His resurrection had no sequel. Then we would derive no more benefit from this than if He had never become man.

It was not necessary for Him to die for Himself, because He was born without sin and the devil had no claim on Him. Moreover, He was Lord over devil and death, so that the devil did not dare to attack Him. Christ might well have defied the devil and challenged him to touch one little hair of His head.[26] This is the way He repelled the Jews in the Garden when He said: "I am He" (John 18:5). No, we must view Him in this light, that this dying and rising again were for your benefit and mine. As He died and lay under the sod as you and I must die and be buried, thus He also rose again for our sakes and made an exchange with us; as He was brought into death through us, we shall be restored from death to life through Him. For by His death He has devoured our death, so that we all will also arise and live as He arose and lives. Therefore Christ is rightly called *Primitiae*, "the Firstfruits of those who have fallen asleep," since He takes the lead and draws the whole throng after Him. For whenever a first one is mentioned, it is implied that more than one are involved. The others who follow, the second, the third, and so forth, are included here, all bound together, as many as have fallen asleep. Otherwise, if Christ had risen alone and no one were to follow Him, He could not be called the First.

And note well that Paul refrains from calling those "dead" who will rise after Christ. No, he says that Christ is "the Firstfruits of those who have fallen asleep." And yet he says that Christ arose, not from sleep but "from the dead." For what was a true and eternal death prior to this and without Christ is now, since Christ has passed from death to life and has arisen, no longer death; now it has become merely

---

[26] The German expression is *ihm ein Haar krümmen*. This idiom is well known from Paul Gerhardt's Easter hymn, *Auf, auf, mein Herz, mit Freuden*, st. 4: *Die Höll' und ihre Rotten, die krümmen mir kein Haar.*

a sleep.[27] And so the Christians who lie in the ground are no longer called dead, but sleepers, people who will surely also arise again. For when we say that people are asleep, we refer to those who are lying down but will wake up and rise again, not those who are lying down bereft of all hope of rising again. Of the latter we do not say that they are sleeping but that they are inanimate corpses. Therefore by that very word "asleep" Scripture indicates the future resurrection.

And what is more than that, by calling Christ "the Firstfruits of those who have fallen asleep" Paul wishes to signify that the resurrection is to be viewed and understood as having already begun in Christ, indeed, as being more than half finished, and that this remnant of death is to be regarded as no more than a deep sleep, and that the future resurrection of our body will not differ from suddenly awaking from such a sleep. For the main and best part of this has already come to pass, namely, that Christ, our Head, has arisen. But now that the Head is seated on high and lives, there is no longer any reason for concern. We who cling to Him must also follow after Him as His body and His members. For where the head goes and abides, there the body with all the members must necessarily follow and abide. As in the birth of man and of all animals, the head naturally appears first, and after this is born, the whole body follows easily. Now since Christ has passed over and reigns above in heaven over sin, death, devil, and everything, and since He did this for our sake to draw us after Him, we need no longer worry about our resurrection and life, though we depart and rot in the ground. For now this is no more than a sleep. And for Christ it is but a night before He rouses us from the sleep.

Now if I know this and believe it, my heart or conscience and soul have already passed through death and grave and are in heaven with Christ, dwell there and rejoice over it. And in that way we have the two best parts, much more than half, of the resurrection behind us. And because Christ animates and renews the heart by faith, He will also surely drag the decomposed rascal after Him and clothe him again, so that we can behold Him and live with Him. For that is His Word and work on which we are baptized and live and die. Therefore this will surely not fail us, as little as it failed Him. No matter when or how God ordains that we die, whether in bed or in the fire,

[27] Cf. Luther's hymn on Simeon's Song, Luke 2:29-32, especially st. 1, line 6: *Der Tod ist mein Schlaf worden.* See *Luther's Works,* 53, p. 248.

in the water, by rope or by sword, the devil, death's master and butcher, will surely see to killing us and carrying out his trade, so that we will not be able to choose or select a mode of death. But no matter how he executes us, it shall not harm us. He may give us a bitter potion, such as is administered to put people to sleep and make them insensitive, but we will wake up again and come forth on that Day, when the trumpet will sound. That the devil shall not prevent, because even now we are more than halfway out of death in Christ, and he will not be able to hold back this poor belly and bag of maggots either.

Behold, thus we must view our treasure and turn away from temporal reality which lies before our eyes and senses. We must not let death and other misfortune, distress and misery, terrify us so. Nor must we regard what the world has and can do, but balance this against what we are and have in Christ. For our confidence is built entirely on the fact that He has arisen and that we have life with Him already and are no longer in the power of death. Therefore let the world be mad and foolish, boasting of and relying on its money and goods; and let the devil rage with his poisonous darts in our conscience; and let him afflict us with all sorts of trouble — against all of this our one defiant boast shall be that Christ is our Firstfruits, that He has initiated the resurrection, that He has burst through the devil's kingdom, through hell and death, that He no longer dies or sleeps but rules and reigns up above eternally, in order to rescue us, too, from this prison and death. Our money and goods and all that we may boast of shall repose in Him at a place which neither devil nor world can venture to approach.

In the face of this, why should we let the devil terrify us and make us so despondent, even though he comes face to face with us and reaches out to us, as though he would rob us of everything; even though he kills wife and child, torments our heart with all sorts of misery and sorrow, and in the end also destroys our body, assuming that he has thereby taken everything away? But he is still far from accomplishing this. He may now take life and limb while we are lodging here in his inn, where he does nothing but kill and slaughter daily, similar to a hangman or a butcher in a barn filled with sheep. And since we eat and drink in such an inn, we must naturally also pay him for our keep. He dispenses no other food than pestilence and every other sickness and pours no other wine or drink than pure poison.

Therefore we can expect nothing else than that he will fill us with this and then butcher and flay us.

But with all that done, he has still stripped us of nothing. For the goods and the treasure which we Christians have are not those which the world seeks and possesses in this life on earth. No, we have already secured our possession against the devil, so that he cannot take it from us. It is in safe custody in this Firstfruits of the dead, who is seated on high, who has ascended from the den of murderers and has taken our life and all with Him. We defiantly boast of that and, in addition, scoff at the devil, saying: "Because you hanker so to devour us Christians and assume that you are acquiring a dainty morsel, go ahead and kill and butcher us, fry us and devour us hide and hair. However, begin behind with this, and then you will have mustard and salt in advance. But what do you have after you have completely devoured us? It will be far from satisfying your insatiable appetite. For you will not find what you are seeking and desiring, and that is the best and greatest part of us, indeed, our whole life and treasure, namely, this article of the resurrection in Christ. Through this we have already been wrested from your teeth and have been moved too far on high. For this treasure does not reside with us or in us — if it did, you would soon tear it away from us — but on high in Christ. There you will have to let it rest unassailed and without any thanks.[28] What does it harm us that you now kill our body? For the only thing you effect thereby is to help this poor sack of maggots out of its misery and arrive at its destination, where the head, the heart, and everything is except all misfortune. That we look forward to daily and that we desire. Then you shall perceive and feel what you have eaten. It will be most distressing to no one but only you. The very pestilence and poison that you gave us you yourself will have to eat and devour and guzzle down, and it will tear both your jaws and your belly, putting an end to your raging." Behold, thus we must fend off and defy all terror of the vile enemy, because he can after all but afflict us with all distress and grief. This he does to distract our eyes and our heart from this article and the Firstfruits, Christ, making us forget whose we are or what we have and what we are called.

In this way St. Paul demonstrated that Christ's resurrection is the reason for ours. He now expounds and illustrates that further with an example, saying: "For as by a man came death, by a Man has come

[28] Cf. p. 88, n. 15, above.

also the resurrection of the dead." That is to say: "Just as Adam was
the beginning, the first man, through whom we must all die as he died,
so Christ is the first Man through whom we are all to arise to a new
life as He arose first." Those are the two persons and the two types
which Scripture juxtaposes. And that is the way God ordained it,
namely, as death came, and still comes, over us all through one man,
so the resurrection from the dead shall come through one Man. Therefore Adam is an image of Christ, as St. Paul says in Rom. 5:14, where
he enlarges on both. However, the latter is far better and different,
indeed, it effects the direct opposite of what its antitype, Adam, effected. For Adam transmitted nothing but death to all men, so that
both he and we must submit to it and cannot escape it. But if that
was to be corrected, God had to have another Man appear, who would
again transfer us from death to life.

Here St. Paul places these two types over against each other. He
wants to say: "Through one man, Adam, so much was effected that all
men must now die, both he and all of us who, after all, did not commit or perpetrate the offense but came into sin and death solely because we are descended from him." Although this happens after the
Fall, yet it is no longer the sin of another, but it becomes our own
when we are born. That is a miserable deal and an awful judgment
of God; and it would be still more terrible if we were all to remain in
death eternally. But now God placed a second Man, called Christ,
over against the first one, so that, just as we die without any fault of
our own by reason of the first man, we shall live again by reason of
Christ and without our merit. And as we in Adam have to pay solely
for the fact that we are his members or his flesh and blood, so we enjoy
our advantage here in Christ also solely by virtue of His being our
Head. It is pure grace and gift, so that we have no works or merits
to boast of here, as our monks and false saints teach. For how should
we who are born in sin and belong to death, being of Adam's flesh and
blood, manage to liberate ourselves by our cowls or other works both
from sin and death, emerging alive from dust and ashes, brighter and
more beautiful than the sun and the rest of creation? That can, of
course, not be achieved by human power and strength or by that of all
creatures, not even by the angels in heaven, but exclusively by God
Himself. There must be another Man who can achieve that and bring it
about, a Man who is called Christ, God's Son and Lord over sin, death,
devil, and over all things, as St. Paul will say of Him later (v. 27). It is

He who acquired this article and initiated it in Himself and presented it to us, so that we, too, might attain it through Him, solely because we are incorporated in Him through Baptism and were called to this article and engrafted in it, so that we will arise and live by the same power and merit by which He arose and lives.

And now since this is not at all our doing, both that we came into death and that we came into life, our consolation is all the stronger, as is also our hope that we shall have life through Christ as surely as we now have and feel sin and death through Adam. For if it would rest with us and depend on us to work our way out of sin and death and to obtain life by our own doing, we could not be at ease our whole life. We should have to torment and terrify ourselves with works incessantly. And after we had thus tortured ourselves to death, and even if one person were to produce the holiness of the whole world, we could still not be certain and sure that we had done enough and sufficient to satisfy God. Therefore God granted us the mercy to impose all of this on one Man, who acquired all of this without us and ahead of us, so that it is assured us and cannot fail us. Therefore we come into this entirely without our doing. Nothing that we do or are able to do contributes toward our obtaining grace and resurrection; although we do and must do good works. This is the same as when we become sinners without our doing and must die. For we had no hand in Adam's eating the apple and falling into sin, although we do admittedly commit sin after the Fall. In that way everything that pertains to sin and to righteousness, to death and to life, resides solely in those two men, as St. Paul now elaborates further.

22. *For as in Adam all die, so also in Christ shall all be made alive.*

Here St. Paul is still speaking only about those who are Christians. These he wants to instruct and console with this article. For although also the non-Christians must all arise, this will not be to their comfort and joy, since they will arise for judgment and not for life. Therefore to hear this article does not bring comfort and joy to the world and the ungodly people of today either. This I experienced in my own case when I tried to be a holy monk and when I was most pious. I would much rather have heard about all the devils in hell than about the Last Day. My hair stood on end when I thought of it. For aside from the fact that the whole world is loath to relinquish this life and to die and is frightened when one speaks of death and of yonder life, we are all submerged in the mire of our own holiness, and we are of the opinion that we might silence God's judgment and merit heaven with our life and works. And yet all that we accomplish thereby is that we become ever more averse and hostile to this Day. I will say nothing of that great vulgar throng which seeks its pleasure and consolation only here, which contemns God's Word and cares not a mite for God and His kingdom. It is not surprising that such people are annoyed to hear of the blessed resurrection; for us, however, it is pure joy, because we hear that our greatest Treasure, over which we rejoice, is already in heaven above, and that only the most insignificant part remains behind; and that He will awaken this, too, and draw it after Him as easily as a person awakens from sleep. There will no longer be any grief or suffering, and neither world nor devil will plague and sadden us anymore. Now they are persecuting and tormenting us, but then tables will be turned on them. Their lot will be everlasting lamentation, but we will rejoice eternally. For since Christ is to be the Judge both of the good and of the evil, they, too, will have to come forth on that Day to receive their judgment and their punishment for whatever they perpetrated in their impenitent and devilish malice against Christ and us.[29]

It is a ridiculous message that St. Paul conveys here, telling us where both death and eternal life originate. To clever reason and worldly wisdom it seems to be a great and strong lie that the entire human race must die for the guilt of another, of one single man. It seems too unfair and too absurd that God should treat this matter so strangely and take this silly position in His judgment. Because Adam bit into an apple, he is supposed to have effected that all men are doomed to die to the end of the world. But what is to be our position in this matter? That death befalls us we can all see clearly. But that this is due to one minor sin sounds too odd. When we explain this with words and compare the two, this does appear disproportionate.

For at the time Adam had, after all, not committed murder or adultery, he had not stolen or robbed anyone, he had not blasphemed God or committed any similar sins, wicked and horrible sins such as abound in the world today. All he did was to bite into an apple, persuaded to do this and deceived by the devil through his wife. Reason asks whether so much importance had to be attached to that one apple that the whole world had to pay for it and that so many fine, excellent,

---

[29] The fifth sermon, preached in the afternoon of Oct. 13, 1532, the Twentieth Sunday After Trinity, ends here.

and wise people, indeed, God's Son Himself, together with all the prophets, fathers, and saints, had to die. Yes, if nothing more than death were involved here, as the world and wise people say, who console themselves over against death with the assumption that it ends all misfortune! If some better fate should await them after death, as they hope, they are willing to accept it too. Still they cannot conclude that with any degree of certainty; and of the resurrection they know nothing whatsoever. But the thought that we all deserve eternal punishment and damnation and suffering in hell because of the sin of someone else, and all of that by reason of just one sin — that is still harder for the human heart to accept. For this judgment on the part of such an exalted Majesty, which is the highest Wisdom and Goodness, seems too unfair, and the action too merciless.

As we have said, we must all profess that it seems so ridiculous that we all must die; however, that this derives from Adam we must learn to believe here. For no human heart or wisdom ever devised or thought this out, that death is a penalty for sin. No, everybody thought and regarded death as man's natural lot, comparable to the death of a dog or a pig or any other animal, or comparable to the rising and the setting of the sun, or the growing or the withering of grass. All things are considered perishable by nature, vanishing again as they came. However, Scripture teaches us that our death and dying does not come in a natural way but that this is a fruit of and the penalty for our father Adam's sin. He offended the Sublime Majesty so outrageously that he and all who are descended from him and are born on earth must die eternally. No one on earth can escape or ward off this calamity.

And again it sounds so absurd and so false to the world, yes, much more incredible, when Paul declares here that in one Man all men shall rise again; that both death and life rest with and depend on one man; that the whole world is unable to do anything in this matter; that no man's power or might, no saint's life, virtue, and work, are adequate reason for rising from the dead; that this is absolutely beyond the ability and the merit of every other human being and is centered solely in one single Man, who was unknown to the world and despised by it, who, moreover, died a most shameful and miserable death. To Him all the world is to accord honor, and He is to be regarded as the One by whom we all rise again. No holy monk, Carthusian, yes, no prophet, apostle, or martyr, can contribute anything toward this or merit it with all his doings. This appears preposterous as we ponder it. It often appeared strange and odd to me myself. It is surely hard to convince the heart of this article. When I behold a corpse carried out and buried, it is hard to go my way and believe and think that we will some day rise together. How so, or by what power? Not by myself or by virtue of any merit on earth, but by this one Christ. And that is indeed certain, far more certain than the fact that I will be buried and see someone else buried, which I know with certainty and behold with my eyes. Therefore this is a sermon for Christians and an article of faith. All who are of the world regard this as sheer fraud. They argue that it is impossible for God to be so foolish and to condemn the whole world without distinction for the sake of one man, or, on the other hand, to save all men without any merit of theirs for the sake of one Man.

For in their opinion, if fair judgment is to be exercised, everyone should die or live as an individual and in accordance with his own deserts, just as a criminal is hanged or beheaded because of his misdeeds. Ordinarily everybody is penalized for his own crime and rewarded for his own piety, it is entirely incongruous that someone should die or be acquitted for the sake of someone else. The belief of the Turks today and, to be sure, of the entire world at its best, would be considered just and fair by the world, namely, that the pious shall rise on the Last Day and live, and vice versa. But that one Man should account for all others and that the question of dying or living of all is dependent on the deserts of someone else, in a manner that all derives from one father and is devoid of any other cause — that is regarded as teaching and preaching offensively and ridiculously. However, it pleased God to adopt that plan. He wants to make a fool of the world and of the wise, carrying out His work so that no one can comprehend it.

For if He did what you and I can understand and sketch out for Him, what honor would He derive from that? Or what sort of a God would He be who let us instruct Him, or who would be directed by us and work according to our wisdom? But as it is, He works in a manner in which His wisdom remains profounder than ours; we have to surrender to it and desist from criticizing. We must say: "According to my wisdom this does not seem good; however, since You say it, it is just and good." Anyone who will not do that but instead places His own wisdom before and above God's and judges

Him accordingly, let him beware what he is doing. We, however, will confine our wisdom to things here below and apply it to cows and horses, trees, houses, fields, etc. In this area you may be smart and judge and rule as you will, and you may stick to your opinion. But we must not interfere with His wisdom and rule. That is too high and far removed for us, since we are under Him and He is over us as our Creator and Lord. Therefore we must give ear to Him and believe what He says, so that His honor remains unsullied and His grace and mercy alone prevail, without any glory or merit of ours.

That is the message which Paul is so fond of preaching and proclaiming. But, as I always say, this is of benefit only to those Christians who are in a position to accept and to believe this article. They feel their sin and death and experience this fact. They confess that they fell into sin through Adam and were cast under God's wrath and condemnation and became forfeit to death. That thought oppresses them continually, and they would like to be free of it. And although according to the flesh they are also loath to die, they are consoled by their desire to be liberated from this, by their longing for the resurrection, and by their willingness to suffer such terror of sin and death in the hope that Christ will free them from these. In their hearts there is nothing but yearning sighs too deep for words and a cry with all their might, as St. Paul expresses it in Rom. 7:24 f.: "Who will deliver me from this body of death. Thanks be to God through Jesus Christ our Lord, etc." It is as though he were to say: "Indeed, I feel the death and the misery which I have from Adam. This pains me so grievously that my heart all but melts in my body. However, to remedy this I hold to the Man Jesus Christ and take comfort in the knowledge that I have life through Him. This is, admittedly, a scarcely perceptible consolation. To console oneself in such deep sighing and longing is but a feeble undertaking, for the heart beats violently and feels nothing but the pressing burden of sin and fear of death, so that it must cry out. Yet it feels no more and can utter no more than the wish to be relieved of this and be saved. Thus the heart must be sustained and nourished solely by its sighing. But it serves the purpose of teaching a Christian to look for the true consolation in such fear; not in himself nor in men nor in any other creature but in the Christ, through whom alone so much has been earned and acquired that sin and death, transmitted by Adam, do not harm us, but that we come into life through it and from it.

The non-Christians and unbelieving saints cannot do this, although they also cry out and are terrified when their hour strikes. But their thoughts cannot carry them so high, nor can their hearts utter such deep sighing, that God should and would deliver them from this for Christ's sake without any merit of their own; no, they must despair in terror and fear. For they do not know this doctrine which tells us how to escape death, namely, that this is effected exclusively through this one Christ. Meanwhile they run to and fro in their fright, first to this saint, then to another. They look for one work here, for another there. But a Christian leaves all of that out of consideration, for he has learned and experienced that there is no help on earth against death, which is innate in us. In fact, a Christian must also bear and suffer death the same as others. And of course it frightens and pains him. But he cries solely to God, believing that He will deliver him from death through Christ. In that way he strengthens himself daily until he passes from this life.

Furthermore we enjoy the advantage of which I spoke earlier, namely, that in Christ death has lost its meaning even today and that a part of the resurrection has already taken place — really the best and foremost part — and that we have received a taste of this in our hearts through Christ, and that we, praise be to God, have arrived at the point where the enemy has practically no more teeth and where he has lost his sword. For if we figure it out, we find that he has already almost devoured the world and has emptied the keg down to the very dregs, that he has killed the larger part of the human race, the head, the chest, the belly, and the legs, almost the feet too. For today we are no more than the last toes of the great image of which Daniel speaks in chapter 7. For the four monarchies, or empires, are already past history, and all the prophets and fathers and Christ Himself with His apostles and saints are all gone. In brief, the largest part of the entire body of Christendom and, in addition, the greatest and wisest princes and lords and kings are gone, so that only the last little drink remains to be taken, and it is only a short leap to the end. It is comparable to the time of vintage. Practically all the grapes have been picked and not more than one or two remain hanging on the vines. Or it is similar to shaking a tree; only two or three apples remain hanging. These pale into insignificance over against the entire harvest or vintage. So death, too, has almost completed his slaughter and has almost finished his reign. But he is not sated until he has also consumed the entire small remnant of pious people.

On the other hand, however, Christ has already brought about life in Himself and His saints, and that almost to the last detail. For He thrones above as our Head and reigns over the entire human race with so much might and majesty that the whole world is as nothing compared with Him. He already owns the greatest part of His body, that is, Christendom, through its belief in His resurrection, so that not more than a leap, yes, a moment, remains until His own, whose bodies still repose in the grave, arise completely. For all of these, excepting a small number, have been taken from their misery, and more than half of them are alive in Christ, because they lived and persevered in the faith. For Christ says (Matt. 22:32) that Abraham and all the other saints are alive in God's sight even though they have departed this life, since we have a God not of the dead but of the living. Therefore death has already been deprived of his power, and he has but few more people left to slaughter; for almost all have already passed through death, and the time is near at hand when God will present us all alive again and cast death and hell under our feet. In short, our head, yes, our back and our belly, our shoulders and legs have already passed from death, and all the hold death still has on us is by a small toe. This, too, will extricate itself soon. Therefore we who have now reached the end of the world have the defiant comfort that it will be but a little while, that we are on our last lap, and before we are aware of it, we shall all stand at Christ's side and live with Him eternally.

Therefore, if we believe God's Word, it must not trouble us if the statement made here by St. Paul sounds ridiculous, namely, that as we all die in one man, so we shall also rise again in one Man. Since we came into sin through Adam without our own fault, and since we could not deliver ourselves from that sin by ourselves, it pleased God in His divine wisdom and goodness to restore righteousness and eternal life to us through one Man who was without any sin. For it was not His will that we remain in sin and death, which would have happened if Christ had not come. Thus this is all sheer grace. Now we no longer suffer any harm from the fact that we die in Adam. On the contrary, we derive an advantage from it, namely, a much better life than would have been ours if we were not able to die. There is only this, that death still seems repugnant to the outer man, our flesh and blood; he approaches it reluctantly. For the outer man cannot do otherwise; it is simply part and parcel of him and inheres in his nature, inherited from Adam, that he fears death and flees from him.

But here he can take comfort in the knowledge that he surely has life in Christ, together with all the saints who preceded him. Christ is already enthroned on high and lives for Himself and for all of these. Therefore we have already acquired more than half of this, both in those who died before us and in ourselves. And yet we received all of this free and gratis. We contribute nothing except that we are baptized, hear the Gospel, and adhere to Christ — all of which is no work of ours but only God's grace. So we contribute nothing to the fact that we fall into sin in Adam except that we are born of him through a father and a mother and cling and stick to him as his flesh and blood. For he has led us all after himself. He is like a person who goes up a high mountain and in the ascent tumbles down and pulls all who followed him down to the bottom with him. And now, as I have acquired death through Adam, I acquire life through Christ. I on my part contribute nothing to the latter; I merely accept this or receive it by faith.

Therefore the grace, the consolation, and the joy are as great here as the misery and sadness are there, indeed, even greater. The benefit surpasses the harm done by far. If someone inflicts a slight injury on me and another compensates me richly for this, what cause for complaint do I have? It is as if a thief had stolen ten florins from me and a rich man reimbursed me with one hundred florins. Therefore when the devil kills my body with all sorts of evil, Christ again restores this to me in a state much more glorious, beautiful, and brilliant than the bright sun. Therefore we must not be concerned about our reluctance to die, but against this we must vividly picture the happiness and the joy that will be ours in yonder life. This will be inexpressibly greater and more glorious than the damage and the woe which we now suffer from Adam.

23. *But each in his own order: Christ the Firstfruits, then at His coming those who belong to Christ.*

Here St. Paul does not discuss the question whether several others arose from the dead and are in heaven with Christ. He speaks solely of Christ as of one Man. For he wants to present this article exclusively and purely according to its substance, making the one Man, Christ, the Origin and the Beginner of life, or of the resurrection.

Therefore, whether several saints, for instance, Enoch and Elijah, ascended into heaven before Christ or whether several people were resurrected by Him or arose with Him is not the question under discussion here. Here we are not dealing *de privata resurrectione,* how one or two arose from the dead, but with the general resurrection and with the Head or the Cause of the same, which is Christ. For it is of no importance to me whether several people rose under special circumstances. But it is very important to know that Christ arose and how or when we, too, are to arrive there, namely, that we shall be led from this vale of tears by Him and abide where He is.

That is what he means when he adds these words. He brackets Christ with all of us who will arise, making Him the Head and the Beginning. He expresses it thus: "each in his own order," that is, one after the other; first Christ, then we. And with that He also strikes a blow at His factions who carried confusion into this article by all sorts of prattle. Some said that the resurrection had taken place long ago or that it should not be expected in the future. They said: "Of course we hear you say that Christ has risen. From this fact you conclude that we, too, will arise. Well, when will this take place? Or who will rise first and who later? For we don't see anyone who has risen, not even Christ Himself." In this way they made sport and a mockery of this article, as though there were nothing to it, or as though their resurrection had occurred only spiritually. To such Paul wants to make reply, saying: "Indeed, my dear man, you expect this to be shoved under your very nose, so that you can gaze at it as a cow gazes at a new gate. The apostles did not see Christ rise either when He was hanging on the cross and was laid into the grave. They, too, had to await the time." Thus we, too, must believe it today without seeing it, especially since we know that Christ has already risen as the Head and the Firstfruits. Meanwhile we must wait for the time when we, too, shall follow Him.

St. Paul says that the resurrection will not take place in this manner, that Christ will immediately take all who died before Him with Himself; nor will He awaken the Christians who die after Him individually and one after the other. No, He was to be the Precursor and the Head, acquiring for all Christians, both those who preceded and those who succeed Him, the ability to live in Him spiritually during their appointed time here on earth. And when the time comes, He will on one day bid all who belong to Him come forth, and then He will lead them with Him. He arose when His hour was at hand. And thus we, too, shall arise when our hour comes and follow Him. For He will not awaken us before all who are His own have been gathered together. And since many are yet to be born, both we and those who preceded us in death must wait until these are also added and death, which slays us daily, ceases entirely and is abolished, as St. Paul will tell us a little later.

That is what is meant here when we read: "each in his own order." These words differentiate between His resurrection and ours. For the order demands that He be the first; He must blaze the trail and produce life. After that He will gather all those who are His members and belong to the resurrection, one after another, so that they all come forth together on one day appointed by Him and live with Him eternally. Meanwhile He alone remains *Primitiae,* "the Fristfruits"; and we who believe in Him live in Him by more than one half until He draws forth also the small remnant completely, namely, our flesh and blood. Thus He remains in His order, and we in ours. And we have the certain hope that since He, our Head, has preceded us, our entire body in one piece will follow Him at the proper time and abide where He is. This will not happen in secret or in some nook or corner, one arising here and another person there; no, this will be a public spectacle viewed by the whole world, when death, sin, and every evil will end and all will be sheer life and joy. Furthermore, our bodies, together with those of all creatures, will possess a new clarity in keeping with His promise. Therefore the question whether several people rose separately is not to be dragged in here, as I said; for in these this is not yet manifest, nor is the final existence which will prevail at that time.[30]

24. *Then comes the end, when He delivers the Kingdom to God the Father after destroying every rule and every authority and power.*

When the hour strikes, he wishes to say, in which we who are Christ's are to rise and follow Him, then all is accomplished, and the end to which Scripture points is at hand. This earthly life with all its misery and misfortune will cease, the vile devil with his rule will come to an end, yes, also both the secular and the spiritual offices will terminate. In sum, all things on earth will come to an end, and that which we together with all saints have desired and waited for

[30] The sixth sermon, preached in the afternoon of October 20, 1532, the Twenty-first Sunday After Trinity, ends here.

since the beginning of the world will be ushered in, namely, that God Himself will be Lord alone and rule alone in us, His children. To this rule there will be no end. He Himself explains what He means with the end when He says that He will abolish every rule and power and will alone be all in all.

The life to come will not be regulated as this temporal life is, requiring man and woman, children, house, fields, menservants and maidservants, and whatever else pertains to the married estate or proceeds from it, such as government, subjects, and whatever other estates and offices there may be on earth. To be sure, man and woman will remain with regard to the nature and person of each, but not for the purpose of begetting children, establishing a home, or providing daily bread, food and drink, clothing and shoes, etc. Every purpose for which God instituted marriage, namely, that husband and wife live together and beget children and then rule city and country and people, is left behind in this life. For wherever the married estate is established, the rest must all follow, entailing everything that pertains to the government of the world. But since the married estate will no longer exist, all the rest will necessarily also terminate.

And then, says St. Paul, Christ will "deliver the Kingdom to God the Father, etc." How is that? Does not Scripture declare everywhere that Christ will remain King forever and that His kingdom will have no end? How does that agree with the statement made here that He will deliver the Kingdom to the Father and subject Himself to Him, laying His crown, scepter, and everything in His lap? Answer: St. Paul is here speaking of Christ's present kingdom on earth. This is a kingdom of faith, in which He rules through the Word, and not in a visible and public manner. It is like beholding the sun through a cloud. To be sure, one sees the light but not the sun itself. But after the clouds have passed, both light and sun are viewed simultaneously in one and the same object. In that way Christ now rules undivided with the Father. It is one and the same Kingdom. The only difference is that it is dark and hidden at present, or concealed and covered, comprehended entirely in faith and in the Word. All that is seen of this is Baptism and the Sacrament, and all that is heard is the external Word. These are the only power and might with which He rules and executes everything.

I suppose that we would like to see Him reign like emperors and kings, surrounded by external splendor and power, and see Him lay

about Him with fists against the evildoers. He does not want to do
that now. He wants to reign quietly and invisibly in our hearts, solely
through the Word. Through this Word He wants to protect and preserve us amid our weakness over against the world's might and power.
And this Kingdom on earth is identical with the one which will later
be in heaven, only that it is hidden now and not open to view. A florin
in a purse or pocket is a genuine florin and also remains genuine when
I take it out and hold it in my hand. The only difference is that it is
no longer concealed. Similarly, Christ will take the treasure which
is now veiled to us, who know nothing of it but what we hear and
believe, and reveal it openly and before the eyes of the whole world.
But nonetheless we surely possess this treasure. A merchant who
holds a sealed promissory note is just as sure of his money as if he
had the cash in his pocket. Here all happens alone in faith, through
Word and Sacrament; here I believe and do not doubt that we are
God's children and the kingdom of our Lord Jesus Christ, that He is
our King who reigns over us and protects us against all enemies and
frees us from every need, even though we do not see this but rather
feel the reverse, namely, that sin weighs us down, the devil terrifies
and harasses us, death kills us, the world persecutes us, and everything
overwhelms and oppresses us. But today the order reads not to see
but to believe, not to comprehend it with our five senses but to disregard these and give ear solely to what God's Word tells you, until the
hour comes when Christ will put an end to this and present Himself
publicly in His majesty and sovereignty. Then you will see and feel
what you now believe. Sin will be erased and drowned, death will be
abolished and removed from view, the devil and the world will lie
at your feet. Life with God will be manifest, and all will be clear
before our view, as an uncovered treasure, such as we now yearn
for and look forward to.

When St. Paul says that Christ will deliver the Kingdom to the
Father, he means to say that He will discontinue faith and the hidden
essence and present His own to God the Father and in that way
openly transfer us into the Kingdom, which He established and now
administers daily, so that we will behold Him most clearly, without
veil and obscure words. Then this will no longer be called a kingdom
of faith but a kingdom of clarity and manifest being. And although
this is one and the same Kingdom — Christ's, who became man that
He might create faith in Him; and God's, for whoever hears Christ

hears God Himself — it is at present properly called the kingdom of the Lord Christ, because God in His majesty is now hidden and has given all to Christ, so that He might bring us to Himself by His Word and Baptism. Moreover, God has hidden Himself in Christ, so that we must now seek and acknowledge God only in Him. But up above, when Christ has accomplished all that He is to accomplish; when He no longer reigns amid our weakness and tribulations but death and sin and all that is against God are abolished; when He has brought us to the place where we behold Him with the Father in divine majesty; when we no longer need to administer His Gospel, Baptism, and remission of sin, nor learn to recognize Him or fear any misfortune any longer; when we will have naught but God, eternal righteousness, blessedness, and life present and visible with us; and when Christ bestows all this on us, so that we will be like Him — then it will really be called God's kingdom.

Thus Paul himself explains and interprets it with the subsequent words, "after destroying every rule and every authority and power, etc." This is to say that Christ will put an end to all, both to the spiritual rule which He now administers in the world, consisting of Baptism, preaching, Sacrament, Office of the Keys, or Absolution, etc., and to the secular government with its estates and offices, such as father, mother, child, manservant, maidservant, lords, princes, peasant, burgher, etc. None of these will be needed any longer. For since the spiritual rule of the Word and of faith will cease, the office of the emperor and of Jack Ketch [31] with the sword must also terminate. Only One will remain; He will be called God. He Himself will be Preacher, Comforter, Father, Mother, Lord, and Emperor. And everything that we must now beg for piecemeal — this item from our father, that one from emperor or princes, or spiritual matters from pastor or preacher — all of that we shall have up there at one time and in a lump. For the preservation of this life demands many classes of people. The father provides life and sustenance; the emperor or prince procures peace and protection; the schoolteacher imparts knowledge and instruction, etc. Over there, however, nothing will be needed beyond having Him. Everything that we must now obtain from many people and that is acquired and preserved with great difficulty and labor will be furnished there.

[31] Luther's term for "executioner" is *Meister Hans.* In English history a notorious practitioner, Jack Ketch, lends his name to the profession.

And yet St. Paul differentiates between the two kingdoms, the spiritual and the secular. Of the spiritual he does not say that Christ will abolish it, but that He will deliver it to God; it will still remain. The secular government, however, will be abolished by Christ, as Paul declares, and destroyed completely. For this was instituted not for the sake of the pious but for the sake of the impious, to resist and curb their malice and villainy, so that the pious may maintain themselves over against them and enjoy peace. And when the impious are all executed, He will also have to discard that office and whatever belongs to it, sword, gallows, death. But this will remain, that we may glory and say: "I loved God and His Word. I was baptized and was a Christian, and through love I served my neighbor." But those people, on the other hand, will be constrained to say: "Now our kingdom is completely shattered, and nothing of it survives." For it, too, was instituted solely for the sake of temporal life and has nothing to do with heaven, nor does it promote toward heaven. The sole purpose of the spiritual life, however, is to take us to yonder life. Therefore the temporal life will be completely destroyed, and nothing of it will remain; but the spiritual life will be transformed into a better and perfect existence, in which everything we now look forward to by faith will be eternal and present.

St. Paul uses three words: rule, authority, power. Everyone is privileged to distinguish here as he will. I differentiate as follows. I think that Paul thereby expresses three divisions pertaining to government; for every secular government requires these three. He calls the first and foremost *principatum*, "rule"; this refers to the supreme lord, for instance, the emperor in his empire, a prince in his land, a count in his county, also the burgomaster in a city as the head from whom all commands emanate. The second he calls *potestates*, "authority." This refers to those who receive the commands from the supreme government and are authorized to issue further commands, such as officials and judges. The third he calls *virtutes*, "power." This term embraces those who carry out and execute the commands, such as the servants of lords and princes, Jack Ketch,[32] and municipal officers. For if both justice and punishment are to be executed, people are needed who put their hand to this task and carry it out. And if it is to be carried out, it must be done by people who do this by virtue of their

[32] Cf. n. 31 above.

title and office. But those who execute it must be authorized by a higher power and not do this on their own. Where this order prevails, it is proper that the sovereign lord governs and rules, the official in charge commands and prosecutes, and the servant carries it out and does it. The same procedure must be observed in the home. The husband must be the master who issues a command to son and daughter which the servants must carry out. Thus the command passes from the father of the family as the sovereign lord to wife or child and to the servants. Those are the three divisions which St. Paul terms rule, authority, and power. These are to be abolished in all estates and classes of government to the far reaches of the world, the highest and the lowest and the intermediate, making us all equal and erasing every distinction among emperor, kings, nobility, burghers, and peasants. God alone will be everything.

All of that God will do, says St. Paul, not we nor the factious spirits, who allege that everything must be equal and that no one must be placed above another. They themselves want to abolish all government and deprive Christ, who alone must do this, of His office. Therefore government must remain until He appears, just as the spiritual offices, pulpit and Baptism, must remain, indeed, as the sun and the moon must remain in the heavens. Therefore no one dare set himself against this or alter it. Christ Himself will do this without any intermediaries, saying to emperor and princes: "You may no longer be emperor, prince, father, master, mistress, etc. Now no human being shall rule or govern anymore, but all the world shall be subject to God alone."

25. *For He must reign until He has put all His enemies under His feet.*

Someone might be tempted to say: "Why did He not do this soon after His resurrection, when He already became Lord over all things and had the power to put all things under His feet?" St. Paul replies to this that Scripture declares that He is to reign and rule beside the secular government, through His spiritual rule (Ps. 110:1): "The Lord says to my Lord, 'Sit at My right hand, till I make Your enemies Your footstool.'" This is our consolation, and it was done for our benefit, that Christ did not strike down His enemies immediately a thousand years ago but postponed this until we, too, should appear; for not all who belong to His kingdom have been born as yet. He must reign in order to gather all the children of God, as Scripture declares elsewhere.[33] Therefore He must first complete His kingdom and not annihilate His enemies before He has brought all into His kingdom who belong there. Following that, He will destroy everything at one time and lay about Him. In the meantime He lets His Word be preached, and He governs Christendom spiritually with Word, Sacrament, faith, and Spirit amid His enemies, who oppress and harass us; and He preserves and protects us against these with the sure consolation that He will put them completely under His feet on that Day; in fact, He has already begun to do this, and He does it daily. For through the Gospel and through Christendom He strikes the factious spiritually, repels the devil, dethrones the tyrants, subdues the raging and raving of the world, deprives sin and death of their strength and might, etc. This is His work which He pursues and in which He engages until the Last Day, only that He now does this piecemeal and by degrees. Then, however, He will knock the bottom out of the barrel [34] and put an end to everything at one time.

Thus we perceive how Christ has taken a hand in the affairs of the world from the inception of Christianity, has placed countries and people under the Gospel and toppled and deposed all who opposed this. Here He dethroned a king, and there He banished a tyrant. This action He often demonstrated on such people mightily also within our own memory; and He will do this still more. For He begins to afflict them in that way here, only to destroy them utterly there. They also experience another heartache. Whereas God assigned them rule and government over body and property, expecting them to restrain and punish evil, the disobedient, and the refractory, to maintain peace and to protect the godly, they attack God Himself, misusing their entrusted office for harassing and persecuting the godly, etc. They refuse to hear or to tolerate the Gospel, and they blame it for causing rebellion and the destruction of country and people. To be sure, the latter does happen. But whose fault is it? No one's but their own, because they will not execute the office commanded and assigned them by God for punishing the evildoers. They venture to punish God's children and to become unruly and rebellious against God Himself.

It serves them right that they thus run their heads against a wall and are toppled in their own might. In Christ God overthrows death and devil similarly; they also had the power to catch and entangle

[33] John 11:52.

[34] *Dem Fass den Boden ausstossen* means to put a violent end to something. Cf. p. 96 above.

sinners in their net. However, when they tried to use their net also for Christ, thinking: "I have devoured so many of them, I shall also devour Him," they were brought up short and they burned their fingers. For He was not the quarry that fit their net. They were warned against going after Him. And that is why He stormed through the net and tore it so that it can no longer hold a Christian. In Acts 2:24 St. Peter declares: "It was not possible for Him to be held." And thus it is also impossible that He or His own might be held by the world, even though the world casts the net over them, intent on their destruction. He takes a hand and breaks through their might and power and everything that wants to hold Him, converting it into a torn and rent net; for He will surely not be caught and captured by anyone. The world should catch and capture villains and rascals with its net. But wherever it goes beyond those bounds and ventures to capture Christ Himself, He breaks through as through a spider web and tears it into shreds so that nothing remains of it. That is what He did first of all to the Jews. They retained no country and no city. They are so completely rent apart that they could not catch a fox, yes, not even a dog. For they would not content themselves with the power God assigned them over the evildoers, but they attacked the godly, they released Barabbas and wanted to catch and kill God's Son Himself.

That is how the Romans and Greeks also fared. They, too, refused to confine themselves to the office assigned them but captured and slaughtered Christians. On the other hand, every idolatry and villainy went unpunished by them. Therefore God tore into their countries so that these crumbled and were destroyed by Goths, Vandals,[35] and Turks. That will happen also to us, because our lords and princes, in disregard of their office, rage against God's Word and persecute, expel, and murder Christians, as though they had nothing to do but to prove their rule and might against God. Otherwise they can tolerate and connive at every knavery and villainy, which will prompt God to say also to them: "You should seize and be quick to punish rogues and criminals and execute your office. Instead, you proceed in your madness and venture to lay hold of My Word, which confirms your office and which makes people pious. And you cry out frightfully that it creates discord and rebellion, although you yourself rage against God and in addition lead a most shameful life. And since

---

[35] The text has *Wenden,* but *Vandalen* is probably meant.

you insist on having rebellion and discord, you are going to get it in rich measure, so that you will not retain a government or a country which is not rent asunder."

And God has already begun with this over the Gospel. How was Hungary and now Austria torn apart in a few short years and despoiled by both friend and foe! Neither they nor anyone else had expected that. And as matters stand in Germany at present, no one knows what will happen to it. For they, too, are inviting this fate. They are carrying things to such a pass that they richly deserve this fate. For they are knowingly raging against God's Word and the acknowledged truth, so that God can hardly tolerate that any longer. And I am worried that He will soon interfere here with His punishment and tear the net apart with His dogs, leaving neither trunk nor head.[36] For He has to date overthrown so many countries and cities that were also great and powerful, yes, He tore the four empires of which Dan. 7 speaks asunder one after another and finally destroyed them. Today only the dregs remain, and He may also soon demolish this last and smallest part. He has destroyed, and still destroys, our enemies and beats them down one after another, singly and piecemeal, lest one assume that He died or became impotent and that we had no Lord who is able to help us. He tears them up and overthrows them, one by one, until they all fall into a heap. Then it will be manifest whose fault it was that secular government and rule foundered — not the fault of the Gospel but of our great ingratitude and contempt for God's Word and grace and for our refusal to accept Him as our Lord. Because we today give ear neither to warning nor to threat, He will also give ear neither to lament nor to cry.[37]

26-27. The last enemy to be destroyed is death. For God has put all things in subjection under His feet, etc.

It is an especially fine and appealing text and a comforting note that he calls death the last enemy of Christ. I could never have extended the meaning of this text so and interpreted the word "enemies" as referring to death, as St. Paul does here. For at first sight these words apply solely to the Jews and the Gentiles who torment the Christians on earth. But like a true painter and carver, St. Paul

---

[36] *Es blieb weder Strumpf noch Kopf* signifies totality of destruction. *Strumpf* here means "multilated remains."

[37] The seventh sermon, preached in the afternoon of Oct. 27, 1532, the Twenty-second Sunday After Trinity, ends here.

fashions a lovely picture and portrays death as it must be portrayed. He refers to death as the words of the psalm do, which read (Ps. 110:1): "Till I make Your enemies Your footstool." In that way we might learn to know and regard our Lord as an enemy of death; His kingdom is intent on engaging death in combat, in putting him in subjection under His feet, until He has utterly destroyed him. I am fond of having Christ depicted and proclaimed thus, showing that He is not a man who delights in wrath and punishment and who deals unmercifully with people, but as one who is a king and who has occupied His kingdom for the purpose of battling with all His might against His last enemy until He has cast death under His feet. Therefore it would be proper to inscribe this verse with golden letters and to hold it before the eyes of Christians constantly. Note that Christ is called an enemy of death and, in turn, that death is called Christ's enemy. And as Christ will execute His other lesser enemies one after another, as I stated earlier, He will also execute this His greatest enemy.

He demonstrated this enmity with a deed when He trod him underfoot in His own person, so that death is no longer able to harm Him. And as He cast him underfoot and overpowered him for His own person, He is also resolved to overcome and utterly annihilate him for His entire kingdom, until he lies prostrate at the feet of all, torn asunder and dispersed like dust so that nothing of him remains to be seen. That is portraying Christ's kingdom correctly and lauding it splendidly and interpreting Scripture mightily. This depicts Christ as sitting at the right hand of the Father and occupying the office in which He battles death and hurls him underfoot for all of Christendom, as He has already done for His own person. In our case, however, this is not fully carried out as yet. But it is already initiated and it continues daily until the Last Day, as I said earlier, so that a Christian is already more than halfway out of death. For his life on earth is nothing other than death; as soon as a Christian is baptized, he is thrust into death, as St. Paul declares in Rom. 6:4. And all who accept Christ are already sacrificed and sentenced to death. They are like people who have already died and are awaiting their resurrection. That is how Christians must regard their position and existence over against the life of the world, which is nothing other than a march toward death; indeed, it is like those who run to their grave backwards, for these live riotously and ignore death until they suddenly tumble into the grave.

But a Christian has already been thrust into death by the very fact that he became a Christian. Wherever he may be, he occupies himself with this hourly. He expects death any moment so long as he sojourns here, because devil, world, and his own flesh give him no rest. However, he enjoys the advantage of already being out of the grave with his right leg. Moreover, he has a mighty helper who holds out His hand to him, namely, His Lord Christ; He has left the grave entirely a long time ago, and now He takes the Christian by the hand and pulls him more than halfway out of the grave; only the left foot remains in it. For his sin is already remitted and expunged, God's wrath and hell are extinguished, and he already lives fully in and with Christ with regard to his best part, which is the soul, as he partakes of eternal life. Therefore death can no longer hold him or harm him. Only the remnant, the old skin, flesh and blood, must still decay before it, too, can be renewed and follow the soul. As for the rest, we have already penetrated all the way into life, since Christ and my soul are no longer in death.

The world knows nothing of such consolation and of such a defiant boast, although it does boast of and pride itself on its possession of much money and goods, great honor, friendship, power. But I challenge you to name one to me who could fend death off or work his way out of death with all of that. There has, of course, been no one who has ever taken as much as a thread or a hair's breadth or a tiny grain or a drop of water with him. There they must lie, unable to help themselves with as much as a breath; and they would, I suppose, lie there forever in unbearable stench if they were not buried under the sod. Not even a small worm is so weak that it is not able to devour the body entirely. There is no king who ever becomes so rich and so mighty that he might take a penny's worth of his crown or his might with him. They must leave all that they ever possessed behind and let themselves be interred in the grave, stripped of everything.

Aside from the fact that not a few have already emerged from death and grave with Christ and have come into life, we have a Man who lost nothing through death and who did not leave as much as a little hair in the grave. Indeed, it was precisely through death that He drew all things to Himself, as He Himself declares, and made all things subject to Himself, so that we, too, shall come forth from the grave in Him and through Him and take all with us that we left behind here. We can glory in that and boast of that over against the whole world, even though it ridicules and mocks faith and Christianity and relies on its possessing enough money and goods now and is able to live as it will in its greed and in all sorts of lusts. But we say: "Just go ahead and scrape, give way to your avarice and accumulate riches as you will. Let us see who can outboast the other. If you have money and goods, power and all that you covet, we challenge you to take one penny with you. I, on the other hand, will show you a Lord who left nothing whatsoever behind in death but took everything with Him and extends His hand to me to enable me to force my way out too. Show me just one such man in the whole world who ever took as much as a thread with him or again brought it away from death! Of what avail, then, is your scraping and boasting of such ephemeral things, which you do not control for a moment when death comes along? You act as though you would possess them forever or as though you would take all of them with you.

Behold, thus Paul teaches us to defy death through faith in Christ as One who is death's powerful foe, who is resolved to do away with death and exterminate it utterly. And death has richly deserved this from Him, because he attacked and assaulted Christ without cause. He attacked Him with the intent of devouring Him. But death met such a warm reception that his jaws and belly were torn apart. Now he must pay and return all whom he devoured. That serves, as I began to say, to console against daily trials and enables us to view and picture Christ aright. It keeps us from being frightened by images and ideas inspired by the devil that tend to deject and sadden us. It permits us to conclude that this is not Christ, as the timid conscience fears and assumes, but the enemies of Christ, vile death and the devil. For here you perceive that Christ is a King for the express purpose of destroying death completely as His enemy. And it surely follows from this that whatever befalls me and is inflicted on me by death is inflicted on me by the enemy of the Lord Jesus. And this vexes Him as much as me and even more than me; for death is not chiefly my enemy, but Christ's, my Lord's. But because I believe in Christ, He takes my part against this His enemy; and now whatever death does to me, he must first have done to Christ. Christ wants to avenge me on death as on His enemy. As Christ overcame him for His own person, so that he no longer gets a sip or a sniff of Him, so He wants to destroy him entirely through me and all Christians, thus tearing him to shreds and annihilating him also in my body.

Therefore you must not worry that Christ would frighten or sadden you, thinking that He delights in slaying and killing. No, since He is hostile to death, He wishes to see no terror or fear but is hostile to everything that intends to distress or scare us. That is the consolation we Christians have in our dear Lord. The world, which relies on its possessions, does not have this. And yet it can take nothing with it. It and all its possessions are in death's power; and it must leave everything to him. But he will not deprive us of everything. If he takes much from us, it is still only whatever we possess here on earth. He retains this body in his inn for a while. However, he must release the soul and whatever we possess in Christ. And in the end he must also restore the body together with all that he took from us.

But why does Paul call death "the last enemy"? Or, what other enemies does Christ have? We commonly speak of three enemies that are both Christ's and ours: world, flesh, and devil, which we feel and understand. In Rom. 8:7 St. Paul says: "For the mind that is set on the flesh is hostile to God." Therefore God will also destroy it with its avarice and care, as he says 1 Cor. 6:13. Thus it is also certain that God will destroy the world. He has already ordered a fire in which it will be consumed and dissolved, as 2 Peter 3:10 tells us. In like manner He has also already sentenced and condemned the devil to eternal fire in hell, for he is God's worst and chief enemy, who instigates every adversity and evil against God's kingdom with lies and murder, also with terror, despair, and unbelief. God has these three foes, all of whom act and contend against Him. He in turn fights against them and arrays His whole kingdom solely against them. With His Word, Sacrament, and Spirit He holds the flesh in check. With these He also repels the devil and his venomous suggestions and all sorts of temptations, and also the world with its raging.

But in addition to these there are also other greater enemies, namely, the Law, sin, and death, by which Christians are harassed the hardest. Without these the other three would be unable to do anything. For if sin and death did not exist, both world and flesh would have to leave us alone. These are the real enemies. They beset us the worst, and it is through them that the others oppress and harass us. For "the power of sin is the Law" (1 Cor. 15:56) and, as St. Paul declares (Rom. 4:15), "the Law brings wrath." He calls it "the bond which stood against us with its legal demands" (Col. 2:14). And Moses he calls a servant and preacher of death and his law a law of sin, which does nothing but reveal how evil man, flesh, world, and devil are (Rom. 4:15; 7:8, 23). Otherwise we would know nothing of sin, as Paul states elsewhere (Rom. 4:15): "Where there is no law there is no transgression." But where sin stands revealed, the Law renders this sin great and grave. And then when sin is felt, it immediately brings death in its train.

Those are the real enemies that St. Paul mentions by name here and cites from the text "till I make Your enemies Your footstool, etc." (Ps. 110:1). But death is called the greatest and the last enemy because all the others point to him; and even when we rid ourselves of the others, death still remains and holds us captive. When man is buried, flesh and blood with their lusts must come to an end. These can no longer assail him. For one no longer beholds an adulterer or a miser running about after he has died. Then the world can no longer try and tempt man, nor can any false doctrine, or a factious spirit, or even the devil himself. And the Law, together with sin, must let him alone. In short, Christ removes all these enemies in or with this life; He comforts and preserves us by His Word against world and devil, also, by remission of sin, against the Law and God's wrath, until we depart this life. Thus these enemies can deal with us only here on earth; after that they have to cease. Death, however, survives all the others and holds us in his power, so that we must remain captive forever and cannot escape. But if we believe, we have this consolation here that we have a Lord who can and will do away also with this last enemy, tear his fetters and bonds to pieces, and furthermore slay and exterminate him. Since He now vanquishes and subdues the other enemies, so that flesh, devil, world, sin, and Law cannot overpower us, we must not doubt that He will surely rid and free us also from the last enemy. Otherwise He would not have effected anything so far; then all the rest would be in vain.

Therefore learn to understand this verse now and utilize it for your consolation and the strengthening of your faith, knowing how to divert all six of these enemies from you and to turn them over to Christ; for primarily they are not called our enemies and they are not that, but they are the enemies of Christ. It is not our being that they assail in particular, since we, as far as our person is concerned and when we are without Christ, are already willingly subject and obedient to flesh, world, and devil, pay no heed to sin, Law, and death, and march entirely under their banner. But they are all Christ's foes; for He is also their foe. It is He whom they are after and whom they have in mind and whom they oppose with all their might. And for His sake they are also hostile to us who cling to Him. And since they are unable to harm His person, they attack us and propose to weaken and to destroy His kingdom in that way.

And now since we have to suffer and pay for Him, He must, in turn, look after us, His members, and avenge us on His enemies. Thus it all centers in the fact that it is He who is battling with these enemies and that He is taking the lead in the fight. Now He has escaped from the flesh. He has soared so high that world and devil can never catch Him or slay Him or harm Him otherwise. The Law in conjunction with sin and death also terrified Him, but now they must lie prostrate at His feet, sentenced and condemned. Now He reigns in the faith, defeats and kills the same enemies in us uninterruptedly until that Day, when we shall see Him destroy death completely and we can no longer find a trace of him and will think that death never existed. Thus we must live in faith today as though there were no sin, no Law, no flesh and blood, no world, no devil to harm us, because we have Christ. We must have a very good and cheerful conscience and be convinced that none of these will or can overcome us, no matter how viciously they may attack, frighten, or oppress us, and that our Lord Jesus Christ has won and retained the victory in us. And as He has already slain the other enemies for His person, has weakened them and daily defeats them in us, preventing them from gaining the upper hand, so He also begins to weaken death in us, so that death no longer gains the advantage over us. It is only the shards and only half of us that death takes away. That is the work and the rule Christ constantly pursues; for that purpose He is also seated at the right hand of God, as the verse in the psalm tells us (Ps. 110:1). It is the Christians' highest knowledge and wisdom to be cognizant of what we have from Him and to learn to understand our glory which God gives us in Christ and to esteem this treasure highly and, on the other hand, to despise the world's fame and splendor, money and goods, honor, power, etc. With these the world distracts us and deludes our eyes to believe that this is something precious, and thus it makes us lose sight of and forget our treasure. But we must be smart over against this and clear our vision that we may recognize and magnify not only the treasure but also our vision and our understanding, "that we might understand the gifts bestowed on us by God," as St. Paul says in 1 Cor. 2:12, namely, such gifts as are greater and more splendid than heaven and earth.

For what greater or more splendid thing can be imagined or desired than to be lord not merely over a city or a country or a kingdom but over all our enemies, over flesh and blood, world and devil? No emperor or king on earth is able to be that. For there is no one who could ward off every evil thought or who could help us to the point where the world with its enmity, power, and might could not harm us. Indeed, even if we had the world with all its might with us and for us, what could it do to ward off trials and temptations of the devil, or to resist him and defeat him? Only a Christian is such a man to stand his ground against the devil and all his angels, and that solely by enduring in faith in Christ. That is surely a treasure without equal in heaven and on earth, in comparison with which all the world with its power is not worth a thought. Therefore we should not appraise such gifts in Christ lightly and regard them as the world and our flesh do, who view Christ as a poor dead idol, who is seated idly above and does nothing among us, and us Christians as poor, weak, impotent, and wretched people. No, we must remember that we, as the text informs us, are lords with Him over everything that flesh, world, sin, and devil are able to do, and, in addition, also lords over half of death. We must adopt such a defiant and arrogant attitude over against all the world, reflecting that we Christians are greater and more than all other creatures — not in or of ourselves but through the gift of God in Christ, in comparison with which the world is nothing and can do nothing. Its kingdoms and principalities are nothing but a paltry possession which it must leave behind and which will pass away with it.

Behold, thus St. Paul proclaims, praises, and glorifies the Lord Christ, so that we can see what He is and does, and what His office and rule in our midst are. These He administers that we may participate in His rule and gain the victory over the great enemies. For He calls them His enemies and regards them as such, not for His sake but for ours. He is concerned about what happens to us as though it were happening to Himself. Thus He says in the prophet Zechariah (Zech. 2:8): "He who touches you touches the apple of My [38] eye," that is, "I am hostile to him who is hostile to you." But if He is hostile

[38] Luther changes the personal pronoun from "His" to "My" to suit his context.

to them, He will surely rescue us and destroy the enemies, for He is powerful enough to do this. Therefore His kingdom exists solely for the purpose of helping us against our sin, Law and conscience, flesh and blood, world, devil, and especially death. He is called Lord, not a lord whom we must serve or who would take something from us, but a lord who only serves us, fights for us, and wards off danger, so that no foe can harm us.

That is the text on which St. Paul bases and presents his argument for the confirmation of the article regarding the resurrection of the dead. For since death, too, is called an enemy of Christ, and the very last enemy at that, He must remove death completely and restore to life those whom death has devoured. The argument for this is, as he said here and again repeats from Ps. 8:6: "Thou hast put all things under His feet." But if everything has been put under His feet, then death, too, must surely lie prostrate at His feet, not only for His person but for His entire Christendom; for Christ is seated at the right hand of God for the sake of Christendom, that it might be His kingdom. And He says that He did all of this not of Himself, but that it is the work and the office of the Father, presented to us for our consolation and to show us His fatherly heart and gracious will, for the Father not only orders and commands that everything be subject to Christ but Himself also places everything under His feet.

For since God hurls both sin and death as Christ's enemies under His feet and makes them His footstool, it surely pleases Him to have sin and death abolished. It is certain that God does not think of killing and condemning us, although we are sinners and are deserving of death, but that He is minded like Christ and will remove sin and death from us and destroy these, so that we might inherit eternal righteousness and life; for it is for that reason that He placed Christ into the Kingdom. Therefore, as I said before, he portrays not only Christ but also the Father as loving and as friendly as a heart may wish for. We are to regard Him no longer as a severe and irate judge, as the devil and our timid conscience always imagine Him to be, but as a friendly Father, who wants to deliver us from all these enemies and who befriends us just as though they were His own enemies, so that He places His Son, following His suffering and death, at His right hand and puts all things under His feet.

Therefore, if you believe in Christ, you must not flee from Him or be frightened; for here you perceive and see that His whole heart, mind, or thinking are intent only on rescuing you from all that assails and oppresses you and on placing you with Christ over everything. But whoever lacks such faith in Christ can never conceive such thoughts. He has to plague and torture himself to death with his own works, by which he wants to reconcile God. For sin and death continue to weigh down his heart like a large millstone. He cannot extricate himself from it but must remain under it, feeling nothing but God's wrath as long as he occupies himself with works. Throughout his life he cannot entertain a cheerful thought, nor can anyone advise or help him. And in the end he despairs completely and is crushed to death by this unbearable burden.

All who want to serve God and deal with Him with their works are of this type — Turks, papists, Carthusians, and other pseudosaints. They cannot see God otherwise than as an irate judge who does nothing but make demands of them and who continuously threatens to punish them. For they are ignorant of the Gospel, which presents Christ to us and teaches that the Father Himself has introduced and given Him to us as a Mediator and has also placed Him at His own right hand to remove all wrath, sin, and death from us. Therefore they must remain encumbered throughout their life with the millstone of a bad conscience, so that they can never lift up their heart to conceive a good thought over against God. And the more they torment and frighten themselves in an effort to help themselves, the worse they fare. For they want to be Christ themselves, and they only anger God the more, because they confront Him without the Mediator. But whoever has faith and is acquainted with Christ as the Man who is seated above and reigns over sin and death, he can rid himself of that heavy millstone on his heart. For he knows that God is no longer angry because of his sin and that He does not condemn him, but that He has placed Christ at His side to extinguish and destroy it like an enemy of God. He beholds nothing but sheer grace and life welling forth unceasingly from the fatherly heart. Therefore, may this text be commended to you so that you may learn to know Christ's kingdom aright and look for all that is good from God the Father, who regards you with friendliness and sheer grace because He works this in Christ and has it presented to all through the Word.[39]

27-28. *But when it says all things are put in subjection under Him, it is plain that He is excepted who put all things under Him.*

[39] The eighth sermon, held in the afternoon of Nov. 3, 1532, the Twenty-third Sunday After Trinity, ends here.

*When all things are subjected to Him, then the Son Himself
will also be subjected to Him who put all things under Him,
that God may be everything to everyone.*

Here St. Paul reverts to and concludes what he said earlier, namely,
that matters will be entirely different when Christ delivers the Kingdom to the Father; faith will be changed into clear sight, the Word
into the essence, dark understanding into light and bright sun. Then
we shall see all our enemies before us, both those we now have on
earth and death in the bargain, slain and destroyed. Paul constantly
stresses the words which state that the Father has subjected everything
to Christ, excepting, of course, Him who put all in subjection under
Him, and that the Son, after subjecting everything to Himself, will
also be subject. These words seem very obscure; but they all tend, as
I said earlier, to point out the difference which St. Paul makes between
God's kingdom and Christ's kingdom, although in themselves they are
one and the same kingdom. Now it is called Christ's kingdom
because we live in it by faith and do not see or hear Him physically
as one beholds with the eyes a king of this world in his kingdom with
crown and great and grand splendor. For it is not yet manifest what
we really possess in Him and what we are to attain through Gospel,
Sacrament, and faith.

But later, when it is no longer hidden but is revealed before all
creatures and when faith ends, it will be called God's kingdom. This
is what St. Paul calls delivering the Kingdom to the Father, that is,
presenting us and His whole Christendom openly to the Father into
eternal clarity and glory, that He Himself may reign without cloak or
cover. But Christ will nevertheless retain His rule and majesty; for
He is the same God and Lord, eternal and omnipotent with the Father.
But because He now reigns through His Word and Sacrament, etc.,
which is not seen by the world, it is called Christ's kingdom. Everything must be subject to Him, "excepting Him who put all things
under Him," until the Last Day. Then He will abolish all of this and
subject Himself with His entire kingdom to the Father and say to Him:
"Until now I reigned with You by faith. This I deliver to You, that
they may see that I am in You and You are in Me, joined together with
the Holy Spirit in one divine Majesty, and that they have and enjoy
visibly in You what they hitherto believed and looked forward to."

Then, says St. Paul, God will be "everything to everyone," that is,
everybody will find all wants that are now satisfied by all things satis-

fied in God Himself. When He will reveal Himself, we will be satisfied in body and soul and will no longer stand in need of so many things as we now do here on earth. In the first place, for the sustenance and preservation of body and life, father and mother, meat and drink, house and home, clothing and shoes, in addition, princes and masters who protect us and provide peace; then, in the spiritual realm, pastors and preachers who teach us and administer the sacraments, who comfort in times of distress and counsel in matters of conscience, etc.; also sun and moon, air, fire, and water for the entire world. Who can enumerate all the items that man requires here on earth for the wants of the body? But over there all of this will cease; none of these wants will longer exist. We will have so much in God that no food, no drink, no malmsey [40] can be so precious or feed us or quench our thirst as well as God Himself will do with the sight of Himself. You will always be strong and vigorous, healthy and happy, also brighter and more beautiful than sun and moon, so that all the garments and the gold bedecking a king or emperor will be sheer dirt in comparison with us when we are illumined by but a divine glance. Nor will we need a patron or any government, money or goods, house or home, or other physical possessions, but we will have sufficient of everything in Him. Similarly, we will have all spiritual gifts, eternal righteousness, comfort and joy of conscience, that no one will be able to terrify us or confuse us or disquiet us any longer. In short, in place of whatever we must now derive from all creatures here and there singly and piecemeal — although this, too, comes from Him and is given by Him — we shall have Him directly, without any flaw and without ceasing.

But the world and stupid people do not understand this. They are given to their notions about this life, as they are accustomed, and they assume that the stomach must really eat and drink and the body must have its nourishment to be sustained at all. They cannot understand that God is able to nourish better by the mere sight of Himself than by all the bread and food on earth, by means of which He now, too, bestows life and nourishes and changes these into flesh and blood, marrow and bone, etc. If He is able to do that now by means of bread and wine, which after all do not possess life, should He not be far more able to do this through Himself as Creator and Lord of all creatures? What would all food and bodily nourishment avail if God

[40] German *Malvasier,* a wine known for its sweetness and named after the Greek city Malmasia or Malvasia, modern Monemvasia.

would not preserve us through His Word? That is what Christ tells us (Matt. 4:4), quoting from Deut. 8:3. For if He gave this human body no more than bread and wine, it would not endure or remain alive very long. The body must first of all have life, it must be healthy and strong and have warmth and strength to digest the food. Otherwise it would not benefit the body regularly to fill it with bread and to pour every kind of drink into it. We observe this when a person is ill and cannot digest his food, indeed, we note this in all people when they die. Otherwise the rich people and the great lords would very likely gather enough bread to live forever, and no one could obtain anything on their account.

Since it is very apparent here that bodily food and drink do not suffice if God does not give His blessing, what will happen there when God reveals Himself? There we will not look at bread and wine; we will neither need nor desire apothecary or medication, but we will have sufficient solely from viewing and looking at God. This will make the whole body so beautiful, vigorous, and healthy, indeed, so light and agile, that we will soar along like a little spark, yes, just like the sun which runs its course in the heavens. In a moment we will be down here on earth or up above in the heavens. Indeed, I believe that everything will become much more beautiful, water, trees, and grass, and that there will be a new earth, as St. Peter says (2 Peter 3:13), which will be a delight to behold. But the preservation of body and soul will be accomplished solely by God, who alone is to be "everything to everyone." The sight of Him will afford more life, joy, and delight than all creatures are able to accord, and you will have to say, "I would not exchange one moment in heaven for all the world's goods and pleasures, even though the latter endured thousands and thousands of years."

Therefore, as I said, the pastor's or preacher's office, too, will be terminated, as will that of princes and secular government and rule. In short, there will no longer be any office or estate. Persons, such as man and wife, will remain, and also the entire human race as it was created. But none of the wants of this life will survive. Everybody will be a perfect human being and have all he needs in God, so that he no longer requires father, mother, master, servant, food, clothing, house, etc.

Now just consider what you would like to have or what you might wish for. Would you like to have money and goods, and abundance of food and drink, a long life, a healthy body, beautiful clothes, a nice dwelling, eternal joy and delight, furthermore, perfect wisdom and a knowledge of all things, dominion, and honor? Just look there; there you will receive enough of everything. God will clothe you more beautifully than any emperor was ever clothed, indeed, more beautifully than the sun and all jewels. If you aspire to be a lord, He will grant you more than you can wish for. If you want to possess acute sight and hearing that reaches farther than a hundred miles, if you want to be able to see through walls and stone, if you wish to be so light as to be in any place of your choice in a moment, down below on earth or up above near the clouds — that will all be granted you. And whatever else you might think of and desire for body and soul, you shall have in rich measure when you have God. For God requires for Himself neither bread nor wine, neither manservant nor maidservant, neither house nor home nor clothes, neither gold nor silver, neither princes nor preachers, but He has sufficient of everything forever in Himself; for He lives in and through Himself. Why, then, should He not do the same in us, that we might have everything solely in and through Him and stand in need of the creatures just as little as He stands in need of anything else? And as God is delighted and pleased as He looks at the creature, so we, too, will need the creature only as a delight for our eyes as a show dish, as we gaze at the beautiful new heaven and earth and praise and love God in these. But in Him all our needs and wants will be satisfied.

But this is proclaimed exclusively to the Christians, who must believe this and look to the future better life. The others, the mad rabble, do not believe anything of this anyhow. Since they despise God's Word, they are not worthy of recognizing this. God punishes them, so that they go along in their folly and blindness and do not accept it. His wrath against them has already begun. For this is the worst and most terrible wrath, that God no longer grants the desire to hear His Word willingly and to give it heed. No greater calamity could be imposed. Therefore it behooves us to let people who will not repent go their way and leave them to God's judgment, for they have already incurred the curse, a greater and graver curse than anyone might wish them. And since they do not want to hear God, they shall also not have Him, but they must be the devil's own eternally in hell, be afflicted with every pain, distress, grief, and misery, burn eternally without a little drop of water with which to refresh themselves for a moment; furthermore, they shall have no light, not even a handbreadth of it or even a thread of it; they must be bereft both of God and of all His grace and gifts, which the blessed will have, as well as of all that was theirs on earth. In fact, this has its inception already here on earth, where they cannot really enjoy their goods. And later they will have to leave them behind so unwillingly. There they will feel the want still more of everything that God is and grants. How can they be plagued more horribly and severely? And yet it is such a common evil throughout the world, among the nobility and among the common people, among those of high and those of low estate, to deride and ridicule this Word of God and whatever is said about life to come and also to persecute it most assiduously. Here we behold the punishment already initiated, the hellish fire ignited and burning over them.

May such examples therefore be a terrifying warning to us and serve to strengthen our faith. May they direct our mind to another life, since we can look forward to such great bliss and inexpressible possessions after this wretched life, when God Himself will grant everything and, moreover, will Himself be all that we can desire. For such is His Word and promise. With it He admonishes us so comfortingly and incites us not to let the temporal, which we acquire or lose here, assail us but over against this learn to treasure the future, the promised lot, as the world spurns it and, in turn, spurn what the world treasures, even if this is money, goods, honor, power, and might. Let us say: "Dear prince, peasant, or nobleman, you have abundant possessions now, you proudly rely on your riches and on your power, and you live riotously; go to it, and be of good cheer. Such husks befit such pigs. In God's sight you have nothing; you are despised and rejected. At present I do not possess your money and goods nor your power; but I know of and look forward to another possession of which you are ignorant. God promised that He would bring me forth from the earth and make me more beautiful than the sun. Then I shall have everything in abundance and beyond measure. That shall be my pride and boast. I shall let you glitter and shine in your worldly possessions, which you must leave behind today or tomorrow when you depart this life wretchedly, bereft of everything."

Behold, thus we must fortify and console ourselves over against the world's unbelief and smugness, with which it offends the weak greatly. We must ignore that and heed what He says and promises: "Just believe in Christ, My Son, and I shall rescue you from death when the world must remain in death forever. I will give you everything your heart desires and adorn you more resplendently than all the stars, when those people will have to abide in eternal darkness." May you esteem that more highly as you see the world boast defiantly of its transitory possessions and despise God and His Word much more than we can prize our treasure. For we, too, are still flesh and blood; therefore we are unable to rely on and pride ourselves so fully on our eternal, imperishable treasure in God as they despise it and boast of their possessions. Yet we must ever pursue this and graft it into our heart, so that we always adhere to it and not depart from it or despise it as the world does.

Behold, that is the consolation we derive from yonder life, that God Himself will be ours and that He will be everything to us. For picture to yourself all that you would like to have, and you will find nothing better and dearer and worth wishing for than to have God Himself, who is the life and an inexhaustible depth of everything good and of eternal joy. There is nothing more precious on earth than life. The whole world dreads nothing more than death and desires nothing more than life. And this treasure we are to have in Him without measure and without end. There the sky will rain down talers and gold, if you should choose, the Elbe be filled with pearls and other gems, the earth yield all kinds of delight, so that, at your word, a tree will bear nothing but silver leaves and golden apples and pears, the fields will bear grass and flowers which shine like emeralds and other beautiful gems. In short, whatever delights your heart shall be yours abundantly. For we read that God Himself will be everything to everyone. But wherever God is, all good things that one may wish for must also be present.

29-30. *Otherwise, what do people mean by being baptized on behalf of the dead? If the dead are not raised at all, why are people baptized on their behalf? Why am I in peril every hour?*

So far St. Paul adduced reasons and proof for this article; now he proceeds to chide his Corinthians for a while, as is a preacher's duty. He does this both to teach and to chasten the refractory. He wishes to say: "You wicked factious spirits and heathen people, if you have a heart that does not believe that we will rise, as Christ has risen, why, then, do you have yourself baptized on behalf of the dead? What does Baptism avail you if you do not hope for another life?" So he remarked earlier: "If the dead do not arise, both our proclamation and your faith are futile." For if there is no other life, why should anyone preach, or why should anyone go to hear someone preach? Such a person would be just as much inclined to put God off entirely as they who believe nothing at all do. If there is nothing to the resurrection, one does not need Baptism either. For no one may be baptized for the purpose of obtaining enough to eat and to drink or for the purpose of filling his chests and granaries. It is true that whoever strives to do only that needs neither God's Word nor Baptism. He can surely live without these, as both peasants and noblemen imagine they can nowadays. And, furthermore, they may well boast that they need no preacher. They would much rather be rid of God's Word entirely; they don't give a farthing for any sermon. This is due to the fact that they have their own god in whom they believe, namely, their florins and fat farthings. These really comprise their life and their heaven. Therefore it is impossible that they should like to hear God's Word or be concerned with the life to come. For that matter, I, too, if I believed — may God forbid — that I die like a cow, would never be baptized, take the Sacrament, or come to hear a sermon. Therefore they cannot be reproached for not prizing the life to come, for paying heed neither to Baptism nor the sermon, for not honoring pastors or preachers. For they live as they believe; they are and remain pigs, believe like pigs, and die like pigs.

Therefore St. Paul declares here: "You yourselves must be big fools to let yourselves be baptized if you think nothing of this article." For if this is void, then let God and His Baptism and Christendom go wherever He wishes and whoever wants to hold Him in esteem, let him do so. For whoever believes thus does not believe that He is God who is able to save from death and that he himself will for one moment following the present life have any advantage. Nor does such a person need Word or preacher. All he needs is Jack Ketch.[41] He is his preacher and his god, who prevents one pig from eating the other, and who, after his death, takes him out and buries him like any other pig in the carrion pit. Those people will surely discover what they despised and ridiculed, when we again see each other with dissimilar eyes and we have attained what we now believe and hope for and they have to howl and cry forever, which, however, will not help them. So the rich man in Luke 16:19 would not believe either while

---

[41] Cf. p. 126, n. 31, above.

Lazarus lay at his door, until faith became palpable and he was tortured and had to behold Lazarus in eternal peace and joy. Gladly would he have given all his riches for one little drop of cold water. But this could not be granted him.

With these words St. Paul wishes to reprimand the ignorant teachers who despised this article with their swinish reason and yet wanted to be regarded as Christians. For there is not a single Christian so stupid and foolish that he could not also say what those mockers regard as particular wisdom: "Do you suppose it is true what the parsons preach, namely, that we will all live again after we are buried and decayed?" Or, as our swine say: "Do you suppose there is another fellow hidden in this one?" This requires — God be praised — no acute reason, but is a truly swinish wisdom, which also the most stupid minds know of themselves. But it was a sin and a shame for these Corinthians to presume to say that and yet to have themselves baptized and called Christians. They would well have deserved a different rebuke from Paul. However, he is not writing to the factious spirits and ungodly people, on whom all admonitions and reprimands would have been lost, but to the small group of those whose heart was not hardened and who could still be converted.

Therefore he wants to convince them with their own action — that they let themselves be baptized — that they must not deny the article of the resurrection. For it is incongruous, on the one hand to accept the validity of Baptism and on the other to reject a future life. Those who have themselves baptized would have to be nothing but fools who do not know what they are doing. There is no pig, to say nothing of Christians, so stupid as not to understand that Baptism serves no purpose if there is no resurrection. But this argument, strong though it is, proves nothing to a mocker. For he will be quick to say: "Why do they do it? They are fools." But among Christians and believers, where one must furnish the other good examples of faith and testimony of such faith by Baptism and the Sacrament, by hearing God's Word and by prayer, there this is accepted as valid and as a strong proof of the certainty of this article, since Christians do have themselves baptized. For it is impossible that so many fine, pious Christians are fools and simpletons; after all, they are just as learned and know as much as the stupid swine, not to say that they possess a far loftier and better mind. And if you are moved by the arrogant talk of swine, why should you not be moved still more by what a Christian, an angel of God, tells you?

"Indeed," you say, "there are so many of them." What does that concern you? Even if there were far more, they are still nothing but swine. Therefore you should rather note how pious, learned, and sensible these are. You will find a wide difference between a Christian and such swine who believe nothing. For a Christian is able to speak so demonstrably and powerfully of God and His words and works that it is impossible for this to be false or void. Those people, however, know no more and nothing more sublime than is intelligible to any swine. Still they want to judge sublime matters with their swine's head, moreover, teach and chide the Christians, who have more sense in their little finger than all of them have in their whole body and who know their swinish wisdom, if it may be called wisdom, as well as they themselves do. Therefore we can conclude correctly: All Christians have themselves baptized; therefore another life must follow the present one. For Baptism and the Sacrament, like pastors and preachers too, do not serve at all for this life. Therefore, if we were confined to this life, we would abstain from Baptism and every other pursuit of Christians. For with that you will not acquire a sack of florins nor a granary filled with grain but deliverance from death, sin, and every distress and the gift of eternal life. That is the jewel, the pearl, the gem of which Christ speaks in Matt. 13:45-46, which a merchant found and for the acquisition of which he sold everything.

But Paul adds a phrase to the word "baptize," *pro mortuis.* This has been interpreted to mean — and so it reads in Latin — that they had themselves baptized "for the dead," that is, for the unbelievers in heathendom. Then they would have been baptized twice, once for themselves and the second time for members of their family. But that cannot be. For in Acts 2:38 Peter says: "Be baptized everyone of you in the name of Jesus Christ, etc." This does not mean that one should be baptized for another. It is the same as that everyone must repent, believe, and profess his faith for himself. Therefore I adhere to the meaning, in concurrence with the old Greek teachers, which we indicated in a marginal note next to this text,[42] namely: In St. Paul's day this article was still novel and was just being spread. It was unknown and unheard of among the heathen, also among the most erudite in

---

[42] Luther's marginal note in the German translation of the New Testament, known as *Septembertestament,* 1522, reads: *Die aufferstehung zubestercken, liessen sich die Christen teuffen uber den todten grebern, und deutten auff die selben, das eben die selben wurden aufferstehen.* W, *Deutsche Bibel,* VII, 130, 29.

Greece, although they did advance to the point where they assumed that the soul lived after the death of the body, without being able to prove this conclusively. However, that man would rise again and that body and soul would be reunited, of that they knew nothing at all. In view of this, it was hard for them at first to believe the apostles' proclamation; and those who believed it had to endure much ridicule. And so, in order to strengthen this article among the people, they had themselves baptized at the graves of the dead in token of their firm conviction that the dead who lay buried there and over whom they were being baptized would rise again. They were so convinced of this that they were, in a manner of speaking, pointing their finger at it. Similarly, we might administer Baptism publicly in a common cemetery or at a funeral. Therefore we read that the congregation at Aquileia had been taught and was accustomed to recite this article in the Creed thus: "I believe in the resurrection of this flesh." This was undoubtedly done for the purpose of teaching and professing also this article clearly and correctly over against the factious spirits.

Since this article was still new, the dear apostles and fathers followed that method of inculcating it both with words and with signs. Similarly, a doctrine must be drubbed into young, ignorant people with ceremonies and external means that they might, so to say, lay hold of it and be so much less disposed to doubt it. Otherwise it is easily forgotten or soon removed from the heart. For that reason they baptized people here at the graves, as though to say: "Here I am having myself baptized in proof of my faith and my conviction that these deceased people lying here will all arise." Otherwise one might think that only a phantom or that different and new bodies will arise, created anew by God. No, it will be this very same Paul and Peter, etc., who died and lie buried here, and, as our Creed states, this very same flesh which is standing and moving about here or which will be interred in the ground. So the very same Christ who was born of Mary and who was nailed to the cross truly rose again. It was He and no other, as He showed His disciples the scars in His hands and His side.

So you see that it is all-important that this article be firmly maintained among us; for if it begins to totter or is no longer regarded as valid, all the other articles will also be useless and invalid, because all that Christ did in coming to earth and establishing His kingdom in the world was done for the sake of the resurrection and the future life. Where this article, which forms the foundation, the reason, and the aim of all other articles of faith, is overthrown or removed, everything else will also topple and disappear with it. Therefore it is indeed necessary to foster and to fortify this article with diligence. That is what these people did with their method of baptizing, and that is what we, too, do with other similar signs. For example, we escort the dead to their graves with honor, walk behind the corpse, sing and pray in profession and token of the belief that these same dead, and we with them, will rise on the Last Day and that these will be the same bodies, though they will be changed and glorified.[43]

Therefore St. Paul entreats us with all these words that we may by all means be assured of the future resurrection. He also gives vent to great impatience as he says: "If this article did not exist, we should indeed refrain from preaching, from administering Baptism, and from the entire substance of Christianity. Why should we cling to something for which the devil and the world are so exceedingly hostile to us? Why should we toil in vain, and why should we remain in that mortal peril to which we are exposed now? After all, there is not a man on earth so stupid and foolish as to subject himself to inevitable danger without reason and to call nothing but great trouble and peril upon himself." To be sure, there were several among the heathen who incurred such great trouble and peril, risking life and limb, but they derived benefits and honor from this and were highly regarded and esteemed by the world. They always had something to motivate them. Thus soldiers and other daring men voluntarily expose themselves to danger in order to gain honor or acquire money and goods. In short, anyone who ventures to risk and to endure something great must surely be aware of and expect some outstanding compensation for which he does this. But the Christians alone are people who endure every danger and misfortune in the world without having anything on earth to motivate them to do that. For, after all, we have neither money nor other goods, neither honor nor favors shown them, but only the reverse, poverty, misery, contempt, animosity. In addition, they are condemned, cursed, exiled, and murdered. They would have to be insane to seek nothing but harm and disgrace and act as though they took delight in having enemies and in being harassed. For even the heathen declared: *Frustra niti, et nihil nisi odium quaer-*

---

[43] The ninth sermon, preached in the afternoon of Nov. 10, 1532, the Twenty-fourth Sunday After Trinity, ends here.

ere, extremae dementiae est, "It is the greatest folly on earth to toil in vain and reap nothing but enmity from it." [44]

And now, since we can expect nothing else but must forgo this life and all it contains voluntarily, so that our life and existence before the world is fitly called *frustra niti,* seeking misfortune without any compensation for it; since we oppose the whole world without profit; since we chasten and reprove princes, scholars, saints, peasants, and burghers with the Word of God and tell no one what he likes to hear, thereby surely inviting everyone's enmity; we must necessarily know of something else to which to hold, something which we esteem more highly than this world's goods, than honor, favor and grace, and all the possessions of the world. Otherwise, thanks to God, we would not be so stupid and foolish as not to prefer to keep our mouth shut too and enjoy the world's friendship, have good and easy times, and live as the world does. But since we are able to spurn all of that and dispense with it, we serve ample notice that our consolation is not based on anything here on earth but has begun to center on another life. We care not that the world derides us and regards us as fools or condemns us and tramples us underfoot. We reply to them: "We are well aware that if we want to be Christians, we cannot identify ourselves with the world; for we were baptized and we preach for the express purpose of angering the devil and of calling the whole world down on us. That is what we sought, and with that knowledge we started this. If we had intended to serve the world, we should have begun this differently. But all of this is done that our Lord may be glorified and that our possessions in Him might finally be revealed when the world with all its favors and grace, honor and goods will no longer count for anything and when we acquire a treasure which no lord or king can touch and which no one will discover, unless he holds with us and also has the courage cheerfully to despise the world with its ways and to stake all on this."

Behold, that is what Paul means when he says: "Why am I in peril every hour?" Although he really says this about the apostles — as he states this about his own person a little later — and although all Christians do not experience the same exposure to suffering and peril as St. Paul and the other apostles or preachers do, yet this truly applies to all Christians: If we profess Christ and live as we should, the world

[44] Luther quotes freely from Sallust, *Bellum Iugurthinum,* ch. 3. The original reads: *Frustra autem niti neque aliud se fatigando nisi odium quaerere extremae dementiae est.*

will become our enemy and attack us as it attacks the preachers, so that we may expect no better fate. This is the common external peril of all Christians, of one as well as the other. But, as I remarked, St. Paul is here referring to the particular peril which he and the other apostles encountered, and which is always the lot of the preachers' office. As he says elsewhere, 1 Cor. 4:9: "God has exhibited us apostles as last of all, like men sentenced to death," or consigned to death. For they must not only bear the external peril at the hands of the world, such as persecution, imprisonment, but over and above this, the devil attaches himself to them and hinders them everywhere, pursues them night and day, so that they must be in constant danger of death and in terror. They feel as though death awaited them any moment. For they must always stand at the head of the fray for all the rest and catch and beat off all the spears and arrows of the devil.

Thus he now says: "What might we be seeking by venturing into such great and inevitable danger, where our life is never safe and there is no joy for us? Of course, I am not doing this for the sake of honor or of favor or of friendship; no, all I accomplish with this is that I incur the most bitter enmity of both the world and the devil and that they harass me unto death. Why should I without any reason want to set myself up as a target for the spears, halberds, and firearms of the devil, all aimed to get me?" Undoubtedly St. Paul had to suffer many a thrust and blow which he felt keenly. To him this seemed like running the gauntlet of spears which strike and stab from all sides. But who would stand up and preach with loaded and primed firearms aimed at him? Do you suppose that I would deliver a sermon for 100,000 florins under those circumstances?

And here conditions were even more difficult and terrible when the devil directed all his hellish quivers and cannons against the apostle. These he had to endure perpetually, as he states very clearly in 2 Cor. 11:23 ff. And yet he remained in his office without wavering, regarding no danger and no suffering so great as to impel him to desist from his preaching. But who would want to live in constant expectation of all this if he were not as sure of this article as he is of his own life? Indeed, I can say for myself, if I knew that no more than honor and goods were at stake here and I could earn the whole world's possessions three times over with this, the world could still not induce me to deliver a single sermon.[45] I would rather crawl nine yards down

[45] Cf. *Luther's Works,* 17, pp. 127, 173, 343.

into the ground than be exposed to such danger. But there is something else in store for us than we may seek and acquire here, something which easily compensates for suffering and misery. Compared with this, as St. Paul declares in Rom. 8:18, all else is to be accounted as nothing. Here we may eat and drink and accept what we obtain, although the world begrudges us that, but it is not for this that we are Christians or that we believe. No, we are awaiting something loftier, something better — an inexpressible, eternal treasure.

31. *I protest, brethren, by my pride in you which I have in Christ Jesus our Lord, I die every day.*

Here he expresses the constant danger he has in mind. He refers this to himself, pointing out his own situation. With one word he composes his true biography, of which the world knows and comprehends nothing. For the world knows no more than it has heard, namely, how he and the other apostles raised the dead and performed miracles and such other works as loom big and can be seen. But this part no one understood but he who himself felt it and experienced it. Even now no one understands it unless he has himself felt and experienced it. Therefore not much is to be said about it here either.

St. Paul affirms this with an oath, "by my pride." He regards this as a strong and solemn oath. It is as though he were to say: "As dear as the pride and honor which I have in Christ Jesus are to me, so solemnly I swear this oath." But Christians know what this pride in Christ signifies and what it is; not to become enriched by 100,000 florins nor to gain a kingdom or empire but to be delivered by Christ from sin, death, and the devil and to be placed into the hope of the eternal kingdom. Indeed, we are already led into this partway. And we pride ourselves on having a gracious God and Father because we are baptized and believe in the Man who can give us eternal life. No Turk, no factious spirit, no papal bishop, no prince, no scholar, no pseudosaint, in short, not the entire world, knows anything of this. This is the pride I take in this article and pledge it, knowing that this will not and cannot fail me. I would not take the world for this; otherwise I would not swear so solemnly.

But what about his statement "I die every day"? The world would say: "After all, I do not see that you were ever buried. No, we see you walking and standing, eating and drinking, moving about and preaching and pursuing your occupation. Is that what you call dying or being dead?" Well, he affirms this with an oath because he wants this regarded as certain. But that is the very thing of which I said that not everybody knows or understands what Paul means with this, what this dying signifies, and how this takes place, that he constantly has death hovering over him and is perpetually harassed, feeling more of death than of life. And yet Paul says that he has an honor or a boast along with this, namely, a boast of life, although he feels this life but feebly and often not at all. Thus death and life, sin and piety, good and bad conscience, happiness and sadness, hope and fright, belief and unbelief, in short, God and devil, hell and heaven, engage in constant combat and contend with each other. It is of such a battle that Paul is here speaking, which he alone understood, for he was a great apostle who incessantly was involved and exercised in this warfare. Therefore it is necessary for him to affirm this with an oath that people believe he is telling the truth, even though others do not feel this so or understand it.

"Now, why should I want to do this," he also wants to say, "since I am not only harassed, taken prisoner, tortured by the world and suffer whatever may afflict me externally" — this he enumerates at length in 2 Cor. 11:25 ff. — "but over and above such danger also engage in constant battle with the devil, wrestle day and night with death, and feel the terror of hell? What do I gain by that? What reward might induce me to incur this needlessly, when I might well be spared all of this? Should I not rather put an end to this situation once for all and have myself buried? Or should I not rather remedy this as the world does, by bidding farewell to Christ and all that is His and by living as the others live, so that the world might leave me in peace and the devil might be my gracious lord? To be sure, I could do that if I wished to renounce the life to come. But since I do not want to do that and since I pride myself on another life, I must be prepared for this reward, that the world treats me thus and the devil pierces and tortures me to death, so that I can never enjoy this life. But even though he slays me daily and does ever so much harm to me, I will not be deprived of this pride, but I will finally defeat him with it and obtain the victory." Now Paul adds an item of his pride or of his danger, although not the greatest, and declares:

32. *What do I gain if, humanly speaking, I fought with beasts at Ephesus, if the dead are not raised?*

This is also a kind of pride, but not a pride such as the world boasts of, consisting in might and strength or in great honor and possessions, but solely one consisting in suffering and in peril of death and in a victory other than the world can obtain, namely, in the fact that Paul was held in the power of death and yet was rescued from it. He speaks of a particular custom that prevailed in the country, especially in Rome. For special entertainment it was customary to take a criminal or a condemned person, build a fenced enclosure in the center of the marketplace, put the criminal into it, and then admit lions and bears or other ferocious wild animals. With these the man had to fight and either ward them off or be devoured by them. This spectacle was enacted when the beasts were very hungry. They were often first chased and driven around to make them all the fiercer. And the people were amused when such wretched people, especially Christians, were mangled by the beasts. They thought that the terrible pain would be a deterrent against Christianity, or they assumed that this would dispose of them. For it was impossible for a person to defend himself against the cruel beasts, except when God occasionally intervened miraculously and saw to it that the fiercest beasts brought in to attack the Christians did them no harm. Indeed, the beasts became so gentle with them that they lay down before them, behaved as friendly as one does with young children, and let themselves be treated like sheep. In that way some were saved to strengthen their faith, but not all of them. Otherwise this would have become too commonplace and would have lost its attraction. But when this failed to accomplish its purpose, the executioner finally had to step in and kill them with the sword.

Now St. Paul glories in this, that he was thrown to the wild beasts to be dismembered by them, but that he nevertheless fought them off and was delivered from them, contrary to the will of the world, just as Daniel was saved when he was thrown into the lions' pit (Dan. 6:16), whereas the others, his accusers, were immediately torn to bits, together with their wives and children, and had their bones crushed by the very same lions. In 2 Cor. 11 Paul relates further that he was often miraculously saved from prison, from danger at sea, and from other perils. So the heathen could not always devour the Christians at will but had to let them live contrary to their own will. They were unable to kill them until it pleased God. This was done that the Christians might observe that God was with them and that they might not be entirely without consolation but could behold a part of life in the midst of death. It was to give others pause, so that they might either be converted or be frightened from carrying out their plans. In that way God has also manifested Himself among us today. If He had not been with us, the pope and his irate tyrants would have devoured us ten times already.

"Well, why should I engage in such mortal combat," St. Paul says, "and fight with wild beasts? Who would do that for the sake of temporal goods and honor? For naught but certain death stares you in the face when one man must fight alone and without any help with raging lions, bears, and leopards. And yet faith had to fight against such a terrible spectacle. And even if I had done it for glory or to please the world, I would still not have reaped any other thanks or any other honor than the world's disdain. The world would have said that I am a sorcerer or that I availed myself of the devil's skill. That is how they treated Christ and would also treat us today even if we raised people from the dead in their presence. Therefore I did not do this in a human fashion or in accord with human understanding in an effort to gain favor with men. And since I am obliged constantly to fight and battle the devil spiritually and must always hover between life and death, and since every evil the devil is capable of afflicts me and nothing but sheer death is mine, I must be aware of a greater consolation than any other person here on earth. That murderers and other criminals incur peril and death is not unusual. They richly deserved this. They strove for it, and they cannot fight or contend against this fate but must despair and perish. But since we voluntarily and willingly and innocently enter into such peril and combat with death, we have to be sure of another life and existence. Otherwise we could imitate the others and talk and do what the world would applaud, or we could flatter princes and lords and strive to become great lords and enjoy good times ourselves. Indeed, this would be the way, if we were looking for no more than the world can bestow. However, we do seek and strive for something other than we find here on earth, something no emperor, king, or lord can give and no scholar or doctor knows and understands. Therefore we speak and act differently too."

Let us eat and drink, for tomorrow we die.

Here St. Paul is speaking in the role of the mockers who ridiculed and derided his preaching with these words. He quotes this saying from the prophet Isaiah (Is. 22:13), who had had the same experience. When Isaiah preached forcefully and chided his hearers in Jerusalem as arrogant and miserly paunches because they despised God's Word and believed in the resurrection of the dead as little as cattle did, they attacked him, opened their big mouths, and sneered at his every threat. They stuck their tongues out at him and jeered at him as a fool, saying to one another: "Dear friend, just listen to what the prophet is saying: that we will die tomorrow. If that is true, let us first eat and drink and be merry while we are still here!" They were surely vexatious windbags to pervert his words like that and indulge in mockery of things that should have frightened them in view of God's wrath and His threat to punish them with all sorts of troubles. However, they do the opposite and use His threats for their jesting and for greater impenitence. They treat death with levity, as though it were no more than a scarecrow. What devil from hell would want to preach to such people, who pervert everything so maliciously? And when one terrifies them with death, they challenge it in defiance of their prophet.

Undoubtedly St. Paul, too, had to hear something similar from his mockers. For this is a common saying which the world and all peasants and burghers and Sir Braggart [46] quote when God's Word is used to frighten them with death and hell: "Oh, the parsons tell us much about death; they paint a gruesome picture of the devil and make hell hot for us. Well, let us have a good drink together while life lasts. When we die, we are dead." That is why Paul quotes their words here, as though he wanted to say: "If it is true that the resurrection cannot be believed, I, too, know nothing better than to speak as they do and mock both God and His apostles. For all that one may say and preach is lost anyhow on those who refuse to believe God's Word and those who do not fear God's wrath. After all, they cannot speak otherwise than they believe, as also our junkers do now, namely: "Do you suppose it is true what the parsons say, that there is one fellow stuck in another? My dear man, when we are dead, we are dead; when the body dies, one fellow dies with the other."

All right, Christians must listen to such mockery. They have to let these mockers have their say until things are cleared up and the time comes when these people will not despise death as they do now. For, praise be to God, I and others have often experienced and wit-

---

[46] Luther's expression is *Junker Scharrhans.* For various uses of this name, see especially *Luther's Works,* 21, p. 133, n. 1.

nessed that our prophecy and preaching was borne out and that neither peasant nor junker was ever so impudent and proud when death confronted him as not to be frightened and angered by it. Then his previous mockery and defiance did not help him against death. For death is adept at making the proudest and the jolliest dejected and cowardly when he greets them but a little with a pestilence. Then their heart and courage droop as they think of leaving their goods and their splendor behind. But if those who do not believe can be frightened so by death, there will surely be far more to frighten them in hell. There they will no longer say as they do now: "When we are dead, we are dead." But they will lie in eternal flames and lament and bewail the fact that they were ever born. They will have to curse and damn themselves for having heard God's Word and for having despised and derided it so blasphemously.

Therefore we should beware of such loose talk and guard against mocking God and His Word thus. For God has a way of punishing such people visibly before they expect it, and He does this as a warning to others. Numerous examples have been observed, which cannot be enumerated here, showing that God strikes about Him fiercely against these mockers who consider it a great delight to speak so scornfully and derisively about the Gospel. These examples should not be forgotten and ignored so lightly. To be sure, God does not always punish in that way. If He did, but few people would survive on earth. But as a frightening example to others, He occasionally indicates how displeased He is with this and what He will do when He thinks the right time has come. But then they will have tarried too long. Today you jeer and carouse; tomorrow you are dead and will not return. And what befalls one may befall all, as Christ remarks in Luke 13:5. There He says about the tower in Siloam, which had killed many: "I tell you . . . unless you repent, you will all likewise perish." Therefore, when God strikes and slays one, He has them all in mind. And He will surely strike them before they are aware of it, if they do not desist in time. How much misery we hear of daily! There are all sorts of terrible misfortunes: fire, water, murder, and sudden death! Even though many are now going their way unconcerned, do you not suppose that God may be postponing His punishment until a time when they have long forgotten the sin? Then they regard themselves as pious, lament and cry as though they did not deserve this. For God does not let punishment follow immediately on the heels of sin but lets people go on long enough and restrains Himself to see if they will reform. However, in the end and when least expected He comes with real terror. The speed of the punishment is in proportion to the body; He is quick to punish an individual or a small group, but He tarries long with a country or a city, waiting till it is ripe for punishment. In the end, however, no one goes unpunished.

Therefore St. Paul gives his warning in the words of the prophet Isaiah. He wishes to use those mockers as an example, as if to say: "At that time, too, there were wicked and base villains who did nothing but jeer at the prophets. But after they had jeered a long time and were now smug and cheerful and no longer thought of what the prophets had said, the time came when God bade the king of Babylon appear, devastate everything, put fire to city and temple, slay whom he could, and lead the rest away into exile. Then they, too, bemoaned their misery and distress; they, too, thought that they were innocent; but they would not think back and view their old list of sins, and reflect how their fathers had merited this and how they had continued in the same sins. They supposed that all was forgotten, as they had forgotten it. But God has a long memory and does not forget, though we may forget." He will also surely not forget how the whole world now sins against the Gospel so wantonly and unabashedly, as though they were free and at liberty to do as they pleased. And when their attention is called to this, they even mock just as though there were no God who sees and is aware of this. But He will get after them when they suppose it is long forgotten, and this with pestilence, famine, war and slaughter, chopping and spearing them like frogs, both young and old, exacting payment for their present conduct. Then they will have to learn how they mocked and recall what we now told them. But God will let them, too, cry in vain, as they let us admonish and warn in vain.[47]

33. *Do not be deceived: Bad company ruins good morals.*

St. Paul declares that we cannot prevent the rude multitude from presuming to say: "If we must die, then let us first eat and drink; when we are dead, we are dead." And when one talks to them at length about the Last Day, they express the wish that they may have enough money to count until that time. But let them have their way and mock while they can. In the end it will be manifest who is really

[47] The tenth sermon, preached in the afternoon of Nov. 17, 1532, the Twenty-fifth Sunday After Trinity, ends here.

mocking the other. They will have more to count than they wish when the list of their sins is held under their noses and they will have to give an accounting that will make them sweat. You, however, must pay no heed to what those frivolous people say, but be on your guard and give ear to what God's Word proclaims to you; for such babble will surely delude and mislead you.

St. Paul quotes this saying from a famous Greek poet, Menander.[48] It refers to civic morality. In rearing the youth one must be diligent and painstaking lest they behold many bad and offensive examples that would harm and mislead them. Even reason dictates that parents be intent on rearing their children properly. Now, just when a father or a mother has devoted much toil and money to their child before it is trained a little and has been taught fine and mannerly conduct so that it knows how to behave sensibly and chastely over against all people, some pernicious animal comes along, an evil tongue says something into the child's ear, or someone displays a bad example that poisons such a young heart and engenders bad blood of which it can never again rid itself. For instance, even when a young lad has been trained and disciplined well for a long time and to the parents' delight, a wild, evil, frivolous rascal comes along and with a loose and shameless remark or example poisons and spoils with a single stroke the whole object of so much care, diligence, time, and expense.

The heathen have experienced it in their lives, and we still experience and witness it daily, how easily and often fine young people, both boys and girls, are so badly misled that it is a shame. An evil tongue can work enough harm and poison to infect and pervert, in a single hour and with a single word, a whole group, one that required ten or twenty years of hard work to train. Therefore the heathen wanted to impress such sayings upon the youth, thereby admonishing each one to guard himself or any member of the family against evil talk or company; for this works murderous harm and ruins whatever is well trained. It is like hail or lightning that ruins the vegetation in the field. And people who take pleasure in poisoning such innocent young people are despicable and devilish.

Now, if evil talk has that effect with regard to civic discipline and pagan wisdom and uprightness, which are taught us by nature and by reason, what might it not do in the lofty and subtle matters of faith,

[48] That Paul was aware that he was quoting this particular version of a proverbial saying is subject to doubt, but the Greek text does match Menander's version in his *Thais* very closely (Fragments, ed. Meinecke, p. 75).

which reason does not comprehend and which everybody nevertheless ventures to discuss, to refine, and to judge? Nowadays this is customary also among the rabble. For instance, such a loose tongue drivels in a group of peasants or burghers: "Why do you give ear to what the parsons preach? Do you suppose that another fellow is stuck in this one? etc." Or Sir John of nobility and the soldiers will bluster: "If I had to bear in mind that I must die and that another life follows the present one, who would want to go to war?" They say: "Let us be merry and enjoy ourselves as long as it lasts. Who knows how things are over there!" Indeed, some who presume to be very smart regard them as fools who preach and speak about this. They say: "People who concern themselves with this must have much time on their hands." Very likely they themselves have something more important to do, namely, how they might buy many villages and castles. A host of people take such words to heart and go their way and no longer think of or heed how they live or die but only how they might accumulate money and fill their bellies. Thus they are all soon corrupted with a single word, that no preaching and chastening longer avails.

But the real harm is done when this reaches the learned and intelligent class of people. They first know how to make this look bad and repugnant. And yet they are able to polish and portray it beautifully to make it glisten. They present it most sarcastically. They say: "Christ and Paul were good, simple people when they stated that there will be another life after the present one. Why should not many fine people on earth, such as emperors, kings, princes, and lords, scholars and sages — especially those living in Greece — have known as much about this as these poor beggars and uneducated men?" A simple person will be quick to take that to heart and think: "Who knows, after all, whether it is true what they are preaching? Should I believe a person whom so many learned and wise people do not believe? Who told him about it?" We have to suffer that and get used to it. Despite all our preaching we cannot prevent such babble and such evil, venomous tongues from following us. St. Paul himself was unable to stop that.

All right, this talk is there, and real evil talk it is too. But to you this should be a warning in God's name not to give heed to it, even though you cannot escape hearing it. You must regard God's Word more highly than the prattle of the whole world, even though this is uttered by the wisest and greatest scholars, emperors, and kings. The more learned and wiser they claim to be, the more they indulge in such talk. For if you do not turn your ears from it but are willing to ponder it, you will surely be assailed and tempted to say: "Who knows? Perhaps there is nothing to it." And if the devil induces you to do that, he has already captured you, as he did Adam and Eve. For his cunning first lures man away from the Word and steals this from his heart, so that he no longers remembers and feels it. Then he injects other thoughts into the heart. In that way he wins the victory. Therefore you must be armed against this and be prepared to take this medicine, or antidote, for and against such poison. And when you hear such talk with one ear, you must counteract it by clinging to the Word with your whole heart.

I myself experienced how perplexing and how painful it is to the heart to hear such people and impertinent wiseacres talk with such arrogance about things and mock so derisively, as though nothing had ever been so surely fabricated as this. Then a person feels constrained to think: "After all, who knows? We find so many great, learned, and outstanding people, the world's elite, and, in addition, the majority, who talk and believe differently. And if this should not be true, it would constitute the greatest deception on earth." Thus I, too, witnessed and observed many who were grievously assailed by the question whether there will be another life after the present one.

Behold, all of that stems from such loose and evil talk, especially where weak and untried hearts are still found. God be praised, I am so armed against this that the prattle of the whole world will, if it pleases God, not harm me. Therefore we must be on our guard with all diligence and always cling to God's Word, on which this article is based. There it has now stood 1500 years and survived. It has indeed been attacked by many babblers and mockers, but it has never been toppled or crushed, whereas all of these vanished together with their prating and died, and no one speaks of them or remembers them any longer. This article, however, still remains and stands as it was proclaimed by the dear apostles and was believed by Adam and all the fathers and saints. And it will be proclaimed as long as the world stands, up to the time when it is materialized and experienced. We will cling to it and disregard that there are a few also among us who speak so virulently about it and mock it. We will take comfort in the fact that they are not worthy of it, and dismiss them as blind leaders of the blind. That is what Jesus called the Pharisees (Matt. 15:14). We will let them prate until they have to stop. They have their reward; they cannot be punished more severely. For if they were worthy of it, they would also believe God's Word together with us. Therefore we say to them as St. Paul did to his fellow Jews (Acts 13:46): "Since you thrust it from you, and judge yourselves unworthy of eternal life, behold, we turn to the Gentiles." You, however, must thank God for granting you the grace, for calling you to this understanding, and for making you worthy of believing it. Let those people go their way with their mocking, their carousing and swilling and living like swine that wallow around among the husks and fatten themselves until they are slaughtered.

You can resist and protect yourself against all sorts of injurious poisons by saying: "I will hear what God's Word says and abide by that; because it is a useful and salutary Word, given by God, which has, moreover, endured since the beginning of the world and will endure to its end, it is superior to such loose prating. I will emulate the example of a pious daughter who, hearing an unchaste tongue, or incited to unchastity by a vile whore says: "My dear mother did not teach me thus. I will rather follow her than another person, for she will surely not teach me anything bad." Or like a pious son who will not give ear to what every villain tells him to seduce him, I will say: "That is not right, for my dear father or teacher did not instruct me thus, etc." As these children conform their lives to the words of the parents and as they conduct themselves over against such poison, lest it harm the heart, so a Christian must cling to the Word of God and reject such pagan and ungodly talk against faith and remain with that on which he was baptized and called, that which constitutes all of Christendom's faith and life.

34. *Wake up fully,*[49] *and sin no more. For some have no knowledge of God. I say this to your shame.*

St. Paul adds these words in order to exhort and warn them the more strongly against evil talk, showing them how to comport them-

[49] Luther translates the Vulgate's *evigilate iuste* with the German *wachet recht auf,* and in his comment he stresses the implications of being wide-awake in the Christian life. The RSV translation "come to your right mind" is based on the picture in the Greek word ἐκνήψατε, "sober up." Luther's German translation of the New Testament of 1546 incorporates his marginal note of 1540 and translates *Werdet doch einmal recht nüchtern.* Cf. W, *Deutsche Bibel,* IV, 373; VII, 133.

selves, lest they be misled. He wishes to say: "See to it that such babblers do not find you drowsy or sleepy or weary and indolent. For so you are already giving way to them, and the door is open to all babblers and seducers. I have often said, and I still say, that this is a most pernicious vice, which is called satiety, or, as it has been called to date but not understood or explained correctly, slothfulness toward worship. In it one is bored with the sermon and says: "Oh, I know this myself; I have often heard it; if I care to, I can read it at home. Why should I constantly listen to the selfsame thing?" They go their way, assuming that they possess the treasure in rich measure, so that they cannot want for it. But St. Paul declares the reverse here: "Beware and be on your guard lest you become too secure and imagine that you know it too well; for you will surely be deceived." For even if a person is on his guard, it will be difficult to prevent evil talk from entering secretly and before one is aware of it.

Therefore it is always necessary to live vigilantly and circumspectly and cautiously, so that we are not taken unawares and work our own harm. Otherwise we might share the fate of those who suddenly and unexpectedly go to the devil. Take an example from an insane man whom I have seen. Whenever he opened his mouth, he would invariably say: "Thousand devils!" also when he stumbled or bumped against some object. His neighbor often warned him to drop those words. He might, the neighbor said, fall perilously and fatally some time, and then the fellow whom he named would come after him. But he ignored this and said: "Oh, if it really comes to that, I myself know very well that I must shun those words." However, not long after this it happened that he crossed a bridge, and before he knew it, he stumbled and fell into the water. And immediately he uttered the customary words: "Well, in the name of a thousand devils!" The devil appeared at once, broke his neck and fetched him as he had desired.[50] These smug spirits may fare the same way. They regard themselves so learned and so safe that they need not hear this or read it or think that the devil comes creeping along stealthily with evil talk and suggestions, making them lose Christ and His Word. And now the devil sways them as he will.

I myself often experienced and discovered that the devil can cunningly lead a person away from the Word. Whenever he notices that I am armed and that I am occupying myself with God's Word, he

---

[50] Luther tells the same story in his *Sermons on the Catechism,* 1528. Cf. *Luther's Works,* 51, p. 143.

leaves me in peace. However, when I give him even as little leeway as not to think of it and to occupy myself with other matters, he comes after me and quickly gives me a blow, which makes my position difficult until I can again lay hold of the Word. What would happen if I, too, were so smug and deemed myself so learned and refrained from preaching or hearing and reading the Word for half a year or a quarter of a year, since I have enough to do as it is to defend myself with daily study and prayer?

Therefore, if you want to avoid being misled, St. Paul says, and losing what you have, you must be watchful and not snore. You must cultivate the Word so that you can maintain your position and defend yourself against this evil pest to keep it from gaining a foothold among you. It does not lie within your power to prevent evil talk from arising and to prevent hearing the world; but it behooves you to be vigilant and not to give way to it but to ward it off wherever it raises its head. For the devil will surely not slumber or snore but will assail you, too, on all sides, wherever you may be. Therefore you must also be on your guard against this, armed with God's Word wherever you are, at home or abroad, in church, in your chamber, at table, and wherever you associate with people. Thus God also commanded His people to write and inscribe His commandments everywhere before their eyes so that they could always behold them and thereby resist all kinds of temptation and offense (Deut. 6:6 ff.).

Such diligent occupation and concern with God's Word St. Paul expresses with the words "wake up" or "be vigilant." He does not speak merely of waking up but of waking up fully, or of being so wide-awake that it can really and blessedly be called that, that is, according to God's Word. The world, too, is vigilant with regard to its affairs, but not with regard to God's Word. But it is true vigilance to be awake in God's Word, with it to repeal and defeat the devil and his poisonous darts. Therefore this does not mean to watch as a city watchman does, to prevent someone from breaking in or working harm; or as master or mistress watches in a home to assure that the servants arise early in the morning and perform their tasks. That is a part of municipal and domestic administration, to see to it that everybody attends to his duties and that all proceeds properly. But here, St. Paul says, we must watch so as not to sin. The world must watch against poverty, against disturbance of the peace, or against enemies, so that all may be well with people and country.

But our watching serves to end sin and to prosper and preserve righteousness; it serves the reign of faith and of love and the extermination of unbelief. This demands that we earnestly occupy ourselves with and cultivate God's Word always and everywhere, snatch it up avidly, hear it, sing it, speak and read it gladly against the despicable satiety and indolence of which I have spoken. Then we will have our castle and fortress well guarded and all holes closed to keep the devil from stealing in. Otherwise, if I or others fail to preach with diligence and if you do not hear it or are practiced in it, imagining that you are well acquainted with it — that is not watching or warding off but slumbering, letting your head droop, indeed, it is snoring right in the midst of the devil's guns and spears and affording him a good and safe place for breaking in and ascending into the castle without difficulty.

That is what happened also to the Corinthians. When St. Paul was no longer with them and many of them became complacent, thinking they were sufficiently informed and knew it all, the devil came among them with his tares and his evil talk against this article, so that they made subtle interpretations here based on their own ideas without God's Word and alleged that the resurrection had already taken place. They did not want to appear to deny this article outright and in contradiction to St. Paul's proclamation — then people would not have believed them so easily — no, they gave it a nice appearance. They took St. Paul's words and interpreted them as seemed fit to them. They declared that these words were not to be understood so crudely as though the dead would all come forth again bodily, but that they must be understood to mean that we had all in Baptism arisen spiritually from our dead life in sin and evil works and had now entered into a new, godly, and honorable life.

That was an extremely sweet poison which spread mightily. And it would still spread if one were to commend this with words and impress it upon people who are not safeguarded by a correct understanding of God's Word. Soon the entire mob would blurt out: "Oh, that is surely true. Until now we did not understand it, nor have we heard it interpreted that way." That is what is done right now with regard to the Sacrament and Baptism. For since they dare not deny Christ's clear words that His body and blood are present, they declare that it is present only spiritually. For how should Christ, they say, permit Himself to be handled and eaten bodily also by the ungodly?

In that way they also treated this article; they daubed their interpretation with a pretty color, so that it appealed to the rabble, especially since it was proclaimed by such as were highly reputed as the apostles' disciples and companions.

And later others appeared who alleged that the resurrection was to be understood not as pertaining to the flesh but only to the soul. In proof they quoted a verse of St. Paul from this very chapter (v. 50): "Flesh and blood cannot inherit the kingdom of God." And since we are flesh and blood, they said, the body cannot rise again. And yet they had to confess that Christ had arisen not only in His soul, but both in body and soul, as He was born and as He had died. Therefore our article very clearly bears the title "Resurrection of the Flesh," meaning that the body that dies now shall come forth again and become alive, just as Christ rose bodily from the grave. That is the correct understanding of this article. It is true that Scripture at times speaks of a spiritual resurrection, namely, when it commands us to depart from sin and enter into a new life. This happens through faith and Baptism while we are still in this life. This article, however, treats of the resurrection following this life and after our death. Therefore it is not relevant to cite that verse of St. Paul here and say that flesh and blood cannot inherit the kingdom of God. It contravenes the clear meaning which St. Paul pursues throughout this chapter. For as we shall hear, he calls flesh and blood naught but the lusts and the evil which inhere in our flesh and blood from Adam, namely, the sinful, mortal being, the evil lusts, and all sorts of infirmities of flesh and blood. For in the life to come everything is to be pure, without sin and weakness. Therefore all the evil in us derived from flesh and blood must perish, so that we may on that Day be completely new and pure in body and soul. It does not follow from this that we will not rise bodily with flesh and blood. Otherwise we should also have to say that Christ did not have flesh and blood after His resurrection.

Such was the evil talk that passed among them. It was introduced not by strangers or by common and base people but by their own brethren, who presumed to be the foremost and the most learned among them and who administered the office in their midst. Paul had to admonish and warn them to be on their guard chiefly against their own brethren. Therefore he concludes with harsh words, saying: "For some have no knowledge of God. I say this to your shame." It is as though he were to say: "Is it not a sin and a shame that matters have already come to such a pass among you, all of whom heard my message in rich measure, that such is taught among you and by your people and that you have become so blind as to have almost nothing left of God's Word? What more disgraceful thing might be said about you than that you, who as my foremost disciples should be best informed and the best Christians, have permitted such unchristian prattle to gain ground among you until many of you disregard God and His Word entirely? Therefore I must exhort you to note how these have fallen, to give you pause lest the same happen to you."

For with the words "to have no knowledge of God" Paul means not to know nor to heed God's Word, since anyone who wishes to know God must learn to know Him through the Word. These people do not do that, but they ignore it. They rush into the articles of faith with their reason and their own notions. They make bold to judge about God and all matters themselves. They will never meet Him there, for the proclamation of Christ and the future life has, of course, not grown in their heads. So, when they hear of the resurrection, they also judge in accordance with their own heads, saying that it is no more than rising from sin and becoming godly. God's Word says nothing about that in this article.

Therefore this is but to go astray and to depart further and further from God and the knowledge of God. It is like a blind man who goes astray in broad daylight, unable to find his way back to the path. And as they who teach depart from God's Word themselves, they also lead the poor multitude after them. In this way one blind man leads the others, until nothing of God's Word is left them and they deal only with their own invented dreams. With these they mislead themselves and others. They say that it is God's decision and will that the flesh or body shall not rise, but only the spirit, or soul; yet this is not His will or meaning at all. Therefore they know nothing of Him. As St. Paul says elsewhere (1 Tim. 1:7), they develop into people who desire "to be teachers of the Law, without understanding either what they are saying or the things about which they make assertions." Therefore be on your guard against such, he wants to say, and pay no heed to their great reputation as Christian brethren or teachers. Rather see to it that you are sure to have God's Word and adhere to it. Then you will not err or stray but know and prove God's will and decisions correctly.[51]

[51] The eleventh sermon, preached Dec. 1, 1532, the First Sunday in Advent, ends here.

35-38. *But if someone will ask, How are the dead raised? With what kind of body do they come? You foolish man! What you sow does not come to life unless it dies. And what you sow is not the body which is to be, but a bare kernel, perhaps of wheat or of some other grain. But God gives it a body as He has chosen, and to each kind of seed its own body.*

So far we have observed how the apostle has taken up this article in good earnest and has worked hard to make it sure and to warn his Corinthians to be on their guard lest they be deluded and misled by dissenting, evil talk. Now he begins to refute their objections, contrived by the shrewdness of their reason. This article does not at all agree with reason. In fact, if one should judge this article in accordance with reason and subjective opinion, much nonsense would result. Thus reason must either regard this article a lie, or it must apply its own subtle wit to it and interpret it to make it somehow compatible.

These were surely sharp fellows whom St. Paul introduces here with their remarks. They not only were able to twist and pervert this article cleverly, but they could also mock and ridicule expertly, as they supposed, when the physical resurrection was taught. They said: "My dear man, what will happen when all rise from the dead? What kind of bodies will they have? Or what sort of an existence will it be?" For figure it out for yourself, if we are all to be revived again, each with his present body restored to him, a teeming world and an innumerable multitude of people will surely forgather. Where will they all find enough to eat and to drink? Where can enough grain, enough oxen, pigs, and sheep be found to supply everyone with food? Just think how many people alone died in two or three centuries, to say nothing of thousands and more thousands of years! They would be enough to consume the whole store of the earth's meat and bread in one day. Furthermore, where will they all find clothing and shoes and covering and all that pertains to the wants of the body? Even now we barely succeed in supporting ourselves with what we have. What, then, will happen when the world becomes so densely populated, when each one has wife and child, house and home, etc., and people will multiply on and on? Then the world will soon become too small even for every person's body, to say nothing of the fruits and the vegetation that the earth must bear for man and beast.

And furthermore, what will happen when we all are to assemble again and live together as we do now? For when I arise, my wife will simultaneously arise, also my children, indeed, also my father and mother and his father and grandfather, and so forth. Also my master or my country's ruler and his father and grandfather. Where will all the emperors, kings, lords, and princes find room? Will they all, beginning with the first member of their family, reign over one and the same country? Will there be as many lords in one city, as many masters, manservants and maidservants in one household as were found there successively over the years? Furthermore, if a man had many wives and must take all of them in again at the same time, how will things be divided if they all live together and are fed and sustained from one and the same inheritance and possession, from father and father down to children and children's children? Who will restore to each what he inherited? According to their reasoning, such and countless other incongruous situations will surely follow if all men who ever lived since the beginning of the world will rise again physically, as we are now. With such questions the Corinthians presumed to be very clever, displaying unusually great wit and wisdom. With it they supposed they had quashed this article and proved that it amounts to nothing, that Paul had not meant it that way, that it had not been understood correctly, and that Paul must be hiding some other meaning under it.

But St. Paul refutes their folly with clear words. He rejects all such questions and clever explanations as to what kind of bodies we will have and how we can make things tally if the body is to eat and drink, spit and cough up, become mangy and scratch, digest and emit stench, be sick and frail, as we are now, and each one again is man, woman, manservant, maidservant, and the like, as before. Paul replies very briefly: "No, nothing whatsoever of this, neither this nor that. But this is the way it will be: Everybody will remain what he was created, whether man or woman. For Scripture says that God created male and female. He will not change His creation. Therefore everyone's body will remain as it was created. But he will not eat, drink, and do whatever results from this. Nor will he beget children, keep house, govern, etc. For God distinguished between creature, or nature, and the offices and estates on earth which were ordained and instituted after creation. The body retains its nature, but the use of the body does not remain the same. For a person's position as manservant, maidservant, father, mother, lord, prince, king is not something that was created, but that is a regulation regarding the creature. Therefore only what was created in man, the different members, will remain, but these will no longer be employed for the bodily needs as they are now. It will no longer be necessary to eat, to drink, to digest, to sweep, to live with husband or with wife, to beget children, to cultivate the fields, to rule home or city. In short, all that pertains to the essence of these temporal goods and is part of temporal life and works will cease to be. That is what Christ, too, teaches in Matt. 22:30: "For in the resurrection they neither marry nor are given in marriage, but are like angels in heaven."

Those pagan and worldly-wise people are unable to understand this, for concerning this life they do not see or think beyond their swinish head. Therefore they proceed to reason foolishly: "If man were to become alive again, he would also have to eat and drink, keep house, etc. Otherwise, how could he remain alive? If we were to meet again and live together under those circumstances, it would be an odd, nonsensical, and confused existence, so that we would all the more wish to remain dead. Therefore there can surely be nothing to it. For according to outward appearances this does not make sense." Indeed, this does not make sense if we consult and ask reason how things will be in that life. Reason knows nothing and can know nothing about that. And it is true, if the life to come would not be different from what reason conceives it to be, I, too, would not wish for it. However, how things will be must be judged not by our reason but by God's Word. And the latter teaches us that not this old, infirm life will come into being, but a new, perfect, eternal life, that the stomach will no longer be in need of food nor the body require anything for the preservation of life, that there will be no distinction of rank, no prince, master, pastor, or subject, as was also said earlier, but that we will possess everything in God, who will be "everything to everyone." Therefore this will be a wholly different, more beautiful, and perfect existence, devoid of all infirmities and wants. Otherwise, what would God really have accomplished, if things would not be different, if man would always have to bear his paunch and sack of stench with him and eternally stuff himself and eliminate, discharge mucus, suppurate, be lazy and be ill? And why should we proclaim this, believe, and suffer, if we could hope for nothing better? But as it is, all of this must pass away with this life, and yet the creature will remain, the body of each one, both as male and female, all in the same estate and position.

However, it is also true, as we shall hear later, that there will be distinctions made also in yonder life, depending upon how a person worked and lived here. For instance, since St. Paul was an apostle and Samuel and Isaiah prophets, and so forth, these will enjoy greater glory than others as men who did more and suffered more in their offices. Similarly, pious Sarah or Rachel will be preeminent before other women and yet will not be a different being or life. Thus everybody will be distinguished and honored in accordance with his office, and yet there will be one God and Lord in all, and there will be identical happiness and bliss. With regard to person, no one will be more or have more than another, St. Peter no more than you or I. Yet there must be a distinction on the basis of works. For God did not effect through St. Paul what he effected through Isaiah, and vice versa. Therefore all will bring their works with them by which they will shine and praise God; and it will be said that St. Peter wrought more than I or others did. This man or this woman lived in this way and accomplished so much. In short, before God all will be alike in faith and grace and heavenly essence; but there will be a difference in works and their glory. It is like fashioning a hatchet, a nail, a key, or a lock from one and the same iron. All are the identical essence, and yet they serve various uses and functions. Similarly, various vessels are made from the same dough or clay.

That is in brief St. Paul's reply to such a question or objection. It extends almost to the end of the chapter and relates both to the kind of bodies we will have after the resurrection and what kind of a life this will be; namely, that the body will arise free of all infirmities, glorified, and perfect, requiring nothing that pertains to this perishable life. And yet there will be a distinction in glory. Paul begins to illustrate that with a few examples. For since reason fails to understand what will happen and refuses to believe the Word and yet insists on spouting its wisdom about it, it is necessary to stop reason's tongue with vivid illustrations borrowed from this life and manner of existence. From these people can see and comprehend that things do not happen as they imagine. As his first illustration Paul takes various kinds of seed that sprout from the soil. He says: "You foolish man! What you sow does not come to life unless it dies. And what you sow is not the body which is to be, etc."

Now he is growing angry over this. He becomes vexed with these inane babblers who were mocking as though they were so very smart. He blurts out: "You foolish man!" It is as though he were to say: "Your own words betray that you are nothing but a fool and that you believe nothing at all; and yet you venture to spout your wisdom about this in accordance with your stupid head. For Scripture calls him a fool who judges God's affairs, not from God's Word but in accordance with reason and the senses, as things appear to sight and touch. Indeed, a cow or a pig can do that too. That is what you are also doing with this article. Because you observe and understand that male and female must unite, keep house, own fields and animals, toil to procure food and drink, etc., you presume to conclude that the same must obtain in heaven. And you fail to see the everyday example of the grain growing in the field year after year. For if you would be governed by your sight also there, as you see the grain lying in the granary or in the sack, and gape to watch any kernel growing there, what would come of that? Of course, nothing at all. It would, I am sure, eternally remain the same. But if the grain is to grow, go and sow it in the field, dig it into the ground, and you will soon see it grow forth again, with an entirely different essence or body. Then you may not say: 'There is my grain, exactly the same as when it lay in the sack.' For it decayed to nothing at all there in the earth. And yet in the process of rotting and decaying, when it was no longer of any use and when it had vanished, it received first of all a root below and a stem or a blade above, and a beautiful ear filled with new kernels. The former kernel disappeared entirely and nothing of it can be found anymore; and yet a new grain emerged from it.

"This you witness daily with your very eyes. It is so common that it is really a shame to present such an illustration. And yet you venture to ask and to debate the question how things will be in the resurrection. You fail to notice that a mirror and an image is here held before your nose which you can lay hold of. For if God is able to work that with a tiny dead kernel, should He not provide us, for whom He created and to whom He gives heaven and earth, with a far different, better, and more glorious essence? Since this is painted before your eyes and penetrates all five senses, you must indeed be a stupid fool. It shows you how every kernel loses its form and body and yet does not lose it; but it sprouts forth again in a far more beautiful form with leaves and stem. Each kernel acquires a beautiful, new body. If you had not observed this before, you would be amazed to death. And in the face of this you refuse to believe that God will keep His promise to us, to awaken us and to glorify us and to make us much brighter and more beautiful than any other creature on earth." Paul will say more on that later.[52]

What a precious artist St. Paul becomes here, painting and carving the resurrection into everything that grows on earth! He encompasses everything with the words "what you sow," namely, all sorts of grains and plants. He employs all of this as an illustration or a painting with which to inculcate this article and everywhere to illustrate it visually. This he does despite the fact that he has already proved it mightily with Scripture and God's Word; that might have sufficed. For whoever will not believe or cannot be persuaded by God's Word and the example or experience of the resurrection initiated in Christ, will very likely be preached to in vain by illustrations and examples. It should suffice a Christian to hear God's Word declare that he will come forth from the earth alive, with body, soul, and all senses. He should regard that as true and certain because God said it. He should not inquire further how this will happen but should leave that to God. For He who is able to raise all the dead from the earth with one word will surely also know how to bestow a form and an essence that will serve and be appropriate to the heavenly, eternal life.

However superfluous it may be, St. Paul enters also into this dispute regarding the question of the how of the resurrection in order to confirm the matter. He proves it and illustrates it with these temporal creatures, namely, with all that grows in the fields, indeed, as we shall hear later, also with the celestial creatures. He who believes God's Word that Christ is risen and that we shall rise with Him is well served by such illustrations. They are like silk kerchiefs or paper bags [53] into which he can place this article to carry it with him. For this is what we use allegories and illustrations for, to lay hold of doctrine better and always to bear it in mind. In that way we have it before our eyes daily and are constantly reminded of it. That is the way Scripture portrays Christ and His Christendom as a bridegroom

[52] The twelfth sermon, preached Dec. 8, 1532, the Second Sunday in Advent, ends here.

[53] The German word is *Scharnützlein*. Luther uses this word in his commentary on his favorite psalm, *Confitemini*, Ps. 118. There it expresses the boaster's derision of the power inherent in "the name of the Lord." He mocks: "Oh, this is a paper cannon, a paper bag!" Cf. *Luther's Works*, 14, p. 74.

with his bride. It takes such a common illustration and metaphor and in it presents our chief article of faith. Thus it is nicely and easily retained by those who believe it. For he who does not previously believe that Christ is our Savior, through whom we become righteous, pure, holy, and entirely one body with Him, is also not benefited by such a figurative portrayal of the doctrine.

So St. Paul here composes a fine picture and metaphor for the bare words and sermon which he had delivered before this on the resurrection. In this way even a simple person can easily understand and remember this article, because this picture is so common and beheld by everybody daily. Therefore, when you see a peasant or husbandman walking along on his field, reaching into his sack and then scattering and strewing something about him, you have a beautiful picture and painting of God's method of resurrecting the dead. But prior to this, it is necessary that you believe this sermon. After that you can imagine and think of God as such a peasant and yourself as a small kernel which He casts into the ground, so that it may come forth much more beautiful and glorious. But God is a much better and greater husbandman than a peasant in his field. He has a sack about His neck filled with seed. We human beings are that seed — as many of us as come into the world, beginning with Adam and extending to the Last Day. These seeds God strews about Him into the soil, as He takes them into hand, woman, man, large, small, young and old, etc. For one is the same as another to Him, and the whole world is no more than the cloth bag suspended from the peasant's neck. Therefore, when God has people die, especially in great numbers by pestilence, war, or otherwise, He is reaching into the sack and strewing a handful about Him.

Well, what does a pious peasant or husbandman do and think when he scatters his seed about like that? It looks like futile labor and loss, and he appears to be a fool who wantonly squanders his grain. But ask him, and he will be quick to tell you: "Why, my dear man, I am not casting it away to lose it and to let it spoil, but I am doing this that it may grow forth again most beautifully and bear and yield far more in return for this handful. Indeed, now it seems lost, scattered into the wind for birds and worms; but let summer come, and you will see it grow forth. One handful will grow into ten, one bushel will yield six others." Such are the peasant's thoughts. They do not dwell on the kernels which fall into the ground to rot. He does not think that they will remain in that condition; no, he looks forward to and awaits the coming summer, which will compensate him fully and in rich measure. He is so sure and certain of the growth of the grain as though he already beheld it before him. Indeed, he is much surer of this than of what he here has in hand. Otherwise he would not be so foolish as to throw it away for no reason at all.

Behold, thus we, too, should learn and accustom ourselves to thinking that it is just like that before God when He casts one handful here and another handful there into the cemetery, or when He seizes me today and someone else tomorrow, always one after the other, and puts them into the ground as His kernels, or seeds. This appears like the end and everlasting decay to us. But God takes a far different view of this and entertains far different thoughts. He does this solely in order that His little kernels might emerge again most beautifully during the pleasant coming summer following this miserable existence. He is as sure of this as though it had already come to pass and had been carried out. But it was recorded and portrayed so nicely for us that we, too, might conceive the same thoughts when we lie on our deathbed, and that we might not be concerned although all we see and perceive is that we will be interred in the ground, and although we hear nothing but wailing and weeping, as though this were really the end. No, then we must tear such human thoughts from our heart and graft these heavenly, divine thoughts into it, telling ourselves that it is not a matter of burial and decay but of sowing or planting of a little kernel, or seed, by God Himself. For here we must not judge according to our seeing and feeling, but according to God's Word. When we sow a physical kernel, we do not think of it as cast in the ground and decaying, but we think of it according to our knowledge of its future condition, although this is not at all apparent yet. Such thoughts are not born of our imagination. Just as we, in our temporal existence, conceive and form our ideas from the work of God, which we behold every year, similarly we are here speaking from the viewpoint of the future life and in accordance with God's Word. And this is true and certain, and it will fail as little when the time comes as His present creation and work on earth fails.

Therefore St. Paul is an excellent teacher who is able to present this article so nicely and charmingly. No other person could have hit upon such a portrayal, evolving a picture of life from what the whole world regards as dead and illustrating this with such commonplace and insignificant things, namely, with all kinds of seeds, or kernels, in the field. Thus when a person dies, he must not be regarded otherwise than as a kernel cast into the ground. If this kernel could see and feel what is happening to it, it would also be constrained to think that it is lost forever. But the husbandman would tell it a far different story. He would picture or portray it as already standing and growing there nicely, with beautiful stalk and ears. And we, too, must let ourselves be pictured thus when we are cast into the ground. We must have it impressed on us that this is a matter not of dying and decaying but of sowing and planting and that in this very act there is to be a coming forth again and a growing into a new, everlasting, and perfect life and existence. In the future we will have to learn a new speech and language when referring to death and the grave. When we die, this does not really mean death but seed sown for the coming summer. And the cemetery or burial ground does not indicate a heap of the dead, but a field full of kernels, known as God's kernels, which will verdantly blossom forth again and grow more beautifully than can be imagined. This is not human, earthly speech but divine, celestial speech. For it is not found in the books of all the scholars and sages on earth. Read all the histories, the books and writings of philosophers and jurists, and you will not find a word or a letter of this painting or hear a speech informing us that a different, a new, eternal life will evolve from death, and that when people die they are but a seed that is sown. No, they will call this eternal destruction and total annihilation, without further hope or expectation. That other vulgar crowd, titled Master Epicurus, found both among the clergy, the nobility, and among townspeople and peasants, talks in the same strain. They say: "Do you suppose there is one fellow stuck in another? etc." For to talk of resurrection and eternal life means to speak a strange and obscure language to them.

But among Christians this must be a familiar, common, and current speech. For Christians are different people. As God's children and companions of the angels, they no longer live or speak in an earthly but in a heavenly manner; and as such they must also employ a different language. Therefore they also have a different teacher, the Holy Spirit, who teaches them through the Word of God to understand and to speak this language spoken in heaven. And now, when I witness the burial of my father, mother, brother, sister, child, or friend, and behold them lying under the ground, as a Christian I dare not say: "There lies a stinking, decaying carcass or dead men's bones, but rather there lies my dear father, mother, child, friend, prince, lord, etc., and today or tomorrow I shall lie there with them. What are they? Nothing but kernels, which will soon grow and emerge immortal and incorruptible and far more beautiful than the green crops in the fields in summer. This is to speak about the subject in a real heavenly language, such as God and His angels employ. Therefore, even if this world is not conversant with such speech and does not understand it, we must nevertheless learn to scrape our tongue and clear our eyes to enable us to view this in the light of God's Word and speak about it.

Behold, this is the painting or picture which St. Paul places before the eyes of us Christians who already believe God's Word regarding this article. He draws almost all of creation into this. He fairly showers and drowns us with illustrations, so that we find examples and illustrations in abundance wherever we look. And every peasant, even though he is unable to read, has this article before his eyes eveywhere and can feel it in his hands. In short, we have as many living proofs of the resurrection as we behold kernels and seeds sown or sprouting in the field or in the garden. And so we say: "Life is emerging from death everywhere."

Go into a garden this very hour [54] to see how things are going, how all sorts of plants and trees are growing there now. You will find that everything is absolutely dead. But if you return in summer, you will find a far different picture. Then all is verdant and is blossoming. There is sheer joy and life compared to this harsh, dead winter. But if we had never witnessed this before, do you not suppose that we would regard it a great deed and miracle to transform one seed into a beautiful apple or cherry tree, which bears a thousand apples or cherries in place of this one kernel? Of course, people do not see or heed that but pass it by and do naught but gorge and swill all that grows. They are like swine that run across a field or wallow in a garden and devour what they find. But if anyone wants to be a swine, let him. This illustration is not presented for swine but for those who are Christians, that they might be delighted at the sight of such beautiful blossoms and fruits and say: "Lo, what a lovely spectacle it is when things are bursting into leaf and blossoming and growing so beautifully! How awful and poor by comparison things

---

[54] The date is Dec. 22.

looked half a year ago, when everything lay frozen and dead in the ground! What a great God He must be who is able to fashion such a beautiful living object from the dead winter? My dear man, what does God mean to show with that, or what does it really signify? This is surely done for our sakes, that we might thereby learn to know Him. He places His work before our eyes to illustrate what He purposes to do with us, for whose sake He created all of this. For since He produces such beautiful new vegetation year after year from a dead kernel and seed, He is much more disposed to do the same with us when we similarly lie buried under the ground and the time comes for an eternal summer to dawn. Then we will come forth far more beautiful and glorious." Thus Christians hold converse with trees and all else that grows on earth, and the latter, in turn, with them. As Christians look at these, they do not think of gormandizing like swine; no, in them they see the work prefigured which God will perform on us. They behold this article comprehended in this spectacle, similar to a precious gem wrapped in a kerchief. This serves to strengthen and confirm our faith previously founded on Scripture. People who do not possess the Word cannot behold such a doctrine prefigured here or interpret it that way, although they, too, witness such work of God in creation and see everything emerging from death, as pagan philosophers indeed did view it and describe it. Therefore we should take these illustrations of St. Paul to heart and let the resurrection make a deep impression on us, so that we may thoroughly learn this new, celestial language.

This is the first comparison with which St. Paul begins to answer the foolish question and nonsensical talk as to what will happen when the dead arise and what kind of bodies these will have. He rebukes their folly based on their crude, carnal, and pagan ideas, for they view and conceive of this only from observations in this life. In accordance with that they presume to speculate and inquire how it is possible for the body to return, since no one can say that the kernel which a peasant sows in a field returns. And yet they must admit that none of these kernels can grow or acquire a new body unless it is first cast into the ground and decays.

"Therefore," he wants to say, "do not keep on asking how God will do this or what form the body will receive, but be content to hear what God will do. Then leave it to Him what will become of it." For as I said earlier, if God can make the essence, He will surely also know how to give it a form. But in order to make this perceptible, Paul submits an illustration. When you see a peasant walking in the field and scattering seed into the ground, He does not intend this to remain lying in the soil — no, then the peasant would rather keep it at home in the loft — but he is prompted to do this mainly by the certain hope of recovering it next summer. He strews it into the ground, even though it must rot and decay there. He knows that it cannot develop any other way. Thus Christ, too, says in John 12:24: "Unless a grain of wheat falls into the earth and dies, it remains alone; but if it dies, it bears much fruit." For only after it has died and lost its form completely does it begin to show signs of life again and sprout out below and above until new grain develops from it.

That is what God also does with us. For He does not cast us into the ground with the intention that we remain there forever and decompose. Yet He must go about it as though all appears to be lost and nothing would ever develop from it. For if the body would not rot in the ground, a new body would never grow from it. But if our body is to receive a new form, we must decay and decompose like the kernels in the ground. "Therefore," Paul says, "you must be a big fool to think that man must remain in the ground and be unable to emerge again because he rots and decays there; or, even if he should arise, that he must retain his present filthy form and become again what he now is. You yourself do not do this when you sow your grain in the ground; you do not expect it to remain there and you do not expect it to retain the same form. No, you cast it into the ground expressly that it might shed its present form. If that would not happen, all would be vain, and your sowing and all your grain would be lost." Should God, then, not be much more inclined to impart a different essence to us — even though He has us cast into the earth now — and to bring His grain forth again endowed with a more beautiful and better form than the present one, so that it will lose this mortal essence and acquire an immortal essence instead, as St. Paul later concludes? For this dead, corruptible grain (which is the body as it lives now) is not fit for heaven until it has first divested itself of its form and been garbed in a new one that will no longer eat, drink, digest, fester and stink, associate with wife and child, occupy itself with house and home, or have other wants. This body will purge itself of all of that in the grave and let it vanish or decay, so that it will be completely purified and glorified. And you fool with your carnal thoughts presume to construct a heaven for God in which the body should daily fill itself and then eliminate again in the same way as it does now. Search your own heart and contemplate your own work. Note what you do with the grain which you sow. That will surely teach you that this will not and cannot happen so, for you must learn from the grain that its decay serves the purpose of imparting a new and more beautiful form to it. If it would remain where it is now, it would never get any roots, much less would it develop stem or blade or ear later. Should God not produce far more with His grain? For He who creates all things and us human beings in addition is a Husbandman different from you. And since He once before created us from nothing, He can also again give us life from the grave and give the body a new form. For it surely denotes greater skill to make something out of nothing than to renew and to beautify what existed previously.

You see, in this way Paul wants to refute the crude, carnal meaning which they inject into this article with the intention of weakening it. His meaning and conclusion are that man's body will be transformed. It will not retain the form it now has. Man will retain only what pertains to his essence, but nothing will remain that relates to this transitory life. And yet it will be the same body and soul with all the members that man had here. But he will have to leave behind all that he required in this world: husband, wife, child, house, home, masters, manservant, maidservant, meat and drink, clothing, etc. These man will need until we have all departed this life, one after another, until this life has ceased and vanished completely and another, more beautiful life dawns, which is to endure eternally. Therefore it is not at all a question whether everybody will live a life or occupy positions in the resurrection as he does now, or how everybody will procure food, drink, clothing, etc.; for God wants to create a new life for the very purpose that all that is perishable be entirely abolished. Death must serve that purpose. He must approach us and say: "Stop eating, drinking, digesting, etc., and lie down and decompose so that you may acquire a new, more beautiful form, just as the grain does which sprouts anew from the soil.[55]

39-42. *For not all flesh is alike, but there is one kind for men, another for animals, another for birds, and another for fish. There are*

[55] The thirteenth sermon, preached Dec. 22, 1532, the Fourth Sunday in Advent, ends here.

celestial bodies, and there are terrestrial bodies; but the glory of the celestial is one, and the glory of the terrestrial is another. There is one glory of the sun, and another glory of the moon, and another glory of the stars; for stars differ from stars in glory. So it is with the resurrection of the dead.

St. Paul applies three illustrations to this article. First, as we heard, he speaks of the kernels or seed. The second deals with the various bodies of all living animals, birds, and fish. The third speaks of all the celestial bodies, sun, moon, and stars. All of these serve to illustrate this article for us and to inculcate it. By the first illustration he showed us sufficiently that the new body will acquire a new form in the resurrection; this will be more beautiful and glorious than the present one. It is comparable to the kernel that grows forth again from the ground and is far more beautiful after it has decayed. It will be a new mode of existence, free of all temporal necessities, finding its full sufficiency in God alone. But in the second and third illustrations Paul wishes to expound the other factor of which I also spoke earlier, namely, the various differences in yonder life. Each body will have its own peculiar clarity; each member will have its own peculiar glory.

This is, in short, St. Paul's meaning: "You can obviously see," he says, "that God created and gave the living creatures various kinds of flesh, such as man, animals, birds, and fish, etc. But they are all of one kind and essence, inasmuch as they are all flesh and are called flesh." To be sure, we Germans and the pope in his language do not apply the word flesh [56] to fish. But among the Romans and the Greeks and all true and natural masters who spoke or wrote about this everything possessing a living body is called flesh. Now, as there are various kinds of flesh and as not all have one form — cattle and other animals on the ground differ from birds in the air; birds differ from fish in the water; and, moreover, in each of these classes there are many varieties, distinguishing the flesh of one from that of another — so there will also be but one kind of man in the life to come, and yet there will be various differences, each one in accordance with the life he lived here and the works he performed. That is the second illustration.

In the third place, after Paul has spoken of all kinds of living bodies, he also speaks of other bodies in general. Thus he briefly

[56] In the dietary sense of the German word *Fleisch*, "meat."

mentions all the physical or visible creatures, gold, silver, fire, water, stone, wood, iron, and whatever other terrestrial things there may be. And then he also mentions everything up in the heavens, sun, moon, planets, and other stars, which he calls "celestial bodies." There are so very many terrestrial or celestial bodies, and yet each one is distinguished in kind from the other. The one is always more glorious and precious than the other: gold is better than lead; silver is better than straw; jewels are better than fieldstones. And among the celestial bodies the sun is more resplendent and beautiful than the moon, and one star is more beautiful and brighter than another. And yet all stars have one nature or body. And everything on earth is also God's creature, the least as well as the greatest and the most precious. Similarly, in the life to come, too, there will be various differences with regard to brightness and glory. And yet all will be of one heavenly essence as one body and as members of Christ. So there are many and various members in one natural body, each bearing its own name and fulfilling its own functions or offices, and yet all partake of the one essence and nature of the one body.

It would be possible to imitate St. Paul and compose and paint many more such illustrations from any part of nature and show how God makes one body from a variety of bodies, each with its own body, but with a difference that makes each distinguishable from others, also within the same kind and essence. For instance, among gems we find different names, varying colors and virtues; in one body there are various members. That forcefully demonstrates the invalidity of the carnal thoughts which assume that things in the life to come must be the same as they are here. For reason says: "Why should one need the members of the body if one does not have to eat, drink, digest, etc.?" But if all the members of the body would still be necessary and be used as they are now, this would become a filthy mode of living and a terrible heavenly kingdom, as was said sufficiently before.

Now St. Paul applies this illustration to his article, saying: "So it is with the resurrection of the dead." He wishes to say: "We shall all rise with body and soul but with a new essence or form of the body and its members. Therefore no one should be led astray by pagan talk and ideas as to how this may agree with reason and as to how this may be done. For if the body is glorified, the members with their functions will also enter a new mode of existence. It will quickly be evident what purpose they serve and for what they will be used, whether or not they will longer be necessary, as they are now, for transitory functions. And yet many differences or degrees of glory will prevail among us. For instance, Peter's and Paul's will be the glory of apostles; one person will partake of the glory of a martyr, another of that of a pious bishop or preacher; each one in accord with the works which he has performed. Similarly, each member of the body has its own honor, the eyes have an honor that differs from that of the hands or feet, etc.; moreover, the sun in the heavens has a brilliance different from that of the stars, and one star is brighter and more radiant than another, making each nicely distinct from the other. And yet with regard to person they are alike and they have the same essence, and all will have equal joy and bliss in God. In the same way all the stars glitter and glisten in the sky, although one emits more and the other less brightness or light. Let this suffice with regard to the comparisons or illustrations that Paul adduces to impress upon the simple that they should not be misled by the crude, swinish ideas that are based on this life. Now he concludes and explains the illustrations with simple and clear language.

42-44. *What is sown is perishable, what is raised is imperishable. It is sown in dishonor, it is raised in glory. It is sown in weakness, it is raised in power. It is sown a physical body, it is raised a spiritual body.*

St. Paul now reverts to the first illustration, which relates to sowing. He himself interprets it. And thereby he removes another great object of offense which severely agitates also the heathen. For they argue or raise the objection mentioned earlier: "In the first place, the Christians must themselves admit that the bodies of even the greatest saints, such as patriarchs, prophets, apostles, are long decomposed completely, with not as much as a speck of dust left of them." That is the way man is sown. When he dies and lies in his coffin longer than a day, he begins to smell and stink. And beyond this time maggots and worms grow in his body. This is so awful that no one can see or endure it. Therefore man has to be buried quickly or be consumed in fire or water and gotten rid of, for he is simply unendurable on earth. Well, such a spectacle is most offensive, and one is forced to think: "How might something come of such a body, which stinks so offensively and putridly, and which, as those who experienced it say, turns into the vilest worms, adders, toads, and snakes? Also, how might something come of those who are devoured on the gallows by crows, in the water by the fish, or who are burned to ashes in the fire and have their ashes scattered abroad? How does that harmonize with this article, with the resurrection of the dead?"

St. Paul says: "Indeed, I, too, know that very well. I have often observed this. But, you must adhere to the word 'seed' or 'sow' as I presented and interpreted it, namely, that it is sown as God's grain. Therefore you must disregard the fact that the body stinks so and decays and that nothing of it remains. You must not be deceived by this. Otherwise you would also have to say to the sower: 'Well, what is to become of the seed? After all, there it lies in the ground and is completely rotted.' He would answer you: 'You are a fool and fail to understand. That is exactly what I want it to do. I would deplore if it were otherwise. For the fact that it decays is a good sign that it will develop as I hope.' The sower cast the seed into the ground for the very purpose that it should lose its form and that new grain should grow from it. He is happy to see it decay and rot. Similarly, it cannot be said of man or of a corpse that nothing can come of him because he has no eyes, ears, flesh, lungs, or liver, etc., and because all has perished. No, Christians must say: 'You fool, it is necessary for the whole body to lose its form and decay with hide and hair and all that it has.' This forces people to say that nothing is left of it. That is termed sowing here, sowing the perishable. Later, however, it will be raised imperishable. Then we will have a new body together with all its members. This can no longer decompose or die or decline, but it will remain eternally hale and hearty, beautiful and fragrant, and possess all that it may desire." That is the first point.

In the second place St. Paul says: "It is sown in dishonor, it is raised in glory." That is to say that it will be worthless and be cast away. It is apparent that no animal's body is treated so disgracefully after death as man's. Pigs and other animals are slaughtered and killed for the benefit of man. Or if they die of themselves, they are taken outside the city gates to the skinner for the utilization of their hide and lard. Man's body, however, is dishonored inasmuch as everybody shuns it, flees from it, holds his nose shut, and hurries it to its grave as fast as possible, whether it be that of emperor, king or prince. Furthermore, it is stripped of all of its honor and adornment, and it lies there naked and bare. The dead raven, on the other hand, is permitted to keep its feathers and the pig its bristles. But no golden chain is left on man's body, not even a thread; it is bereft of everything. It is wrapped only in a linen cloth lest anyone see it lying there so shamefully. And then it is quickly buried so that it does not remain on earth. That is the disgraceful thing man becomes as soon as he dies. Although a mother would be happy to keep her son or a king his only heir and adorn him gloriously, this cannot be done. The sooner man can be put under the sod, the better. It would be a bold man indeed who could remain alone with a corpse.

But a Christian must not be disconcerted by all of that. After all, you are not now assailed or dismayed by the fact that you have a nose under your eyes and that this nose is rendered so filthy by nasal mucus and other impurities, to say nothing of the belly and the whole body with its sweat and rash and all kinds of filth. You do not hate your body for all of that, and you do not disdain it, but despite the fact that it is such a great object of stench, you adorn it most painstakingly with velvet, gold, pearls, etc. Therefore learn to think here, too, that this article is not necessarily in error because the body is treated so shamefully and dishonorably. No matter how dishonorable or worthless it is at present, it will return in a form so honorable and precious that its future honor and glory will surpass the present shame and dishonor many thousand times. Every creature will be amazed over it, all the angels will sing praises and smile admiringly at it, and God Himself will take delight in it. This is why it is described as "sown." It is like the seed. That too, must submit to being cast away so shamefully, to being scraped into the ground, and to having feet tread over it at the place where it will later grow again. The same process is experienced here, because it is really the work of God. He Himself wants to create it anew, so that it no longer remains frail and filthy as it is now but becomes perfectly pure and precious.

In the third place, we read: "It is sown in weakness, it is raised in power." For the body is so weak now that it must suffer all sorts of things when but an illness, yes, a little abscess or a fever, comes along. And when it lies prostrate, it is unable to chase away, if I may say so, even a louse or a flea; it must permit worms and all kinds of vermin to eat it. There is not enough strength present to warrant saying: "He is able to do that," but only: "He must suffer that." In view of this, reason asks how that body might rise from the grave again after it is completely consumed and turned into dust, a body which even now while it is alive is so frail and weak that it is felled by a little pestilence or by an abscess. All right, if you refuse to believe, go your way and remain a pig. We, however, know that later and at the proper time the body, weak and devoid of all strength and power though it may now be when it lies in the grave, will be so strong that with one finger it will be able to carry this church, with one toe it will be able to move a tower and play with a mountain as children play with a ball. And in the twinkling of an eye it will be able to leap to the clouds or traverse a hundred miles. For then the body will be sheer strength, as it is now sheer feebleness and weakness. Nothing that it decides to do will be impossible for it. It will be able to defeat the whole world alone. It will become so light and nimble that it will soar both down here on earth and up above in the heavens in a moment.

At present and until that Day arrives, we look forward to that in faith. Meanwhile we rest under the sod, unable to move a hair's breadth from our place. We must remain where we are bedded and suffer all to tread over us with their feet and all those awful worms to gnaw away at us and consume us. And yet we must not let that dismay us but be minded as the peasant is who sows the kernels in the ground and buries them down deep, letting them rest there until they rot. There these kernels become so weak and perish so thoroughly that they are entirely useless. But nevertheless, when the time comes and summer appears, they come forth again and sprout beautiful blades and shoot into full ears, each of which bears 20 or 30 kernels for that one rotted kernel. And they withstand wind, rain, storm, and all kinds of vermin — unless God inflicts a special calamity.

Behold, this is what such a small kernel or seed, which has no inherent strength and which earlier, when it was sown, could not move or leave the ground the width of a straw, is able to do. Now it is so astir and active that I often have asked in amazement how it was possible that an object as tiny as a mustard or poppy seed could bore its way through the ground which a peasant only with difficulty penetrates with a stake. And the seed is not assisted in this; it bores through irresistibly, although it may encounter sand and gravel and although the ground may be hard and dry. In view of this, should God not be able to do that with us, in accordance with His Word, that we come forth with a new strength when He wants to raise us up? Should we not have sufficient strength to penetrate the ground, even though huge fieldstones were lying over us? Should we not bring sufficient strength and power over all creatures with us, so that all must give way to us and lie under our feet?

Paul concludes with the words: "It is sown a physical body, it is raised a spiritual body." This seems like an unusual saying to us, for we have not preached and stressed this article very much. Still it should be current and common in Christendom, since St. Paul speaks of it and treats it with great diligence. But this does not have a familiar ring especially to us Germans. Nevertheless, we will have to familiarize ourselves also with the language of Scripture. Scripture uses the term *animale corpus,* "a natural body," or a body such as is born on earth, which for its natural preservation or sustenance requires meat and drink, clothing, fire, water, air, wood, iron, as we have it recorded also in Ecclus. 31.[57] For the term *animale corpus,* which we translated with natural body, is derived from the Hebrew נֶפֶשׁ, *anima,* which is very generally used in Scripture. It refers not only to a part of man, as we Germans speak of the soul, but it refers to the whole man as he exists with his five senses and as he maintains himself with meat and drink, house and home, wife and child. In short, a natural body is nothing other than physical life as it is lived by every animal. In good clear German we might call it *einen viehischen Leib,* "an animal body." For in point of physical life there is no difference or very little difference between us and the animals. They have bodies just as we do, bodies that perform the same natural functions that our body performs. They, too, live in accordance with their five senses; the only difference is that they have no reason.

Such a natural, or animal, body, which sustains itself, digests its food, expels the remnant, and is, moreover, corruptible, wretched, and weak, is now sown, as St. Paul says, when it dies and is buried, to the end that a new, spiritual body might emerge from it, which will not live for this natural life, require neither food nor cover, have neither wife nor child, nor satisfy any physical wants. And yet it will be the same physical body. When it is called a spiritual body, this does not imply that it no longer has physical life or flesh and blood. No, then it could not be called a true body. But when it is called a spiritual body, this means that it will have life and yet not be a body that eats, sleeps, digests, but a body that is nourished and preserved spiritually by God and has life entirely in Him. And then, when the body thus lives spiritually in God, it will sally forth into heaven and earth, play with

[57] The Weimar editor suggests Ecclus. 31:12 ff.

sun and moon and all the other creatures, and also be delighted by this. It will find such content and bliss in this that it will never think of eating and drinking. It will be a completely spiritual existence, or life, of the whole person, covering both body and soul. It will issue from the Spirit and will come immediately from or through God, so that we will be illumined by Him and know Him not only with regard to the soul, but our whole body will be pervaded. It will be as clear and as light as the air; it will see and hear sharply to the ends of the world. We will need nothing else for life or the preservation of life. And yet we will have a true body. This is comparable to the stars that are now in the heavens; they are so constituted that they need nothing for their existence, and yet they are physical creatures. To be sure, they have no terrestrial body but a celestial body.[58]

Thus St. Paul wants to banish all pagan ideas and the offensive picture that inspires these, portraying man as an abject and impotent being. This views a Christian merely in his external aspects; it sees him dying like a cow or a pig. No one was ever wise and learned enough to differentiate in that point between man and any animal. "And it is true," St. Paul says, "I myself see this and am well acquainted with that wisdom which you present from your pagan reason. Indeed, there is not a cow which cannot see it. And if mocking this article makes a person smart and erudite, I am a doctor already, or will soon become one." But a Christian must be acquainted with a wisdom different from this swinish wisdom, so that he does not judge and believe as matters appear to the eye and as every cow understands them. He must believe what God's Word teaches about those things which he now neither sees nor feels. A Christian no longer says that man departs this life and dies to perish, that man is nothing but a frail, corruptible, and foul being. No, according to true, divine understanding and in celestial language he says: The corruptible, dishonorable, and weak is sown that it might arise incorruptible and in glory and power, and that the animal, terrestrial body might become a spiritual, celestial body.

Therefore we must learn to impress this upon our minds to be confirmed in our belief and not doubt this, because we are called by God through Baptism and the Gospel to Christ and possess the promise of eternal life, since we believe that the Savior arose from the dead for the purpose of raising us, too, on the Last Day and presenting us as

[58] The fourteenth sermon, preached Jan. 19, 1533, the Second Sunday After Epiphany, ends here.

glorious and resplendent as He Himself is. In this way we can comfort, sustain, and fortify our hearts. We can already toy with such thoughts and find joy in the prospect of the beautiful, glorious life which we will receive there. For this serves to warm our hearts to the idea and to forget the temporal life, lest we cling to it as though we want to remain here forever, as the world does. Then we will find our comfort and our reliance in something loftier than in this life and transitory goods, which are, after all, uncertain from hour to hour. We must rather get used to comforting and delighting ourselves with the lofty and inexpressible treasure which we shall receive.

44-45. *If there is a physical body, there is also a spiritual body. Thus it is written: The first man Adam became a living being; the last Adam became a life-giving spirit.*

To confirm what he said about the natural and the spiritual body, St. Paul here quotes a verse from Scripture. With regard to man's creation, Gen. 2:7 records: "The Lord God formed man of dust from the ground and breathed into his nostrils the breath of life; and man became a living soul." St. Paul translated the Hebrew term "living soul" with the Greek word ψυχικός, "natural body." But as I said earlier, the word "soul" does not convey the proper meaning for us Germans. However, we must show the Hebrew tongue the honor to adopt its mode of expression occasionally, because we cannot reproduce it better. Thus what Moses calls a living soul and St. Paul here terms a natural life or a natural man are one and the same thing. Earlier I showed that the Hebrew word for soul really signifies what we call the life of the body or a living body, that is, a human being or an animal which pants and breathes.

Accordingly, later in Moses we often find the term "every living soul," that is, every kind of animal with a living body. He also says of Jacob (Gen. 46:25-27) that he moved to Egypt with all souls who were in his house. That means nothing else than as many living bodies as were with him. We also find the same in the New Testament, for instance, in Rev. 18:11-13. This passage prophesies of Babylon that no one will any longer buy of her or sell to her human bodies or souls, that is, living persons, or slaves. Moses, too, only wishes to state that God infused the five senses into man and provided that he eat and drink, digest and do whatever else the body requires. Taking it from the Hebrew, St. Paul calls all of this ψυχικός, *animalis homo.*

Now St. Paul draws an antithesis or relationship from this text, saying: "When Moses declares that man was created, first, to have a natural body, or to live a natural life, he implies another body, or life, which is not natural but spiritual." These St. Paul contraposes and infers the following *per antithesin:* "If a person has a physical body, he must also have a spiritual body." So he distinguishes two kinds of life, the one for which Adam was first created, which is called natural, and the other spiritual, which will come into being later. For Adam was first created for natural life. But as this life will cease and another life will follow, so that man will live anew, the latter cannot again be a natural life but must be a spiritual life. Christ makes the same distinction in John 3:6, where He says: "That which is born of the flesh is flesh, and that which is born of the Spirit is spirit, etc." He applies the word flesh to the whole human being born of flesh, encompassing body and soul, reason and senses. If he remains nothing but that, he does not belong in heaven. If he is to get to heaven, he must be born of the Spirit and become completely spiritual, both as to body and soul. This constitutes a life far different from the present natural one. And yet it remains the same body, or person.

Therefore Paul now poses two different Adams, or two persons, making the first Adam an example or image of the other. The first Adam, he says, is created for natural life. From him we inherit this natural life. Father and mother cannot impart more to us than that, or God through them. The other Adam, however, will have and will bestow another life. As you bear the first Adam and feel and touch as he did, by means of which you live the natural life, let me tell you that you will also have the other, the spiritual Adam, when the former ceases to exist.

Thus you must learn to understand the words "natural" and "spiritual" correctly and distinguish in accordance with their usage in Scripture. Here the body is not to be distinguished from the soul, as we customarily do when we hear the words spirit or spiritual. No, we must understand this to mean that the body, too, must become spirit, or live spiritually. We have already begun to do that through Baptism, by virtue of which we live spiritually with regard to the soul and God also views and regards the body as spiritual. It is only that the body must first depart from this temporal life before it becomes completely new and spiritual and lives solely of and by the Spirit. Thus our Lord Christ, the other Adam, was transported into the spiritual life through the resurrection, no longer living for bodily wants as He did during His sojourn on earth. And yet He has a true and genuine body with flesh and blood, such as He had when He showed Himself to His disciples. For His person He has achieved the celestial, spiritual life, so that He might also initiate this in us and complete this fully on that Day, as St. Paul will demonstrate further.

46-47. *But it is not the spiritual which is first but the physical, and then the spiritual. The first man was from the earth, a man of dust; the second Man is from heaven.*

Here you note that St. Paul always juxtaposes the two expressions "natural body" and "spiritual body." He does this lest someone understand this to mean — as some heretics do on the basis of the words that follow later (v. 50): "Flesh and blood cannot inherit the kingdom of God" — that only the spirit, or the soul, will rise and be saved on the Last Day and that the body will remain in the ground. They began to say that already at St. Paul's time. They interpreted this as referring only to a spiritual resurrection. They said that when man is baptized, he has already been resurrected; that this does not at all pertain to the body. "That is not the way it is," Paul wants to say; "for I am declaring plainly that it is to be a spiritual body, the very same body that was previously a natural, or animal, being and led a natural, or animal, life. If it were true that the soul alone is saved, this would create a fine muddle. Then we could blame Baptism that we are sinners and that the body remains condemned to bear its punishment. In accordance with that we could say that it is not the soul but only the body which sins, and that, despite this, the soul could not be saved since the body is still present. But there is nothing to that. For we are baptized not only with regard to the soul; no, the body is also baptized. So the Gospel is also preached to us, and we are blessed thereby, not only so far as the soul is concerned but also in regard to the whole person, also the body. Likewise, not only the soul but also the body receives the Sacrament of Christ's Body and Blood. Thus the body accompanies the soul through Baptism and the Sacrament, and on the Last Day it will abide where the soul abides.

Therefore we adhere to the clear words of St. Paul which state that it will become a spiritual body but that it was a natural body previously. Of course, we should like to see — as St. Paul declares elsewhere, namely, in 2 Cor. 5:4 —also the body become perfectly holy and pure at once when we are baptized, when we hear the Gospel, and when we partake of the Food, so that we would no longer be cumbered with this filthy bag around our necks. But that cannot come to pass before that Day, when a completely new essence comes into being all of a sudden, not only in us human beings but also in all other creatures. In the meantime we must put up with the animal body. And during this time we will not become so spiritual that we can feel it and lay hold of it, but we must apprehend this solely by faith. For God, who has promised us this, is surely adequate guarantee that He will not let us believe and hope in vain.

St. Paul says: "The first man was from the earth, a man of dust; the second Man is from heaven." That is to say that we are, beginning with the birth of the first man Adam, nothing but flesh and blood and entirely earthly; for as Scripture says (Gen. 2:7), he was "formed of dust from the ground." Paul here refers to that statement. If you have read that in Scripture and are able to believe such a miracle, that God made that Adam from and of earth, then you can surely also believe that He will make a celestial body from the other, the heavenly Adam. Just place a clod of earth next to a living human being. Then ask yourself what comparison there is between that clod of dirt and that beautiful living picture which is Adam? Yet the latter is nothing more than that same clod of dirt converted into blood, flesh, veins, bone, eyes, ears, head, etc. If God can make a living person with all his members and powers from this dirt, should He not also be able to form a spiritual, celestial body from the present natural body, which already possesses the nature or the essence of the body?

Furthermore, where did our first mother, Eve, come from when God formed her from a bone of Adam? What a beautiful picture she presented at that time prior to the Fall as compared to the bare bone or rib? Indeed, if we were to figure out how all people derive from father and mother, who could believe such a genesis possible if experience would not convince us of that? Should God, then, not be able to produce that same body again from the grave and make it more beautiful than before, since He applied His Word, Spirit, and work to it? Therefore I may well say to man now as God Himself says to Adam: "You are dust, and to dust you shall return" (Gen. 3:19). All men are from the earth and must return under the earth. However, they shall not remain earth. But as God once formed a beautiful person with body and soul of earth, He will make him far more glorious and beautiful the second time. Now God lets man decompose in the ground to have the terrestrial essence vanish as something merely ephemeral and corruptible, also weak and impure by nature, and to become a new man of heaven, who is no longer terrestrial but completely celestial.

Thus St. Paul again resorts to God's Word and work to oppose the mockery of smart spirits who ask how anything might be made of the dead, impotent, and decomposed body. He says: "I will indeed propound a more difficult question than yours. What was Adam in the beginning but a clod of dirt? He was far more unlike a human being than we will be when we are lying in the grave and are to rise again. Furthermore, how totally unlike each other are a rib, or bone, and a beautiful live woman? And how unlike are a little drop of blood and a living person who will become a great and famous king on earth or a great and holy apostle, prophet, and martyr in heaven? And yet also Scripture does not title such otherwise than Abraham's and David's seed. Even Christ is called thus, only that He was not begotten by a man. If this reflected any wisdom, I suppose that I, too, could ridicule and mock this most expertly. I could say just as absurdly as some crude philosophers: "My dear man, let them preach what they will; but don't ever believe that flesh and blood will get to heaven. See for yourself where you come from, etc." Yet I have to confess that the difference is far greater here where I need not believe but where I see before my eyes and feel the work God does on man when He creates him for this life. Moreover, the sun would have to shine long and all the forests be collected and ignited and all creatures melt away, before it were possible to make a man from a clod of dirt. Therefore it should not be so difficult to accept also this article, since it is far easier to make a celestial body from what was previously a terrestrial body.

48-49. *As was the man of dust, so are those who are of the dust; and as is the Man of heaven, so are those who are of heaven. Just as we have borne the image of the man of dust, we shall also bear the image of the Man of heaven.*

Note how the apostle emphasizes this article and enlarges on it with many words. He wishes to anticipate those shameful preachers who were already at that time beginning to be heard. Again he juxtaposes the two men, Adam and Christ, as he did elsewhere earlier. He calls Adam the first terrestrial man but Christ the first celestial Man.

He makes them both our prototypes and concludes that we must all become like the celestial Man, Christ, as we are now like the first terrestrial man, etc. But the words "as was the man of dust" and "as is the Man of heaven" must not be understood as referring to the sin of the first man, Adam, which we inherited from him — as several have interpreted this — nor to the righteousness which Christ possesses and which we receive from Him. No, we will remain with the meaning with which Paul began to speak here. For here he does not treat of our relationship over against God by reason of our sins or our piety, but solely of the natural and the spiritual life of the body.

Therefore this is in brief the opinion: Just as Adam lived the natural life with the five senses and all sorts of natural functions of the body, so all of his children from the beginning of the world to its end live, one just like the other. For the words "the image of the man of dust" mean that we all bear with us the same form and essence and live and do in every respect as Adam and Eve lived and did. They led the same kind of life, they ate, drank, digested, eliminated, froze, wore clothes, etc., as we do. Therefore, in external aspects there was no observable difference between them and us. Later, however, we shall divest ourselves of that image and essence and receive another's, namely, the celestial Christ's. Then we shall have the same form and essence which He now has since His resurrection. Then we need no longer eat, drink, sleep, walk, stand, etc., but will live without any creatural necessities. The entire body will be as pure and bright as the sun and as light as the air, and, finally, so healthy, so blissful, and filled with such heavenly, eternal joy in God that it will never hunger, thirst, grow weary, or decline.

That will indeed be a far different and an immeasurably more glorious image than the present one. And what we bear there will be far different from what we bear here. There will be no dissatisfaction, no annoyances, no hardships to bear, such as we have in this lazy, lame image, where we must bear and drag this heavy, indolent paunch about with us, lift it, and have it led. No, there it will swish through all the heavens as swiftly and lightly as lightning and soar over the clouds among the dear angels. St. Paul was intent on impressing these thoughts on us so that we might accustom ourselves already to rising into that life by faith and remember what we are hoping and wishing and praying for when we recite the article: I believe in the resurrection, not only of the spirit — as the heretics said — but also of that very flesh, or body, which we bear on our necks. We believe that it, too, will become a celestial, spiritual body. For what St. Paul discusses in this entire chapter with so many words is only an explanation of this article. He teaches nothing but what these two words contain and convey: "resurrection of the flesh."

50. *I tell you this, brethren: flesh and blood cannot inherit the kingdom of God, nor does the perishable inherit the imperishable.*

St. Paul has almost finished his sermon now. He has said enough about this article. However, he adds another item, by way of supplement as it were. He wants to confide a secret to them, revealing how things will be on the Last Day when we are to rise. But he prefaces this with a brief warning, as though he were to say: "You heard the wiseacres and factious spirits preach against this article and ask derisively: 'How will this take place? What sort of bodies will we have?' Therefore I counsel and warn you faithfully to be on your guard against flesh and blood and whatever human wisdom and ideas may suggest. Do not suppose that you will obtain or retain this article in that way. For it is not recognized otherwise than from heaven by faith, which the Holy Spirit must bestow. In short, be governed by that, lest you think and live as flesh and blood does, which believes nothing at all and lives as though we would remain here forever. Strive to obtain the resurrection. For such carnal, worldly ways and thoughts do not belong in heaven; they must all cease and vanish."

For as I said earlier and have often said elsewhere, Scripture applies the term "flesh and blood" to man with his whole being, as it is inherited from Adam and develops in accordance with reason, if it is not renewed through Christ and faith. A person who lives thus and remains in the old Adam knows and understands nothing of God, but invents a god and portrays him in accordance with his own ideas, missing the mark entirely. That is the way the monks picture their god. He is seated above and pays heed to their cowls and orders. Therefore such a person cannot comprehend this article either. The smarter he is with regard to reason, the less he esteems it. Therefore be on your guard against such people; for when they would be smartest, they are nothing but flesh and blood, and flesh and blood does not belong in heaven, nor can it enter God's kingdom, but it must perish completely and decay until an entirely new man develops from this.

That is, in short, the correct meaning of this text. If someone were to say in view of St. Paul's declaration that "flesh and blood cannot inherit the kingdom of God," that only the soul, or the spirit, and not the body will arise, as a number of heretics concluded, he is directly contradicting St. Paul's doctrine throughout this whole chapter. For Paul does not say that the body will not rise, but that "flesh and blood cannot inherit the kingdom of God." And behold what asses and imprudent fools they are who arrive at this strained interpretation. The text clearly states that it "cannot inherit the kingdom of God." They flit over this and see only the words "flesh and blood" and no more. Then they add their own ideas and say that flesh and blood will not rise. St. Paul never intended to say that nor could he say that, because he stated so plainly and clearly in the text immediately preceding this one that a true spiritual body will rise. No, he says that flesh and blood does not belong in God's kingdom. Christ Himself says that too in John 3:3 ff.

It is one thing to rise physically or with flesh and blood and a far different thing to enter God's kingdom, or heaven. For also Judas, Caiaphas, and all the damned will rise physically, but they will not enter God's kingdom. And what could be clearer than St. Paul's words, which state that flesh and blood, which is sinful now, cannot come into heaven? As Christ also says (John 3:3, 6): "Unless one is born anew, he cannot see the kingdom of God," for "that which is born of the flesh is flesh." But the flesh and blood which is baptized in Christ, even though it once was flesh and blood, is now never called flesh and blood, for it is born anew of the Spirit. In a natural way it is flesh and blood, but not spiritually, because it has been purified by Christ in Baptism and received into God's kingdom. Therefore it can no longer simply be called flesh and blood, except in an external and physical sense. For the term flesh and blood really applies to the old man in accordance with reason, as descended from flesh and blood, who no longer knows or understands anything, who is without faith and God's Word and without Christ. Thus Christ says to Peter in Matt. 16:17: "Flesh and blood has not revealed this to you, etc." Therefore it does not belong into the kingdom of God. But it does not follow by any means, nor can we conclude from this, that flesh and blood will not arise on the Last Day. The reverse must rather be deduced from this. For precisely because flesh and blood cannot enter the kingdom of God, it must end, die, and decay and rise in a new spiritual essence, so that it may enter heaven. Therefore St. Paul admonishes them as Christians to be such new men, lest they be found to be flesh and blood on that Day.

I am saying this that one might note how such spirits, who everywhere presume to be masters of Scripture, stray so precariously and stagger. When they spy a word, they gape at it with open mouth and eyes and see or hear nothing but it. So the Anabaptist faction sees no more in Baptism today with their mouths, eyes, and ears than mere water, and then they gush and say: "Water is water. How could water benefit the soul?" They can see water as a part of Baptism; to be sure, a cow can also see that. They suppose that they are displaying great wisdom when they are able to say: "Water is water." But the other, the chief part, they cannot see with open eyes, namely, the words: "He who believes and is baptized will be saved" (Mark 16:16). They have filled their mouth and eyes so completely with water that they are unable to behold both water and words. And it serves them right that they disgrace themselves with that and are struck on their heads with their own swords.

51-53. *Lo! I tell you a mystery. We shall not all sleep, but we shall all be changed, in a moment, in the twinkling of an eye, at the last trumpet. For the trumpet will sound, and the dead will be raised imperishable, and we shall be changed. For this perishable nature must put on the imperishable, and this mortal nature must put on immortality.*

That is the last part; in it St. Paul wants to impart a secret to them. For he is a godly apostle and has their welfare at heart. He would like to see them understand this article well, remember it, and not be led astray by any loose talk. Therefore he confides something special to their ear, something not recorded anywhere else, namely, how things will go on the Last Day. For since he said that no one can enter heaven with this perishable animal body and that a new spiritual body will have to come from this natural body, someone might fret and ask what will happen to those still living on the Last Day. Will they remain thus, or will they also rise, though they are not buried and do not decay as the others who died previously?

Paul reveals this secret by way of reply. He says that this is the way things will happen: "We shall not all sleep, but we shall all be changed, etc." That sounds as though not all of us will die. In fact, some people did juggle the words to mean this. However, St. Paul's meaning is this, that the Last Day will come as suddenly as a snare — as he said elsewhere (Luke 21:35) — before anyone is aware of it and when the whole world feels secure. Then all will be changed in a moment. That does not negate that we must all die. No, Paul says that we shall not all sleep. That is to say that those who are struck in the final hour will not depart this life as a person does otherwise on his deathbed, nor will they be placed in a grave or buried under the soil. For Scripture applies the term "sleep" to those who are placed into coffin and grave. These people, however, will pass from this life into yonder life without being buried in a grave. They will simply be transformed, or changed.

The Greek word found here means chiefly to change so as to be moved from one place to another, for instance, from the water to dry land, from the earth into the air. Similarly, then we, too, will be found elsewhere and in a different condition in the twinkling of an eye. The very hour before we were here on earth in a house or on a field. Suddenly we are removed from table or bed or from our work, as we happen to be walking, standing, sitting, or lying, so that we are dead and alive again in a moment, changed in every way, and soaring up in the clouds. Those are the changes Paul has in mind here. To be sure, he encompasses also the other changes *qualitatis,* of the form. Of these he already remarked earlier that the body will put on a different dress, that is, that it will be glorified and bright, much more resplendent and beautiful than the sun. But that will not happen while the body is still sojourning in this inn and garbed in this dress. No, it will first be divested of everything and become naked in the same moment and be burned to powder and be carried away.

Paul explains this himself in greater detail in 1 Thess. 4:15-17, where he says: "We who are alive, who are left until the coming of the Lord, shall not precede those who have fallen asleep. For the Lord Himself will descend from heaven with a cry of command, with the archangel's call, and with the sound of the trumpet of God. And the dead in Christ will rise first; then we who are alive, who are left, shall be caught up together with them in the clouds to meet the Lord in the air, etc." There he points out that everything will happen together and in the twinkling of an eye. The dead will be removed from their graves, and we will be carried away with them, however or wherever we may be found. We will be torn from this mortal life and existence, and all will be glorified together. That is what Paul means when he says: "We shall not all sleep." It cannot and will not happen so slowly, with one always burying another until we all die, one after another. No, we will all be gathered together at one time, and all will be changed together; but this will not happen without the agency of death. Still, God will manifest His omnipotent might and majesty. All that is on earth will be consumed in a moment. The whole world will lie in ruins and be changed. We will be near and with Christ forever. The others, however, who did not believe will be thrust into eternal torment. And this God will do, Paul says, through the last trumpet. For prior to this, "the Lord Himself will descend from heaven with a cry of command," as 1 Thess. 4:16 declares, and He will bid the archangel blow the trumpet, which will resound through heaven and earth. This will cause everything to fall into ruin and all the dead to be awakened.

This is the secret and hidden fact which Paul confides solely to his Christians. For the worldly-wise can and shall not understand it, but they must make would-be-wise remarks about it and deride it. The Christians alone shall know and comprehend this. To be sure, God will not carry this out on the Last Day in a manner that might be intelligible to you now. In fact, there is no other article of faith either which can be understood or comprehended by reason. We cannot even understand our own nature in body and soul, which we see before our eyes and feel. We cannot understand how it happens that we see, hear, talk, think, grow, etc. What, then, might we understand of such lofty things which we cannot see or feel, things that we must apprehend solely by faith?

Paul continues: "For this perishable nature must put on the imperishable, and this mortal nature must put on immortality." He stays with this theme until he arrives at the beautiful text with which he will close. He wants to say that we will not only be enraptured and be carried heavenward and leave all that pertains to the necessities of this life behind, house and home, clothing, shoes, etc., and see all that is on earth perish and burn to ashes, but we shall also put off all that is inborn of the perishable essence, eating, drinking, sleeping, so that we need no longer toil or labor. All of that must be cast off in a moment and be renewed to eternal glory and splendor. We will be changed, not only with regard to place but also with regard to our body, which will then remain unchangeable and imperishable.[59]

54-55. *When the perishable puts on the imperishable, and the mortal puts on immortality, then shall come to pass the saying that is*

---

[59] The fifteenth sermon, preached Saturday, Feb. 1, 1533, ends here.

written: Death is swallowed up in victory. O death, where is
thy victory? O death, where is thy sting?

"Out of the abundance of the heart the mouth speaks" is a common
saying.[60] St. Paul is able to speak about this article at such length
because his heart is filled with it and he is so convinced of it that he
regards all else as nothing by comparison. If his heart were not filled
to overflowing with such thoughts, these words would never occur
to him. Therefore they sound so hazy and strange and incomprehensible to others who do not occupy themselves with such thoughts. But
whoever concerns himself with these matters and reflects on another
life will, I am sure, comprehend and understand them; for Paul speaks
of this subject as though he were already face to face with it. And
because Christ is risen and gives us His resurrection against our sin,
death, and hell, we must advance to where we also learn to say: "O
death, where is thy sting? etc.," although we at present see only the
reverse, namely, that we have nothing but the perishable hanging
about our neck, that we lead a wretched filthy life, that we are subject
to all sorts of distress and danger, and that nothing but death awaits
us in the end.

But the faith that clings to Christ is able to engender far different
thoughts. It can envisage a new existence. It can form an image and
gain sight of a condition where this perishable, wretched form is erased
entirely and replaced by a pure and celestial essence. For since faith
is certain of this doctrine that Christ's resurrection is our resurrection,
it must follow that this resurrection is just as effective in us as it was
for Him — except that He is a different person, namely, true God. And
faith must bring it about that this body's frail and mortal being is dis-
carded and removed and a different, immortal being is put on, with
a body that can no longer be touched by filth, sickness, mishap, misery,
or death but is perfectly pure, healthy, strong, and beautiful, so that
not even the point of a needle can injure it. That will be the power
and the effect, or, as St. Pauls says here, the victory gained by Christ,
which will completely do away with and purge our sin and death with
its attendant frailties, perils, and sufferings of the body.

Note how St. Paul speaks about this life and existence. He views
it not as man himself but as a dress that he must wear now but dis-
cards later and replaces with another. He makes no more of death and
grave than he does of taking off an old torn garment and casting it

60 Cf. Matt. 12:34.

away. To him the resurrection is like putting on a beautiful new garment called *immortalitas,* incorruptibility or immortality. It is spun and woven by Christ's victory. For the victory of Christ, who overcame all in Himself, was wrought for the purpose of clothing you with it and of cleansing you from your sin and death, so that nothing of your corruptible body remains or of anything that the devil infused in you or that derives from him, all sorts of misfortunes and frailties, error and folly, everything except your natural and true body as created by God. For God did not create man that he should sin and die, but that he should live. But the devil inflicted so much shameful filth and so many blemishes on nature that man must bear so much sickness, stench, and misfortune about his neck because he sinned. But now that sin is removed through Christ, we shall be rid of all of that too. All will be pure, and nothing that is evil or loathsome will be felt any longer on earth. However, this is not brought about in any other way than that we first shed this old, evil garment through death. We must be divested of it entirely, and it must turn into dust.

When that comes to pass, Paul says, this will be fulfilled; now we say: *Scriptum est,* but then we shall say: *Factum est.* The time will come when that which is now always preached and spoken about will actually happen and be carried out. And what is that? It is the fact recorded in the words: "Death is swallowed up in victory." St. Paul states that these words are found in Scripture; I really do not know where in Scripture. They seem to be taken from the prophet Hosea, chapter 13:14, where we read: "Shall I ransom them from the power of Sheol? Shall I redeem them from Death? O Death, I will be your poison. O Sheol, I will be your plague (or pestilence)." That is to say: "I will kill you and do away with you." For in Scripture poison and pestilence are regarded as a deadly evil, which quickly destroys and kills a person, for instance, when he is stung by the most venomous adders or when he gets a high, virulent fever or contracts the pestilence. It is natural also for the bite of a snake to bring about a fever. St. Paul may have had that in mind and paraphrased it with a few words.

However, I believe that St. Paul's eyes ranged further and that he wished to include, in addition to Hosea's statement, all similar ones contained in Scripture; for instance, above all the chief verse from which many others are derived, Gen. 3:15, where God says to the serpent: "I will put enmity between you and the woman, and between your seed and her Seed; He shall bruise your head, and you shall bruise His heel." In the Hebrew we find the same word for both *zertreten* and *stechen*.[61] That word really means to bite as a serpent bites as it shoots the venom in. It means to say that the serpent will bite Christ's heel, but He, in turn, will bite its head, that He will be a mortal venom and a pestilence for it, as Hosea interprets from this text. And this verse now prompts this proclamation of St. Paul: "Death is swallowed up in victory." For our Lord Christ brought it about that the venom and the bites of the devil were deadened and completely swallowed up by Him, who crushed his head, that is, who stripped him of all his might and power. In this way we can relate all similar verses found throughout the prophets to this one. They all flow from this one and into this one, so that all of them comprise but one text. For according to His rich Spirit He melts many verses into one and molds a text from these which is supplied by all of Scripture and expresses the meaning of all of Scripture.

Thus Paul now wants to say: "After Christ has accomplished the purpose of His resurrection, then all that is recorded of the victory will be fulfilled, namely, that by means of it both death and hell will be swallowed up and exist no longer." Then one may say: "Death, where is your sting? Hell, where is your spear?" Then this will no longer be proclaimed or heard and believed, but we ourselves will feel and experience it. Then the word will no longer be *Fiat* but *Factum est*. Then we will be face to face with what is now presented to us in words. In the meantime we must cling to this verse and know that what it says will surely come to pass.

Now note these words. Note how forcefully he speaks of death on the basis of Scripture. He pictures him as entirely swallowed up and devoured, with nothing remaining of him who himself devoured and swallowed up all men on earth. We hear furthermore that He Himself will be a poison to death and a pestilence to hell, which will consume all the poison with which the devil killed and destroyed people. For this poison is nothing else than the curse which has passed on to the whole world. It was blown and beaten into us by the devil, and we must all die from it. That is the drink he offered Adam and we all partook of with Adam when we were born. It has coursed through our body and all its members, and it also manifests itself externally by

61 Luther's German Bible renders the Hebrew word שׁוּף with these two words, which mean respectively "crush" and "sting," or "bite."

means of all sorts of distress and sorrow. However, Scripture discloses a salutary medicine and a precious antidote, given us by God in the Word, in which He assures us that He will kill death in return and that He also gives the devil a drink with which he will have to drink himself to death forever. He himself will have to devour his poison, curse, sin, hell, and death which he attached to nature, while we will be saved from these eternally by believing and adhering to the Seed.

"I Myself will do that," He says; "I will be your death and your pestilence." He applies these ugly words, death and pestilence, to Himself; and yet they are so immeasurably comforting. For note what and whom He refers to with these words. He is not a foe of nature. No, He shows that He wishes to help nature and subdue its enemy, death and devil. He has compassion with our misery, for He sees that we are now drowned by the devil's poison and by death and are so submerged in it that we cannot extricate ourselves. He wants to wreak vengeance on him as on His own foe, who poisoned and spoiled His work. Therefore this is a real divine antidote, not taken from a physician's pharmacy but prepared by heaven and given to us through Christ's resurrection. It will be harmless for us, but it will kill and ruin only him who gave and served us this poison. And now, when we begin to believe the article of Christ, the potion is already mixed and drunk which eliminates the poison that he injected into my heart and conscience and also into my body. Now we are saved from the curse, and the same poison which we have in us is now poured out for the devil, so that he has to eat death by us. Thus we have drunk a salutary medicine in Baptism and the Sacrament, which expels and removes our poison. This does not kill me but the very enemy who intended to kill me with it. You see, that is why God employs such figurative language and calls Himself a poison, not a poison for us poor people who once were cumbered with death and pestilence, but a poison against the poison of death and hell. Now we who feel such poison and plague can take comfort from that, assured that God befriends us so greatly that He completely removes these from our body and soul and feeds these to devil and death, that his belly is rent by them.

Poison and pestilence are a death which does not kill suddenly and abruptly; but it kills nevertheless. It gradually makes its way through the whole body until it reaches the heart. That is the way God also treats us. He does not want to carry out the victory over death and devil all of a sudden, but He has this proclaimed for a while for the sake of the elect who are yet to be born. So He begins to mix and prepare the potion to be a *purgatio* or a medication for us, to refresh and to invigorate us but to be poison and death for the devil. This is comparable to a potion prescribed by a physician. This is conducive to a patient's health, but it is poison to a fever. Thus He could well call His medicine or antidote a poison or a pestilence. Here, too, it is true that one poison expels another, that one pestilence kills the other.

This also applies to Christendom now, when Word, Baptism, and the Sacrament are administered and nothing is proclaimed but that Christ died and rose again. That is the only prescription or *purgatio* for our sin and death. That we must take daily and let it work, in order to drive the poison from our heart and take us from death and hell to eternal life. He promised us that; and He commanded us to proclaim it and to believe it. Thereby He brings it about in us daily that it penetrates like a leaven (as Christ says in Matt. 13:33). Then the heart grows and grows in faith and learns to despise and overcome this life and its hardships.[62]

That is the victory by which death is to be swallowed up, so that we need fear death no longer or remain in it. For the heart is already saturated by the Gospel, which shall be poison and pestilence to death. It weakens death from day to day and deprives him of his strength, until he is submerged entirely and disappears. For although he is not yet entirely swallowed up in us, the victory gained by Christ is already present, and through Gospel, Baptism, and faith it has become our victory. On the Last Day, when we have taken off the old, terrestrial, perishable garment and put on a new celestial one, we can destroy him completely with this victory. Then we will remain in life forever; then we will behold and perceive life as we now behold and feel the reverse, namely, that death is in us and that we are stuck in death. The victory appears to be his alone, as he as the lord of the world devours and consumes one person after another up to the Last Day. But nevertheless we know from Scripture that victory was wrested from him by Christ, who began to swallow him up in Himself. And through Him we, too, are spiritually victorious over him. Later we will bury death also physically and do away with him entirely, so

[62] The sixteenth sermon, preached in the afternoon of April 14, 1533, Easter Monday, ends here.

that nothing will be seen or known of him any longer. Instead, we will have nothing but life and bliss.

Then we will really begin to glory joyfully and defiantly and say and sing: "O death, where is thy sting? O hell, where is thy victory?" That is really snapping one's fingers at death and hell and saying: "Dear death, do not bite me, but show your anger with me and kill me. I defy death and hell and challenge them to touch a hair on my head! [63] Where are you now, you vile man-eaters?" Then there will be naught but making game of death, hell, and devil. And as they now boast and jeer at the whole world, saying, "We defy you to escape us!" tables will then be turned. Then we can vent our anger on them and defy them forever and say: "Now let us see what you are able to kill! Of course, you have been enjoined from killing. Now it is your turn to lie there ignominiously and be ridiculed in the bargain." This has already begun through Christ on His own body. He sings this song of defiance against death and hell uninterruptedly: "Dear death, once upon a time you crucified and buried Me too; and you trampled Me underfoot. You assumed that you had gained the victory and had devoured Me. But where are you now? I defy you to pursue Me further!" For death has already been drowned and swallowed up entirely on His body, with not as much as a speck of death's dust remaining on Him. Now we who believe in Him share in this when the hour comes in which we see and feel how death and hell are entirely swallowed up and exterminated. At present, however, we await the hour, assured that this will surely come to pass and that we can already defiantly rely on Christ by faith over against sin, death, and hell.

56-57. *The sting of death is sin, and the power of sin is the Law. But thanks be to God, who gives us the victory through our Lord Jesus Christ.*

St. Paul places these words at the end to explain by the way, as it were, what sort of a sting he has in mind and what kind of a victory it is that swallows up death. He concludes his chapter as he began it, with a brief sermon on the power of Christ's resurrection. He portrays death with a spear with which he slays people. This sting, or spear, he calls sin, and the sharpness or power of sin he calls the Law. These are obscure and odd expressions for us, too. But that is proper

[63] Cf. p. 109, n. 26, above.

for those who strive and hope for another life. For the others, the great mass of people, neither feel nor heed what sin or death is but go their way unconcernedly until they go to hell suddenly and before they are aware of it; in the same way they also fail to understand this language. The Christians, however, must learn this language on themselves as people who daily feel what sin and death are and what power they possess.

Thus St. Paul now calls sin death's spear or weapon, as though he were to say: "If it were not for sin, death would surely have to desist from slaying. But the fact that he does slay us is due to sin. Therefore, whoever is to slay death must do more than merely slay him, namely, first of all slay that which brings about death, and that is sin. It follows that sin is death's weapon and spear, or sword. For as long as a person goes his way and neither feels nor heeds sin, he does not feel and fear death either. But when the hour strikes that man must fidget and die, sin soon appears on the scene and tells him: "Alas! What did you do! How you angered God!" When that really strikes the heart, man cannot endure it, he must despair. And furthermore, if this condition lasts long, he must die in despair. For it is impossible for man to endure a bad conscience when it really lays hold of him and he begins to feel God's wrath. Thus we see some people dying suddenly or committing suicide because of such terror and despair. For this is a sting or a spear that penetrates the heart, so that soul and body have to part over it.

This is what St. Paul means when he speaks of sin, namely, not just an act that is done or committed is real sin, but the sin which is alive and strikes terror to heart and conscience. For while sin lies dormant and neither bites nor plagues us, it is no real sin. But when it is aroused and agitates the heart, it cuts and pierces, so that no man can endure the sting, even though it issues from a slight transgression, unless he is comforted and again healed by the Gospel. If you ask: "Where does death come from?" or: "How does death frighten people so easily and kill them?" you are told here that nothing else but sin does that. Sin is nothing but spear and cannonball, indeed death's thunder and lightning, through which he carries out his work.

But where does sin come from? Or how does it happen that it is so very strong and able to kill and slay? St. Paul says: "I shall tell you: 'The power of sin is the Law.'" Who has ever heard that said about God's commandment and law, which, after all, was given and instituted as holy and good by God? And still St. Paul can say that sin would be feeble and dead and could effect nothing if it were not for the Law. The Law renders sin alert and strong and prompts it to cut and to pierce. If it depended on us, sin would very likely remain dormant forever. But God is able to awaken it effectively through the Law. When the hour comes for sin to sting and to strike, it grows unendurable in a moment. For the Law dins this into your ears and holds the register of your sins before your nose: "Do you hear? You committed this and you committed that in violation of God's commandments, and you spent your whole life in sin. Your own conscience must attest and affirm that." In that way sin already shows its power. It frightens you so that the whole world becomes too confining for you. It agitates and strikes until you must needs despair. And there is neither escape nor defense here. For the Law is too strong, and your own heart abets it, which itself denounces you and condemns you to hell. Therefore sin requires nothing else than God's law. Where that enters the heart, sin is already alive and able to kill man if it wants to, unless he lays hold of this victory, which is Christ, our Lord.

If the Law has such bad results, why, then, did God issue it? Would it not be far better if there were no Law? To be sure, it would be better for us. And yet it cannot be dispensed with. For it is incompatible with God that He should be pleased to let us have our way and do as we wish. It is true that He is longsuffering with us all before He manifests His wrath. He permits many people to follow their own course, who never feel the Law and sin or ever think of God's wrath, but, instead, disdain the Law and sin and, moreover, deride them, no matter how one threatens them with death and hell. But finally God is constrained to show them what both the Law and sin are able to do, to deter them from making sport of it. To be sure, God may wink at this for a while, but when the hour comes in which the Law really raps at your door to find you at home and demands an accounting, it will not be so easy to ignore it. Then one begins to lament and wail: "Alas! What did I do? What will become of me now?" Then we observe the meaning of the words: "The Law is the power of sin." That is why St. Paul elsewhere [64] also calls it a law of death and an office of death, which proclaims death and is the cause of death. Even if there were no other sermon or rule, the entire world could be preached to death solely with this.

[64] Cf. Rom. 7:6; 2 Cor. 3:7.

For the one follows the other: When the Law shines into one's heart and reveals sin, the latter imediately becomes alive and strong; and sin brings death with it. Therefore it is pertinent to say that sin is the sting of death, that sin alone, and no one else, kills. But sin comes from nothing else than the Law. This does not mean that the Law first creates and makes sin. No, sin is existent already before the Law appears, and it remains with us, because it is born with us and we are conceived in sin. It means that sin is not properly recognized and felt unless this light is kindled in the heart; nor can sin attain its power unless it is awakened by the Law. But when the Law appears, it shows us that we are completely steeped in sin and lying in God's wrath, so that we must say, as St. Bernard says of himself: "I thought I was sitting in a rose garden, and am not aware that I am sitting among murderers.[65] But it becomes unbearable when the heart feels this; for it beholds and feels nothing but spears aimed and hurled at it, so that it must die. That teaches us effectually that works do not avail to atone for sin or to silence the Law. For it holds man in its meshes, from which he is unable to extricate himself. He can neither ward it off nor render it satisfaction, no matter how he may run hither and yon and do what he will. The more he torments himself with works, the worse it becomes.

St. Paul's words, however, point out how this is accomplished: "Thanks be to God, who gives us the victory through our Lord Jesus Christ!" That sermon is different from that of Moses, for it reveals the Christians' consolation against death's sting and sin's power. It is true and necessary and right that the Law reveals your sin and accuses you; and sin, in turn, has the right to kill you and death to devour you. That is beyond dispute and argument. For both your own testimony and God's Word are against you there. However, there is help in the fact that the Man Jesus Christ has come and has assumed and borne our sin and death, which we had justly deserved, and that He now steps forth in our behalf, confronts the Law, sin, and death, and says: "I am of the same flesh and blood; these are My brothers and sisters. What they did I did; and I paid for it. Law, if you want to condemn them, condemn Me. Sin, if you want to bite and kill them, bite Me. Death, if you want to consume and devour, devour Me." That is what happened when He stood before the judge, Pilate. There He was accused and sentenced to death as a sinner.

[65] The reference is probably to *Meditationes devotissimae,* ch. 14: *Inimici mei animam meam circumdederunt: corpus, mundus, et diabolus.*

Therefore He also calls Himself a sinner in Scripture. In Ps. 41:4: "O Lord, be gracious to Me; heal Me, for I have sinned against Thee." Also in Ps. 69:9: "The insults of those who insult Thee have fallen on Me," that is, "Whatever they did against You to deserve death, that I did." Therefore also the Law attached itself to Him and condemned Him, sin crucified Him and pierced Him to death, and death carried Him under the sod. They did everything to Him, everything they were capable of. For God "did not spare His own Son," St. Paul declares in Rom. 8:32, "but gave Him up for us all." They all tested their might on Him.

But thereby they failed by far to accomplish what they had intended to do. For through the very event by which they expected to exterminate Him and to win the victory He emerged again and said to the Law, sin, and death: "Do you not know that I am your Lord and God? What right do you have to accuse and to slay your Lord? Therefore you shall do this no more; but, rather, I will accuse and condemn you and dispatch you so thoroughly that you will henceforth have no claim on anyone who believes in Me. For what I did, I did for their sake." For His own person this would not have been necessary, and they would have been obliged to let Him go unharmed. But now He has stepped into our place, and in our behalf He has let the Law, sin, and death pounce on Him. He has not only removed these from us, but He has also vanquished them completely and cast them at His feet. Now they are overcome for us and no longer have any right to or power over us. In that way we have a complete victory in Christ, now spiritually by faith but later also physically and visibly.

Now a Christian must learn to apprehend this and to avail himself of it when the battle is joined and the Law attacks him and tries to accuse him, when sin wants to slay him and thrust him into the jaws of hell, and when his own conscience tells him: "You have done this, and you have done that; you are a sinner and are deserving of death, etc." Then the Christian should answer confidently: "It is unfortunately true that I am a sinner and that I have surely deserved death. So far you are right. But still you shall not condemn and slay me. Another, who is named my Lord Christ, shall stay your hand. You accused and you murdered Him innocently. But do you remember how you vainly dashed full tilt against Him and burned yourself and thereby forfeited all your rights to me and to all Christians? For

He both bore and overcame sin and death not for Himself but for me. Therefore I concede you no rightful accusation against me. I can, rather, justly assert my rights against you for trying to attack me without cause and despite the fact that you were already condemned and overcome by Him, which deprived you of any right to assail and accuse me. And although you may now attack and devour me according to the flesh, you shall not accomplish or gain anything by this. You must eat your own sting and choke to death on it. For I am no longer the man you are looking for; I am no longer a child of man, but a child of God, for I am baptized in His blood and on His victory, and I am vested with all His possessions.

You see, in this way Christians must fortify themselves with this victory of Christ. With it they must repel the devil. They must not give way to him in a dispute, but say: "How dare you accuse and harass a Christian? Do you not know who my Lord is and what He is able to do?" There is nothing better — for anyone who can do it — than to deride and defy him and say cheerfully: "If you want to be a villain, go ahead, but take heed and do not bother me! and do not expect any thanks for this either.[66] If you are so eager to sting and to strike, go up to Him who is seated above and do battle with Him. If you have any designs on me, lodge your accusation there, before your Judge and mine, and let us see what you will accomplish." But he does not want to go there, for he is well aware that he has lost out there and that he is already sentenced and slain by Him. Therefore he avoids going there as he avoids the cross. Nor does he go to the impudent, wild, and coarse people who are unconcerned about sin and death, for he already owns these. No, he wants to attack only us who seek Christ and who would fain be rid of sin and death. He is intent on tearing Christ from our heart and on frightening and oppressing us with sin and death, so that we might despair and surrender to him completely. Therefore we must again rebuff him and point him to the victory which is ours in Christ. In that way we must embrace Christ and hold to Him, so that the devil cannot approach us; for he knows very well that he is unable to accomplish anything if we but cling steadily and firmly to this by faith.

This is the beautiful sermon for Christians which shows us how we, through Christ's victory, rid ourselves of sin's sting, which kills us, and of the power of the Law, which drives this sting into us. And it

[66] Cf. p. 88, n. 15, above.

shows us that in the end this sting will be completely destroyed in us. And now St. Paul appropriately concludes with a song which he sings: "Thanks and praise be to God, who gave us such a victory!" We can join in that song and in that way always celebrate Easter, praising and extolling God for a victory that was not won or achieved in battle by us — it is far too sublime and great for that — but was presented and given to us by the mercy of God. He had compassion with our misery, from which no one could rescue us, and He sent His Son and let Him enter the battle. He laid these enemies, sin, death, and hell, low and retained the victory. He transferred this victory to us, so that we may say it is our victory. It is just as if it had been gained by us. The only condition is that we must accept this sincerely and not give God the lie, as they do who presume to overcome their sin and death by themselves. Nor dare we be found ungrateful for this, as vulgar, false Christians do, but we must keep this in our heart in firm faith and confirm ourselves in this and always be engrossed in such a message of thanks and sing of this victory in Christ. And in faith in this we must cheerfully depart this life, until we experience this victory also in our own body. May God help us to that end through the same dear Son. To Him be glory and honor forever.[67]

Amen.

[67] The seventeenth sermon, preached April 27, 1533, Misericordias Domini Sunday, ends here and concludes the series.

LECTURES ON
1 TIMOTHY

Translated by
RICHARD J. DINDA

The Lectures of Dr. Martin on the
First Epistle to Timothy

CHAPTER ONE

I⊤ is the intention of Paul [1] that we should be rich in the Word of God (1 Cor. 1:5), because our adversary, the devil, prowls around (1 Peter 5:8). Therefore it is not only pleasing to God but also necessary for us that we abide in the Word of God, and we have no other weapons (Eph. 6:10-17). Lest we become lazy, then, we want to devote ourselves to our food, and while we have the light, we want to give attention to the light; because the time will come when we would be glad to study if we could. I have taken up the Epistle to Timothy, in which Paul establishes not only the bishop but all the ecclesiastical orders. The epistle is not didactic, and it does not strive to establish basic teaching. Rather, it establishes the church and sets it in order. And yet, in the midst of this process Paul does not neglect to add very important doctrinal subjects. It was characteristic of the Christians to be daily involved with these subjects.

1. *Paul, an apostle.* So also we generally write to our friends differently from the way we write to strangers. After all, our friends have observed our habits of speech, and from such habits they have looked into our heart. Paul maintains this usage to address his disciples in more familiar fashion than the rest of the churches, which he addresses quite timidly and respectfully because of his reverence for Christ. With his disciples Paul also speaks a bit more confidently. You know why he boasts this way over his calling, because it is every preacher's own certain boast that he knows he is pursuing the doctrine commanded to him and demanded of him. So those who do a bad job of teaching sin on both sides. On the one hand, they have the authority and the ministry, as in the case of the papists, but they do not teach; the factious spirits and heretics, on the other hand, run into it, but they do not have the call. When the call is present, genuine doctrine should also be present, so that one can teach, etc. The call is as significant as the doctrine. For where there is a legitimate call, our Lord God does not let the Word fail. For example, however wicked the papists may be, they still do preach Christ's suffering and

[1] Luther began these lectures on Jan. 13, 1528.

all the articles that we also preach. So they do have the call. In fact, the Gospel gives such dignity to this ministry that it may be of service to what remains of the Word. There is, then, a very great power resident in the call. Where it is a legitimate call, there God is not completely absent. In a marvelous way He calls and draws those who are His, even though the wicked keep on sinning. But the call never exists without doctrine. On the contrary! Where there is no call, damage is almost always involved. We read in Jer. 23:21, "I did not send you." He always reproaches their very doctrine whenever he reproaches their running and rashness. Indeed, even Enthusiasts preach a little of the Gospel. So Paul is not boasting in vain that he has been called to preach. Now, we have either a divine call or a human one. Our calling today, unlike that of the apostles, does not come directly from heaven. Rather, the state calls, or I do it myself. Also, there are fraternal calls through men. Yet they also come from Christ, because I am called in this way the same as if Christ were calling. After all, we must be subject to each other in love. So Paul boasts more than someone else might because he is an apostle "by command of our Savior," and he says in substance: "I have a call from heaven. I have been called miraculously." This is something that had to happen in the primitive church.

Of the Lord our Hope. This is an addition and a note of familiarity. He does not speak thus to the churches. That calling of his indicates many things, as if he were saying: "My dear Timothy, you know me." Later, in 2 Tim. 3:10 ff., he says: "You know my teaching. You have observed all of the many things I have suffered and the false brothers I have had. You have seen from how many directions spies have set up attacks on me. And you know, too, that I have no hope other than Christ. You have worked together with me in persecution, and you know that I trust in no man. So I write to you in a more familiar fashion, because Christ is our Hope."

2. *To Timothy.* He also writes this way to Titus. *My true child.*[2] He distinguishes this son Timothy from his other sons. In another epistle (Phil. 2:20) he commends Timothy because, as he says, "I had no one like him, . . . They all look after their own interests." In sum he says: "This is my best-loved son. He does the same things I do, is

---

[2] Luther here comments on the Latin word *germano* ("my own true"), which does not occur here in the Vulgate text; *dilecto* is used instead. But in a similar emotional situation in Phil. 4:3 *germane compar* ("my own true yokefellow") is used.

interested in the same things, endures the same things, etc. He mirrors his father in all his ways and mannerisms." He also writes (2 Cor. 12:18): "I sent Titus to you. . . . Did we not take the same steps?" Furthermore, his other sons did not have so close a relationship. Timothy was his son not in the flesh but by the Spirit, for Paul had fathered him in the Holy Spirit through the Word.

Grace, mercy, and peace. This is the forgiveness of sins, peace, joy, and the soul's freedom from care. He clearly distinguishes between these and gifts of the world. He also adds a third word which he does not generally use in his letters to the churches — "mercy." Why does he add it here? Every theologian has been established as a bishop of the church to bear the troubles of everyone in the church. He stands on the battle line. He is the prime target of all attacks, difficulties, anxieties, disturbances of consciences, temptations, and doubts. All these hit the bishop where it hurts. Still greater trials follow. The princes of the world and the very learned seek him out. He is made a spectacle for both devils and angels. So then, it is enough to pray for two things for the rest: that they be in grace and peace; yet for a bishop one must add "mercy," not only that God would deign to give His grace that he might have forgiveness of sins and peace but that He would have constant mercy on him, that He would heap many gifts on him with which to serve his brothers; also, that God would grant him mercy because he constantly endures great tribulation. Were he to have no other temptation, it would be enough that he must battle with devilish heretics, who direct their efforts to turn away the hearers and brothers — a most troublesome situation. Satan meets him on the field and assails him in a spiritual battle. Satan takes from him the beautiful statements of Scripture and corrupts them, just as he did with Christ in the desert (Matt. 4:6, 10): "He will give His angels charge," and "if you will worship me." The office of a bishop is a great responsibility, one that Christ first held in the church. Therefore there is need to abide in prayer; that is why one must pray for grace and peace. Each man has his own temptation. But the bishop is the womb of the Lord Jesus, in which he carries others through the Word, to comfort the sad, convince the foolish, and teach the unlearned.

From God the Father. Because that peace which exists in our conscience is deeply involved in troubles, nothing is less apparent in Christians than peace. Yet it is a peace from God the Father and from Christ, who was crucified, as well as from the Father of the Crucified. "In the world you have tribulation" (John 16:33). Therefore where that peace is preserved, it signifies the peace of Him who was crucified. Whoever wants the grace of God must have it spiced with the wrathful madness of the world, Satan, and his own flesh. Mercy must be surrounded with the base cruelty of the world, the flesh, and the devil.

3. *As I urged you.* Here you see two things. First there is the example of Paul — an example that he reveals to us in his great concern. Whenever Paul goes away, he cannot rest until he writes an encouraging letter. He did hardly anything else for the 24 years during which he was an example to all the bishops to have concern, not just when they are present with the Word but also in prayer, etc. — to think how they may preserve their hearers, the churches, in the true faith, lest they fall away because of tyrants or bellwethers. This is an example of apostolic solicitude. The second thing we see is his warning to us not to feel smug. It was not for nothing that he wrote to the Thessalonians (1 Thess. 3:8, 5): "Now we live, since you stand fast," and "We sent . . . to you for fear that somehow the tempter had tempted you, etc." What forced Paul to write this way was that he knew the fury and cleverness of Satan, as he says there: "Why, where I am present, he rises up against my face. What would he not do if I were absent? He never sleeps; he never stops." Paul's request is not absolute. "As I exhorted you" would have been better.[3] *Remain.* He approaches Timothy in friendly fashion. He avoids a word of command. He does not say, "I commanded you," but rather, "I urged, I exhorted." After all, in the church the arrangement should be that each man be a joyful servant of God. No one in the church ought to be forced; such compulsion does not please God. Under the guidance of the Spirit, a willing people ought to act freely — not as the pope has learned, to go at everything with thundering threats. That is the way of Moses. In the church he advises the disciples that their service should be joyful, voluntary, and free. *Remain.* Why? To do nothing? To make money? No! Rather "that you may charge." This is an elegant expression. Obviously to charge those false teachers and his hearers not to preoccupy themselves. "You should do the work of two men: of an evangelist and of a teacher. Charge them not to teach; charge the pupils not to listen," because we cannot resist them.

---

[3] Luther means to say *hortatus sum* would have been a better translation for the Greek παρεκάλεσα than the Vulgate's *rogavi*.

If we close the mouth of one, ten more appear. We cannot avoid the false apostles and false teachers. We are not allowed to kill them, as the papists do, but we may teach against them with mouth and Word, even though we may not battle them with the sword. If they do not come to their senses, let us avoid them; let us abandon them to their own inclinations. So it is bearable when he says, "that you may charge." "To teach any different doctrine" is an elegant expression. In Acts it is translated differently — "to speak in other tongues." We Germans also speak this way: *Johannes Hus ist ein ander und neu Paulus.* So also here: "You should charge them not to become new authors who are teaching something different and better." With this expression he means the arrogance of the false apostles, because they cannot be content. They cannot stay in the pattern. They cannot, as Jude says (v. 3) "contend for the faith which was once . . . delivered." For wicked men will come, and they will not persevere. They always have this fault of teaching something different and new. A wicked spirit, not rooted in solid doctrine, causes this. It always looks for something new and a better doctrine. "Timothy, you tell them to remain in their former pattern, lest they develop sects." This fault the new author, the Gentile Cato, has. The religious call this the vice of singularity, as in the case of the monk who was discontent with his own rule and wanted a hair shirt. In my order the older monks used to fight hard against singularity, and that was good. The same thing happens in senates and legislatures. When the head man does not want to stay in the realm of the usual but wants to be wiser than the rest, he upsets everything. Bishops do the same thing. We must not hope, however, to be free of such disrupting influences. Therefore the bishop and those of us who are in the offices of the Word must be urged to charge Christians to remain in their former pattern, which was handed down from the apostles.

4. *To occupy themselves with myths.* Paul again speaks of myths deprecatingly when he speaks of a very spiritual spirit. It has to be the Word of the Lord; the flesh is of no avail.[4] He firmly calls them myths, because everyone who departs from the doctrine once delivered does not teach the Lord's Word but myths which are his own dreams and mere poison. Today the Enthusiasts teach nothing but myths, because they depart from the doctrine once delivered. They are therefore heterodox teachers who, with much boasting, teach only

[4] Cf. John 6:63.

myths. He attaches this word scornfully to their boasting, where they boast about revelations, spirits, and absolute truth. Is salutary doctrine mere myths to Paul? No. Their hearers must be admonished not to be impressed with words like "glory" and "God." They make a great show, but actually it is all myths.

With genealogies. They were involved in these too. These have nothing to do with Christianity or Judaism. The Jews were of the opinion that they were a separate and unique people; that if any of the Gentiles were saved, they had to participate in the Jews' rituals. This is what they used to call incorporating with the Jews. That is where the power lay to preserve their people, genealogy, and polity; to know how many proselytes they had. It is an article of faith and an absolute necessity to know of what tribe you were born. You see, Moses makes distinctions among the tribes, and that is the reason for the necessity. They consider that article of the same significance as the Enthusiasts consider bread and wine. Even if some of this still existed, it is not important now. There is no longer a distinction of tribes or differences of title. As a result, we now have infinite and unending genealogies. Still, it was necessary for Christ to have been of the tribe of Judah, because so it was written. But what they later observed among the other tribes is of no importance. In this way, they develop many thousands of superstitions from one example. After all, what need is there for the other tribes to be designated along with the tribe of Judah? Let it be void the moment Christ would come. This is the way they distinguished their people from the Gentiles, as the great question arises in Matthew and Luke: if we ignore faith in Christ, do the Jews still stand in that glory? You are inferior people, because the Jews are sealed with a certain number and you are not. Thus [5] miserable souls of the Gentiles have perished because of such worthless ideas, and they cannot be brought to a definite end.

These [6] are outstanding precepts and descriptions of wicked doctrines — that wicked doctrines place high value on their titles and are called spiritual precepts, the traditions of Moses and the fathers. But they are actually pure myth. That would be enough, but this is the worst of it, that they carried the condition that they never achieved the goal. Later on (2 Tim. 3:7) he writes: "They will listen to any-

---

[5] We have read *sic* for *si.*

[6] The lecture of Jan. 14 begins at this point.

body and can never arrive at a knowledge of the truth." Hellfire is in the human tradition, as Paul writes to Titus (1:14), "of men who reject the truth." It would be tolerable to keep human tradition except that it gives rise to questions. Let what is doubtful be doubtful. So he has given the genealogies the genuine description — "endless." This is the way our Enthusiasts first began to have doubts about the Sacrament. Now they will slide along from one error into another, and finally they will slip so far as to deny God. Thus one question always gives rise to another. This is what happened with the decrees of the pope. One decree generated 10 more, and one council generated 10 others. Our theologians had the same experience with the *Sentences.*[7] Meanwhile, what result has come from losing a genuine knowledge of Christ? As he says later (v. 5), "The aim of our charge" is that one believe in Christ and love his neighbor. Here you know what is involved. Beyond this there is no way of finding the goal.

How many rules and prayers and strange regulations have the monks used? Having abandoned the chief doctrine, they generally devote themselves to inconsistent and endless doctrines. Not only do they go on endlessly; they also require fruitful creativity, provide a good deal of work. They generate endless questions, the one rising from the other. He wants to say: "You keep us mighty busy with those questions of yours. They beget as their offspring another question. That is, they produce one doubt after another." That is wonderful fruit indeed! Scholastic theology was like that, with everything uncertain and yet requiring great effort. One teaches, or he learns, the fundamentals of Scotus, and later he has nothing except uncertainty and doubt. But if I believe in Christ, I love my brother, I carry my cross; I am not tossed on an uncertain sea, but I have this confidence, that my call is God-pleasing, because that is His Word. First, these genealogies are unending. Second, they are restless and uncertain. This is the restlessness of a reed stirred by the wind — a great achievement. The Enthusiasts are so busy with these thoughts that they do not listen. Satan has blinded them and now possesses them.

Rather. It is the customary trick of all false doctrines to neglect "godly edifying." They have a head swollen with their own thoughts and their heart obsessed with their own speculations. We have enough

---

[7] Luther often criticized the proliferation of the *Sentences.* Cf. p. 85, n. 12, above.

examples of this today. The Enthusiasts write one book after another. In these they teach faith and love, but they urge that which they have in their heart. Then Satan assails them. He allows them neither time nor place to think about anything else, because they want to bring this to the people. When this occurs, they want to edify, but nothing happens, so they never do edify. "Godly edifying" occurs in Paul's writings as in 1 Cor. 3: "I have built upon stone," [8] and in Eph. 2:20: "Christ Jesus Himself being the cornerstone." To edify is nothing else but that I be planted and prepared by the Word of faith and love as a habitation for God so that I begin to believe that through this faith Christ lives in me and I am built on Christ. Timothy, then, should urge the good bishops that this faith, etc. They say, however: "The matter of faith is easy. We have to dig into and carefully investigate the Scriptures." He describes very carefully the character and genius of the spirits. When they have given much thought to their own ideas and then are asked about faith, there is no answer, no "godly edifying" that relates to God or the things of God. God is the Builder. But Paul does not mean this here. He means instead that which relates to God, that is, the spiritual edifying in Christ. He asserts that to build is to urge that faith carefully, to root it, to protect it, that people may grow in faith and love. All people are children, sucking infants in their faith, for faith overcomes death and holds this life in contempt. To be so built on Christ is [9] to be firmly fixed, so that we hold not only gold but also life and death in contempt. We have this doctrine still written down on a tablet but not yet expressed in life. You haven't reached the highest level of doctrine, have you? Yet we are all Christians.

5. *The aim of our charge* looks to this goal, that you not doubt, etc. This is the aim of all charges and laws — of God as well as of man — in all the world. It is the law of a good conscience. This is a beautiful text. "The aim" is not to increase questions and to leave consciences unsure after all their difficulties but to bring consciences to the point that they know this for sure. This is the "aim of our charge": that they know how their relationship with God in this world stands. The man who knows languages well certainly can come up with a word, because he knows the "aim" of languages. When he hears a strange statement, he says that it does not relate to his language. So, too, in spiritual matters. When a man knows how he stands with God,

[8] The reference is perhaps to 1 Cor. 3:10: "I laid a foundation."

[9] We have read *est* for *et*.

with people, with the devil, and with sin, he sees every aim. That no person can do from human traditions. Were a Carthusian monk to wear a hair shirt for a hundred years, he would not realize his aim, he would not know how to please God. But if anyone believes in Christ and loves his brother, he is certain that he is pleasing God. Then he is satisfied and content. But if a Carthusian keeps his rule, he still is afraid that it is not enough, that is, that it is not the be-all-and-end-all of certainty, that the rule does not have an end, that the rule does not mean what he is striving for and what he stands in, and that the law thus does not come to an end and make no further demands.

What is the "aim of our charge"? *Love.* This is the full thunder-clap against a human doctrine that cannot reflect love from a pure heart, etc. Paul gives a beautiful description: a faith from an un-pretending heart is the tree, or root. Its fruit is love. With individual phrases, he punctures wicked doctrines.

First, *a pure heart.* What is this? Titus 1:15: "To the pure all things are pure." What value is there in your teaching people by genealogies and myths the purities of the Law (as also the Enthusiasts do) but not the purities of the heart? The pure heart simply does not get stuck in anything, not in shamelessness, properly called greed and lust. This expression has a wider application. You see, a pure heart loves nothing except God, as Christ explains in Matt. 5:8. I have an impure heart when I become attached to anything beside the mercy of God. A psalm says: "They purify my raiment, etc." [10] But what is inside? Outside they are righteous, but inside they are abominable, because they trust in their own works, and from this they develop their own laws, etc., and think: "If I keep these laws, I have a kindly God; if I don't, He will be angry." This is the most impure and wicked heart of all. Even the prostitute's heart that keeps thinking about a man is not so shameless. This is the heart of a man who takes his own merits to heart. He evaluates God according to the image which he imagines in his heart. He sees neither his own sin nor the righteous-ness of God. The Law therefore demands that you have a pure heart, that you reject all your own righteousness, that you place no con-fidence in righteousness, power, or wealth, but in the mercy of God. The pure heart, then, is one that knows that it is saved solely by the

[10] The passage Luther had in mind has not been identified.

mercy of God and that it is special for that same reason. That heart says: "No matter how holy and learned I am in my life among men, I still live as if I didn't know this. I occupy thrones. I live with David. But I live as if I were not aware of that. I live as if I had no honor. My heart is free of the pleasure in those things, but I cling to the mercy of God." And this heart sees God and knows how God feels about the desires and later the power of an angel, of man, of the devil. Purity of heart brings this about. The others say: "Only if you are circumcised will you have protected your family lines." But this man sees neither sin nor righteousness, neither God nor man. In Isaiah a beautiful garment was wantonly smeared when someone threw a handful of manure into his eyes. Yet it didn't bother him. This is not illumination but blinding and blurring of the eyes.

Second, *a good conscience.* When a heart in sin has been purified of all the things we have already mentioned, then there is immediately a conscience which says: "I trust only in God's mercy, which sin does not sting." If sin does sting it, yet it does not lose faith. It is a conscience which trusts in and clings to the mercy of God. First, the heart must be pure; then follows a good conscience. To summarize, they run along side by side.

Third, if the heart is pure, the conscience is sincere. But what does *faith* do? This is a rebuke against the doctrine of wicked men who even boast of their faith. But their faith is partly pretended, partly genuine, because their heart is not pure. If it were genuine, it would make them have a pure heart and a good conscience. Indeed, they do boast of such a heart and conscience, but it does not follow that way. Faith, then, purifies hearts. Next, it is the nature of faith that it establishes a good conscience toward God and all men; for it teaches me that I must trust in Christ alone as Savior, because His suffering has redeemed me. Where this condition exists, purity of heart follows shortly after. That speaks the rule: "My own energy does not save me." In this way all those idols in which I have trusted fall down. This pure heart is not pure in the sense that it is so in its own thoughts. That I have called an impure heart, as if an artist were composing his own work, or as if a mother were performing her function. But the pure heart must abandon the world, which is a woman, etc. The pure heart is to cut off all these things and look to itself alone. Some people have, with Satan's help, a softness — tears, for instance. But those spiritual consequences, as the monks call them, are very suspect. A man can do his work and his wife can cook, and both can have very pure hearts because they can say: "My Lord God, this work pleases You. I am performing my task according to Your command." They believe that God is in the midst of their ordinary business. On the other hand, a monk has an impure heart. Christ was a light amid the spittle and uncleanness of the body. Yet, He had the purest heart. The world is that which comes from the devil, avarice, for example. He has a pure heart who has the Word of God and trusts alone, etc. The false prophets, then, are the most impure when they boast about their purity most. Of course, they feel smug; they act boldly, as did Peter and Paul. They dare with great stubbornness to do their own building. That, to be sure, is a stubborn conscience but not a good conscience. They always take their own works first. This disturbs the conscience, as is written in Ecclesiasticus.[11] It listens to no man. It never comes back. It goes along weakly with the pious. This is not the case with the bold. Sincere faith believes in Christ alone. This is God's building, when people are instructed toward a sincere faith, a good conscience, and a pure heart. Once they have these, then follows the end and result of that knowledge — love. God has loved me; therefore I also, etc. Paul cannot omit the chief points. This is to build silver, gold, and precious stones; you bring in false teachers; you have taught well.

6. *From these.* He intends to describe the Gospel of those theologians. To be sure, they do teach these things,[12] but they are inconsistent spirits. They have false pretenses. They let this their own meaning of the Law remain and neglect faith, love, and the good conscience. They have something else before their eyes: that they keep asking to whose tribe you belong, that one must find and serve holy God. That is what *swerving from* is, swerving away from the scope and aim of the charge. They fabricate for themselves another faith, another intent of the Law. Moses says: "Circumcise your sons. Separate those tribes." The Law, therefore, demands those works. Because they do not see that the Law leads to an acknowledgment of sin and to thoughts of our own weakness, they are led away from faith into works. *Into vain discussion.* We have already heard this in the lec-

[11] The Weimar editor suggests Ecclus. 9:18, but the reference is probably to Wisd. of Sol. 17:11.

[12] Pure heart, good conscience, sincere faith.

tures on Titus.[13] They are not theologians but prattlers.[14] They do not want to teach about God. Rather they teach empty talk, gossip. To neglect faith and yet to teach — what could that accomplish except something of this sort: it has the appearance of piety, but it is empty talk? In such talk the heart cannot have confidence. On such talk it cannot stand firm. And with such talk it surely cannot establish for itself the serene calm of conscience. This is what I have not been able to see. The saintlier I have been, the more uncertain. So I say: "Despair of all things. Throw yourself on Christ. He cannot fail you." Then I know where I must abide.

7. *Desiring.* Oh, how beautifully he gives it to them. He does not keep quiet about their attractive appearance. They are empty talkers, but most people don't realize this, for they are very learned *teachers of the Law.* With that title they strip the apostle of his authority. You see, when Paul was converted, he was a young fellow. He had not yet become a teacher of the Law but was still a student. "We are teachers of the Law, and this makes a big difference among the common people, for they look at our appearance and not at our doctrine." But Paul gives them the needle. "They desire" — they boast that they are such men, and among the Jews they are respected as such men, but actually they are not, because they do not have the "aim" of the Law. To be sure, they see, as above, but they do not understand — and Paul connects this very neatly — what they state and decree. There are two things which the teachers of the Law do: first, they speak; second, they teach from Scripture. However, they do not understand Scripture on the law of circumcision. The text given by Moses is a good one, but they do not understand it. They assert their own doctrine, but they do not understand it, because they do not see the end of the Law. Whatever strange language they cook up and use they do not understand. "Look, Moses says: 'Whoever has kept this work.'" This is their law. There are two things: they err as to the sense of Scripture, and they bring in a new sense. Thus today our Enthusiasts say: "This is the body . . . ." The wording is correct. But then they add their own interpretations. That becomes their law, and yet they remain uncertain.

[13] Luther had lectured on the passage in question, Titus 1:10, the previous Nov. 19. Cf. *Luther's Works,* 29, p. 35.

[14] Luther contrasts *theologi* with *mathaeologi,* a word patterned after the Greek ματαιολογία used in this verse and meaning "idle talk." Cf. *Luther's Works,* 13, p. 81, where Luther applies the word to Zwingli.

Without understanding.[15] Paul is speaking from experience about the wicked teachers who discuss Moses' allegorical words of Scripture but certainly do not understand them. It is necessary, then, that they set up something out of their own heads and arrange the words into their "correct" sense according to what they have imagined. Afterwards they say, "This is God's Word," and "Verily, He says." And they say this because they do not understand what they are setting up. They are very eager to teach, for they have more than a mad passion solely for the applause and good will of the people if they have these. The more this passion pursues them, the more daring they become. But they become daring not at their own risk but at the risk of others. They begin a doctrine which they have not tested at their own risk. But once they have begun it, they run away. So it is with Carlstadt, Müntzer, and Zwingli. Thus no good teacher who boasts of the Spirit sneaks away when danger appears. They are daring until they are among their own kind. Müntzer was a man of supreme boldness. But after he was captured, he became a follower in all things. Our dogma is indeed very precious because of what we read in Matt. 16. Yet we are very timid and cannot become so daring. I used to be afraid of everyone and would yield to everyone when I could, until I saw clearly. Christian truth, therefore, has humble and timid declarers. Granted that they have a most sure doctrine, yet they are weak in the faith, apprehensive. We carry this treasure, not in iron chests, but in small clay vessels. Today I stand, etc. So it is with trembling that we busy ourselves in the presence of God with our salvation. That is, they declare and assert and are proud and stubborn. To be sure, they teach the words of the Law, but they do not understand them. They assert what they do not understand. The Arians read the text "was the Word"[16] but did not understand it, and they kept finding their own interpretation there. I really hate teachers who are bold at another's risk. I love those the more who begin at their own risk and lose their life as they confess their error.

8. *We know that the Law.* This is a fine passage about the understanding, or knowledge, of the Law. Paul explains it more fully in Rom. 7. Now the false prophets argue: "Why do you condemn us for our doctrine? We are not following human traditions or human interpretations. We establish our idea on Scripture and the Word of God."

[15] The lecture of Jan. 15 begins at this point.
[16] John 1:1.

They believe they have overcome. Let them follow along with us in Scripture and let them grasp Scripture. This is the war against heresy, against heathenism, against human traditions. They make this objection to Paul: "When we teach the Sabbath and genealogies, we are teaching the Law itself. Thus we teach, not our words, but the words of Scripture." "The flesh does not profit" (John 6:63) and "He sits at the right hand of God" (Mark 16:19). That they use Scripture as we do gives them a very wicked weapon. The battle, then, is over the correct use of Scripture, not over Scripture itself; as Paul here battles not over the Law but over the use of the Law. So also we now are not fighting over the remission of sins through Christ, for we are in agreement there. Rather, we are battling over the exercise of forgiveness of sins and justification. They say: "There is no active redemption except on the cross. The flesh? It is abominable that you say that there is forgiveness of sins in the Lord's Supper, since it takes place on the cross alone." They have a foolish spirit. We say: "The remission of sins, considered as the miraculous act, took place on the cross, where Christ accomplished this. But whom would this forgiveness benefit? There it is a matter of pure action. He reconciled the Father with His blood, tears, and death. But if this were not preached, as Christ says in the last chapter of Luke (Luke 24:47), who would benefit from the fact that this forgiveness has been obtained and accomplished? It would be of no use to me if it were not applied." They do not see what the remission of sins is and what its function is. When someone says, "Look, Christ has done this for you," then this is applied to me through the Word. Or he may say: "Eat this bread, that is, His body." Likewise they say that in the Lord's Supper Christ does not die. Therefore He has not been eaten on our behalf but has died on our behalf. Isn't this sheer madness? Remission of sins does not walk around on earth or in heaven. It's something which has already been accomplished. They are not separating the function of forgiveness from the achievement of it. Another example: Christ's birth has taken place. But preaching it brings the incarnation into my heart. Now I use it. Unless the Word be preached, there is no use for it. So also the act of the remission of sins took place on the cross. Who uses it? No one. But in the Lord's Supper we say, "Eat this body and [drink this] blood shed for the remission of sins." I say this: We have a battle with heretics about the use of Scripture. We say that they abuse Scripture and that we have the right meaning. Here the Sacramentarians distinguish concerning the Law and the use of the Law. To the Christian the Law is most sacred. Because it is divine wisdom, it is a very fine and sacred thing. The fact of the matter is this: both the wicked and the pious man have the Law. Both have a very good thing. But they disagree over its use. The former misuse a very sacred thing. We teach that one must use it correctly. Meat and fish are things, the created works of God. The only battle there is is over their misuse. They were not created for this, so that we might be justified by them, but that we might continue to live because of them. Their use? To receive them with thanksgiving for our enjoyment. So also a good wife or good husband is a very fine creation. The pope does not deny this. He forbids wickedness. In our case, on the other hand, he says it is a sin if a priest marries. He places righteousness in celibacy. We say that God gave us wives and husbands that we might use these creations of His and give thanks. Gold and silver, too, are fine things, but everyone grabs them up for his own use. The same thing happens with Scripture. The Enthusiasts use the Word. The papists have the very Gospel itself, but they do not use it. The same is true of the Enthusiasts. "We know." There is no argument here as to whether the Law is good or bad. So they are arguing that we condemn their doctrine, and condemn it, as also the Law, with the judgment: It is not a good thing. But they are not using it well.

If anyone. That's where the trouble is, in its use. We must note this point well. In my first book [17] I treated carefully the matter of the use and the actual achievement, but the Enthusiasts remained unmoved. His work was finished, but Christ added His command to preach. As far as I'm concerned, separate the act of His passion from preaching, and its treasure has been stolen, and it becomes useless. Everything is good if one puts it to good use. So He establishes as means the Word, preaching, Baptism, faith, the sacraments, reading, that He might by every means bring things into use. If this is a matter of the mind, it concludes: "Christ is on the right hand of the Father; He is not dead." They here confuse the function with the act. This is also what the Jews have done.

What is the "lawful use" that knows that "the Law is not, etc."? To sum up all of this: Use the Law as you wish. Read it. Only keep this use away from it, that you credit it with the remission of sins and righteousness. Beware of making me righteous by the Law. Rather, use it to restrain. You must not give the Law the power and virtue

---

[17] Luther is referring to Part I of his treatise *Against the Heavenly Prophets,* published in December 1524. Cf. *Luther's Works,* 40, pp. 92 ff.

to justify. But you are teaching this — that there is a righteousness of works and of the Law. But boasting is excluded (Rom. 3:27). "If . . . by works"; but that's what you believe. However, "the righteousness of God has been manifested apart from the Law" (Rom. 3:21). It is a spiritual misuse of the Law if anyone wants to make men righteous by it, if anyone teaches that men can be justified by the Law and by works. It is a misuse of the Law if one wants to teach what he does not know and assert what he does not understand. It is a very unhealthy misuse to say that the Law is laid down for the justification of one who is not subject to the Law. This does not happen by the Law. Its work and virtue is not to make an ungodly man righteous. Even less can such a man be ruled by it. Were the Law laid down for the righteous man, this would be to tell him that he is not yet righteous. We have a similar argument in Gal. 2:17: "If in our endeavor to be justified in Christ we ourselves are found to be sinners, is Christ then an agent of sin? Certainly not!" If this is our situation and this is not sin and the righteousness of Christ does not abide and we must be led to the Law, then we have sin from Christ; because if a believer in Christ must be considered a sinner also through the Law, then it follows also that he is not justified through Christ. This would be to destroy and wipe out faith. Among the ungodly this point about the Law and its relation to the just man is not clear. They say: "Well, then we don't have to do good works." If, as [that text] says, we are righteous in Christ, no sin is found [in us], and we have no need of the Law, for the Law does not justify us, but grace does; and if [the Law does] not [justify us], then it is not given to us and has no effect on us. When we teach through the Gospel that men are justified by Christ, we are at the same time teaching that this does not happen by the Law. The Law, then, is very sacred, very fine; but it does not justify. It frightens, it accuses; but it does not justify and does not free one from death. If I were to say it does justify, corporal food would also give nourishment for eternal life. If I credit a given creature only with the things for which [18] it was ordained, I do well. So the Law is abused when I assign to the Law more than it can accomplish. Good works are necessary and the Law must be kept, but the Law does not justify. They say, however, "Unless you are circumcised" (Acts 15:1) and "It is necessary . . . to charge them to keep the Law" (Acts 15:5). What about this? To be justified by circumcision is to misuse the Law al-

---

[18] We have read *quae* for *quod*.

ready. The Anabaptists say: "If you are baptized, you will be saved." In the first place, in Baptism we are baptized with the Word, which is spoken and in which there is great power. But they hold also the Word in contempt. There they declare that only the applying of water justifies. I am not speaking about an abuse which tells lies against the Law but about the misuse of those who treat the Law and teach others but whose mouths misuse the Law. The new doctrine, however, says: The Law is neither here nor there. If you believe, you will be saved. The Law no longer condemns anyone except unbelievers. The Law does not justify unless you believe. Before, it justified and condemned externally like the civil law.

9. *Not for the just,* because he has what the Law demands and he has been established without it. The Law frightens and causes trembling — these are the spiritual effects of the Law. It really has a double function: in an external way to repress violence and spiritually to reveal sins. It restrains the wicked to prevent their living according to their own flesh, and it shows the Pharisees their sins to keep them from pride. Satan, every wicked theologian, and even nature cannot bear to have their works condemned. Those who have the firstfruits of the Spirit have the battle to fight against confidence in our own works.

This disease is an innate thing in us. From it develop all the monastic orders. "If you keep this, I promise you in the name of the Lord eternal life." Consequently they perform these works, because they hope that God will pay some attention to them. This disease has deep roots in us. All the saints have the job of cleansing themselves of this disease with the help of the Holy Spirit. Thus when the Enthusiasts come to us, they find in us many things which please them. God laid down this law; therefore He wanted you to be circumcised. There the reasoning is compressed and binding. But the Gospel says, "God wants His commandments to be kept, but this does not make one righteous. 'Love is the fulfilling of the Law'" (Rom. 13:10). "I am not aware of anything against myself, etc." (1 Cor. 4:4). I must say with the heretics: "We are unworthy servants," [19] that is, I am not justified. They do not know that so lofty a justification is required. One does not fulfill the Law except with deeds — not with the heart. The Holy Spirit says, "He wants such things done by you, but in such a way, etc." You see, it is written (Ps. 143:2): "Enter not into judgment with Thy servant." Who is the servant? "The one who keeps Thy com-

[19] Cf. Luke 17:10.

mandments." Justification, however, is to believe in Jesus Christ, the Son of God. Human reason neither grasps nor finds this Gospel, but this is hidden knowledge. Men say, "I do works; therefore I am pleasing. I preserve my decency." These are the empty inventions of seducers who mislead men by works. It is one thing to fulfill the works of the Law; it is another to be justified. We assign righteousness not to the Law and its works but to grace alone, which is offered to us through Jesus Christ. The Law does this: it teaches that one must do works, serve his brother, and recognize his own sin. These are good things, are they not? To be humble in knowing oneself, to do good for one's neighbor — these are wonderful. But you want to add: This is to be just before God. Those who do not use the Law lawfully, that is, as the Law ought to be used, should not exalt the Law beyond that which the Law is or can be. You are using the Law not according to its lawful function but as if it were grace and the Holy Spirit. This use of the Law is one that is "for the just man." You false prophets err when you teach that the Law is laid down for the just man. That, you see, is contrary to the nature of both the Law and righteousness. The Law is laid down *for the lawless.* This gives the Law both its civil and spiritual functions: that wicked man is restrained and is led to a knowledge of himself. Those are the two functions. By its civil function it restrains crass sinners who rush in before they reveal all things as free. This must be the Law with its own punishment. Many people are greedy, and yet they live with a beautiful and holy appearance. Paul in Rom. 1 assails the Gentiles for their crass and manifest sins. In chapter 2 he assails the very decent-appearing Jews who beneath their hypocrisy kept encouraging the worst sins so that these holy sinners are put to shame. Rom. 2. There we have the true use, and you should not assign more to the Law than to restrain and humble the proud saints that they may be led to understanding. When this occurs, there is no further function of the Law. Why, then, do you preach that one is justified thereby? The just man ought not have the Law except as a restraint and to reveal his sin. But it does not take away sin. But in the case of manifest sinners, it restrains; in the case of secret sinners, it reveals. In the case of the just man, it cannot restrain, because there is nothing to restrain; it cannot reveal, because he has done nothing concealed. It is the good use of the Law to restrain and to reveal sin; but it is misuse thereof to say that it takes away sin.

We have treated [20] these two points: the Law is good, and it was
not laid down for the just. I have also mentioned that we understood
those two points as characteristic for recognizing Christians. The
wicked do not understand that the Law is not for the just man. Against
this, Rom. 13:10 proclaims that love is the critical point of the Law,
and beyond that it says (Rom. 7:16): "The Law is good." The two
functions of the Law are to reveal sinners and restrain them. The third
function, however, to remove sin and to justify, is limited to this: The
Lamb of God, and not the Law, takes away sin. It is Christ who removes sin and justifies. Consequently, we must distinguish between
the function of the Law and that of Christ. It is the Law's function to
show good and evil, because it shows what one must do and reveals
sin, which one must not commit. The Law therefore is good because
it shows not only evil but also the good which one must do. But beyond that it does not go. It does not kill Og and King Sihon.[21] It
merely reveals good and bad; Joshua [does the rest].

For the just. To what extent just, since the Law is not laid down
for justification? These two ideas clash: for the Law to be laid down
for the righteous man and for him to be righteous himself, since the
Law reveals the sinner or the good man for this very purpose, that
it may provide for an inquiry into sin. Augustine says: "It is not that
two plus three ought to be five; two plus three is five. So also it is not
that the righteous man ought to become righteous; he is righteous."
When we therefore take away this word "ought," we also take away the
Law. The righteous man has what the Law demands, and so the Law
is not laid down for him. "The Law is good, if anyone uses it lawfully"
(v. 8), that is, if he knows that it has not been laid down for him.
And this is to know Christ, "the Lamb who takes away" (John 1:29).
Whoever therefore understands Christ in this way understands also
this: every man is justified through Christ; therefore he cannot be subject to the Law, because he has righteousness before God and men.
From this reasoning and way of speaking, we must understand the
following. Paul is speaking against the false prophets who wanted to
justify men by works and the Law. He says, "You ought not impose
the Law on them. That's why Peter asked, 'Why do you tempt God?' [22]
You want to burden them with the Law for this purpose — as if they

---

[20] The lecture of Jan. 20 begins at this point.

[21] Cf. Num. 21:33.

[22] Cf. Acts 15:10.

were justified thereby, although they already are justified." If one doesn't know Christ, he cannot understand this idea. For this reason the papists are of course stuck in works; they always have the idea that the Law is necessary. Had anyone of us written this passage of Timothy, he would be a heretic a hundred times. For us, the law of love has been laid down, and the ceremonial laws have been given because of love. In fact, the Christian is the servant of all men. He is subject to every law. What about the Law, then? We are subject to every law, but we submit voluntarily in brotherly love to all laws of all men, but we do not, like them, lay them down for justification. We distinguish the Christian life in faith and love. Faith is queen over every law. The Christian wants to be justified by grace alone. In this way he is free from all laws. But the false prophets want to impose the Law on the conscience: "If you do this, you will be holy." But that is where faith should rule. That is what Paul speaks against. On the other hand, the Christian is subject to every law. He bears the Law and the burdens of the Law according to the old man. He seeks as his slavery the good of his neighbor. This is where Rom. 13 and John 3 come in.

This idea clashes with the seducers of the *Sentences,* who want to put works into the place of grace. It is impossible for them to know what they are talking about. When you take that understanding away, they know nothing except the works of the Law. Therefore they necessarily do not understand "the things about which they make assertions" or as far as that principal part is concerned which involves the Spirit and faith.

It is laid down for the unjust. Here you see Paul carefully treating the function of the Law. It does not go into the kingdom of Christ but into that place where Christ is not — the kingdom of the devil. There there is need for the function of the Law, because the ungodly do not understand, or do not wish to understand, the Law. It performs its function to that end, that it restrains and reveals sins so that a person seeks justification, which comes through faith. The idea of Paul is very clear when used correctly: that, if anyone uses the Law in this way, he is restrained in his civic life, he is righteous before the world and is convinced that he is a sinner and understands what good he lacks. Thus the Law does have its function. That is how Moses struck down the two kings.[23] Paul does not intend to list the whole gamut of sins, but rather several, as one says, "If any."

23 Cf. n. 21 above.

For the unjust. I do not know how to distinguish correctly here. He uses six general expressions. Then he follows with undistinguished forms to describe types of sin which are against God as well as against men. In the first place there is "the lawless one." In 2 Thess. 2:3, 8 Paul speaks thus about Antichrist as one who acts as if he were outside of Law and obeys no law. The *disobedient* is not subject to the Law, obeying neither God nor man. Another may explain it in another way: whoever lives a willful life, obeys no one willingly, whether they be public magistrates or others whom he owes obedience. Those are the general ideas. The Greeks call such a person "lawless," one who does absolutely anything he pleases contrary to God's law. The *ungodly* operate against both God and man. These are the two who do not believe; they hold in contempt faith, the Word, and everything else. As he who neglects and despises his neighbor sins against God in faith, so he also sins against his neighbor in a cruel manner and without faith. These are the *unholy* and also the *profane*, as was Esau. As there are those who disobey God and men and, like the ungodly, neglect the glory and respect of God and men, so also these are in themselves an unspiritual people who have no decency in their lives. This happens in the papist sphere when priests live in fornication, lust, greed, and uncleanness; they do not live holy and chaste lives. When they are simply profane in themselves with respect to their food, they live outwardly in a coy boldness. These include flirty girls and disobedient boys who are irreverent and profane. This relates properly to one's own person, that is, to a person who is wicked or irreverent toward himself or against himself. That's the way the peasants and the laymen are now. They do not distinguish among preachers. "Let him work as I do." They make no distinction between the sacred and the profane. They live in their own lust and filth. These are the general sins. The following are the particular ones — those which are better known.

10. *Kidnappers.* There are many kinds of thievery. There are rustlers, who steal cattle; embezzlers; sneak-thieving magistrates; the sacrilegious, who steal something sacred; the kidnapper, who steals people, as when one takes a slave or servant girl, a son or daughter, and forces him into work or slavery. If unchastity is involved, it is called rape. This is a rarity among us. The nobility does this when a father hangs [24] his son. Among the Gentiles this was common, because the condition

[24] The Wolfenbüttel manuscript has *aufffangen* for *aufhangen* and so would be translated "kidnaps."

of slaves was *leibeigen*.[25] *Perjurers.* Among the Gentiles theirs was also a general and common sin, as was also lying. There is also that very shameful sin of males among the Gentiles, both slave and free. Here Paul is designating the manifest and obvious kinds and types of sins against which the Law is laid down. Let each person see whether or not the Law is laid down for him, whether or not he is a just man.

Sound. It is a peculiarity of Paul to call the Gospel "sound." "Whatever else [26] you cultivate I consider types similar to this." What is "sound" militates against those sins. There they fight against themselves; the Law is not for him who is established. The Gospel is opposed to them as if the Gospel were the Law. It is the Gospel that brings the "Lamb who takes away." Therefore when they take away the Gospel, they are all named as foes of the Gospel, because they are bringing in sins. If the Gospel takes away sin, it is opposed to sin.

11. He overflows with the happy, spiritual words *of the blessed God and of His glory.* "Of glory," because there is preached there pure confusion and the glory of God alone. Every man is a vain liar according to Rom. 3:4. "The Holy Spirit will convince, etc." (John 16:8). Therefore He confounds all men. So it is that a man of confusion and of the glory of God shows mercy, goodness, and all things through Christ, as Rom. 8:3 tells us, in His own Son "in the likeness of sinful flesh." Is it not glory to have poured forth all the bowels of His mercy and limitless love by doing good? So Paul glorifies, praises, and applauds that blessed God. He is blessed who alone has immortality and blessedness, as if Paul were saying: "We are all simply wretched and condemned to eternal death. But God was not just the one and only God [27] but a God who pitied us in our wretchedness and poured out His blessedness upon us."

"Who is believed because he is believed" is exactly the same as *with which I have been entrusted* and "to me has been entrusted this responsibility." [28] Paul here glories in a certain righteousness and holiness of his, that God, as he says later, considered him a faithful man to whom He gave this responsibility. This is not a boast over the certainty of Paul's word. It strikes us as a chilling phrase: "Paul, an apostle" (v. 1) and "the Word has been entrusted to me" (cf. v. 11). I have

---

[25] *Leibeigen* describes a slave as being "owned in body and life."

[26] We have read *reliquum* for *reliqui*.

[27] Cf. Deut. 6:4.

[28] Cf. 1 Cor. 9:17; Gal. 2:7; Titus 1:3.

said that we have no rest or peace unless we know [29] for sure that we have the actual Word of God. It's a great thing to know that one has the very sure and infallible Word of God. This is a gift we cannot explain. Before we were in the Gospel, we were carried about by every wind. Even those who have the Gospel are not certain but wander here and there as the sects do. They have doubts about this Word. They cannot put forward such a boast. I would not rejoice as Paul did over the "glorious Gospel of the Great One," entrusted to me. I know that I have it; that is, I know that I stand upon the Rock, and that I hold all the gates of hell in contempt, even though Satan assails me quite enough. But when the heart has doubts, Satan has won. Thus these boasts of his are certainly spiritual. The Word is a treasure, but not like the treasure of men. He recommends carefully that we must not take up the Word as if it were man's. It is easy to receive the Word, but to receive it as the Word of God, who lives and is blessed forever, that is a truly great thing.

12. *I thank Him.* The Greek here gives the idea that Paul has been strengthened for Christ or for obedience to Christ. Neither idea is foolish — that Paul be brave in his ministry in the Gospel of faith. The second sense is that I be brave in Christ. If grammar demands rather the first sense, the emphasis should remain on the word "strengthened." [30] Earlier, we also had to declare this in Titus.[31] This "strengthening" is required to make something sure. He is saying: "The Word has been entrusted to me, but others are teaching it. But they do it coldly, as men who have doubts, men who have not been strengthened. This Word which we teach, however, wants to be so persuasive that no one doubts it. So I thank Him because He has not only given it to me but has also strengthened it in me lest I run in vain or in uncertainty, Gal. 2:2; 1 Cor. 9:26, like those who teach it and do not know if it is true." Thus in our time many have kept that Word only because of novelty and because heretics have arisen. They have not received it as the Word of God. These are vainhearted people who are bound by an enthusiasm for new things. This Word wants us to adhere strongly to it. God gives it that we may be strong in it. One is strengthened by his practice in teaching, testing, battling. Earlier, in

[29] We have read *scimus* for *simus.*

[30] The Vulgate text has *confortavit me,* but Luther has the Greek ἐνδυνώσαντί με in mind and therefore uses *roboravit me* here.

[31] In the lecture on Titus 3:8, held Jan. 20, 1528. Cf. *Luther's Works,* 29, p. 86.

the Epistle to Titus,[32] we have "that you insist on these things." We do this to strengthen our own people, who are not strong and sure and fully persuaded but are easily misled because they have no zeal for the truth and do not take this seriously. That is, the Word makes me strong for Christ so that I have no doubts, and we should let that count for something that someone can give thanks to God. Anyone can let the spit fly in public and be considered a learned teacher. But to teach with this confidence is indeed a rarity.

Because He judged me faithful by appointing me to His service. Again this is pure boast about his certainty: "I have this great duty in spite of and against Satan." God causes him to have success in his work. If anyone still has doubts, he is lazy and slow to work. The Enthusiasts crack such lame jokes [33] and present such pitiful arguments. Not only do they not strengthen with their foolish bits of worthless information, but they even move me to sympathize with them because of their uncertainty. There is no blessedness in their teaching, "it is but toil and אָוֶן" (Ps. 90:10), because they are uncertain. But they will boast just the same. *Faithful.* Paul has not become a saint now, has he? This happens because of divine reckoning, as in Rom. 4:3. His sin is taken away. Thus we become faithful when God reckons it to us. In that grace of His I live from His Gospel. Let others boast of their own accomplishments. I am sure that I have the Gospel of the blessed God. Then the Lord has looked on me as a faithful man. It makes me rejoice from the bottom of my heart that the blessed God has looked on wretched me. Because He wants me, a faithful man, to preach, I shall do it. This is boasting over the certainty of the Word. Whoever has this certainty can be a happy man and can teach others with good results.

I said yesterday [34] that it is the great blessing of all Christians and especially of those in the ministry that they are sure that they have the Word of God. Out of that certainty follow peace of heart, rejoicing, thanksgiving, and an entire life that becomes more bearable. On the other hand, whoever lacks this certainty is without peace and comfort. At this appropriate moment, Paul goes on to state this exceptional example of God's grace and mercy — the example of himself. This is one of the most glorious passages that Paul treats here with word and

---

[32] Cf. n. 31 above.

[33] Luther uses the German phrase *reissen so lame Zoten.*

[34] The lecture of Jan. 21 begins at this point.

example. He speaks words of life and salvation and adds this very
effective example of himself. This is opposed to sin, death, devils,
princes, the flesh, and the judgment of God, which is the most serious
of all, just as the Law is and our conscience, which is divine wrath or
desire for judgment. Opposed to all these this is a very beneficial and
useful passage. So note it well.

13. A *blasphemer:* a proud man, one who treats another badly,
a harmful and violent man, who does violence to people. This is the
first "virtue" Paul mentions. These are his "merits" which preceded
God's grace. This is his way of arriving at grace. Our sophists weaken
this text. They say that although this miracle did happen to St. Paul,
yet we must not make this a general rule. That gloss Satan invented
so that that text might not remain in the church. That venomous gloss
has abolished that text: "The Lord will not do with you as He did with
Paul," against the clear text of Paul, "that in me He might display"
(v. 16). Still their gloss prevails: "This is an ideal, a sketch, that others
might believe more firmly in Christ." Paul says that this did not happen as a miracle but as a general example. So we must first abominate
that terrible gloss. This does apply generally. After all, "whatever was
written," Rom. 15:4. To whomever grace comes, it comes as it did to
Paul — without merit, because that is how we have lived. I was a fer-
vent saint; I celebrated Mass daily; I confessed to the world with body
and soul; I kept preparing for sacrifice whatever sacrifice I, a wicked
man, could make, because there on the altar was crucified the Son of
God; and I wanted to redeem others with my good works. If we compare this with Paul, we certainly outstrip him. But there you have out
and out blasphemy against the doctrine of Christ, for I am saying:
"I want to be Christ. I want to be counted like Him. I make you
a sharer and brother of all my good works, my vigils, my Masses, as
if I were a Christ who wanted to take away the sins of the world."
Is not this blasphemy against God? No one can therefore boast that
he has received grace because of his own merits. To be sure, merits
have appeared, but we were never worse than when we appeared the
best. Paul never chased after Christians like a thief. Instead, he was
a zealot. He performed his work as though engaged in the highest
office. Therefore grace came to him through mercy. We have crucified Christ, blasphemed His holy name and doctrine, despised His
blood. This same thing happens today in the papacy. There is nothing
worse than the Mass, which was a marketplace where we sold a good

work. This sin is not avenged yet, nor can it be, but eternal death and
the Last Day must punish it. Just as grace came to Paul, although he
was sinning greatly, so also grace is offered to all sinners, lest anyone
lose hope. Paul is set down here as an example for our comfort so
that, if we believe, we may know that Christ is merciful and longsuffering. After all, we do have a command to hope as well as a prohibition against losing hope. The first is the command that one should
hope diligently in the Lord Jesus. Holy Scripture urges this everywhere by commands and promises as well as by examples for hope.
Paul was a blasphemer. With his words he sinned first against the
Gospel because he condemned it as heresy. We also have done this.
Had God not given us His light, we still would be doing it. You see,
whoever does not know Christ cannot keep silent when he hears that
Christ condemns his works. I condemned Hus and Wycliffe, [35] who
wrote against the pope and good works. I thought they were pure
poison. That's the way people are who still must be converted.

A persecutor. "Not only did I condemn that doctrine, I did it with
a violent hand." He was guilty of much blood, for he kept killing, he
kept delivering judgment, he pursued his intent to conquer the church
as church. He killed very much. It was mass murder. It is a great
comfort to know that the greatest apostle was involved in so many sins
against the First Commandment that he blasphemed God's name and
caused it to become worthless. Later he had good men imprisoned
and robbed them, separated families and especially was responsible
for the death of St. Stephen. "I made the statement: 'He should be
executed.'" This comfort of Paul belongs to all of us wretched sinners.
It is not a miracle. It is rather an example. Whoever gives it his consideration cannot lose hope, because it is too strong an example. You
are no more devout than a bandit. In fact, the bandit is a better man
than you. He kills people and carries off their bodies. Paul carried
off both their bodies and souls. "I used to force them to blaspheme."
He compelled them to recant; he confirmed many in their own wickedness; he terrified many. So Paul therefore came to grace with as great
a burden of sin as we — we who have been leaders in doing and

---

[35] Jan Hus, Czech reformer (1369—1415), was influenced by the writings of
John Wycliffe (1320—1384). Both were condemned to a fiery death for heresy
by the Council of Constance in 1415, Wycliffe posthumously. For Luther's own
defense against the charge of Hussitism leveled at him by Johann Eck in the
Leipzig Debate, 1519, see *Luther's Works*, 31, pp. 321 f.

preaching wrong things. If we have not been that bad, still we have restrained and hindered the Word of the Gospel; we have sacrificed Christ in the Mass. There really are no baser rascals in the whole wide world. In blasphemy are included all the sins against doctrine and the soul. Therefore we should not despair because we are blasphemers now. He was a persecutor of men, he caused separations from wives and children and the destruction of homes, he made widows and orphans. Paul has written a good case against himself. He was violent, harmful. And he even considered this legitimate. He did not repent. He went on with hard intent and violence. There was a heaving sea of sins in Paul. He is the greatest sinner we can find in Christianity. *Of whom I am the foremost* (v. 15) is really true, because here rapine, blasphemy, and holy teachings come together. He abuses the power of his teachers and magistrates.

16. *I received mercy.* "I was presented with mercy." In Greek it reads: "But I also was such a one. That's what I became too, such a lost scoundrel was I; in that condition I received mercy." He cannot say: "He gave this to me according to my merits." To bestow mercy on a person who has such "virtues" ought to be a further sin. To clash with well-known truth and to be unwilling to believe it is dangerous. Paul very likely did not know what they believed and anticipated. He only heard them preach against Moses and abrogate the Law. "I was ignorant and an unbeliever on top of it" (v. 13), that is, a heathen. There are others who know what is being taught, but they don't believe it. Unfaithfulness can stand beside understanding, or knowledge. For instance, I can know what the papists believe, but I don't believe that. They hear us teach "faith alone," but they attack the idea. Paul was not entirely ignorant of that doctrine. Similarly I was [not] ignorant of what Hus taught.[36] Whenever I heard the name Hus, I was afraid. I dared not trust myself when I once came upon a sermon of his clipped to a Bible. "I received mercy for this reason: I was ignorant. I began to see myself as a fool, and I did not believe." Paul here is making something of an excuse for his blasphemy. Does this, then, take our comfort away from us? No! It strengthens our comfort. There are such persecutors as the emperor and Ferdinand,[37] who simply do not read or hear what is taught. They are ignorant and unbelieving.

[36] Cf. n. 35 above.

[37] Charles V and his Brother, Ferdinand I of Bohemia. Cf. *Luther's Works,* 16, p. 258, n. 10; 17, p. 188, n. 12.

For such men we pray. As for Erasmus and Emser,[38] who resist solely because of an eagerness to resist, and Zwingli and Oecolampadius,[39] who fight against the truth which they feel they do not have, see 1 Cor. 4:3.[40] Paul was not like this. To them the truth is offered to bind their conscience, but they are unwilling to believe. In this way Carlstadt was overcome in his τοῦτο, yet he did not yield.[41] To be unwilling to believe when the truth is known is to sin against the Holy Spirit. This is the attitude of Korah.[42] They sin obstinately against the truth. By the grace of God, we are not such people. We admit our blasphemy. Yet we have been moved not to blaspheme the truth but to rejoice over it. Therefore we hope, even if we have been ignorant. Now we can say to the Lord: "You converted Paul not because of him himself. From this I can draw great confidence in the Lord that all of us may presume upon Your mercy and longsuffering." Because this is the sure Word of God and we rejoice in its truth, we are sad when someone is misled. "Love does not rejoice at wrong" (1 Cor. 13:6). Thus the conscience is sure that Christ converts. If He was merciful then when we crucified Him on the altar, He is more merciful now. It is our comfort that in our terrible blasphemies and crucifixions He has remembered us and gives us light. "I want to abound in mercy toward you," Matt. 23.[43] It is forever indescribable that that mercy renders such good gifts for such evil deeds. If we will be ungrateful, He will give us sects, every article of faith will directly pass

[38] Against Desiderius Erasmus (1466—1536) Luther wrote his treatise *The Bondage of the Will* (1525). Cf. the introductory remarks in *Luther's Works*, 33, pp. 8 ff. Against Jerome Emser (1477—1527), formerly Luther's teacher at Erfurt, Luther writes in his letter "To the Leipzig Goat" (1521): "I will overlook it that you are writing against me because of your pretense to learning and wisdom." Cf. W, VII, 263.

[39] Ulrich Zwingli (1484—1531) and Johannes Oecolampadius (1482—1531) were in the forefront of the opposition to Luther's teachings concerning the Lord's Supper.

[40] "And even if our Gospel is veiled, it is veiled only to those who are perishing."

[41] Andreas Bodenstein von Carlstadt (1480—1541) rejected the Real Presence in the Lord's Supper with the explanation that Christ's "This" (τοῦτο) in the Words of Institution was accompanied by the gesture of Christ's pointing to his own body, as if to say: "This is My body, which I shall give into death for you. In remembrance of it partake of this bread." At Luther's insistence Carlstadt later withdrew this interpretation, but he always felt closer to Zwingli's teaching than to Luther's. Cf. also *Luther's Works*, 29, p. 33.

[42] Cf. Num. 16.

[43] Perhaps Matt. 23:37 is meant.

away, not because I have done this out of stubbornness, not because I have resisted the well-known truth, but because I have acted like a fool.

14. *Overflowed.* Where sin abounds, there grace abounds all the more (cf. Rom. 5:20), namely, in me. *With the faith.* Here the man pronounces himself holy. "I was the foremost and worst sinner of all, a murderer and a shameful scoundrel." Yet for these he received very rich grace beyond what the rest received. He received both grace and love. The greater the iniquity, the greater the grace. Because Paul was a greater sinner than Peter, he received more grace than Peter. "The grace of Christ has abounded, because I have been guilty of such a flood of sins. What is that grace? It is overflowing forgiveness. It is also a gift. I have received a twofold blessing: forgiveness and grace and in addition the gift of the Spirit — faith and love." Grace is that favor and beneficence of God which forgives sins and does not remember them. Second, that man must be restrained to cease his sinning. This is what faith and love do. Grace causes God to be favorably inclined; faith and love cause man to be holy. The first is useless without the second. To have other words, works, and ideas — that is what the gift causes. Grace is not alone; it comes in such a way that faith and love are joined to it. It creates a new man so that I believe in Christ. It makes me more effective because I am given a faith which is effective through love in Christ. You consider Paul the worst sinner and the greatest saint because the greatest iniquity was in Paul. He, therefore, who was the worst, became the most beloved servant. If I have been a robber, a murderer, an oppressor of widows and little children, I must say: "You have set up Paul as an example. I do not contemplate examples of wrath and desperation set down for the terror of a 'hard head.' " God has given no example for our despair. God says and does nothing to lead one to lose hope. He does give examples of His wrath. Those examples have to do with confounding stubbornness — a serious sin in the world, because for the most part the world holds Him in contempt. If the weakhearted take up these examples of wrath, they begin to fear and to lose hope. They misuse those examples. You see, they were not written to encourage the loss of hope but to inflict a blow on the stiff neck. If sin and the fear of judgment vex you, you should avoid all Scripture that sets forth examples of wrath. Such examples do not apply to you, because you are not stiff-necked. Rather search Scripture for that which comforts you and

nourishes hope: David, Manasseh, Moses, Aaron, Mary Magdalene, the dying thief. He permitted few pure saints to live long. Yet He preserved John in such a way that He did not have to perform miracles. All the others He permitted to fall into grievous sin, so that each should have nourishment for his hope. It is a great thing to hope in God, so that He may bestow the kingdom of heaven without cause. Therefore He overwhelms us with so many examples to enlarge our heart and encourage our hope. The hardhearted and quarrelsome have the example of the flood, Sodom, and Saul. We must divide the Word correctly: comfort must be given the weakhearted; on the other hand, those opposite must receive a threat. Otherwise they will be overwhelmed, as 2 Cor. 2:7 says, for the command is certain and does not fail: "I am the Lord." The Lord forbids despair under penalty of eternal death. Where there is stubbornness, one must inflict a blow on it. This is an excellent example for consciences that feel that they have sinned much. Not to be killed yet — although this may be nothing — nevertheless lends encouragement. If I look at my sins, they are nothing when compared with those of Paul. According to the Spirit, however, Paul is nothing when compared with me. Were the Lord to give pure examples of mercy, that would be useless because of the hardhearted and stubborn. We see what the wicked are doing today. Yet He offers them mercy. That is a useful text, salutary to all wretched consciences. So praise God among the saints. This is the right way to honor the saints. Heavenly Father, the more we see the papists and the more You have magnified and listed the sins of Paul, the greater is Your mercy.

15. *Sure.* There stands the rule and text by which Paul himself was saved. The rule "He came, etc." is greater than Paul's example, which is the best kind of teaching. This passage has quite often been life and salvation for me. So Paul praises it with a beautiful preface. He speaks with great certainty. Oh, who else could speak with such assurance! This is a very trustworthy and certain statement. Then, *worthy of full acceptance.* This we should receive. Where are those who are full of dead men's bones? [44] I can say this in the midst of the tyrants' prisons, in the death of the devil, because Paul swears and declares that this statement is certain, this Christian rule "Christ has come." Whoever grasps this comprehends Christ correctly. We looked at ourselves before the judge and into the rainbow and invoked Mary

[44] Cf. Matt. 23:27.

and Barbara.[45] I loved the Virgin more. We kept reading these words, but we did not note them. Praise God that we are over that; *mit allem Fleiss und Willen* we should accept these words, that is, we should accept them by every means, with every effort, with all our heart. After all, this does not disappoint, because this Word is sure, it is also saving. No, this Word transcends evaluation! Human reason shudders at the greatness of the gift, because I am to believe that God gives me eternal life for all my sins, as I said earlier. But this is too much! The greatness of the past Gift makes possible also the gift which is yet to come. Because this has happened, because God has given His Son, therefore the other will happen. Even if I am not worthy, it is still true. Were I unwilling to glorify God in His promise, I would still be willing to glorify Him in the Son He sent. I would want to say that His blood is worthy of redeeming me from sin and death. Nothing except eternal life can be the reward. Rom. 8:32: "He who did not spare His own Son but gave Him up for us all, will He not also give us all things with Him?" These words are beyond evaluation and incomprehensible. The Gift that has been given is very great, except that it is not yet revealed. Eternal life is not as great as Christ. From the very magnitude of the Gift I have received I perceive the greatness of the gift which God has yet to give.

Christ did not come to judge, to destroy, but to give Himself for the salvation of sinners. Therefore let no sinner lose hope. Rather let him despair who does not want to be a sinner, as the self-righteous. The sinner has the opportunity to hope because "Christ has come." Like the devil, the law of Moses condemns. We do not need Christ to condemn us, nor was He sent to condemn; and yet we receive Him thus because we have neither read nor understood Scripture.

Of whom I am the foremost. Here there was an argument; that is: "I consider myself the foremost for the sake of humility." He said this in all seriousness. "I know of no greater sinner in the church." David was a great one, but Paul perpetrated more than David, who neither persecuted doctrine nor misled. Let the text stand then. So Paul is saying: "I comfort all sinners. I stand here to sustain you. None of you can compare himself with me."

Yesterday [46] we heard that Paul called himself the foremost of all sinners; that we who know we are sinners console ourselves with this

---

[45] Cf. *Luther's Works,* 17, p. 140, n. 3.

[46] The lecture of Jan. 22 begins at this point.

salutary text; and that God does not condemn sinners but rather sends
His Son to save them. As a consequence, no cause for condemnation
has been left among men. Otherwise sin would seem to be the greatest
cause. You see, if we cling to Him, sin and the commandment have
been washed away by Christ. So the man who complains that he is
burdened with sins deceives himself, or lack of faith is the reason
for his condemnation. He describes this beautifully here, saying that
God loves and pities sinners. This is an essential passage which demands frequent use, especially in temptation and in the peril of death.
At those times one has the real proof of that passage. When people
are without tribulation, it cannot bring pleasure. Under the pope we
have lived quietly. No one hated us. In that situation this passage was
foolish and dull. When the hour of trial draws near, then we remember this Word of salvation. Therefore the Word is willing to do battle
against death, because as the Word of life and peace it is a battle
against fear, Satan, and tribulation and as the Word of God it is a
struggle against the devil, and the spirit with the flesh that adheres to
it is saved.

16. *For this reason . . . for an example.* Here Paul is saying that
this occurrence is not *per se* a miracle but a general example. As an individual thing, this passage speaks of special prerogative. Therefore
all comfort is taken away. But when it is written as a comfort and
example for me, then it applies to me, so that I may glory in this passage, not just Paul, who has reached his goal. "Therefore," he says,
"He has had compassion on me," so that it might not have a secret
and individual privilege, but that "Jesus Christ might display," that is,
that all Christians, who are sinners, might know "from my example"
what sort of a Person Christ is: The Lord is long-suffering, patient, etc.;
He can forgive and is willing to forgive our countless sins. "Therefore
I have been set up as an example for the whole church that all may
fix their eyes on me as an example of His long-suffering mercy."
Patience. Every kind of patience. "He could endure my murders, blasphemies, seductions, crimes of violence. I used to force people to blaspheme, revoke, and deny Christ." *Those who were to believe.* This
warms Paul's heart. Before this he blasphemed; he drew many away
from Christ. "Now," he says, "I have received mercy, and I have re-
paid it. Where I once alienated one from Christ, I have brought a
thousand to Him, because my ministry has not been in vain. Those
who previously became hardened because of my madness now are
forced to be ashamed."

For eternal life. We believe in Christ not only for this life but also for that which is to come. You see, we believe in the Conqueror of death, the Destroyer of hell. No one believes in Christ that Christ may fill his belly. We know Him not according to the flesh. There stands Paul before us, with glory in thanksgiving in remembrance of the good he has received and for the evil left behind. He abounds in spiritual affection, and this makes him very sure not only that he must avoid sins but also that, in place of sins, many fruits have been given to him — fruits which the Lord has given him. As a result, his spirit abounds in rejoicing, and he gives thanks. This also describes our joy. John writes in his last epistle (3 John 4): "No greater joy do I have," because truth is in the purity of the Word.

17. *To the King of ages.* This King has no peer. First, He is the King of ages. With one wink of His eye He holds the eyes and crowns of all kings in contempt. They are the kings of an hour. They do not rule for a hundred years but for a man's lifetime. This is a unique King, who rules from the beginning of the world throughout all ages. The other kings are kings, but they are nothing, for He is the same for all ages. Others die. So do we. He alone has immortality. He is the One who does not die. Also, He bestows immortality on others. He is *invisible.* The eye of neither flesh nor spirit sees Him. *To the only wise God.* Also, He alone is wise. This is blasphemy: that if God alone is wise, then all are fools, and where God is not present with His wisdom, there there is pure foolishness. Kings aren't fools, are they? But God takes away not only their power but also their wisdom, their sense of justice. By the wisdom of God we who are in Christ have wisdom. But this wisdom comes from God — of course, from His Word. Those who have the Gospel have the wisdom of God. They are wise in God and from God. Wherever His Word is not present, there neither God nor His wisdom is, but pure foolishness. Paul says that the world considers our God a fool (cf. 1 Cor. 1:21), that no one is interested in this, and that "claiming to be wise, they became fools" (Rom. 1:22). But we glory in God, that He alone is wise and portions out His wisdom among His people. Through the wisdom of God they learn many things, a wisdom that is a certain quality resident in the soul. This, however, is said very briefly in Scripture. Wisdom in Scripture is sacred. It is the Gospel. It teaches you to know God, the counsel of God, and the Son of God incarnate for you. Such wisdom is hidden from the world. Only faith grasps it. Afterwards one

can grasp wisdom wastefully. Wolves learn from a wolf. But true wisdom is meditation as to how I shall live forever, how I shall possess and have God. This is in the Gospel alone, but that wisdom is foolishness in the world's eyes. The Book of Wisdom sings the praise of the Gospel because it describes the example of the Israelite who clung to the wisdom and Word of God. But to the world he is simply a fool, and all the rest are wise. In 1 Cor. 1:25, however we read: "The foolishness of God is wiser than men." Paul is moving along in the Spirit. He is saying: "They live as if destined to be eternal conquerors, but my King is immortal. I thank my God." So far Paul is giving thanks.

18. *This charge.* Before this we heard Paul urge Timothy to command that they refrain from new doctrines. Now he is exhorting Timothy himself. Satan prepares his traps through false teachers, through our own thoughts of public insults, and privately when he misquotes Scripture for presumption or loss of hope. Satan does not sleep. What sort of charge is it? As follows: *in accordance with the prophetic utterances.* The text is obscure. I don't know what Paul intends here. He clearly says that Timothy should do battle in the prophecies. We are not sure what sort of prophecies these are. We take it as just that: that they are prophecies, that is, the books of the prophets in which Timothy himself must be trained. Indeed, it is a good idea that the one who cares for souls ought to pay attention not only to reading the prophets but also to giving the prophets to the crowd and to the people of God. I really do not know what these prophecies are. The text reads: "Certain prophecies went out about you." "There was a prophecy about you. You have much of the testimony of the prophets who prophesied." And also, as he says later (cf. 1 Tim. 4:14), "by the laying on of hands and in the assembly of the elders" Timothy was ordained as a teacher of the church. To this I want to apply these prophecies: "That you remain firm, that you be watchful according to those prophecies by which as by an endowment you were commissioned to serve as a soldier," that is, "Timothy, my son, see to it that you respond to your calling which you must fulfill. There was a prophecy about you when you were called and ordained. See to it that you are zealous in that calling. Do not be lazy." He appears to speak not about the writing but about the words of the prophets which were spoken over him. I do not know what their custom was for ordaining such teachers. Read something about it in

Acts 13:1-4. One reads exegetical notes concerning these things, such as "according to the custom at ordinations" concerning Ezek. 3, to the effect that then the promises were read, because the responsibility of refuting, rebuking, teaching the faith, and feeding souls was now given to the ordinand. Isaiah has something of this sort (cf. Is. 6). So you see, for that time that was the method, that he spoke and then added the prayer that God might give to him according to those prophecies spoken about him. In this way the pope sets forth to the bishops and to the emperor the articles to which they must swear. Those are the words of the prophecies, although this can be better interpreted. Paul can be saying: "when you are told what you are to do."

By them. That is, "by the prophecies as they have been described to you. Not only should you stand firm in them; you should also fight." Paul has the custom of freely using military terms with which he brightly illuminates the Old Testament. About the old wars he says many things that were merely figures of speech. "Remember that you have been appointed to read for seven hours and that you read, etc. But see to it that you conduct yourself like a soldier. You must stand in the front ranks. You are a soldier. You have weapons and sword in hand. You have been set up in a place of war. See, then, that you fulfill those prophecies which have been prescribed for you. May you be a good soldier. On behalf of souls, hurl yourself into peril of life, body, possessions, and all things." You see, a bishop must teach the ignorant, comfort the weak; he must be patient with them. He has been set out for the convenience of others, so that he lives for others rather than for himself. Satan then attacks through false teachers, with bothersome hardships, and by false interpretation of Scriptures based on private thoughts. Therefore watch that you may remain firm in them. *The good warfare.* This is a Hebraism, how one wages this warfare. It is a salutary training. He should thus be a soldier under Christ that His words properly come to prominence. He who teaches well is a good soldier. In the Word the ignorant are taught, the sluggards aroused, foes overcome and consoled, although he says this rather of the general public than of the service that is useful for the brethren. These are very burning, powerful words. The factious spirits also fight. They fight more diligently, more ardently than we do. But theirs is an evil service, they are devils, because they desert the Word of God and follow their own thoughts.

19. *But holding faith.* This he inculcates carefully. This is the one word Satan attacks: faith. If the word is "conscience," he cannot abide it, and he cannot endure anything good. Rather he tolerates people like the Enthusiasts and the factious spirits. They accomplish much, and he helps them. But where there is a true conscience and faith, he becomes a fool, so that he gives not a penny for God. The Enthusiasts are full of good works, but they blaspheme in doctrine. On the other hand, the godly give and serve less. Now they do more good works than formerly, and they give more. Where a single florin is given now, it is more than 10,000. But even if one gives but a penny to others, it has been done in truth. He does this from a good conscience. *Faith.* Faith is to believe in God and thus to have a conscience secure in Christ. You will not produce a good conscience by being a soldier. You will be a soldier by teaching, etc., but watch out that your good conscience is not on account of these; yet you will have a good conscience in this service as a soldier. Were we not sure about the Word, why should we work and suffer? A good teacher is a very pleasing member to God, a very displeasing one to the devil. Next, God does not allow the Enthusiasts to fight against us with strong arguments, so that you may preserve a good conscience not only within yourself but also among others. How? Be a soldier! He will strengthen you through the Word. Later on (4:16) he says: "Save yourself and others," as much as lies in the office. We believe there must be an enthusiasm for this office in everyone and that we must strive to keep the faith. This the Enthusiasts cannot do; they follow their own speculations. *By rejecting conscience, certain persons.* What they did I do not know. Some persons reject this good conscience and faith. These are the light and wind-blown spirits who, when they once hear, know immediately. Later they become smug, but soon the devil overcomes them. Already the Enthusiasts have gone back to that point that they are beginning to deny Christ. Zwingli says: "The Son of God did not die. Christ has redeemed us insofar as He is a man. Divinity cannot suffer. If Christ suffered for us, He is denied as Christ by those very words." They are worse than the Jews, they have been so captivated by their thoughts that they cannot escape from them, nor do they cling to the principal position of faith. They deny original sin, Baptism, and now Christ's sacrament. That is to reject faith and to have no concern for a good conscience. *They have made shipwreck.* Mark well this passage

against the smug and presumptuous. Stand firm on the main article
so that you stick to it in faith. Works will surely follow in due time.
If this item fails, immediately danger — shipwreck — is near. If Christ
fails, shipwreck occurs. To preach the rest of the doctrine does not
help at all. In this way, the papists have become shipwrecked, and
all have gone to the devil.

20. *That they may learn.* What they did I do not know, because
he does not write what they taught. In Corinth there were certain
people who kept denying the resurrection. I believe they were Juda-
izing, because they denied Christ as the Son of God. After all, it is
for this end that Satan rages, because he is unwilling to cease the
attack. Through Arius he fought against Christ concerning His divinity; through Pelagius, about His humanity. Now people deny that He
is the Son of God and that He is one Person. To be sure, they confess
Him with their words, etc., but they rip and divide Christ into two
persons as if doing this out of zeal, lest they mix the two natures.
It is true that we must not mix the two persons. By the same token,
we must not divide the two natures, although I may not say, "Divinity
is humanity," yet God is man. To reject faith and a good conscience
is to fall presently into shipwreck. This is an excellent metaphor from
ships. In a single word he points out what the world and the sea are.
We are carried into the midst of perilous storms. With trembling we
must remain in the Word. Immediately a shipwreck occurs. So it is
not that we are safe. Rather we are serving as soldiers. We have
not been set up in a place where it is safe to leave the Word of God
and hide it under the bench. Instead the Word is essential. There
must be no sleeping, so that the Word is always in our heart. Before,
when we were in shipwreck under the pope, we were at ease, because
no one opposed him. Now he sends the sectaries on our necks and
crowds us.

At the end of chapter 1 [47] we hear how Paul gives Timothy this
command, that he wage good warfare by keeping a good conscience.
He gave an example about those who rejected faith and a good conscience and suffered shipwreck. These he consigned to Satan. This
example he wrote to strengthen us and to terrify the spirit sects, because it is a rule that whoever has started to neglect faith and conscience soon becomes a heretic and is forced to be zealous. On the

[47] The lecture of Feb. 3 begins at this point. No lectures were held the week
of Jan. 27, for Luther was away at Torgau those days. Cf. W, *Briefe,* IV,
No. 1216.

[W, XXVI, 30, 31]

other hand, whoever turns his enthusiasm to this end, that he have faith and a good conscience, remains safe from heretical thoughts. Paul therefore finds that all heretics rise from this source, that they begin to weary of this general doctrine of faith, love, and the cross. Because they are unaffected by this doctrine, they find new doctrines every day. He wants to say: "Those who find new dogmas are those who have no concern that they have a good conscience before God and that they walk in faith." We experience this daily. That you hold a good conscience and faith is a very noteworthy statement. That is, you should so walk in your enthusiasm that you keep your goal before your eyes, that you hold a good conscience before God and faith. Spiritual self-love will surely leave a person alone; but if others cannot resist the temptation to go into shipwreck, either they follow the inventions of others, or they themselves think up new ideas. In this sin they have underestimated those two points, because they reject good conscience and faith. As a result, they have fallen into shipwreck. This the Enthusiasts do today. If they were living a life dedicated to harming neither God nor their neighbor, they would be glad to call a halt. They are caught up in speculations and new dogmas. This is what we call "shipwreck of faith." The man who begins to hold a worthless conscience and faith is not in a little danger but in the greatest and most terrible peril, because he is not merely breaking a leg in this shipwreck but is drowned completely.

I have delivered. What it means to deliver to Satan you find defined in other places. I believe that the apostles, too, employed this deliverance to torment people's bodies, just as one threatens the person who ravishes his stepmother. Take a look at that passage. Although he has not done it, he has begun to do it, but in such a way that they might forbear to injure their souls. That is, he is using his power to chastise, not to kill; to edify, not to destroy. This is one way of delivering to Satan — that Satan may harass and punish physically. Another method is to excommunicate, to denounce, so that one is outside of the church, as Matt. 18 has it. I believe that Paul is here speaking about the first method. I believe that Hymenaeus and Alexander were that obstinate and were frustrating doctrine that much. They were not wretched specimens. They are special. They were not, like the princes of Abiron,[48] poor fools. They were very noble people, and they caused great damage. Therefore, because

[48] Abiron, or Abiram, was a fellow conspirator of Korah's. Cf. Num. 16:1.

they hold great power, Paul has made this attack by his authority as an apostle.

That they may learn. Our chastisement ought to be a medicine, for the kingdom of Christ is one of mercy. It does not chastise to destruction but to salvation. It does not kill. It holds no sword except a spiritual one. It keeps a man under Satan, yet it does not deliver him farther than to recover him from the snares of Satan. It wants to have him chastised in such a way that he returns. We have no other punishment. Let each Christian not look for vain glory. Let him not seek new and unusual things. Rather let him teach the pure Word of God. If he blunders, he is not guilty of one or two mistakes, but he errs endlessly. This develops into shipwreck. A slight error in the beginning becomes a very great one at the end.

In the first chapter Paul instructs Timothy how he should remain firm in purity of doctrine and wage that warfare in sound doctrine by resisting those who teach otherwise. Then he instructs him to remain steadfast in faith and a good conscience and to help others in the same faith and conscience. In the next section, he instructs Timothy how to live externally in the church and how he ought to train Christians — as well as himself — in their moral way of life.

CHAPTER TWO

THE first moral work of love among Christians is toward civil office. True Christians therefore do not say no to a public officer, even though he is an unbeliever, much less to a Christian one. Our rebaptizers say that Christians cannot hold public office. On this subject Paul speaks in great detail. We must note every syllable. The first fruit of love is to be that you Christians respect every public officer in the world and that you pray for them, because you hear what it means to keep the realm in peace. When a good magistrate fails or is upset, then nothing good is left in this life. Then you will be unable to come to love, to obey parents, rear children, or support the wretched. We must forget about all fruits of love if public offices do not stand firm in peace. In time of war you must anticipate your death at every moment; the inviolacy of virgin, wife, and all property is in peril. God has His will in peace; in the opposite condition the devil has his. Therefore it is the first work of Christians that we respect all public officers. There was a time when I had so narrow a mind that I would not dare to include in my prayers such important matters as praying for kings. My mind, you see, was afraid to ask for such great things. Thus the importance of matters frequently dampens the ardor of the petitioner. It is the gift of the Lord Himself that more is given (for example, public officers) than the very gift we are asking for. We ask that He preserve all things He has thus delivered and are now actually in hand. Because our God is so great and gives such great gifts, He wants us to ask for great things. His goodness is infinite, it pours out without measure. We must pray: "I am indeed unworthy to ask. But I consider not my insignificance but Your greatness, for You give invaluable gifts." It is a shame to pray to God for a mere pittance.[1] From the very greatness of the gifts the confidence to ask for great things grows. He gave His Son. Our petitions —

---

[1] Luther uses the German *Parteke*, a word he seems to have introduced into literary German. It is thought to be a diminutive form developed from the Latin word *partem*, which was one of the cries used by schoolboys as they sang before the houses of citizens and begged for alms of food. In his *Sermon on Keeping Children in School* of 1530 Luther makes a special point of the fact that he, too, was a *Partekenhengst* ("crumb collector") during his student days in Eisenach. Cf. *Luther's Works*, 46, p. 250.

peace in the world, wisdom for magistrates — are far inferior to a prayer for eternal life and remission of sins. Let everyone then expand his heart and pray not to a simple little God but to the God of the heaven and earth He created. So He will give great things to those who ask for great things. Christians who understand that these are the gifts of God pray. Let this be the first fruit of love, that you pray. You see how Paul urges this fruit of the Christian faith.

1. *Supplications.* These are prayers with which we pray for evils to be averted, so that when I pray for a prince, I shall say: "God, the evils which threaten his official position are countless. There will be great danger in the Council of Ratisbon.[2] Satan will call the participants away from serious matters so that they discuss trifles. They will finish no business. Neither peace nor harmony will result. They will not end preparation for war against the Turk. The princes will arrange whatever pleases them." It is the duty of Christians to see whose fault it is that nothing happens in meetings. We must pray that God would instill a good spirit so that they consider all good and salutary things. There will be infinite evils at Ratisbon if we shall not have prayed that the Lord would stimulate them to thoughts of peace. The clergy are bent on wars. Were we to pray, we would accomplish something and would do battle against Satan in the midst of the princes, even though we would be absent in body.

Prayers. These are requests for good things: that the Lord would remove every lamentable condition with which Germany is being oppressed; that instead of those evil men He would give prudent, wise, pious princes who are eager for peace. In this way we pray for the kings of France, England, and Bohemia.[3] They are good gifts of God, but the devil is in their midst. We must do what we can.

Intercessions. These *postulations* are properly intercessions. We correctly apply them to our enemies, according to Matt. 5:44, who do

[2] When the political situation in Germany in the 1520s seemed to make it unlikely that the Edict of Worms (outlawing Luther and exposing him to a death by violence) would be enforced, various additional efforts were made to suppress the spread of the Reformation. A meeting and agreement at Ratisbon (Regensburg) in 1524 ostensibly aimed at reforming the church, but among its provisions was a strict implementation of the Edict of Worms. The politics of the day brought failure to this effort, too, but it was a first step toward the Ratisbon meetings of 1541 and 1546, in which the Catholic-Protestant dialog broke down completely.

[3] Francis I, king of France 1515—1547; Henry VIII, king of England 1509 to 1547; Ferdinand I, king of Bohemia and Hungry since 1526 and administrator of Germany since 1521. See also *Luther's Works,* 17, p. 188.

not seem worthy of our praying for them. We must, however, pray for our enemies. Here is the reason. If you have prayed that God remove evils but one or two who are persecuting all honorable things and the Gospel still stand in the way, then you pray for them: "Lord, forgive them. They do not know what they do," lest He should lay the fault to their charge as to people who do not know, etc. Let them place Christ before themselves, as Stephen did (Acts 7:56-60). "Pray for those who persecute you" (Matt. 5:44). First, we must pray for all public officials, whether they are ours or someone else's, that He take evils away from them and give them good things. We must also pray for tyrants, who persecute us and hinder our prayers when tyrants and sects hinder the fruit of the Gospel. We pray: "Pay no attention to what Duke George [4] or Zwingli does. Rather listen and permit Your Gospel to be sown and to produce fruit."

Thanksgivings. This also pertains to Christians. Gratitude always merits the receipt of more; ingratitude drains the fountain of divine goodness. Gratitude consists of more than the expression "I thank you, Lord God." It also involves acknowledging first that it is a gift of God, that a person knows that peace, which today holds sway here in Germany, a type of government, and the security that allows one to marry are pure gifts of God. It is a gift of God to have a king and a state and the pest without poison, etc. After all, Satan wants the air polluted, all the land burdened with pestilence and death. That this does not occur is a gift of God. We have so many kings and peoples, so much produce, food, and property, purely out of His goodness. This gratitude consists not only in our words alone but principally in our acknowledgment of the blessing we have received. Those people are rare who make such an acknowledgment. Thus no one gives thanks, nor do people pray. Even those who pray with their mouth do not make this acknowledgment. Gratitude must be involved with prayers, because one must confess the gifts he has received. Phil. 3.

For all men. The Christian ought to ask for great things and include all men in his prayer. God gives and bestows great things. He wants us to pray for great things. At that time there were heathen magistrates, and the "all men" included also Turks and Tartars. Yet for these we must also pray, and especially for kings. Still, we do

[4] Cf. *Luther's Works*, 17, p. 188, n. 13.

pray once a year for the pope and the emperor,[5] but this is not a habit. We have few words of prayer, but if one sees a thing, he ought to have a prayer for it: "O God, may You be kindly disposed to all men, especially to princes, and more especially to our princes." This is a great prayer if it comes from a good heart.

2. *That we may lead a quiet and peaceable life.* If we pray for public officials, this is the fruit: to lead a placid, quiet, peaceful life. Extend this expression then, and you will discover how great a thing peace will be. In that condition we can build, plow, fish, sail in safety, walk, sleep, eat, have chaste wives and children who apply themselves, feed our herds. Those good things which we have because of God's great blessing no one considers as good things. Indeed, God bestows them, but He preserves them through public officers. In time of war there is no peace. One cannot go in or out. Not a hair of one's head is safe. In this case no one considers that these outstanding benefits are preserved by a good civil authority which ought to be keeping watch so that peace might endure. It is a great gift to live in peace and quiet. What a wretched state of affairs it was when the peasants were revolting! Everything was filled with the fear of death. There was no thought of plowing. I am sure that Satan plans something similar to stir up a war through the princes and bishops that will be worse than that of the peasants.[6] The power to begin a war is in our hand; to stop it is in Another's hand. They might be killed in one month. We must pray for the wicked papists not only for their own sakes but that peace may not be upset, that preachers may not be checked in their duty, and that the Word may not be taken away. We must pray for public officials; when they have peace, we have peace, too. So we must pray also on behalf of evil men.

Godly and respectful in every way. Let our prayer not be a carnal one, a prayer that seeks our own ends. We must not pray to live in wealth but to ask that godliness and dignity may be able to exist through this peace. The ungodly use peace for shameful wickedness. We use peace that we may more quietly be able to discuss the Word, extend the faith, and bring up our children in spiritual, corporal, and moral discipline — in Christian discipline. He has said both, a godly

[5] A special collect "for all who govern states" was featured in the Mass of Good Friday. But this petition was in position as well as in form subordinate to the collect for the pope in the same service.

[6] Possibly an allusion to a league of Catholic princes and bishops supposed to have been formed in Breslau in 1527.

and respectable, that is, upright life. The man who watches out for indignities and shame holds before himself an upright life. His words, gestures, things he sees, every disposition of his body, garb, and food — all these are honorable. The inconstant man is one who walks dishonorably, since he acts the fool in his food, habits, and words. He is not σεμνός ("honorable"). Instead, he is shallow and shameful. Let us teach the faith, let us increase the hearing of the Word, let us spread the knowledge of Christ. Let us be concerned for what belongs to the kingdom of God and to moral matters. Let us be serious toward men and do nothing that offends but only what edifies.

3. *This is good and acceptable.*[7] In this way you see the apostle make a distinction between doctrines in order to consider human doctrines as useless myths, although he generally marks them thus, and they are vain and useless in their effort to brand sound doctrine as heresy. This is sound, as if he were saying: "These things one should have learned. These things are useful." The flesh follows another dogma. It is his entire intent to keep us on the royal road and in sound doctrine. There is never sound doctrine unless one has seen temptation. This, he says, is teaching empty doctrines. But this is good and useful. What is more, it is "acceptable." Thus we read in Titus 3:8: "I desire you to insist on these things." In the pope's kingdom they do not care what is acceptable to God or what is sound. They care only for a great and different work. If a work glitters with a bright show on its surface, they do it. But we do something when we know very certainly that it pleases God. It is a very beautiful life when someone knows that his life pleases God. Such a person Satan tries to carry off. This passage is an excellent commendation of a true good work. There is no profit in wearing a hood. And what does it profit this and that fellow to be shaven? Besides, this is not acceptable to God. What is acceptable to God is to pray for a magistrate *in the sight of the Savior.* The passage causes much debate. It is much discussed in nearly every disputation even today. Different exegetes explain it in different ways. Those who cause arguments should be avoided. You see, our doctrine is the kind that people cannot grasp except with calm minds. It is the water of Siloam;[8] it is the serene spirit, it wants to be taken up with kindness and gentleness. But if one is contentious, Scripture is opposed to him.

7 The lecture of Feb. 4 begins at this point.

8 Cf. John 9:7.

4. *God wants all men to be saved.* Elsewhere we read (John 13:18): "I know whom I have chosen." If anyone wants to be agreeable, he has a hundred arguments which they may oppose. They want only that to be heard which they themselves say. To such people, then, say, "Farewell." We must answer (1 Cor. 11:16): "If anyone is disposed to be contentious, we recognize no such practice." On the other hand, those who really want to learn are quiet and at peace. If you say something twice to someone, he should look for another teacher, because our doctrine is the sort which brooks no contention. The Holy Spirit, then, must not fight against Himself. In this vein Augustine says: "No one saves except the one God. Nowhere is there salvation except in God." John, the illuminator,[9] that teacher, is reported as saying: "All in this city." [10] This is an exclusive proposition that is expressed in universal terms. Every man is an animal,[11] therefore only man is. In the same way: He causes all men to be saved, therefore He is the only Savior. This is a strong idea and appears to have confirmation from the text:

5. *One God.* Here the exclusive proposition connects with the universal. That is: No man saves; or, God alone saves. The good and godly heart will not laugh. This is a very fine statement, for outside of God there is no salvation. God is our God. He is salvation. Whatever good happens to anyone comes from God; whatever evil, from Satan. *All men* (v. 4). That is, He is their Salvation. God saves them with His goodness. Then He also makes these things come true. There is the question whether this means eternal or temporal salvation. We can take Augustine's statement either way, because no one saves except God alone.

I think he is speaking about general salvation. He saves from the perils of adultery, fornication, poverty, error. Whoever now has escaped some peril escapes as God saves him. Ps. 107 confirms this idea. There God lists all their perils and their many works. He lists prison, poverties, captivity, the perils of the sea; and everywhere He says: "You shall confess, etc." He is speaking about the most general salvation. Paul says in ch. 4:10: "He is the Savior of all men, especially

---

[9] Cf. *Luther's Works,* 22, p. 62.

[10] The reference may be to the "all" in John 1:7: "That all might believe through Him."

[11] *Omnis homo est animal* was a common example of the "universal" proposition in Aristotle, e. g., *Prior Analytics,* I, 25a, 25; II, 91b, 5.

of those who believe." That passage clearly distinguishes between "all men" and "those who believe." The latter He saves eternally, but not the former. Accordingly, when we make a distinction of salvation between faithful and faithless people, we must draw from those passages this conclusion, that Paul here refers to general salvation. That is, God saves all the faithful, but He does not save the faithless in the same way. After all, He gives the victory even to wicked kings, but to David He gave a singular victory. To him, while he was still a mere lad but a pious one, He gave the throne of the kingdom. God preserves from plague both the ungodly and the godly. He gives both the light of the sun. Is this not a general statement? He tells us to pray for all men, because such a prayer for men is acceptable, even if they are wicked. The grace of God is one and the same, even for the faithless. We must therefore pray not only for the faithful but for all men. That prayer offered for them is both heard and pleasing, because He wants it so and desires to save all men. God wants to be asked that we may gain this request from Him, as Paul says Rom. 3:29: "Is He not the God of the Gentiles also?" He commands us to pray, and He accepts our prayer even for the wicked, because He is considering the following: that through our prayers He wants to save even the wicked, to give peace, wife, etc. Prayer for all men is acceptable, because He desires all men to be saved. Paul is not speaking about God's incomprehensible will — a topic forever secret, as here regarding the will of His command. There is a will which is hidden and reserved for Himself. This He points out to us in word and deed. His other will He reveals with many signs. Therefore we take this passage to refer to the will of His command or work, not to His hidden will. The contentious man, however, does not agree. From the material we have just treated and from other passages which agree you see this, as below in chapter 4 and in the psalm.[12] Why? Because He wants to save all men. God pours out His blessings so that doing this good thing — giving rain, for instance, to all men — pleases Him. It is therefore our duty to pray that the rain come. Satan, on the other hand, has his delight in the wicked, who desire to disturb this peace.

And come to the knowledge. This also refers to the will of the precept: "God wants all men to be saved." He wants to illumine all men under the sun, because He Himself shows the light of the sun

---

[12] 1 Tim. 4:10 and Ps. 107, as above, p. 261.

to the whole world. If they wish to ask us: "Why does He make some people blind?", that is God's hidden and incomprehensible will. However, I see the sun shining as a sign. In this way He wants "all men to be saved." You see, He causes the sun of Christ to rise in the world. He has given us the command that we illumine all men: "Go and preach to every creature" (Matt. 28:19), that is, He exposes to absolutely all men the light or knowledge of the truth. This is nothing else than that He wants all men to know this. After all, the Gospel comes that men may know the Gospel. Many do not know it. This relates to His most secret will. But His will which He has given us to teach is incomprehensible. These questions are too deep for you to explore. Adam broke his neck over them. This is beyond us and means nothing to us. We must think about those matters which have been expounded and given to us, for instance, the fact that He has given light to all men, and what they do not perceive with their eyes has still been expounded.

Thus Paul's statement is very simple. It is our job to pray that we may have a quiet life; that there be one salvation; that a prince have a safe rule and realm on earth; that a husband have a safe home and wife; the state, a safe magistracy; the housefather, a healthy crop. Next, we pray that all men may know the truth; that they may know the source from which they receive their blessings. You see, through our prayer and thanksgiving we indicate that these come from one Man. But these things do not bring one to a knowledge of the truth.

5. *For there is one.* Here we have the explanation: these things belong not only to Christians but to all men. Therefore we must pray to one God on behalf of all men. He must reveal Himself to the Gentiles that they may know how to have this Word of salvation and all good things. *Mediator.* What is the knowledge of the truth? It is to know the one God, from whom come those temporal blessings. He is clearly setting down a twofold salvation. There is a true God, who saves all men with a general salvation; and Christ the Mediator, who saves with an eternal salvation which also comes from God but through Jesus Christ. After all, Christ was not incarnate to have kingdoms, wives, and children. We have those gifts without the death of Christ. In those prior things God is our Savior without Christ. However, in our eternal salvation God is not our Savior without the Mediator. You see that Paul is speaking about salvation in general. This he then divides into temporal and eternal salvation. No matter

what he assigns to God, this is salvation left to God through Christ. Some people select other gods, but we know the God of all men. He has not left Himself without witnesses that they might see the one God, but this is because they do not know Him.

Between God and men, . . . 6. who gave Himself as a ransom for all. It is not clear whether this "for all" means for all men or for all those who are redeemed. It sounds as if he were speaking only about the faithful, because he seems to be making a distinction between temporal and eternal salvation. That is, he seems to say that all who are redeemed are redeemed through Him and not another. Whoever wants to argue may go his own way. He appears to be making a distinction here between faithful and faithless men. Yet he speaks about the faithful in such a way that there is no man among them who makes satisfaction for himself but through Christ. This is a very beautiful passage about redemption, about which Paul is happy to write. He speaks of redemption, or of the price of redemption, which means the price by which captives are ransomed. As Christ pays His life and head for our life and head, He has become the Price by which satisfaction is made for divine justice and wrath on our behalf. Some people [13] think that Christ's death has been set as an example, a type, an ideal of Christians. This is preaching scarcely half of Christ. He truly is the Price of redemption, which God elsewhere calls the forgiveness of sins. The wrath of God is real, not imaginary. It is no joke. Were it false, mercy would be false. You see, as wrath is, so is the mercy which forgives. May God avert that joke from us. When genuine wrath is at its highest, so is genuine mercy. Thus most truly has Christ taken the wrath of God upon Himself and has carried it on our behalf. He takes this upon Himself not only as an example, but He is the very true Price which is paid for us. If He has placed Himself in His own Person to turn away wrath from us, He has established Himself as the Price for us. If He is the Price, He has given not gold or silver but Himself. But here come the new Enthusiasts and Zwingli, and they say: A man, not the Son of God, has suffered for us. They make the Savior nothing more than a man. They go so far as to say that as God He does not suffer and that therefore only His humanity has been given for us. As proof they use this text, "the man." This passage we must observe as the rule and must explain other passages according to it, as, for instance, Phil. 2:7

---

[13] A marginal note suggests that Erasmus may be meant.

and the passage (John 6:63) "The flesh is of no avail, etc." The figure ἀλλοίωσις [14] is a matter of case for case, number for number. The city which I establish they have upset when the word for one nature is used for the other and also in the case of "Son" in Rom. 8:3, where the words "the Son of God" are taken for "man." Rather, one ought to say: whenever the word for one nature appears, whatever is said about the one nature must be understood as referring to the entire Person. Here, for instance, "man" is the word for one nature; yet the whole Person is referred to. This must be kept in force, etc., whenever the word for the part is attributed to the whole. "The Ethiopian is white," because he has white teeth. "He struck the son of the king," but this fellow says: "No, because he was struck in the leg." In all matters we must note the manner of speaking. Grammar ought to set the norm of speaking. The sophist says: "No. He struck the leg of the king's son." But this limb along with the son is one person. They cannot be torn apart in nature. It is the true Son of God and Son of Man who is crucified. It is said in truth: the Son of God is crucified, not as concerns the divine nature but according to the Person.

I had begun [15] to treat the point concerning the communication of attributes, for that error creeps in with the others, and according to that device Christ, the Salvation of the whole world, will be lost. He will follow us who have been redeemed through His humanity alone. That error wants this word used as confirmation through ἀλλοίωσις, that is, through an exchange. Consequently it has been taken up into an article of our faith and has been set forth in sacred literature that Christ is God in true substance and nature.[16] If that article stands, it follows inevitably that whoever harms one limb of this Person harms the whole Person. He divides that Person, as it were, into two persons.[17] He says that His humanity suffered, but not the divinity. This has outward appeal: "The divinity cannot be

[14] For the definition of this figure of speech, cf. *Luther's Works*, 37, p. 206, n. 63. Luther wrote a parallel discussion of this figure of speech in his *Confession Concerning Christ's Supper* (also February 1528). See *Luther's Works*, 37, pp. 206—214.

[15] The lecture of Feb. 5 begins at this point.

[16] Perhaps Luther has in mind the "He is God, . . . of the substance of the Father, . . . perfect God . . . equal to the Father with respect to His Godhead" (Athanasian Creed, pars. 29—31).

[17] Cf. the Athanasian Creed, par. 32: "Although He is God and Man, He is not two Christs but one Christ."

killed." It does not follow, however, that therefore the Son of God was not crucified. Whoever bows down to worship Christ worships the Son of God, because he touches and worships that Person who is God. When I strike the king and touch his arm, I have not struck his skin. "You have struck the tunic with which he was clothed and covered. They did not crucify God but someone clothed as God." *Man.* When we hear a term such as this, nature will be such that when people have the term on their side, they let it stand as it is; but if it is against them, they take pride in their full sacks. Then the term signifies a part of that Person, because it is the word for the human nature. But because that Man is in substance a divine Person, "man" here has to mean man in a sense other than elsewhere because of the union of persons.

Mediator. Unless you know this, you will lose Christ. Peter said: "I struck him." The Enthusiasts say: "How could you? You know that a man is composed of body and soul. How can you touch the soul? Therefore you have injured only the flesh." The flesh and soul are one person. These are statements from nature. When someone hits a dog in the leg with a stone, because of the injured limb we say that the whole dog is injured. This is synecdoche. In passing, I wanted to warn about this: in what sense Christ is Man in regard to His Person and yet is the Mediator, even if you were to separate Christ's divinity from His humanity. Christ entered into glory. Here Christ is taken for His human nature according to ἀλλοίωσις. But "Christ" signifies the entire Person, who is the Son of Man and Son of God. Yet this was before He was glorified. Yet it is truly said that the entire Christ is glorified, although in the other Person. "I live by faith" (Gal. 2:20) even in that Man, because He is one Person. I will attach myself to Christ as to the Person who in work and practice cannot be separated. They can separate Him in their speculations. If I prostrate myself before Christ, I do so before the Son of God as well as before the Son of Man in one Person. Without apology the expression issues from Christ and is directed to the blind man. John 9:36-37: "Who is the Son of God?" "And you have heard Him, etc." [18] There Christ says that the blind man is hearing and seeing the Son of God. I see the very Person, who is truly God. I look at a man; nevertheless, his intellect is his better part. Yet I hear him. I hear that person which is a real spirit, even if I may not see his reason

---

[18] The conversation between Jesus and the blind man is abbreviated.

and intellect. I see that part — the part of the flesh — joined with
reason. We must listen to grammar, to the *usus loquendi* about matters, and to sophist keenness. This deceived Wycliffe, too.[19] They
look at the reason for speaking but not at the manner of divine opera-
tion. Therefore it deceives them. Christ is established as one Person
consisting of God and Man. No suffering, no work can apply to Him
without our saying that it touches His entire Person.

6. *The testimony to which.* Our translator [20] has added certain
things which are not in the Greek.[21] Although the Greek does not
have "to which," yet it does not seem to have been a bad addition.
This is an unfinished statement: "the testimony at the proper time."
Both a verb and a genitive construction are lacking. So he added the
pronoun "to which" and "was borne." There is a similar passage in
Titus, but in different words. "He manifested" (chapter 1, at the
beginning). This is a similar statement in different words; that is,
God promised that salvation "ages ago." There appears to be something lacking in this text, too, perhaps "As God had promised from
eternity," or something like that, as in Titus (Titus 1:2). "The testimony at the proper time," obviously, He has revealed, He has made
manifest, because Christ is the testimony at the proper time. This is
not in tune. He did not give Himself as a testimony at the proper
time, but He revealed Himself. I explain this from Titus 1. Christ is
"the Mediator between God and men," as this was foreordained from
the beginning. About Him testimony has been manifested and revealed at the proper time. Furthermore, a testimony of this sort
(you will read it well this way) has been revealed at the proper time.
Rom. 16:26 and Eph. 3:5 both speak this way. This is an excellent
passage. Christ has two functions: mediation, or redemption, and
a testimony about the forgiveness of sins and mediation. This, too,
our Enthusiasts do not understand. The one is an act; the other,
the use of the act. I have written against the Enthusiast Carlstadt in
a book to answer his charge: "You new papists, you make new mistakes. You teach that there is remission of sins in Baptism, in the

[19] In his *Confession Concerning Christ's Supper* Luther wrote at some length
about the deception logic was able to achieve in Wycliffe and the sophists when
they neglected to heed the force of grammar. Cf. *Luther's Works,* 37, pp. 294 to
303, especially p. 301.

[20] The Vulgate.

[21] For *testimonium temporibus suis* the older Latin Bible had *cuius testimonium temporibus suis confirmatum est.*

Gospel. But Scripture says something else. The only thing we know about the forgiveness of sins is that it occurs on the cross, not in Baptism." [22] That is where he misleads the naive. Note well this passage and others like it. They distinguish between redemption as an actual act and redemption as it is preached. Had Christ been crucified a hundred thousand times and had nothing been said about it, what profit would the act of His being brought to the cross have brought? But when I come to this, I must draw this act into history and publish it for all the world. Also, if anyone had seen this, he would not have thought that the work of redemption was taking place there. The work is fulfilled on the cross, but no one knows of the redemption except the Father and the Son. Therefore to the act also the use of the act must be added, that it may be declared through the Word and that one may hold it by faith and, thus believing, may be saved. Paul's intent, then, is this: to the work of redemption belongs the Word of preaching, which does nothing else but impress the work of redemption. "You have urged this passage beyond measure. No one, etc. Answer me. You credit the remission of sins to the Gospel, to Baptism, and to Scripture. But the forgiveness of sins lies in the shedding of the blood." Who has placed those words in your mouth so that you know that this is the redemption from sins? You did not see it on the cross. You heard it, but through the Word. They say: "Christ completed the redemption with a single work." Yes, but He distributes it, applies it, and tells it by testimony. There is a testimony in Baptism. We are baptized into Christ. His Word is present. I am baptized into Christ the Crucified. In Baptism, therefore, there is a use of redemption — an application of its use. In this way the Gospel is the spoken Word, but it gives and brings this that Christ is, etc. Thus the Word of God brings out the remission of sins. Therefore there is remission of sins in the Gospel. This one fact — that Christ once, etc. — is divulged and spread in the Word. Thus there is remission of sin in the Sacrament. No one says that Christ is crucified in the Supper and in Baptism, but we say that in the Eucharist His body crucified for us is given to us, as the words say: "And He said: 'Take this.'" This word "Take" — this word offers me Christ crucified. Satan makes the following ridiculous remark: "They don't want the remission in Word and sacrament. They establish it

[22] Cf. Luther's *Against the Heavenly Prophets* (1525), *Luther's Works*, 40, especially p. 146.

in their speculations." They say that neither water nor bread saves us, but Christ crucified. But it profits nothing unless we receive in the Word that which in Baptism, in the Sacrament of the Altar, and in the Gospel brings this Christ to me. And wherever the Word of the Gospel is, there is the remission of sins. Therefore, Christ redeemed us once with a single work, but He did not pass out redemption with a single means. He gave it out through the medium of washing in Baptism, through the medium of eating in the Sacrament of the Altar, through the media of comforting the brethren, of reading in the Book, that the fruit of His passion might be spread everywhere. I would be happy to know those who comfort one who has been afflicted. They must do this through the Word of consolation. Who will say, then, that remission of sins is not in the Word? So Paul preaches and boasts wonderfully that he is justified by the Word, in which the treasure of our redemption has been enclosed and through which it is offered to us. When Paul made this commendation of Christ, he says that one thing is necessary: that a testimony must be revealed in which that redemption is brought near and distributed. Without that vehicle and channel, redemption would not come to us. No one thinks of it in this way. "A testimony that has been revealed." Actually, redemption has been foreordained and fulfilled in its own time. Thus the testimony has been fulfilled in its own time, but without the Word it would remain in darkness. Human reason cannot say that a man who dies is God, is the Redeemer of the world from its sins and who gives eternal life. To be sure God sees this, but not we. Therefore we must have the testimony of the Word to announce this to us. It is then that I get another thought. Wherever the Word of God is, then, there is the forgiveness of sins. After all, the Word is nothing else than the declaration of the forgiveness of sins. This is the conclusion which the Enthusiasts have to draw against us: "They have Baptism, the Eucharist, and confession; they comfort — but all this is without the Word." But we say: "The Word is our Baptism, etc. The Word has announced the whole thing to me."

7. *For this, this testimony, I was appointed a preacher.* To preach is to convey with great glory and boasting. Paul is happy to boast of his ministry, because it is his grace as a teacher to know for certain that he preaches the Word of God. I preach this Word in which is conveyed the treasure of redemption. The Enthusiasts who have read and listened to our material do not wish to see this. Human reason neither hears nor grasps it. On the contrary, whoever does

hear and grasp this gets this from God. Also, Paul has been appointed for testimony. To be sure, they say that Christ was crucified, but that He was not crucified in confession or Baptism. Therefore in these there is no remission of sins.

A teacher. See how he boasts with a full supply of spiritual boasting! Why? "I cannot boast enough concerning my apostleship; always more boasting would be necessary, for I have more people who want to be teachers." Today, too, we must have such boasting in the face of such great errors. Still I know that I have the Word, that it is true, that you are wrong, and that my Word will stand against all the gates, etc. (Matt. 16:18). "What great pride and boasting are in these men! That's the way they want to change us, but etc." This is a lofty title, that is, "I teach the faith and truth, I teach the faith and the Gentiles. Others teach myths, genealogies, foolish thoughts and grand notions. I teach faith and the truth, that is, this is the use of that redemption. Through my testimony comes faith that man is justified through faith, that is, through the knowledge of all things." In Titus (1:15) we read: "To the pure all things are pure," and here in chapter 4: "Everything created by God is good" for those who believe and understand the truth. Whoever believes in Jesus knows that salvation rests on Christ. And after that everything else is free. Works never do anything toward justification. Others are "always learning but never arriving at a knowledge of the truth" (2 Tim. 3:7), because they have been deprived of the truth. Concerning dress, eating, and service to the brethren one should know that one must not hope for salvation from them. That's the kind of teacher I am.

8. *I desire then that . . . the men should pray.*[23] Paul has said this often, and he feels free to insert that passage about the redemption of Christ. In this is God's chosen tool which the passage on redemption especially urges. If indeed God has established Paul, He has also established him to teach outward practices and ceremonies. He knew that in the future people would go after legalism and would neglect the principal theme of redemption. He wanted people to pray for all men. Because of this, he here takes the opportunity to digress. If one must pray for all men, then he is concerned for all men. After interjecting the digression, he returns to the topic of the beginning of the chapter. *I desire,* he says. We are not certain whether he is speaking here about public or private prayer. One can

23 The lecture of Feb. 10 begins at this point.

take it to mean both. Yet he appears to be speaking especially about public prayer, when someone comes to hear the Word, at the same time to kneel there, lift up his hands, and pray to the Lord, whose face remains before us as we pray the Our Father after the singing. So I take this to refer to public prayer. I desire, then, that the men should pray, especially in public; and that they pray thus also in every place but especially where the Gospel is taught. In one city there were many churches — in fact, as many as there were houses. Paul writes in Titus (1:11) that people were "upsetting whole families," and in Philemon (2) he writes to the church which is in the house of Archippus. It is his intent, then, to say that those churches ought to be in harmony, single-minded, praying in one spirit. People thus separated by households should not separate themselves as far as their souls are concerned. In any home or church the men should begin to pray. They should be the first to pray. This is what happens in the church; when the priest reads that public prayer, the congregation responds, "Amen."

In every place. That is, the congregations should pray at the same time and should help each other with prayers for each other, so that there should be no place which prays against another place. If you wish to take this to refer to private prayer, that's fine. But in private prayer women are not excluded. Neither sex is, as Christ indicates in His prayer in Matt. 6. But because Paul here separates men from women, he seems to refer to public prayer. Also today Jewish men are separated from women. We, too, preserve this custom. The student and priest read the Psalms softly and simply. That is called public prayer. Women did not participate. Now they read and sing but do not pray. *Lifting pure and holy hands.* We live not with Judaic purity which water washes. Rather we live with purity of life or work. Whoever wishes to be involved in sacred matters ought to approach them with pure heart, mouth, and hands, that is, such as are pure of blood, murder, rapine, theft, all burnings and injury by which one injures a neighbor. This describes a ceremony that we ought by no means neglect: that in prayer we lift up our hands, according to the Psalm: "I lifted up." [24] That gesture which

---

[24] Ps. 25:1; 86:4; 143:8 use the expression *levavi animam meam,* but *levavi manus* is apparently not found in the Psalms. In Gen. 14:22 Abram says to the king of Sodom: *Levo manum meam ad Dominum,* but this is in the sense of "I have sworn to the Lord." But regarding the psalm passages listed above, one should remember Luther's statement a few lines later: "When the soul is lifted up, the hands are lifted up."

the lifting up of hands signifies is recommended in sacred literature. People have let this fall into disuse among us fools and hypocrites. We do not do it as the prayers are being sung. Where there is serious prayer, it is an excellent ceremony of prayer to lift up the hands. In the Greek church, they say, this custom still endures. When the soul is lifted up, the hands are lifted up. Also, Christ says (Mark 11:25): "Whenever you stand, praying," or, when you prostrate yourself, as did David; that is, pray with a good conscience. He is referring to a hindrance to a prayer that accomplishes nothing. As Peter says (1 Peter 3:7): "Bestowing honor . . . in order that your prayers may not be hindered," yield to the woman, tolerate her idiosyncracies. You see, if you don't do this, there will remain a disharmony between you. While that continues, you cannot pray. Whoever cannot pray for the forgiveness of sins cannot pray for anything. As we read in Matt. 5:24: "Leave your gift." Whoever feels that he has offended his brother either by word or deed, in act or body, cannot lift up, etc. He has hands filled with blood (cf. Is. 1:15). Wash them! First clean your fists! That is, first be reconciled with one another, in order that your prayers may become more harmonious, that is, harmless; or, if harmful, then that they may be reconciled. What is said in Ecclus. 28:3 — "A man retains another man's sin and yet asks God for pardon" — will not occur. *Without anger or quarreling*. This is his explanation of the meaning of purity of hands. What is it? There should be peace and love between brothers. If there is anger and quarreling, then prayer is hindered and the hands are impure. Therefore take care that everywhere there be peace, love, purity. "You pray, but not well. Therefore you receive not because you are impure" (cf. James 4:3). Whoever offends by anger with which I am irritated and offended ought to bring about our reconciliation, and he who is offended ought to be reconciled. This I still keep in my heart, my own thinking, about which Rom. 1:21 says: "In their thinking they become futile." This is the sharp memory, as when one philosopher tries to nullify the argument of another. When two people engage in dialog in such a way that one struggles to overcome the other, to strive with his cunning to establish his own points and refute those of the other, it is dog-eat-dog, that is, quarreling occurs. Paul turns a neat phrase here. He wants to speak about very bitter quarreling. When a man who has been wronged turns this over in his heart, he suffers a bite. He is wounded as he thinks how to bite back or prick back most sharply. For example, this occurs where two people are arguing and both want to be right. On both sides one can see the sting, as when two roosters attack with very sharp strikes. When these thoughts are in a man's heart and keep him busy, when he dwells on them and they fight back, then no good prayer takes place. You see, I am thinking, "I shall have revenge for his answers." Such a person entertains a false idea. He is considering how to avenge an act or person. Thus he is disturbed by such thoughts, and he cannot pray, because he does not forgive his brother his sin. Because you do not forgive, you are not forgiven. From anger follow those wranglings. "I will bite back that it may be seen." Where the Catholic teaches correctly: "My foe does nothing but make a false charge." This is well said. Provoked by anger and wrath, he does this to jeer with his insults. He again loses patience: "I charge you. I charge you," and it's dog-eat-dog. Therefore one ought to stand firm in peace and forgiveness of sins toward his neighbor. See Matt. 18 regarding the servant.

9. *Let the women be sensible.* Here Paul seems still to be speaking about public prayer. I have no objection if anyone takes it to refer to private prayer, but it is better to take it as public prayer. The women should be properly arranged, correct *in their apparel.* It is a Hebraism to speak of "adorning oneself in clean garb with modesty and propriety." Here the passage is the same. There are some who treat this passage in the following way: they allow no cleanness to mere women. Rather, women ought to walk in squalor. This they say against those who want them adorned. As we see below (1 Tim. 3:2), a bishop must be a man who is κόσμιος ("dignified").[25] The word κόσμιος is applied not to property but to one's way of life. The bishop's deportment, ought to be pure. This refers to his way of life, not to his property. He denies any adornment of property. This is not a matter of silver. He is adorned, then, in regard to his behavior, lest it offend or harm someone. As Scripture has spoken about the purity of hands,[26] so women ought to walk that they may not offend someone with their adornment. Rather, as we say in the proverb: *Zucht der Weiber ist der schönste Schmuck.*[27] Simple garb and adornment is more fitting for a woman than a wagonload of pearls. I do

[25] The Vulgate translates this Greek word with *ornatus* ("well-ordered, adorned").

[26] Cf. Ps. 18:20, 24.

[27] "Decency is women's most beautiful adornment." Cf. Prov. 11:22.

not want to interpret this too scrupulously — that rich clothing is forbidden to women. Here we must make exceptions for weddings. I have seen a marriage which intended to be Christian. Here Paul is speaking about a woman's everyday life. He condemns those women who parade in luxury, who wish to be dressed in the most beautiful clothing to allure lovers day after day, who go about everyday as if it were Easter. As for the fact that a woman adorns herself in honor of her groom but goes about in common fashion otherwise, etc., Scripture commends the adornment for a spouse, etc. He is saying that it is superstition to wear rags at a wedding; it is contrary to the ritual of the area and to the custom of the people with whom we live; provided, of course, that no excess occurs, if this has been the mode of dressing for weddings or festivals. Rather, Paul forbids the surrendering of self to elegance, the pompous pursuit of adornment. He does not demand the rigor of superstition. After all, a queen must bedeck herself, as did Esther. If she clothes herself with care and good taste, she is not decorating herself but acting in accord with the custom of and allegiance to the people with whom she lives. If it were the custom, then it would be a matter of choice for her so to adorn herself or not. In allegiance to her groom, in honor of her wedding and husband, she should dress otherwise than one dresses in church, where one ought to wear proper clothing. There is one way of dressing for a dance; another way for church. Paul is speaking out against pomp and excess, a passion for fashion with which so many are so affected that they cannot fill their eyes. If they see adornment today that they did not see yesterday, etc. — this is to desire dress because of pleasure or passion. Such are the little ladies who are not acquisitive, etc., but they do have a passion in dress. If that were to come to the Sacrament today, I would not permit it, so am I against the pleasure of and passion for dressing. Whatever there is in clothing, food, drink, homes we can keep with good conscience. "In the church." How? Not for passion or pleasure but for "apparel," that is, edifying apparel, which offends, entraps, or scandalizes the eyes of no one. He does not want them to wear filthy clothes. Filthiness is not religious scrupulousness, as St. Francis says. A Christian can have clean and pure clothing, as the Jews do. He explains the term *modestly*, that is, that there be modest and temperate dress. *Sensibly* does not speak about filth when one reads what he ought to read. Formerly women walked about with neck bared all the way to the middle of the back. This was immodest dress. Elsewhere half the breast is seen. They have high-heeled shoes, etc., so that they can show off their bodies. Rather, they ought to have clothes to conceal themselves, to cover the neck. Our women walk about with their faces nearly veiled and everything covered very neatly, with their furs, so that almost nothing of their limbs or skin is seen. All this ought to be hidden in church in order that they may walk modestly. Monastic garb comes in here. In this everything is concealed. This is very modest dress. Thus I praise long coats and furs highly. Also young unmarried women ought not wear their locks braided but have a veil when they participate in the Sacrament. I find no fault in our women. I could bear that young women come with their hair veiled, but this is contrary to custom. There should be modesty in dress. Otherwise, in public, modesty is the rule. Clothing should not be too expensive, with too much gold or pearls; a woman should be clothed and adorned with proper modesty and chastity. Let her walk thus at home. He explains *not in tresses*,[28] "braids." Paul wants women to veil their braids. Here [29] there is no need to prohibit this practice. In France they wear their hair unbound and with open braids so that no one knows who is married or unmarried. Perhaps this is how Greek women wore their hair. Among our people married women veil their hair and braids. When they do this, they veil their locks chastely and modestly, so that it may not become material for watchers to think shameful thoughts.

With gold. A woman ought not display gold in her clothing or coat. Here it becomes very clear what custom Greek women had. They were haughtily resplendent in all of these adornments. I don't want them to wear these things in church. Weddings are something else, that is, where it is a matter of some expense, as when a lady wants to wear a velvet gown. This indicates not a Christian woman but a brash one as she goes to the Word, Sacrament, and prayer. She does not want to submit.

10. *But in that which befits.* Here he explains what he means by clean and decorous clothing. They dress in such a way to be the sort of women who have a zeal for piety and who practice good works. If they overdress, it means they are self-seekers, they feed their own eyes, they irritate others. This is to be eager for the vanity of this world and to desire a badge for praise. Our women ought to dress so that one can

[28] Luther quotes the older text *non in tricis* for the later *non in tortis crinibus.*
[29] I. e., in Germany.

recognize that not one of them is seeking clothing. She goes about, covered everywhere. She does not dress expensively. Whatever is left she spends on the poor. So it appears that they are concerned about God and their neighbor and do not seek their own praise. This is one rule about controlling women in public. We need not fear that they overdress when they go into the kitchen but when they go out in public, when they gather for prayer, and when the Word is about to be taught. Against the superstitious, the pompous, the brash, Paul condemns overdressing both in public and in private. I am not against dressing up in honor of one's bridegroom, but not in church, which is another matter. In the former case it is a custom of the person or of the people with whom we live, and it is done in honor of the bridegroom. But in church they should be covered. Good people have held to the middle ground. Brash and superstitious women must not be admitted. Now follows another rule — about teaching in the church.

11. *Let a woman learn in silence with all submissiveness.*[30] I believe that Paul is still speaking about public matters. I also want it to refer to the public ministry, which occurs in the public assembly of the church. There a woman must be completely quiet, because she should remain a hearer and not become a teacher. She is not to be the spokesman among the people. She should refrain from teaching, from praying in public. She has the command to speak at home. This passage makes a woman subject. It takes from her all public office and authority. On the other side is the passage in Acts (8:27) about Queen Candace. We read many such examples in sacred literature — that women have been very good at management: Huldah, Deborah, Jael, the wife of the Kenite, who killed Sisera.[31] Why, then, does Paul say here that he deprives them of the administration of the Word as well as of work? You should solve that argument in this way. Here we properly take "woman" to mean wife, as he reveals from his correlative phrase (v. 12) "to have authority over man," that is, over her husband. As he calls the husband "man," so he calls the wife "woman." Where men and women have been joined together, there the men, not the women, ought to have authority. An exceptional example is the case where they are without husbands, like Huldah and Deborah who had no authority over husbands. Another lived in Abela.[32] The evangelist

---

30 The lecture of Feb. 11 begins at this point.

31 Cf. 2 Kings 22:14; Judges 4:14, 17.

32 The wise woman of Abel of Beth-maacah (2 Sam. 20:14-21).

Philip had four unmarried daughters, etc. (cf. Acts 21:9). He forbids
teaching contrary to a man or to the authority of a man. Where there
is a man, there no woman should teach or have authority. Where there
is no man, Paul has allowed that they can do this, because it happens
by a man's command. He wants to save the order preserved by the
world — that a man be the head of the woman, as 1 Cor. 11:3 tells us.[33]
Where there are men, she should neither teach nor rule. She rules in
the home and says: "Be quiet," but she is not the master. This maxim
was spoken against Greek women, who have been and now are more
ingenious and clever than those in other countries. The Jews and Arabs
do not honor their women in this way. The Turk considers women as
beasts. Not so with the Greeks and us. Miriam seemed wise to herself;
she rose up against her brother and her "man" (cf. Num. 12). They
should be with all submissiveness. Then comes the teaching, and Paul
does not entrust the ministry of the Word to her. He considers this the
greatest thing that goes on in the church. You must always understand
this with the condition that men are present. Paul says this that there
may be peace and harmony in the churches when the Word is taught
and people pray. There would be a disturbance if some woman wished
to argue against the doctrine that is being taught by a man. The
method of 1 Cor. 14 has now perished. I could wish it were still in
effect, but it causes great strife. Where a man teaches, there is a well-
rounded argument against a man. If she wishes to be wise, let her
argue with her husband at home.

12. *To have authority.* That is, she ought not take over for herself
the heritage which belongs to a man so that a man says to her: "My
lord." She wants her own wisdom to have priority, that whatever she
has said should prevail and whatever the man says should not. We say:
Paul is saying with power what is to be said. He is not speaking about
real physical domination, but about the authority of the word, that she
should be right and have the last word, that in the church her word
ought to appear wiser and more learned and thus of greater authority
than that of her husband. So also in the home.

13. *For Adam.* Paul skillfully arranges this example of his that he
may not appear to be speaking off the top of his head. This is the way
God has ordained it. The principal role belongs to the man. Adam
was first, etc. Therefore the greater authority lies in the man rather
than in the woman. *Then Eve,* that she should be, etc. Secondly, this

[33] The Weimar text reads "Cor. X."

situation stands not only because of what God intended but also from
the history of Adam and Eve.

14. *And Adam was not deceived,* that is, was not involved in the
lie. Here Paul appears to gather arguments with considerable concern
on behalf of man's dominance. Yet they are true: (1) God Himself
has so ordained that man be created first — first in time and first in
authority. His first place is preserved in the Law. Whatever occurs
first is called the most preferable. Because of God's work, Adam is
approved as superior to Eve, because he had the right of primogeni-
ture. In human affairs it can happen that a later work can be better.
It also happens that whoever does not do evil does good. In Scripture,
however, this is not so. (2) Experience. Not only has God's wisdom
ordained this, but there was more wisdom and courage in Adam. And
by this one sees who is wiser and rightly preferred. But Adam was
wiser than Eve. Experience has been witness to this. Therefore Adam
is approved according to God's creation and man's experience. These
are the two arguments. Paul thus has proved that by divine and human
right Adam is the master of the woman. That is, it was not Adam who
went astray. Therefore there was greater wisdom in Adam than in the
woman. Where this occurs, there is the greater authority. One point
here indicates that Adam was not deceived. We do not know that
Adam would have sinned had he listened to the serpent. Adam sinned
knowingly, but he wanted to agree with his wife and please her. He
thought that it was not so important a matter, etc., although Paul may
seem to point to the fact that he wants to explain that Adam had not
been addressed by the serpent, since Adam had received the command
from God written in his heart. This, too, is an argument: God gave him
the command directly, but to the woman through the man. He presses
this idea, that Satan did not attack Adam. Therefore Adam was not
deceived by the serpent. Yet this is a very simple statement. The serpent did not deceive Adam, because it did not tempt him by speaking
with him. Therefore Paul is correct in saying that Adam was deceived
not by the serpent but by the woman. He believed that this sin was
an insignificant matter, not realizing that, if he fell, he was falling away
from the command, from God, even from life. This he was not considering. He did not have that knowledge of good and evil. That is, he
persevered in his dominion over the serpent, which did not attack him
but rather attacked the weaker vessel. Therefore, etc. He has written
quite carefully how cleverly Satan treated the fearless person and at-

tacked the weak one, just as he does today. *But the woman was deceived and became a transgressor,* that is, she became the cause of transgression. There are three arguments here: (1) that Adam was formed [first]; (2) that he was not deceived; (3) it was not he but the woman who brought on transgression. Paul uses the argument which we have in Genesis (3:16): "Because you have done this, you will be under the man. In punishment for your sin and transgression, you must be subject to the man and suffer the pains of childbirth." Thus that ordinance of God continues to stand as a memorial of that transgression which by her fault entered into the world.

15. *She will be saved.* That subjection of women and domination of men have not been taken away, have they? No. The penalty remains. The blame passed over. The pain and tribulation of childbearing continue. Those penalties will continue until judgment. So also the dominion of men and the subjection of women continue. You must endure them. You will also be saved if you have also subjected yourselves and bear your children with pain. *Through bearing children.* It is a very great comfort that a woman can be saved by bearing children, etc. That is, she has an honorable and salutary status in life if she keeps busy having children. We ought to recommend this passage to them, etc. She is described as "saved" not for freedom, for license, but for bearing and rearing children. Is she not saved by faith? He goes on and explains himself: bearing children is a wholesome responsibility, but for believers. To bear children is acceptable to God. He does not merely say that bearing children saves; he adds: if the bearing takes place in faith and love, it is a Christian work, for "to the pure all things are pure (Titus 1:15)." Also: "All things work together," Rom. 8:28. This is the comfort for married people in trouble: hardship and all things are salutary, for through them they are moved forward toward salvation and against adultery. *If they continue.* This means whatever a married woman or a mother and her children do. *In faith.* Paul had to add this, lest women think that they are good in the fact that they bear children. Simple childbearing does nothing, since the heathen also do this. But for Christian women their whole responsibility is salutary. So much the more salutary, then, is bearing children. I add this, therefore, that they may not feel secure when they have no faith. Rather, they should continue — along with their children — in faith, etc. But how they can take care of this as children, etc., see chapter 5, if you have done your job and instructed your children and

have done what you can. Let Isaac be wicked against the training of his father, let the defeat be not in Abraham but in his son. See to it that your children do not persevere in faithlessness because of your negligence. See to it that they are not corrupted or that you do not allow them to be corrupted, if it is your fault that they have not continued "in faith." See to it that they do not hold in contempt the Word, faith toward God, love toward neighbor, holiness toward themselves. That is, a woman ought to live in holiness, according to 1 Thess. 4:5, "not in the passion of lust." That is, she should not befoul herself with another's husband or unclean morals. A man should be content with his own wife, for she is his own body, and in relation to her there should be reverence and holiness. *With modesty*, with moderation, good common sense; sensible, well-mannered. People see modesty or a composed mind when there is modesty of body, a person who can deal with matters sensibly. I interpret it with "sensibly" *(vernünftig)*, to be temperate in doing all other things — in speaking, in managing; that a person may sensibly and skillfully manage affairs. Thus you see how he wants Christian women to behave in public life, in the home, etc. If the Lord were to raise up a woman for us to listen to, we would allow her to rule like Huldah. This first part has spoken to husbands and wives. What follows is the description of other estates — of bishops and of deacons.

CHAPTER THREE

1. *The saying is sure.*

Paul now goes on [1] in his instruction for preachers, estates, or orders in the church. As he has here spoken about the husband, etc., in a general directive, so now among all the ranks of the church he has preached the ministry of the Word. Therefore he establishes what sort of a man a bishop must be. The passage is known from the Epistle to Titus, since it is one and the same word. *Pha* in Hebrew, or the apostolic *pa.* [2] No one ought to be in doubt about this, but one should stand with firm conscience, that is, on it one can rely and die. What is this? *If anyone.* This is a passage for dealing with the call. You see, Scripture everywhere warns us away from rashness in entering the ministry, Heb. 5:4; John 10:1; Jer. 23:21. It does this because everywhere one requires some call. Paul comforts. Here Paul saw that there were many fickle, big-talking false teachers who kept rushing about in all directions, saying that they were driven by the Spirit, by wisdom, and by their talent. This temptation used to bother the Carthusians: "Look, you have a talent from the Lord, and you are not investing it for profit." In this way they would cause them unrest. Those who are in the ministry think about the austerity of their life. Paul himself bursts into the middle of these confusions and shakes them up: "This is true. Would that you had such men to pursue the office of a bishop, the ministry." So also we can say today, "Would that we had!" Thus this is a passage which both confirms and concedes. But you have his words before you in a splendid expression, because this is a "noble task." If this text did not stand firm, the Enthusiasts would have won the battle. Paul does not say "a noble thing," but a "noble task, undertaking." The office of bishop in the church, then, is a noble work, a very good function, which has many good works in it. Where are these men? He is one who is eager and exerts himself to do well. See whether the Enthusiasts are the kind of people who delight in doing good. See whether they have an affection for gentleness, hospitality, generosity; whether they show this willingly, with enthusiasm, or

[1] The lecture of Feb. 13 begins at this point.

[2] The manuscript leaves space after both italicized syllables, possibly for completion later of words imperfectly understood.

whether they take this kind of life by choice. I always see many of
the sort who seize the office of teaching in contempt of all good works.
They are looking for glory. Paul does not speak in this tone. Rather,
he says: whoever aspires to the office of a bishop must be from his
heart a righteous man, sincere, good to the core, a model of piety.
Thus it is a duty, although a difficult work, for it is exposed to all
styles of life, the most contrary of all, even to detractors, and the incumbent is exposed to every peril of life. It is easy to fall into error
while teaching and comforting. If God Himself were not driving such
a person, he would prefer to withdraw into the desert. Thus Moses
refused the ministry six times to which God called him (cf. Ex. 3 and
4), until God became angry and said (cf. Ex. 4:14): "Look, Aaron will
come out to meet you." God had to thrust it upon him in anger. Because the ministry is so important — a situation where one is exhibited
as "a spectacle to the angels," according to 1 Cor. 4:9 — he must absolutely be strong, firm, and good who says: "I see that the erring brethren do not understand the sound Word. They are my brothers. I shall
run into that fire. I shall oppose those errors and iniquities of Satan."
For people with aspirations like that the sights are set mighty high.
Our Enthusiasts run without being called; but to be of service to
a brother as a matter of indulgence is a serious matter. "You have been
unfaithful in a little thing" (cf. Matt. 25:21). If someone does not
hazard his bread and substance for a brother, how will he risk his life
and salvation? Meanwhile they say, "I mean it from the bottom of
my heart." They are not seeking to look to their conscience. Rather,
they are seeking their own glory. Paul says (Phil. 2:21): "They all look
after their own interests." The heretical false teachers do not go where
no one has taught that way but where Paul has set the foundation.
They build with stubble and hay and violate the temple of God. That
is how our Enthusiasts act. Paul, then, wants to say: "I should judge
this man to be the kind who preaches the Word with a pure and confident heart. He does not sin; he is not spendthrifty." On the other hand,
if he is a greedy accumulator, he sins and boasts of his doctrine. "Doctor, heal yourself" (Luke 4:23). This is a concession: truly, whoever
aspires to the bishop's office must make one take heart, because he is
not looking for his own glory that he might perform a miracle in the
world, as our Enthusiasts do. But here there is error. "Even if no one
else wishes to, I want to serve the wretched people with that which
the Lord has given," he says if he looks about with guileless eye. For

bishop means "watchman," "visitor," that is, one who goes to visit, who visits to see people. He looks around to see what is being taught and how people live. He watches with open eyes that no false doctrine breaks in or that there be no person who does not listen, who holds his teaching in contempt, etc. A papist who tends to his job of overseeing is properly something of a bishop, not one who merely wears the badge of office and sits in his palace but one who goes out and visits the sick, the grieving, the lonely, the sinners to help them. He is exposed to the weaknesses of all men, because he himself is weak and in need of comfort. That is, a person who has a desire, who has an interest, to see which people might believe, etc., that is, the man who has aspirations to serve the weak, surely desires a good work. A father has aspirations for obedience, for a magistracy. He has aspirations for a very fine thing. There is a difference between those who aspire and those who simply have a desire. That is, the latter do not look to see who is being taught but who is pouring out his own wisdom. Their stomachs are ready to burst. Carlstadt never asked his hearers to become more learned. Thus he is another "Twin," [3] but that he might appear to be an opener of the sacred groves. Such people write and teach to gain exposure for their own doctrine. In the public ministry one should see to it that others learn. If people would only say: "Thank you. That was a good lecture, because it produces fruit in the hearers and not merely admiration." They only flaunt their own wisdom; "they look after their own interests" (Phil. 2:21), not the fruitful instruction of the brethren, and so a good work is not a good work. May one aspire to a call, and do they not lack a preacher? One certainly may have such aspirations. But see to it that they themselves desire this work. Then you can volunteer, and then you will be called. After all, Paul speaks this way: "If you hear that there is need of a preacher somewhere, you can tell the people in charge, 'If there is no one else available, I would, etc.' If you offer yourself as one who is ready and if you have the recommendation of your brothers, so that the people in charge may accept you, etc., we should not make an exception of the office of the episcopate." A word about aspiring to be a bishop. The pious aspire to that office with trepidation. They do not come freely and teach, but they are forced into it, even as I. If God and the people consider that I am useful to the people, I neither aspire to the office nor ask for it. I do not offer myself to do this if He could send

[3] Cf. John 20:24-29.

someone else in my place. Those are the best who aspire to the office and see its errors and needs. In me the aspiration is secondary. If this is what people want, they chase one away here, another there; therefore, etc.

2. *He must be above reproach.* This is the first quality he must have. The man who wants to investigate, correct, and teach others should be above reproach. To be beyond comparison is shameful for a teacher; that is, that he is beyond accusation and can neither rightly nor justly be accused. After all, there is no one who is above reproach before God. Paul writes: "I am conscious of no evil" (cf. 1 Cor. 4:4). Let the Our Father stand: "Forgive us." Before God no one is above reproach, but before men the bishop is to be so, that he may not be a fornicator, an adulterer, a greedy man, a foul-mouthed person, a drunkard, a gambler, a slanderer. If he is falsely accused, no harm; he is still above reproach; no law can accuse him before men. Samuel and Moses are good examples. Samuel said, "If I have defrauded anyone, etc." (cf. 1 Sam. 12:3). There he showed how innocent he was, as far as men were concerned. Moses spoke this way before Korah (cf. Num. 16:15). To live this way, that you do not harm your neighbor by theft or adultery, means that no man can accuse you of anything or say: "You have stolen from me; you have raped my wife." St. Jerome says: "A bishop must be the sort of man whom no sin has contaminated since his baptism."[4] Therefore he himself was never a bishop. Nor has anyone else been! It is monkish superstition to grieve over sins, a bishop tortured by weakness. *The husband.* We have said enough about this in the Epistle to Titus.[5] Here the papists say he must be the bishop of one church. Others say that bishops must have a wife, that a person cannot be a bishop unless he is married, and that today it is necessary that everyone of them be so, etc. *Temperate.* These are the priestly robes, the royal adornment, the gems and precious stones of our Aarons. *Sensible,* wide-awake and sober, so that he is not drunk with sleep, a snorer given to sleep. κόσμιος, "proper." As I mentioned above regarding women,[6] they should have dignified dress, that is, a bishop ought not to go about like a vagabond or a mercenary soldier but ought to appear with dignity as befits him. He should not be seen with torn shoes, mountainous mane, ragged shirts, and torn sleeves,

[4] Cf. Jerome, *Adversus Jovinianum*, Book I, ch. 35, *Patrologia, Series Latina*, XXIII, 270—271.

[5] Cf. *Luther's Works*, 29, pp. 18—21.

[6] Cf. p. 273 above.

but he should wear respectable clothes. That is what κόσμιος means. As I said above about women: covered in every member.[7] Let this be his covering, that he walks with proper garb. σώφρων, *vernünftig*, he should be, to handle the situation nicely. He should listen and answer gently. He should advise prudently, he should not insist on his own way. He should use good common sense so that it will be a pleasure to behold it. He is not noisy. He is not rash. Everything is done with good common sense. φιλόξενος, hospitable. He is a cheerful host to brothers who come from everywhere — from churches in other places. He gives them food and drink; he washes their feet. Indeed, the bishop's home should be open to foreign brethren, but not to just any vagrant. At the time of the Roman Empire this was not so, and the political community of the Jews in a very fine way wrote letters of recommendation for their brethren. We read about this in John's last epistle (cf. 3 John 10). From this passage it is clear that the bishop had control of a common treasury. I would not want us to have one. Even Augustine did not have this, because he said that we should look after our own things. The bishops converted that money which belonged to the poor into horses and attendants. It is better, then, in a corrupt time not to have money. Thus a person remains without fault and loss of reputation. We do not apply the requirement of hospitality to parish priests. They are forbidden to be hospitable. After all, they scarcely support themselves, so meanly and poorly are the ministers of the Word fed. Whoever has the means should be hospitable. Were we to have the means, we would be hospitable. *An apt teacher.* Does this mean he should be trained at the university? He should be eager to teach and qualified to teach. Better yet, he should teach carefully. He should not be the sort of man who lectures once a year at the university. It is not the bishop's job to teach in the pulpit. Rather, he should teach so that he trains a student when he inculcates things, so that his voice shows earnest care, so that his listeners improve, not so that he himself is in the limelight. This expression does not appear in Titus. The title "teacher" is great if it is not perverted. A teacher and a speaker differ. The former teaches so that a thing may be understood. The latter speaks, but there is no understanding. In the church people should teach and educate. Erasmus does not teach. Even if he teaches, he muddles about. Thus the Enthusiasts are not teachers, because they don't strengthen consciences. But a man teaches when

---

[7] Cf. p. 275 above.

his hearers understand what he is saying. Paul wrote to Titus (1:9) "so that he may be able to give instruction." He teaches what they must learn. At the same time he instructs them in doctrine. Then he "refutes those who contradict" (Titus 1:9). There the opposing party is false. I would prefer that the translation "an apt teacher" stand, but it has fallen into abuse, because the apt teachers have been put off in the universities. The Enthusiasts are filled with empty talk, but they do not teach, because nothing is definite with them. That is, he is an apt teacher who hands down what people must know.

We have heard [8] that a bishop ought to have this gift, that he teach well and cheerfully. This is the chief responsibility and duty of the bishop: the ministry of the Word, even though our people regard religion most cheaply.

3. πάροινος, *drunkard*, one who is always eager for wine or drink. It is not that he should dislike wine, but that he should not be a drunkard. Paul is writing to Greeks, where there is no beer. He seems to make a distinction between the drunkard and the alcoholic. Those who must drink constantly are alcoholics. And yet it is not good that a bishop be drunk even once. This can lead to a fall, as in Lot's case (cf. Gen. 19:33). But Paul condemns constant drinking. *Violent.* This he ought not be — a snappish person who lashes out with his tongue. He is not speaking about physical violence. After all, you know that in a meeting one must observe this rule, that faults should be attacked in a general way, so that no one is named personally. There are seditious preachers, and there are two methods of attack, one in general. One must not preach against the government so as to spare the people. On the contrary, we must censure orders of every kind. Through sedition the contrary is usually done. The public official listens freely, so that he may punish the people. This is the way to encourage sedition. If both are attacked, some preachers today win the minds of the common crowd over in this way, but they overlook how much malice men have. The Enthusiasts used to think that they would restore the republic with the common crowd. The second method is in the presence of the congregation. This occurs with formal testimony and judgment. Paul witnessed before all (cf. 1 Cor. 5:3). If they do not listen, they must be excommunicated. He selects certain persons whom he brings into public light. Yet Christ says (Matt. 18:15-18): "Tell him his fault between you and him . . . tell it to the church."

[8] The lecture of Feb. 17 begins at this point.

The faults are not corrected when someone is brought to confusion in, that is, before, the whole congregation. Rather, people get worse, and minds become irritated. He is a snappish preacher who strikes a person in private. One must strike against public faults, but not private ones, for that is to sow the seeds of sedition, discord, anger, and jealousy.

"Greedy of filthy gain." What sort of gain is filthy? That which comes from filthy profiteering like gambling and usury, which demean the bishop. He ought to have the necessities of life and keep his accounts honestly and without blame. Paul writes this way to Titus (Titus 1:7). *Gentle.* This means fair, or, better yet, accommodating. This is a bishop's outstanding, most honorable, most universal, and greatest virtue. With it he wins the minds of men. With it he accommodates himself to the ways and interests of all people. He is burdensome to no one, approachable to all. He can skillfully adapt himself to the people. He can explain all things, endure all things. He does not proceed strictly according to law. The young regents want to rule according to laws — an impossible thing. They should rule according to ἐπιείκεια, "fairness," according to the just proportion of laws, so that the magistrate may keep the laws under his will. You see, people are different, but the law is impersonal. A situation can occur in common, and he can preserve justice, etc., where the law is against both parties. The one loses because he is hindered by some misfortune; the other, because of his wickedness. One must be punished; the other not. This is to deal with people not according to severity. Let them manage their affairs so that a person does not waste a dollar for the sake of a penny, that he does not throw the baby out with the bathwater. A bishop should be very fair, very obliging, so that he can easily tolerate people and accommodate himself to their ways, for they are not all of one kind. He must impose obedience upon all men and yet be a burden to no one. "Let all men know your forbearance," Phil. 4:5. ἄμαχος, *not quarrelsome.* Our people today are still plotting wars. I do not think that Paul is simply prohibiting battles and warfare. A bishop should also not be a contentious man who likes to quarrel with people over a penny or a nickel. Such people should not go to court with their fellow citizens and brothers, but if they inflict a loss through a lawsuit, he should be long-suffering. How our divines follow this rule we can see. *Lover of money.* "Greedy" is a good translation. Avarice is a shameful fault in a bishop. Paul censures it severely and calls it idolatry (cf. Col. 3:5). A bishop ought to be a gentle person, available to all for encouragement. Therefore he cannot be greedy or, as they say in Greek, eager for money.[9] He should not be thinking how to gather a great treasury. "If we have food and clothing" (cf. 1 Tim. 6:8)! The princes learn this quickly, this fault, etc.[10]

4. *He must manage his own household well.* That is, he manages well who rules well his own household. Yet Paul is speaking not only about piety but about courtesy as well, that his house is well managed in this way, that he has a serious and disciplined home. Paul explains this in this way, that the children, servants, and maids are well mannered in customs, clothing and behavior, that it be a virtuous household. There one does not enter for illicit love and to carouse as in a tavern. He means that the family should abstain from foul language or singing. That household should follow the road of disciplined decency. That is, he can keep them in discipline. If he does not control his own household and if he cannot discipline his own children and family, how will he discipline others outside the family? His own household should be settled in its behavior — disciplined. *Keeping his children submissive and respectful in every way,* in an honorable fashion, that is, when man and wife do not go about frivolously, like harlots and scoundrels, but nicely appointed in clothing and also in words and deeds. Villainous behavior in the streets does not become them. They ought to behave as befits their own person. If their children and household ought to be honorable in manner and appearance their behavior ought to be respectful too. That is, everywhere with polish and seriousness everything should take on an honorable appearance. The bishop cannot endure it in his family that they curse, use frivolous language, disparage others, and swear. So, if you were to see a servant having fun and running after his wife — well, that's not impossible. After all, that is a physical and civil matter. Those, however, who are unwilling to be obedient he may cast out. Levi sinned. The reason was that he did not control his own household. This is an argument *a breviori:* if one cannot control the smallest part — the persons and things that are around him at all hours every day, then [what can he

---

[9] Luther is referring to the ἀφιλάργυρον of the Greek text, which is translated with the Vulgate's *non cupidum.*

[10] Luther means to say that the princes soon discover that covetousness is a fault of the preachers, and so they provide a salary so small that the preachers hardly have bread enough. This is confirmed by the added comment above the line *et deinde dant ut vix habeant panem.*

control]? Paul is speaking not about power but about diligence. Should one see a bishop's household singing dirty songs or hear the maids swearing, this is a sign that he is not taking care of his family, that he has no concern for vices and virtues. As a consequence, he will not qualify for controlling the church. Greater concern is required there in the church than in the home, because there there are no parents. Our bishops have explained this to mean: to build the house well and to increase the inheritance of Christ. The world does this if it leaves its children wealthy and constructs its houses well. As we commonly say, possessions waste away. On the other hand, to bring up children who are well educated and settled — that is the better part of economy. Gathering treasure is not. That is, how will he be diligent to correct faults in the church? Paul is speaking about care in control, not care in gathering property, because he talks about diligence in caring for the household, that it be pious, live a God-fearing life, be upright and honorable.

6. *He must not be a recent convert.* This means he should not be newly converted, a novice, recently trained. *Without conceit.* He has this not only from the Holy Spirit but also from experience. He has sent some preachers and disciples, who did not do well, who were so smart and holy. Their ministry is too learned, too holy, or too unlearned. If we have an uneducated bishop, it will not do at all. If he is too learned, it is of greater benefit to have an uneducated and unwise man. His life then does less harm, because he does perform baptisms, he does read the Gospel. Even if he does not help much, at least he does not hinder. Those new saints and newly taught people stir up sects and make a show of their own teaching. These are like young colts that don't know their own strength. So they do not know the measure or limit of their own wisdom. They preach the most difficult passages of Scripture; according to whim and will they transmit them to others. These are dangerous teachings, and they are not useful, because they do not accommodate themselves to their hearers. They do not keep them in mind but have regard only for what they are teaching. I have seen many such men. Some of them I have seen sin in their wisdom, others in their eloquence. This is merely to make a show of eloquence. It does not profit. But to the uneducated masses a bishop must speak with a very plain and direct eloquence, the way one speaks to his children at home. A new teacher cannot achieve this. Paul therefore says that novices are dangerous preachers. When I first

became a monk, I was ready to take heaven by storm. These are vessels that foam and run over. Therefore one must select those who have lost the yellow about the beak.[11] Such a person will bring himself down and teach what he has thought salutary for people and to the extent that this can be grasped. Paul and Christ speak this way — with the simplest eloquence. I shall obey gladly — but Erasmus does not — so that the common people may understand. Where people are learned and know Hebrew and Greek, show your knowledge. They can judge more things than you can know. We must take note of that expression ["a recent convert"]. I would not have believed that there was so much power in this expression. Timothy and Titus were young men, but they followed Paul very closely. He is speaking not only about one who is a young man in age but also about him who is young in understanding and the knowledge of Scripture; he speaks especially about the age in understanding and in saintliness, when a person is a newcomer in the Scriptures. I shall give an illustration. I had this fault when I first got into the Scriptures. Speculations seemed to me to be the very best ideas, and no one understood them except me. That's the way it is for those who are fresh newcomers in Scripture. They don't have the patience to teach the little things. They must grasp the text of 1 Peter 4 and the anathema of Rom. 9. Those are dangerous theologians who are carried away by a fervor and ardor for new doctrine and want to have something special. Those Satan can drive where he will, as we see. The novice is he who is new to Christian doctrine, whether it be a newness of age or of practice, he who is new either in age or in knowledge or understanding. Holy Scripture does not want to be understood by knowledge alone but also and certainly wants to be inculcated through experience. Let a man make the test to see what he has presented in his trial without practice, faith, love. As far as the cross and the remaining virtues are concerned, let him test whether he was present with his theology. Novices are those who read and carry on their reading when we are reading the Gospel and the Epistle. They know more than I. They are all my teachers, so that I know nothing more. They simply grab up a doctrine and burst into a lecture. The exegesis of Zwingli is nothing here. Zwingli reads the adages and history of Erasmus. He shows off his knowledge and reading ability. How does this profit people? They are not saved because of his

---

[11] The yellow color about the beak is characteristic of extremely young birds. Luther is fond of this figure for immaturity. See also *Luther's Works*, 15, pp. 27, 64.

doctrine, are they? Such men are carried along by a fervor for doctrine, but they are not caught up by an enthusiasm to serve the brethren. The people must learn that they are smart and holy. I am happy and willing to have uneducated bishops, until they are tested and the whole Bible is too limited for them. We read in *The Lives of the Fathers:* "If you see a young man who is striving to get into heaven and already has one foot in heaven, draw back." He who wants to be too learned and holy makes a mockery of the whole thing. Thus with a fervor for new doctrine he seeks grace. He has not yet been mortified. Such people show off only themselves, and they teach no one. These certainly are fitting words: "That he not be swollen up and puffed up with pride." *Condemnation of the devil.* This is an ambiguous text. Does it mean here the condemnation of the accuser or of Satan? If it is the condemnation of Satan, let him not fall with the same fall by which Satan fell; that is, that fall which the devil suffered when he fell from heaven with Lucifer (cf. Luke 10:18). Paul generally calls the devil "Satan." These are his words: "Satan hindered" (1 Thess. 2:18). Peter calls him "devil"; so does Mark. In Paul there is a more frequent use of "Satan"; "devil" is the Greek word and the common word, "the slanderer" *(calumniator).* In German we say *Lästerer.* We have preserved that word in its common sense. We force no one into our interpretation. This is a savage and serious statement. "Satan" — that is, let him fall as Satan fell, and that can stand, although I would gladly not hold to this interpretation because of its fierce brutality. The Enthusiast rarely if ever returns. He pleases himself with his own inventions, and the applause comes. Then he falls irrevocably. Like Lucifer's fall from heaven, this is not a human fall but a devilish one. He is blinded with vainglory, so that afterwards he never recognizes himself. Because he has sought the zeal of God and the salvation of his neighbor, he looks for little works and makes himself aprons.[12] I have prayed since the beginning of my preaching that God would free me of this fault. Our Enthusiasts are blind and lazy to the point of staying with what they have once thought. That fall of Satan is common in the church, and not in the church of the commonest people but in that of the finest. Lucifer was one of the noblest angels. Thus in this fall not the common people but the very learned, the most enlightened, are involved, and they fall just as Satan did. In this way that statement can stand, but I am not fond of it because of its sav-

[12] Like Adam and Eve, Gen. 3:7.

agery, nor do I like to pronounce it. τυφωθείς.[13] The poets invent
Typhoeus, a huge giant who used to carry on warfare with heaven.[14]
Such are the neophyte theologians. They revolt against the Word and
command of God. They think that they are standing firm, and they
fight against God. When someone slips into adultery, blasphemy, or
slander and when he realizes that he has fallen, he is not fighting
against God; he has fallen away from God. But such people think just
the opposite way. They are the real Typhoeus, for they become so dis-
dainful and proud that they even fight against God. That is the sin
against the Holy Spirit. This sin is not like any other. It is a horrible
sin that can assail the neophyte. St. Antony heard about a certain
young man, etc.[15] Let him come here to this ass. Alas, I consider this
man similar to a ship purchased at great expense which never can
come to harbor. So it happened. Likewise the fathers sent out people
who worshiped gods, but they sent out serpents, etc. The fathers kept
on reproving them and gave them a good going-over, because the
fathers worked very hard in the church against the pest called spiritual
pride.

We have treated [16] this passage "not a novice" and have said that
we must relate it not only to age but also to doctrine. You see, those
who are newcomers to the doctrine of the Gospel have not yet been
trained and mortified, as is necessary for one who should teach usefully.
Those men are crude, unmortified. They are delighted by a fervor for
glory. They watch for miracles, with no consideration as to whether
or not they are beneficial. "Lest he be puffed up" I said was an ambiguous text. First, we can take the statement as referring to the fall of
Satan, that is, to falling irrevocably. But here we have kept the words
in their general use. You see, Paul almost always uses this not for
Satan but for "slanderer." The first meaning is in itself true, but it
is uncertain in this passage. However, we may understand this to mean
an accuser in a general sense, because when the novice seeks his own
ends, he easily falls into the condemnation of his enemy and slanderer,
and because we preach divine, holy, and sacred things and presume to

[13] This is the word in the Greek text which the Vulgate translates in super-
biam elatus ("puffed up with conceit"). The sound of this Greek word reminds
Luther of the giant Typhoeus, or Typhon, of Greek mythology, who came to
grief when he presumed to launch an attack on heaven.

[14] E. g., Ovid, Metamorphoses, V, 353, Vergil, Aeneid, IX, 716; Horace,
Odes, III, 4, 53.

[15] Cf. Luther's Works, 24, p. 65.

[16] The lecture of Feb. 18 begins at this point.

lead people to heavenly life. Our adversaries hear that we boast of our holy doctrine. Being jealous, they immediately watch all our deeds and words with malicious eyes, and when they have taken hold of something, why not blow up cheeks [17] and say: "They teach divine matters, although they live very disgracefully. Look how their life matches their teaching!" Even if we live in very holy fashion, we are still exposed to the false charges of all men. Therefore we must be particularly careful to have first the sound Word and then a blameless life for the sake of our adversaries. But who can stop everyone's mouth, when his adversaries can tell lies about him? In this situation Paul responds that he is not discussing the fact that anyone can avoid the slander of his foes but that one should not provide an opportunity for his adversaries to charge him deservedly: "He teaches love but is himself puffed up. He gives imperious orders to the brethren. Is this the way to teach humility and love?" The lie of the slanderer is unavoidable, but his judgment is, etc. The second meaning is the one which we have followed. In German we have taken the devil generally as the slanderer. Because doctrine now has been placed on a mountain by force, as it were, they watch us with spiteful eyes not only in our words but in all our statements and deeds. Satan watches by day to slander us through heretics, the pope, and the sects. Where they weave a single thread, they corrupt the whole thing. We are in a very unfortunate situation. If we have defeated the pope in a hundred thousand lies and vices and if they have a single virtue, they become puffed up. "Under the pope there was peace — the highest virtue, and with one little piece of paper, etc." [18] This virtue they cherish against all faults. They can cover up, etc. If, on the other hand, we should gleam like the sun from the sole of our feet and they have found a single fault, they disgrace the whole body. We must be completely humble and holy; but if there is one blemish, they have it. Thus they are completely evil; and yet we are overcome. Since the situation is like this, we who are exposed to the tongues and ears and eyes of everyone must live a life that cannot be fairly faulted. "Watch every act and deed, On this vain talk will feed"; [19] and "Lies do not last long." If a bishop wants to be puffed up and yet teaches the modesty which he renounces, and if he is

[17] This is probably an echo of Horace, *Sermones*, I, 1, 21, the "puffing-out of cheeks" being a stock burlesque representation of anger.

[18] The reference is obviously to Luther's having disturbed the peace with his sheet of the 95 Theses.

[19] *Hut dich fur der that, unnutzem gewesch wird wohl rat.*

a newcomer, he can never keep from becoming puffed up and proud. You see, the knowledge of Christ is a great thing, and he knows what the whole world does not know. Cf. 1 Cor. 8:1. Therefore bishops ought to be well-trained old men, learned not only in terms of their age but also in terms of their training. Man's ability to understand wears gray hair, and wisdom belongs to venerable old age. This relates not simply to age but also to respect for doctrine. Where there is a spotless life, there is old age. I have always understood the wise men. The man who is trained in a good life and in good sense is not puffed up. He will humble himself easily and will close the mouth of his accuser with the good examples of his humility and love.

7. Moreover, *he must be well thought of by outsiders.* Here he takes up what he has been silent about. Some theologian of the church might answer: "What is it to us what the heathen think or what the papists think? We live in such a way that the church does not judge us, for it is founded on love and gladly endures the criticism: 'You bear it . . . if a man puts on airs' (2 Cor. 11:20). The heathen, however, do not do this." Paul says: "It is especially fitting for you, O bishop, to care what the heathen think about you. You see, you have been exposed in your ministry to men and women. Therefore you ought to live in such a way that the heathen are forced to close their own mouths. This is the way you can gain and convert them. If you live in such a way that you are faulted, you frighten them away and force them to blaspheme the name of God." Cf. Rom. 2:24. Therefore "well thought of." Paul also wrote to Titus (2:8): "Having nothing evil to say to us." Thus the heathen will say: "People wrong them." Pliny wrote to Trajan: "There is a certain sect, etc." He commends the Christians because they live good and holy lives.[20] There those Christians closed the mouths of Pliny and of Trajan himself: "Let men say what they want about those Christians; they are humble and have every good intention." So a person compares his own shameful life with that of the Christians and is converted. Why does Paul talk about what outsiders think? *That he may not fall into reproach.*

Here, too, this still seems to be taken generally for a slanderer. My Aristarchus [21] always wants it to refer to Satan. I envy no one for what

---

[20] Pliny, *Letters,* X, 96.

[21] Luther is probably referring to Melanchthon, whose work he repeatedly praised. Cf. *Luther's Works,* 54, p. 156. The present tribute compares Melanchthon to the famed ancient Greek librarian, grammarian, and critic Aristarchus of Samothrace (c. 220—c. 150 B. C.). In a letter of 1516 addressed to Spalatin,

he has done better. Here Paul sets forth two matters: lest he fall into reproach and the snare. That word indicates clearly enough why he speaks about a slanderer. After all, Satan doesn't care about reproach. But because one is accused of a certain thing, it has a way of happening among men. That is, a slanderer should not have just reason to accuse. Look — let a man so live here, and let us be careful of reproach, lest we fall into it.

The snare. This sounds like something belonging to the devil. He usually traps us with snares. But "net" is still interpreted as referring to men. That he falls into reproach, and falls in such a way that he cannot escape, can convince and overcome with witnesses. There is no place for escape, no room for excuse. The snare is the certain knowledge and evidence of a crime, which can convince with compelling force. Earlier I mentioned that a bishop can live blamelessly before the world but not before God.[22] Here, too, Paul intends a blamelessness before the world. It is true that whoever is not sincere in his faith and the purity of his heart does not escape falling into obvious wickedness. If he is greedy, he cannot cover up his greed to keep it from breaking out. If he is proud, he cannot hide and conceal it. It must show. If, then, he can live blamelessly, it is a sign that his soul is blameless before God, but not completely. He now follows with instructions for deacons.

8. *Deacons likewise must be serious.* Deacons were men who also preached occasionally. We read in Acts 6:1-6 that they chose seven men in the church to be in charge of providing for the poor and the widows. Those deacons also at times preached, as did Stephen, and they were admitted to other duties of the church, although their principal responsibility was to care for the poor and the widows. That custom has long ceased to exist. In the papist church the man who reads the Gospel is a subdeacon. The distribution of goods and the care of the poor have been relegated to the hospices. The truth of the matter is that there ought to be chaplains and common funds. I am more pleased that doorkeepers have the wherewithal to feed the poor than that we have it. I mentioned the reason a little earlier — that the eyes of all are upon us. There ought to be deacons for the church —

Luther apologizes for presuming to bring such famous men as Erasmus, Lyra, and Stapulensis "under the whip of Aristarchus" but defends this literary and theological criticism as being in the interest of the salvation of the brethren. Cf. *Luther's Works,* 48, p. 26.

[22] Cf. p. 284 above.

men who should be of service to the bishop and at his recommenda-
tions have control in the church in external matters. "Serious" is honorable. That is, let them walk in seemly clothes and behavior. Let
them use seemly language and act the same way. Let everything
about them be honorable, because this befits the propriety of their
persons. They should not be frivolous and behave like mercenary
soldiers or a Junker with proper hat, proper home,[23] proper household.
Not double-tongued. This is the voice of experience, not just that of
the Holy Spirit. This fault is usually found in the deacons who are
at hand for the bishop. Through those mediators Satan achieves it
that they speak well of him to his face and then disparage him.
I learn from experience. The devil prompts them to draw the crowd
to themselves, and he converts[24] it to his person; to make himself
a source of wonder, to be praised more than the bishop himself, to
make gains. Those are the fellows for you. They say one thing to the
bishop's back, another to his face. They accomplish nothing good in
the church. Those tongues are more harmful than all swords, you can
depend on that. They are not tongues at all. They are pure angels in
my ears, but behind my back they are the worst devils. Whatever the
bishop does, it stinks. Be sure to tell the people. I am ill disposed
toward them; they are full of poison. If I say, "There is something in
you that displeases me," such a person is silent. Paul has had experience with this, and so have we. What our experience has given us is
an understanding of these passages. I never knew who was a neophyte
and who was double-tongued. What happens when one is unable to
get rid of this? They draw the common people to themselves; they
make themselves wonderfully famous; they make pastors stink. I say,
"Just be the pastor." In our day, it is necessary for pastors to be poor
men. Drinking is a fault of the Greeks and of our people. A drinker
cannot take care of the church and of God's Word, as I mentioned
earlier.[25] *Greedy for gain.* To be greedy for gain means to concentrate on those skills which disgrace a deacon's life and doctrine; to
concentrate on pursuits other than his life and doctrine.

9. *They must hold the mystery of faith with a clear conscience. Da
soll die Frau ausfleissen.* Here Paul is using figurative language. The
apostle should preach so as to call the idea of Christ a mystery. "This
is a great mystery, and I take it to mean Christ and the church" (Eph.

23 For *dona* we have read *domo*.
24 For *convertant* we have read *convertit*.
25 Cf. p. 286 above.

5:32). This is a beautiful figure of speech — "the mystery of faith." That is, he should have this faith in a clear conscience, as we saw earlier in chapter 1:5: "love from a pure heart." It is as if I were to say about money: "Take this treasure, these delights, this money." In this way Paul makes frequent use of the word "mystery." The reason is this: he does not call this a holy mystery in vain, because it is exactly that. Just as money is properly a treasure, so faith itself is a mystery. They must have a mystical faith, a faithful mystery or a mysterious faith, because faith is a sacred thing. A sacred mystery is a hidden thing, as faith is very mysterious. This is not because faith merely lies hidden in the heart, but it is the nature of faith that it works in secret and operates invisibly, because it is, as we read in Heb. 11:1, "the conviction of things not seen." That is, they should be the sort of men who are not affected by visible and tangible things but who are studious and earnest, who live in hope, who place their faith in what is to come as if it were already present. This is to see a sacred thing that no sense of the flesh perceives. The world does not see it, but deacons ought to have this ability. Those who don't have it judge according to persons. Visible things affect them. That is, they ought to concentrate on that sacred, hidden mystery. They ought to fix their heart on heaven; they ought to think about heavenly matters; they ought to hold present and temporal things in contempt and set their hope on the future. In his figurative language Paul calls it the "mystery of faith," and he teaches that it is a hidden thing. In 1 Cor. 2:9 he has the phrase "what the heart of man has not conceived." That is, you have a life and faith that is sincere, unpretended, in short, pure.

Where faith is unpretended, there the conscience is clear. The double-tongued have empty husks of faith. They have faith on their tongues and in their books. This, however, is only the language of faith; it is not the mystery of a faith which teaches sacred matters. That is the faith they ought to have. Paul is a Hebrew, and his construction is a Hebraism. The measure or rule of faith is a Pauline phrase, as is the mystical, hidden faith.

10. *Let them be tested first.* Mark this passage well. He has made these statements from his experience. This is not just the Holy Spirit dictating. First the deacons should be tested. All the more should bishops and professors be tested. How should they be tested, and with what test? According to what they are, can do, and actually do. Earlier we said that the bishops should be tested by those who, etc.[26]

[26] Cf. p. 290 above.

The acid test is that a recommendation be required from those who know them. You see, the deacon takes care of the people and is the bishop's steward. He should be tested first. But how do I know that they are blameless? How do I know which are not of bad reputation or which only care for useless things? So one may be able to gather from the testimony of his neighboring brethren who is a good and faithful man. We must not call a deacon because of his appearance or because he is friendly. We do not test him in this way. If, however, we try to find out from testimony whether he is good, serious, diligent, and the kind of man who gladly pursues piety and is happy to listen to preaching, then we are testing him. One will be able to determine this from the testimony of his brothers and neighbors. We must not take people into the ministry unless they have this testimony. When the apostles were sending out the brethren, they did not send them out without letters of recommendation, as we do in the case of our monks and bishops. This is an apostolic ritual. *Then let them serve as deacons.* He imposes neither the office of teaching nor the qualifications of the bishop on deacons. Instead he gives them the responsibilities for supplies or financing. They should be serious, not double-tongued. They should not sow disharmony within the church. They should have a talent for bringing harmony, for increasing concord, peace, and the reputation of the bishop. They should not be drinkers but be attentive to their business.

11. *Their wives* [27] *likewise must be serious.* The natural function of women, to have something flighty about them, they have by nature. After all, they are the weaker sex. All their members have by nature been afflicted with weaknesses. Therefore there is a greater need for them to learn to be serious, to have the sort of clothing and behavior that befits the honor of the wife of an elder and that is proper for the wife of a deacon. They should be examples for other wives. *Not slanderers.* This is where women are strong. Wherever two women are together, this most natural fault is also present. They like to talk about other people and about bad people. Here we must watch for the singular discipline that they be settled women. If they are unwilling to speak good about those who are absent, they should keep quiet altogether. Here you see what *diabolus* means.[28] When they

[27] Luther here reads *uxores* for the Vulgate's *mulieres*. In his comments he uses the word *mulier* but obviously in the sense of *uxor*.

[28] Namely, that *diabolus* is to be understood in the sense of "slanderer," as Luther points out above. Cf. p. 291.

come to visit a woman in childbed, they gossip about a third person. This Paul also has from experience and not only from the Holy Spirit.[29] *Not given to wine.*[30] They should not be lazy or sleepy, drunk with both sleep and drink. Rather, they should be temperate in their food and drink. They should rise early in the morning, not for the sake of dancing, merrymaking, eating, drinking, and dressing up, as if they were still young girls, but to cook and to serve their husbands. This is what we read in Titus (Titus 2:3-5). *Faithful in all things.* In German, *treu.* He tells us what this means. Whenever they have been established as the wives of deacons and have the duty of doling out something to the poor, they have the opportunity and situation for faithlessness and treachery to be able to use their mouths or hands for deceit. A man can do something for his own convenience, and his wife can help him in this. Also women are clever in swiftly bestowing favors on those they like and in slandering others, that is, both in word and deed. Paul is speaking about outward loyalty, which ought to be trustworthy in an office. They should speak evil of no one. They should not take away alms but increase them. Thus such a person receives the same treatment as widows do. She settles the younger women. Thus Paul is referring to greedy, deceiving, wicked women, who have piled up things to their own profit and have neglected other people.

12. *Deacons.* He wanted to add this; he forgot it above. So he repeats it here that they should be *husband of one wife.* We have explained this earlier in the section on bishops. He seems to be speaking contrary to the law of Moses, where one was allowed to have several wives simultaneously. The Greek church limited this so that a bishop was allowed only one wife. Today they still preserve this idea. Chrysostom left the matter in doubt. We understand and know that Paul was of the Jews and was writing to Jews. (Also the Romans did not consider polygamy a dissolution of marital contracts). Paul, then, is writing to Jews who had several wives, that is, not to have two at the same time. So the deacon should have control over his children, not in temporal matters — which is the smallest part of governing a household — but that they may be well settled in faith and in external discipline. Thus deacons should have a family which not only works well but is settled in good habits. He adds the promise:

[29] Cf. p. 297 above.

[30] Luther reproduces the text in a negative way. Instead of *sobriae* ("temperate") he says *non vinolentae.*

13. *For those who serve well, etc.* You have heard [31] about the arrangement of the office of bishops and deacons, along with their wives. You have heard what sort of men Paul wants set up in the church. The rest is the promise which he connects to this: "For those who serve well, etc." This promise which the deacons have can be taken generally to refer to bishops as well as to deacons. Paul strengthens them in this way that each is established in his own service. Yet he seems to be speaking especially about deacons, and he seems to be encouraging them. To be sure, the sense is: deacons belong to a lower order; inequality generally causes discord; and, since the lesser envy the greater, they become double-tongued. Paul now wants to interject this promise and make them content with their lot. He says in substance: "Even if you do not have duties as solemn as bishops, yet you should be content with your rank. Before God you will not be lower than bishops, as if bishops were better people." This encouragement is particularly necessary for stopping envy, because everyone considers that the other's neighboring flock or grass is more fertile. What my neighbor has is better. No one is content with his lot.[32] Everyone measures his evils, not his blessings. On the other hand, to someone else his evils are good and not bad. He does not see what great inconvenience may be attached. This is our nature. The farmer thinks: "How wonderful it must be for the rich to have horses to ride; and they have such good food." But what a pile of worries, anxieties, and jealousies they have! The others consider this a very wretched life. Demosthenes would have preferred death to the life of public service.[33] Augustus said, "Give your applause. I have finished." [34] That's how unusual it was to rule the state and not die a violent death. Were I to consider my good days and someone else's evil days, my condition would please me more. The serf has it better than his master. The serf sits in the barn, while the prince stands on the wall, for the prince defends the farmer, not the other way around. But the serf doesn't see this. It happens the same way in the church, when the flesh and nature enter at the same time. The deacon wants to be the bishop: "I know as much as he does, and I can preach as well as he." That's the way they act today too. That

---

[31] The lecture of Feb. 20 begins at this point.

[32] Cf. Horace, *Sermones,* I, 1, 1-3.

[33] Cf. Plutarch, *Lives,* "Demosthenes."

[34] Suetonius, *Augustus,* 99. The quotation is in the form of the announcement of actors at the conclusion of a play.

rivalry Paul forbids everywhere. "Let us have no self-conceit," Gal.
5:26. Let us not rival each other except in good. In this way, then,
he now comforts deacons and wants to make them content, etc. Let
each serve faithfully in his own vocation. If someone else has a
loftier situation, let him not be jealous or despise his own lot. "You
should be careful that you serve well." They should be good men,
not double-tongued. "If they serve well," a marvelous text! If deacons do not seem to have so important a position, they nonetheless
have the highest position in reliance on and faith in Christ. It is
enough that they remain in faith toward Christ. That deacon can
be free if he knows that his work pleases Christ and that his diaconate
is as pleasing to Christ as is a bishop in his bishopric. Therefore he
should comfort them that they may minister willingly and well and
not be jealous. If some who are jealous do this because they consider
that they have a gift of eloquence and good appearance, they have
no [35] confidence in pastors who do not have the same blessings. This
is to ask for an official position from the world and the flesh. "Give
thanks! You can be as rich in Christ as a bishop." What is it to me
that I do not have the same function? It is enough that I have the
same wealth as he — or even greater. What would the farmer ask
who has $1,000 in the bank? He doesn't want to live in the city and
beg. "So you, O deacon, minister well. Be a good servant. You are
very rich. Paul gives a high recommendation to your position. Although on the surface these offices appear unimportant before the
world, yet deacons have an excellent position in faith and in Christ."
And also great confidence. If they have served well, they are sure
that they are reckoned among Christ's faithful people. They also have
fulfillment, because they know that they please Christ. In this way
I please Christ as much as the king of France. Why do I need other
pomp and garb? I have the same Christ. So everywhere Paul is concerned that no discord should arise among those who serve — discord
that Satan stirs up to hinder peace and harmony. What causes divisions now? Jealousy and envy. No one wants to be lower than anyone else. No one thinks that he is content with his position. Yet in
trust and faith he would be content with his works. That's the way
things are, it appears.

14. *I am writing these things.* Again he includes a commendation
with a promise in order to offer encouragement. Thus he commends

---

[35] We have added *non,* as the context seems to require.

the church. This is a great title. Note it well. This is an outstanding passage about the church. You see how greatly concerned he is. Although he hopes to come soon, yet he worries that Satan may come and stir up discord, and that something bad will come up amid the bishops, deacons, and their wives, as I mentioned earlier.

15. *If I am delayed,* "because I don't know, because to will is ours." [36] He calls them "the household of God." These are all bright and beautiful words. That is, this is where God lives through the Gospel and the Word. Where it is preached, there is His sanctuary. James writes about both types.[37] Here Paul speaks of God's household because he has heard the Word of God from heaven. *Of the living God.* It has this title because it is His house. You see what a critical matter it is to hold the church in contempt or to neglect it. When one despises the church, he despises God. Also, whatever the church does God does. Here the pope keeps this text in mind: one must listen to and respect the church because it is "the column and bulwark, etc." That is, it is in the church that one finds the truth. Thus the church has been built and firmly established, like an immovable column. Therefore the church does not err, because the Third Article says: "I believe in the holy Christian church." The pope abides in the church, therefore it is impossible that he be deceived by error, that he have a blemish. There lies the distinction: in what the church is. Before the pope and his bishops were there, the church was in existence. Where the church is, there is no hypocrisy, no false doctrine. It does not allow it. It walks in the midst of truth. It has the genuine, legitimate, Christian sense and spirit of the Word of God. Not all who call themselves the church are the church. It is one thing to be the church; another, to be called the church. If the Word of God is present in its purity and is active, the church is there. If not, it is an evil seed, as we see in Luke 8. Such are in our midst. And yet, the true and holy church nevertheless remains. Under the pope there is the true church, yet he and his bishops are the evil [38] seed. God has preserved Baptism, the Sacrament, and the church which He uses to declare His Word. The elect have remained firm in the faith, as Christ has promised (Cf. Matt. 24:24), and the others have been misled. The church is the foundation throughout the whole earth.

[36] Luther is referring to Rom. 7:18: "I can will what is right, but I cannot do it."

[37] James 2:1-9 recommends impartiality to rich and poor in the church.

[38] The word *malum* is added from the context.

See to it that you walk in such a way as to establish firmly your
bishops, deacons, and their wives. *The pillar.* Truth is always opposed to falsehood. He is not only speaking about the truth of words
but also of the matter and of life, where there is no hypocrisy. As
doctrine is, so also is life. If the doctrine is filled with lying, life is
hypocritical. In the church doctrine is pure, and therefore life, too,
so that the truth of both doctrine and life are preserved. This will
happen if you are firmly established.

16. *The mystery.* Almost all the Greek texts have "God is." [39]
Here the interpreters quarrel as to which it should be. I am no judge
of texts. However, because our translation [40] has "manifested" in the
neuter, it appears that the text did not read "God." I should prefer to
have the ancient text "which" stand, namely, "the mystery," rather
than the reading "God was manifested." It does not matter whether
one reads one or the other, although the earlier text, etc.[41] Some say
that this was added because of the Arians. They themselves have
rejected other stronger texts as commentaries of this text. Paul shares
particular concern and anxiety for preserving pure doctrine against
Satan, who brings into the church hypocrisies and spiritual scandals.
You see, the entire strife between the Catholics and heretics is over
religion. What do they say with their doctrines, their religion, their
worship, their religious scruples? If a man were to stay with that true
and unique religion, that would be enough. But Satan wants to add,
etc. We have enough religion. It is sufficient and obvious. What if
Satan practices other cunning tricks? We ought to stay with the
former assurance. Paul states that that religion is great enough and
well-enough published, that it works against those fanatical doctrines. He seems to be discussing the same thing as he does in
Rom. 1:4, where he mentions "by the spirit of holiness." There he
calls it "clear," definitely declared. It was declared powerfully to
the righteous so that there might be no excuse, as if we were ignorant
of that religion. That doctrine did not remain in a corner but was
manifested before God, the angels, the flesh, the spirits, and every
creature. What could become better known, inasmuch as the Spirit
has already revealed what had to be revealed? What shall we
add to this except what Paul says: "This is foolishness; the whole

---

[39] The preferred reading seems to be ὅς ("who") rather than θεός ("God").

[40] The Vulgate.

[41] That is, "ought to have preference."

thing has already been revealed. Whoever wants to have the mystery has enough." He sets this against the would-be-wise spirits, who desert the general mystery set forth for all men and seek a new one. *We confess.* Above I mentioned what a mystery is: that is, a hidden, or sacred, matter, the mystery of religion as well as religion.[42] Earlier we talked about those who have that very faith which is a mystical thing. Here we have a religion sufficiently great, which has been revealed, etc. *Mystery.* This he added because of his zealous advice against the fanatical spirits. If they want to be mystical, they have enough. In this way he opposes our devils, who pretend to know many things, who go off on their own speculations and strange ways. Yet they know nothing about the character of faith, love, and the cross because they have had no experience with them. I judge with confidence that the spirits have experienced no spark of what it means to believe in God or to be a correct influence on their brothers. Such a person boasts of his many mysteries as he sets up false ones, and false wisdom has a way of setting itself in opposition voluntarily. It is a matter full of contention. If they want to teach many great mysteries, let them teach those things which have not been hidden but which are yet very secret. There is room enough in every direction for publishing and declaring. Therefore when it was declared by the apostles, it was through miracles, as we see in Rom. 1:19 f. How was it declared? *It was seen.* Surely it has been published throughout the world, so that we knew it for sure, and people had mysteries enough. It is religion, but not a hypocritical one; it is a mystical religion, not the kind of cackle the Jews and Enthusiasts emit, who go about like ghosts and apparitions. This is a commendation in which he commends our religion. No one can deny that it is "great," because it is plain as day. It is a sacred and substantial religion, a true worship, which is not hypocritical. Now it is declared how it was manifested: *In the flesh.* I call Christ the very reality of Christ — Christ in the spirit. To have Christ in the person is to have nothing. Rather, we must make use of Him. The Enthusiasts say: "Christ is on the cross. Therefore He is not visible in the Sacrament, in Baptism, in the Word." That is an ignorance of Christ; it is to not know how to use Christ. To have merely the fact of Christ is to speak metaphysically of Christ, as I say about Him that He has flesh and hair. Rather, the function for which He died is remission of

[42] Cf. p. 297 above.

sins. The use for which He baptized is in the sacrament — for the forgiveness of your sins. The thief would not have had the remission of sins had he not come to the Word "today" (Luke 23:43). Just to look at Christ accomplishes nothing. The Word is added in the Sacrament, and through it His Passion becomes spiritual and is poured into our hearts, etc. But Christ once believed must still be believed, that is, with the reality His use in spirit. I don't want the Christ the Enthusiasts have. They have the sort of Christ that makes them hold the Gospel and the sacraments in contempt as symbols. They keep this for themselves that Christ suffered on the cross, but this they must believe happened in spirit. Where do they get this foolish notion from? Through the Word? They want to oppose others. Christ is among them not in His work and energy. This mystery has been revealed through the Word. Yet He is not palpable. We do not see him. None of our senses catch Him; and yet we must believe. Therefore this is a mystery. There is nothing more hidden; there is nothing more apparent. If I must apprehend this, it is indeed obscure, and yet Christ is more apparent than the sun. Here we have some clear contradictions. It is "great" through its publication, through the Word, through signs and miracles. Nothing has been more hidden through its comprehension. After all, human wisdom does not grasp it, the flesh flees from it, and reason abhors it. Let them wrestle with it; that will give them something to study so that they may forget the other uselessnesses. I call Christ a mystery in fact, work, or spirit. I do not do this as the Enthusiasts do. They call Christ a mystery in spirit, so that a person can perceive it. But to have Christ known and possessed, to make use of Him, as what He Himself has done — that function we have in us. But because no one knows Him except the man who feels Him in his heart, He is called a mystery. It is a magnificent mystery because it is so well known, so clear.

I believe that "flesh" here can be taken for the personal flesh of Christ. I think, however, that Paul says this in general: that Christ indeed appeared in His own proper Person, yet it would have been of no avail, had He not appeared through the Word. As Simeon said (Luke 2:30): "Mine eyes have seen." We also read (John 1:29): "Behold the Lamb of God," that is, this has been revealed everywhere through the Word. If you wish to interpret this as referring to Christ's flesh, that's fine, but it would have been useless [without the Word]. I interpret this as the combining of the personal flesh and the external

Word, by which He is preached to our carnal ears. This, you see, is the flesh. "In the flesh" means, then, among carnal men, because it must remain in this way so that this mystery may be similarly very hidden and very well published.

Justified in the Spirit. Not in the flesh but in the Spirit. Here he distinguishes justification from, etc. That is, as Luke writes about the publicans (7:29): "They were justifying God and were being baptized." It means to approve His Word, to declare it right. Also, we shall confess that we are unrighteous. We read in Ps. 51: "Against Thee, Thee only, have I sinned." To be sure, Christ's work is published everywhere; however, it does not justify everywhere, it is not accepted everywhere, and not all people believe in it. The Holy Spirit justifies everywhere, that is, He is considered a holy and salutary reality. This the world does not do. It condemns this mystery. Neither do the heathen, the sects, wisdom, or justice. Only the Spirit justifies. That is, they believe that Christ is the power for justifying in spirit. Others believe otherwise. But this is a strained and complicated statement; the former is far more simple. Christ is revealed to the carnal eyes of all men, but He is not received except where the Holy Spirit is. All this points to this: He is declared through the Word and is not merely justified in the heart, but it follows that I confess, as Anna did in Luke 2:38. "I believed, and so I spoke" (Ps. 116: 10; 1 Cor. 4:13). They justify true religion with words and signs.

Seen by angels. This they explained in this way — that the angels sang when Christ was born. But I take this to mean all the angels. That is the angels always saw Christ carrying out the works of Christ! Whatever He did, He did on behalf of someone. Angels, men, the flesh, and the spirit know this. *Preached among the nations.* Not only among the Jews was this mystery revealed but also among the Gentiles, to whom it was not promised. It came to them through the Word. *Believed on in the world.* Behold! Also everywhere! "Preach the Gospel to every creature," we read in the last chapter of Mark. The world has accepted it. He is speaking about faith, unless it is not believed. Not only to the Gentiles has it gone but through them into the entire world.

Taken up in glory. Not only did He live and accomplish a resurrection, but He is still doing the works of Christ. Here is the final summary: false teachers and theologians are diligent in investigating new dogmas. Each boasts of his own mysteries. Were we to remain at this point, it would be enough. It is not that they pretend that it is a secret. Yet they themselves want to teach secrets. However, it is quite clear: He appeared alive after life. And so Paul thus warns us in order to preserve pure doctrine in the church of God.

CHAPTER FOUR

I<small>N</small> the last section,[1] he gathered into a sort of summary the doctrine of religion in such a way that the world and all who err and perish are without excuse. After all, the mystery of religion which ought to be preached and taught has been sufficiently declared. Therefore Paul urges this, that one should preserve sound doctrine in the church against various other theologians. Not yet satisfied with having stated the fact, he goes on with very clear words and depicts the doctrine that will develop and will be opposed to sound doctrine. To believe in Christ and to be justified by faith is the principal point of the Gospel. This idea Satan hates most of all; therefore Christ and the apostles observe it most of all. Therefore they urge that they preserve this pure point. Thus the entire epistle is directed against the spirits that are about to deny Christ. Thus Paul here describes the people who will in the future teach against the faith and this principle of religion. This happens immediately if a contempt for it develops. Nothing stirs the man whom this passage does not move. Had they read this text, they would have been careful, but, etc. He himself does not want to prophesy; he calls upon the Spirit to witness absolutely. "I am not the only one who says this, but all the apostles, the spirits, all Christians establish it. That is, it is the responsibility of the Holy Spirit, who is in the bodies of the entire church. This has been foretold not only through the apostles but also through the evangelists and theologians. That is, this has been said openly, publicly, everywhere. I am not the only one to say it." What is this?

1. *In later times some will depart.* The Greek reads: "They will apostasize." This is apostolic. The nature of this departure from the faith is that it is a stubborn departure. More than this, there is a resistance to sound doctrine, just as heretics do. Not only do they depart in such a way as to deny faith, but they also stir up opposing sects, and, as they battle against sound doctrine, they become seditious, as Korah did (cf. Num. 16). Not only did he depart from Moses in such a way that he refused to be obedient, but he also strove to abuse Moses and to establish himself. They strive and they battle so that the church is abused and destroyed as they set themselves up.

[1] The lecture of Feb. 25 begins at this point.

Our Enthusiasts are not content to let us alone. If they could, they would suppress our words and not leave a syllable. In this way Müntzer left not a syllable. That is, they not only depart but sharpen their horns against heaven. That is, this point of redemption will suffer. Not only will the doctrine of redemption perish in the church, but they will do battle against it so that in its place they will establish works. This Deuteronomy could prophesy (cf. Deut. 18:22). So also we can establish this point afresh. When we have established a chapter, we have theologians who neglect the principal point and bring in new, death-dealing, iconoclastic doctrines, as those earlier theologians and Müntzer also did, who taught that this had to happen. They are so immersed in works that redemption itself perishes. To sum it all up: Where neither faith nor the Holy Spirit is present, there works are again reestablished. We feel sure that because the majority is without faith, therefore works influence the majority. Peter, who fell because of excessive conformity, declined food. There he was confirming the laws of Moses — the idea that works are necessary (cf. Gal. 2:11-21). A majority — in fact, the entire Council of Jerusalem, with the exception of Paul — had the same problem. This passage is used by St. Jerome. Gregory, too, uses it. The Pelagians forced Augustine to use it.[2] Otherwise it is nowhere in all the doctors. They pretended that they do not know that redemption by Christ is our righteousness, and they set up the righteousness of works and confidence in the flesh. He then explains this more broadly and beautifully in his own words. He has depicted it well elsewhere (2 Tim. 4:3-4): "They will turn away from the truth." "Their ears will itch, etc." It is the nature and experience of the masses that they acquire an aversion to sound and solid doctrine. Their ears willingly itch for something else, for they now have been prepared for and driven to the "deceitful spirits." If one is not afire and is not seriously moved by the righteousness of faith, he becomes disgusted and opens the door for the devil: "Faith is a cheap thing," because it is spoken of in terms of its itching. It is a precious thing! This is admonition enough.

Of error. This point has been treated sufficiently elsewhere.[3] *Of*

---

[2] In 1538 Luther is reported as saying: "Augustine writes nothing especially good concerning faith except when he fights against the Pelagians. They awakened him and made a man of him." Cf. *Dr. Martin Luthers Sämmtliche Schriften,* XXII (St. Louis, 1887), 1392.

[3] Luther may be thinking of his treatise of 1522 *Avoiding the Doctrines of Men,* in which 1 Tim. 4:1-7 is discussed as one of the "Reasons from Scripture for Avoiding the Doctrines of Men." Cf. *Luther's Works,* 35, pp. 136—140.

demons. Some people want to make this out of it, that "of demons" means that he calls false apostles superhuman beings who have been inspired by demons. I am not aware of this practice in sacred literature. Everywhere Paul uses "demons" for Satan. In Corinthians (1 Cor. 8:4) he speaks about demons to whom food was offered. So also here, demons has the same meaning. This is a choice hidden word. "They will depart . . . to doctrines." These words no one understands unless he is spiritual-minded, because now follows

2. *Through the pretensions.* This hypocrisy, nevertheless, presents an attractive appearance. Unless the spirit is certain and pure in the righteousness of faith, one cannot understand or judge Paul. What Paul calls "of error" must appear as the Spirit of truth. "To depart from faith" must mean to defend faith. In this way the apostates of faith have the name that they are the true church, that they are defending the faith against heresy. Thus the pope has this title; he rules the church and battles against heresy. We who are true Christians are the apostates. Therefore we must look at these words carefully with the apostle himself bearing witness, because he says, "through pretensions." Where hypocrisy exists, there is so good an appearance that the whole world is deceived, except those who have the Spirit. There is nothing which looks better than hypocrisy. It carries the title of God, Christ, righteousness, truth, church. It has the applause of the whole world. The papists have these titles. When they read them, they thought that they had to fight for the faith. *Of liars.* This deceives the world, the attractive appearance, the pomp of titles, works, and praises, because they tell their lies. Nevertheless, they have the power of error. This, we read in Thessalonians (2 Thess. 2:10), is hypocrisy. To them it is effectiveness, for hypocrisy is the effectiveness of error. If such a person were to say, "I am the devil, the father of lies," who would accept him? He would be without effectiveness. But he says, "I am truth, the Holy Spirit, God, Christ, Scripture. Here is the Word of God, the Gospel." There it becomes an effectiveness. Also, good works must be added. Now he will have the power to be able to be very effective in telling his lies, as if he were speaking words of exceptional truth. This is what hypocrisy does. We are called hypocrites, liars. *Whose consciences are seared.* This "seared conscience" has caused much debate. Almost all interpreters pass it by. We shall explain, to the extent that the matter itself and the nature of other statements allow. It is not the natural con-

science. "They fear where there is nothing to fear" (Ps. 53:5).[4] We
have the same idea in Matt. 15. It is the nature of all hypocrites and
false prophets to create a conscience where there is none, and to cause
conscience to disappear where it does exist. There is no fear of God
before them, etc. That is, they do not have a god who is God. "In
vain do they worship Me (Matt. 15:9)." In the Hebrew, this is fear.
Consequently, the fear of God is located much more in the conscience
than on the outside.[5] From the conscience comes every doctrine, according to the way in which the conscience is influenced. It lives
according to what it teaches. Thus it has a god who is not God.
Thus it errs both in doctrine and in worship. The erring conscience
is seared. That is, it is seared by cauterization. Just as men or sheep
are branded, so those consciences are branded by a false idea of doctrine. With fear they create a conscience where there is no conscience.
Paul, then, is speaking about conscience according to the words he
has proclaimed. These are the "doctrines of demons." Every doctrine
creates a conscience; so this should be a false conscience and false
idea about God. A monk imagines God sitting in heaven to look at
his works and righteousness. In this situation he must live according
to this rule and perform these works. If he does not, he commits a
mortal sin. There he causes an erring conscience. That is, a conscience is brought in by force. This is not natural. The metaphor
pleases me very much. It pleases me that he should call it a "seared"
conscience, as if it had been branded by a hot iron. He does not say
that the conscience has been cut off but that it has been branded to
testify of the efficacy and power of that doctrine, as if he were saying:
"Fire is burning the flesh." Thus these men should have a righteousness of faith with greater enthusiasm, concern, diligence, and ardor,
as if it were branded on them. He wants to say, then, that the martyrs of the devil suffer more than those of God. That conscience endures because of great exertion. At the same time he indicates that
the erring conscience is born of great exertion; much trouble and toil
is involved, so that people must burn themselves over it, as it were.
They are drawn away from faith to works, which pull them in different directions day and night. This agrees with the sense of Scripture:
"They fear where there is nothing to fear." "They fear me (Matt.
15:8)." Also, "You will serve other gods." This is real searing. Every-

---

[4] The text has "Ps. 13."
[5] For *fonte* we have read *fronte*.

where it is called trouble and toil. Here are two special evils: first, the false conscience and, second, the restless conscience. The false conscience comes from sin where there is no sin, and with great toil. This is to work in vain.

3. *Who forbid marriage.* For the sake of example he has emphasized two things that cannot escape us. The papists who have been restrained sin against the Holy Spirit. Their sins have come to that end. We must greatly praise the Holy Spirit because He has set down this rule. He has not set down rules about food and clothing. This surely has hit the pope, because under him these two are prohibited. They make the excuse that this should be taken as reference to the Tatians,[6] because they condemned marriage. Let us admit this: Although the Tatians did condemn and didn't want marriage because they said that no Christian should marry, they argue that the "he sows to his own flesh" of Galatians (6:8) means to take a wife. Therefore "he will reap corruption." I would like to respond to this. But they do not play the game fairly that Paul finds here. Look at the apostle and what he wants to say. He is speaking about those apostasies which militate against the righteousness of faith. Against that point they introduce as much hypocrisy as they can, as the pope does. Thus he teaches that virgins in the monastery and celibate priests have a holy state. You ought to give rewards to virgins and celibates. Thus the pope has established celibacy as the kind of life that would open heaven. There Christ is lost. Not only heaven does it earn but also eternal life. Chastity is looked upon as if one must earn grace thereby. Take a look at the pope to see whether he does not teach everything this way. Whoever is obedient to the pope will be saved; whoever removes anything, etc. This is a curse against God and Peter and Paul. This constitutes searing a conscience, when men are forced to fulfill commands with great zeal and yet do not succeed. Hypocrisy develops from it, and they go against faith. He has seduced the entire world with chastity and the Mass. It is a very great thing in the papacy not to have a wife. Prostitution was condoned in the hope of future penitence, that he could provide indulgences for cases while others could not. He made it a part of the rule that a priest may not marry. However, he rescues himself as follows: "We force no one into the priesthood. We do not forbid it to the laity. If we did compel anyone, we allow free access to the priesthood." We say: "That state

---

6 *Luther's Works,* 44, p. 283 and n. 39.

of the clergy has been left free for heaven. You have not left it free but have formed countless kinds of monks, associations of men, priests — all of them deprived of this freedom." He leads no one into it! "You have come of your own free will. You have taken your vow out of your own freedom. Now keep it." You have not yet closed the apostle's mouth. If I should want to remain chaste, I could not except through my vow, which restrains me. You see, it forbids my taking on this state along with the ignorant. Yet I should have this freedom, because neither God nor man forbids these things. Here the captive assembly and the pope declare that there was a true prophecy about this very point. But Christ has left it free. "Whoever can," we read in Matthew (cf. Matt. 19:11). They forbid marriage. *And enjoin abstinence from foods.* "This relates to the Manichaeans, who used to forbid the killing of animals and picking of fruit for food, with the exception of apples. If there were some fruit on a tree and they would pick it, they would make the tree cry. But those handpicked Manichaeans had been sent to cleanse the world. Therefore this is not a reference to the pope." [7] Look at their decrees: they prohibit more kinds of clothing and foods than the Jews, who do not forbid all kinds of meats but only pork and cloven-hooved animals. "We totally forbid on some days, etc." They do this to deceive the erring conscience, because a man tended to think: "God wants this," and so people would build up a guilt complex for themselves regarding their eating. Wine they still have let remain. *Which.* With this word he destroys even the authority of Moses. "You have foods. You may eat them. So, eat them! God has made them." He does not say "all animals," but "food." After all, there are many beasts we don't use for food. Snakes, toads, certain birds, cats, and crows are not considered foods. God neither forbids nor commands their consumption. What is useful as food we ought not forbid. We use meat, butter, etc. No god, then, ought to forbid them, for they, along with other created things, are counted as food. So with this word, he goes back to Moses: "And God saw that it was very good" (Gen. 1:12). Therefore one cannot forbid them without doing injury to their Creator. He cannot say that meat, butter, milk are bad. In hypocrisy, however, one must register a certain awe with these things to make men look righteous.

[7] Luther is apparently quoting the interpretation others gave to this passage, but he does not indicate any specific commentator. Cf. *Luther's Works,* 44, p. 283 and n. 40.

Yesterday [8] we heard a magnificent point and text on behalf of Christian liberty on the opposite side. All other things — all externals — are free. Only one thing is needful (Luke 10:42), and that is the general truths of faith: to believe in God and to love one's neighbor. Anything which is not faith and love is totally free. All general dogmas militate against this freedom. Granted that in the beginning they began to teach something beyond faith and love, they had to in order to fight against these prohibitions. So it is impossible to add something to our doctrine. He sees this as the future development. This is why he so carefully impresses this freedom with his great proclamations. There is power in hypocrisy, because those false apostles present the appearance of apostles, the appearance of theologians. Paul concedes: there is a spirit, there is a doctrine, there is a departure. But what kind? It is apostasy, not from wickedness but from faith. Although they are capable of many different things, they want to appear to be anything else rather than an apostasy. The sum of righteousness is faith; the sum of the Law is charity. There there is need for the Spirit, who knows those who remain in the fullness of the Law and who will make their judgments easily. They are of the Spirit! They boast of the Spirit. They want to appear Spirit-filled. But they are "deceitful spirits." Thus they flaunt their doctrine, they want to be useful and teach it. There is nothing less in their mouth than to urge men to have confidence in their spirit. But this is devilish doctrine. So Paul says that such a one speaks pure lies, pure hypocrisy. And this is an effective lie; it spreads like cancer, because it has the look of the Spirit, of doctrine, of departure from wickedness, though it goes exactly in the opposite direction. Beyond these concerns, I see a grammatical stumbling block. Here the context says more. "Lies" seems to be construed with "demons," as if demons speak lies and have their consciences seared and forbid marriage. The text is construed as follows: "Giving heed to erring spirits and to demoniac doctrines of those who speak lies in hypocrisy." [9] With this Hebraism he sets up a hazy grammatical construction to which we are not accustomed. In Latin we express this with possessives, so it is a stumbling block. Yet he manages to let it have its effect. Paul clearly offends in another construction. He has "who forbid marriage and abstinence from foods" without connecting verb. Here Paul

---

[8] The lecture of Feb. 26 begins at this point. The text is obviously incorrect in registering Feb. 25. See p. 308 above.

[9] Luther arranges the Latin words so that the syntax of the Greek text dominates.

seems to watch his grammar too little. They do not prohibit abstinence but command it. Paul intended to say: "They forbid marriage and abstain." The text evidently is in harmony, because it advises against censuring the spirits that forbid foods. In many places in his epistles Paul has a way of being forgetful of the rules of grammar because of the fervency of the Spirit. He has his own ἀναπόδοτα,[10] for that one has to make allowances. It is impossible for those who are speaking in the fervor of the Spirit to observe the rules of grammar at the same time. Italians intent on expressing something offend in their language. In this prophecy we have at the same time an exhortation that we avoid those things. I could not be warned away from monkery by a warning more serious than that. In the first place, faith is attacked, and the devil is operating here. Whatever you want to do in your monastic order, he teaches because you owe it to works that your people are saved, this is diametrically opposed to faith. Why, then, should I be in a monastery, which faith does not influence? In the second place, the spirit is erring doctrine. Not only does it take away the doctrine of faith, but it also misleads into error about an error. This is not simply a single error. If anyone once errs, there is no stopping, as in the papacy, where they began to make the Mass a sacrifice, a salable work. The Mass was first used for the dead, for whoremongers, the greedy, and usurers. There was no limit to the abuse of Masses. Then food, obedience, and chastity came next. The Enthusiasts wandered away from faith, the Sacrament of the Altar, and Baptism. They fell at original sin. All of Christ became nothing. I tell you: If you have been snatched away from true doctrine once, there is no limit to your erring. In the third place, it is a doctrine, but Satan invented it. It came from hell. In those three words you have Paul's lament over the situation. The effective cause is its author, the devil. The fruit of this doctrine is to err without limit, to have the devil as your master and to err without limit. Then it produces great difficulty and bother. To err is always to have the devil as your master in your greatest crisis and difficulty, and then to lose faith and Christ, your Head. Should anyone digest this passage carefully, he would receive thorough instruction against wicked theologians and Satan. Who would want to remain in the clergy? God created those things for food. This they cannot deny, even as the pope does not deny that they are all foods. If this

---

[10] Rhetorical devices in which high emotion causes a speaker or writer to produce incomplete sentences, or sentences "without apodoses," that is, without concluding clauses.

is true, Paul concedes that God created them. Therefore they are both useful and lawful. God did not produce them that they should be saved up. They are there for the taking, not for a prohibition. Quite to the contrary, the pope has forbidden it: "Thou shalt not eat." Here there is a substitution of God to this effect, that this should not be saved up but be in complete use. It is His ordinance that man should use those things. Why then does the pope rage against the Creator who, he confesses, has created them? Yet he rages against them and prohibits them and militates against this text and against taking those foods. "Don't take them." He forbids their use. He does not forbid them because they are wicked. After all, he knows that God created them and that they are good. In hypocrisy he does this, however; that is its effect. This accomplishes nothing for the righteousness and salvation of the body, because milk and eggs and the finest foods do this. Therefore he sought salvation. Next, he was unable to seek righteousness, because righteousness is not found in foods. Rather, he sought hypocrisy. Those holy men do not eat meat or eggs, but only fish. That hypocrisy misleads them, and they believe that it is holiness. He should prohibit fish and wine. Fish are aphrodisiacs, and wine is a thing of luxury. Paul makes those situations which lead to luxury very bad; therefore the pope sought hypocrisy. Had he sought righteousness, he would have taught faith and love. Therefore he sought hypocrisy; and thus his is the doctrine of demons. *To be received.* Not just to lie there, but one is to use it. Therefore should they carouse day and night? But the text has "to be received with thanksgiving." Paul preserves freedom but condemns abuse. He does not say "for abuse and excess" but "for use," that we may know that it is by divine authority that one may and should eat it. If the pope prohibits this, I say: "I can and should eat by divine authority. Were I to abstain, I would both sin in hypocrisy and tempt God, because He has given us these things to receive. If He were to give us a bridge over the Elbe, etc." This abstinence does not please God. Rather, He wants us to do this soberly. We ought to receive food with thanksgiving, that is, we should acknowledge that this is God's gift. This does not stop with words, yet it is a good thing; and it is given so that you may know that you have something to eat by divine goodness, not only good food but good food with the will of God, so that you may do the right thing by it. Paul brings in the abuse and the undisciplined stomach. Next he encourages thanksgiving. Whoever eats this way, etc., while he eats, he gives thanks to God, Rom. 14:6. You see, he realizes that God has given him this gift to use, so he uses it with a clear conscience. *By those who believe.* He adds that text, and again he omits what he ought to have added, as in Titus (1:15): "To the impure . . . nothing is pure." In Titus he has both parts, but here only the one. This is what he wants us to understand about the other part: "What do I have to do with the faithless, for whom He has not established this? After all, they do not receive with thanksgiving." Paul stays with the other part. For those who believe, God created food that they might realize that the faithful alone may use it. On the other hand, the unbeliever here creates a bad conscience if he takes a wife and eats food, the saints and other rules being their measuring sticks. Such people have on their side the authority of holy men. "Ambrose and Augustine abstained, therefore we must abstain. He did it, therefore we must do it too." But God has taught it. That's why we must do it. We must do what the Word teaches, not imitate what has been done. If Christ did anything, we must follow it according to His Word. We ought to imitate a saint if the saint has done something according to the Word of God. Then I imitate to obey the Word, not the doer. It is a doctrine of demons when a person makes a rule out of a deed. Ambrose abstained from marriage. That is an act, but he did not teach this. We have to do nothing to imitate the saints. Rather, we must watch whether their example has the support of the Word. We need not watch to what extent we must follow the example. We would do nothing just because Christ did it. And as He has given me no command, may this person not move, no matter how great and how lofty the examples of the holy fathers might be. I do not care what they did; but I shall listen to what they taught. *And know the truth.* Wisdom pertains to faith; it teaches us to believe in Christ. Knowledge is a matter of external affairs. It is a mark of godliness that it cannot be bound; all external matters are free. Whatever Moses commanded and bound I know is free through Christ. According to 1 Cor. 8:9, they did not care about weak consciences and kept binding their own. Therefore this is properly a matter of liberty. But "knowledge puffs up" (1 Cor. 8:1). We must use it so as not to offend a brother. Because I believe in Christ, that matter is not unjust. Therefore I use it in keeping with my freedom. Yet I keep an eye out, lest I offend a brother.

4. *For everything created by God is good.* He confirms his own statement with divine authority and uses Gen. 1 as proof: "And God

saw that it was good." If these things are good, they are neither bad
nor forbidden. He created the beasts, the sun, the man, and said: "It
is good." What God has said is good, you should not say is evil.[11] The
Greek word is καλόν, not merely "good," but "outstandingly good."
These things are very precious. They have been created for many
advantages, that is, they do not serve a single advantage only but various advantages. Why, then, the human temerity to want to make good
things bad? But He did forbid them to the Jews, and in setting down
the law we forbid many allowable things, not because of the things
themselves, but because of inflexible persons. Christian liberty is good
and necessary, but [not] for the wicked. He ordered the Jews not to
eat rabbits. He did this because of careless people. Why do magistrates forbid good things? Because of evil men, who use good things
very badly. A sword is a good thing, but if you give it to a wild man,
it becomes very harmful. To the question as to why God forbade the
Jews, etc., say, "The Law is not for the righteous man." So also the
sword, Rom. 13. If the pope wants to give laws, let him give them to
the wicked. Why does he upset free and righteous consciences? He
should make a distinction and set laws for the wicked, the hardhearted,
and the unrestrained. But to set down laws in such a way that people
will die eternally unless they obey them is a doctrine of demons. There
are no such laws. In fact, we cannot establish enough laws against
this. Thus consciences cannot be free enough from laws, because
they burden themselves with laws and scruples. On the other hand,
this is how the wicked act: "Crush the foolish with law upon law. On
the other hand, free them from every law." Because the papists are
hardhearted and do not wish to listen to the Gospel, let them listen
to the devil with his laws. *And nothing is to be rejected.* This is the
negative confirmation of that affirmative statement, "which God created to be received." Now we have the negative, "Nothing is to be
rejected," for this would be to tempt God and fight against Him. We
simply recognize that this is a gift of God. We do not eat like pigs.
Both positive and negative have been confirmed by the authority of
Moses — both what we should receive and what we should not seize.
Even if there is something unclean here, yet we have the Word and
we say a blessing with which we acknowledge this gift of God, yet
so that this is firm in our heart: Even if there is something of the poison
of Satan, yet this creation has been blessed by the Word and prayer.

[11] Cf. Acts 10:15.

This should be written in red: Even if the pope prohibits it and I have a scrupulous conscience to tell me, "It is a prohibited food," I would say, "Let us speak a Word of God over it." If there is something spoiled here, it is not that there is a real pollution, because the thing created is good, and "nothing, etc." God created it also to be used. Paul, however, is speaking about those people who still consider foods unclean. We read in Romans (cf. 14:14): "There is nothing unclean in man, etc." He says this because of those people as if to say, "I have taught that every creature and every food is good and blessed; but you will find some who think differently. Against these scrupulous consciences, read the Lord's Prayer and the Word, and you will feel secure. If there is anything unclean here because of your conscience, come, my brother, and let us say an Our Father over it." Now his wonderful and outstanding commendation of this doctrine will follow.

6. *If you put these instructions before the brethren.*[12] Here is a golden testimony eminently capable of comforting us. It is also a recommendation of pious doctrine, such that it relates preaching not only to the immediate locality but to all places where it establishes deacons and all men. You see, it ties together everything that Paul teaches in this epistle. First, he teaches the fundamentals of redemption. Next come the orders and ranks of the church, as those of bishops and deacons. Then he speaks of husbands and wives in general. He also teaches us to beware of erring spirits and doctrine, etc. Now he ties them all together: "If you put these instructions, etc., you will be a good minister of Christ," not only a good one but also one who pleases God and has the favor of men. Of this testimony we can also boast with a good conscience, because we teach nothing about the gifts of God other than what Paul prescribes in this epistle. After all, we teach first the fundamentals of redemption; then, that bishops, etc. We do not teach tonsuring, different garb and ceremonies — pompous things — but solid and genuine matters. Next we resist those spirits which bring in new ceremonies, scrupulous saintliness, those unclean celibate and impure ceremonial laws. We resist rules which demand abstinence from certain meats but allow double helpings of fish; which demand abstinence from milk but allow one to swamp himself with wine. Such "fasts" are not pure. We, too, then, take part in the proud boast that by the grace of God we are Christ's ministers pleasing to God. We all rejoice in the Lord over this testimony, which can confirm our con-

[12] The lecture of Feb. 27 begins at this point.

sciences, however weak our lives may be. To be a good minister of
Christ is certainly a beautiful title. A deacon is a minister of the
church. *Nourished on the words of the faith.* See Paul's statement
earlier (ch. 3:6): "He must not be a recent convert," a new transplant.
I have mentioned that this especially relates to newness of vocation
rather than of youth. Now he commands Timothy with that doctrine
to say that he is trained and practiced in that doctrine. They are not
such recent converts. They are not quickly blown by any wind at all,
nor are they open to the tricks of every spirit. Novices are easily misled
into any error. They are not yet experienced in how capable of wickedness human wisdom is. Why "nourished on the words of the faith"?
This is a Hebraism. That is, nourished on the doctrines which Paul
teaches. That faith they have. In Christ, who is propitious, they are
free of evil. There is also a measure of faith, that is, faith brings along
a measure or division of gifts. Where there is not faith, there are no
sound words. The "words of the faith" are those analogous to faith
or in harmony with faith, so that they do not militate against religion
or the basic concept of redemption. Other words are words of faithlessness about a hood. I would teach love. "Nourished" by faith is this:
"You have taught a sound doctrine, which is proper to a faithful man,
or to faith. You will not preach the wisdom of the flesh or the pride
of spirits. You will stay on the royal road, which is the way of faith.
Whatever the faithful person says and does, that you will do, too."
The Lord gives men like this. He also speaks the word of faith. This
testimony is so precious because all that has been preached — sound
doctrine — is very good and precious in the sight of God, etc. It makes
a minister pleasing in the church and in the world. However poor and
comtemptible a minister may be, the message he proclaims must be
enough. What you see here you see from what he has said earlier.
I would not accept the riches of the world in exchange for this testimony of good or sound doctrine. *Which you have followed.* "Which
you have adopted. You have heard and seen me. You have read Scripture for a long time. You have trained yourself to find this doctrine
coming together from all parts to form a unit." From the gathering
and discussion of learned men understanding and reverence freely
arise, so that afterwards one becomes sure that this has the Word of
God and nothing else does. Novices take up a single passage of Scripture, not collections of passages, which make a person sure. In the
latter case one becomes certain because against such a passage no
objection can be raised.

7. *Godless.* This means profane. Things contrary to this doctrine
he calls empty, silly, womanish myths. Why this? Old women are in
the habit of gossiping, being more garrulous and talkative than young
women because they have seen and experienced more. They were the
very instigators of the Trojan War, according to Ovid in his *Heroides.*
They want to pour out everything at the same time. Stories are special
delights for this sort. It is natural for them to tell stories and relate
their own histories. They do not rest until they have had their say.
They cannot have peace until they pour out what is in their heart, etc.
Paul compares wicked doctrines about celibacy and prohibited foods
to those useless, womanish tales. There is no greater profit in them
than vain bother. In this way that doctrine brings nothing but vanity
and bother. Indeed, it works a severe hardship in vain. *Train yourself
in godliness.* This passage also has been exposed to corruption. "I have
taught you this sound doctrine. Now see to it that you practice it
in your work. 'Train yourself.' Godliness is the worship of God. Train
yourself to worship God." First, the level of exercising godliness is
without doubt the teaching of others. "Avoid myths. Rather, train
yourself by teaching." The largest part of εὐσέβεια ("godliness") is
devoted to teaching. Whoever teaches the Word of God correctly
should train himself for godliness. He does not lay the Word down
in his napkin, as a lazy slave does (cf. Luke 19:20). He keeps it in
use so that it may not rust or rot away. Rather, let him declare it every
day. We read in John 15:2: "He will prune." For the man to whom
God entrusts this work God stirs up enemies — his own flesh and the
devil. God gives him many people that that gift of the Spirit may not
lie idle but that the man may walk in the training of the Spirit. "You
have the gift. You have been nourished" (v. 6). Elsewhere he says:
Be urgent in season, etc." (2 Tim. 4:2). Keep at it. Don't become
weary or lazy.

8. *For while bodily training is of some value.* He does not condemn this, but bodily training is far inferior to training in godliness.
Isn't it godly to exercise one's body with farming and the work of his
hands? Also, in all the other duties of magistrates there is physical
exercise. Why does he make a distinction here with this training? He
is speaking about physical exercise, first, so that he speaks about bodily
training — fasting. The self-righteous believe that it is the greatest sort
of piety that they wear distinctive clothes. Fasting and the like — this
bodily training leads to the breaking and controlling of the body. This
is good, but two points of moderation are involved: first, that there be

no hostility here; and second, that one place no trust in this kind of
life. Therefore Paul says that it is "of too little value." This pertains
to the latter idea. He neither condemns nor encourages the manner
in which each trains his own body. If you relate this to the work of
hands, there have to be those who know their craft. This is good training, but it is "of some value," because it provides food and drink. It has,
however, no comparison with the exercise of godliness, because such
training involves inviting to and increasing the kingdom of Christ. You
see, teaching, comforting, exhorting, praying, and writing are the exercising of godliness whose fruits stream over to other people. "In such
practices train yourself that you may enrich many souls, etc." This is
true godliness. Of course, the other exercise is worth something too,
but it profits only you. There is some fruit, but it is little in comparison
with this. If a person reads or preaches, he accomplishes more than
if he were to fast. If there is some fruit, it belongs to me, because
I am chastising my own body, and I profit no one else. To work in the
faith is a good work, God-pleasing, but it is nothing in comparison
with this, because it bears no fruit for the other person. But to teach
others, to instruct them, visit them that they may know Christ and
grow in Him and avoid sin, to preserve discipline in the church and
at home — this all produces fruit for many people. See to it that you
do not fall into that wisdom in which the monks are involved, for they
serve only themselves. Paul [13] and Antony [14] had an excellent reputation; they lived in the desert, but they lived for themselves. Paul, Antony, you were saints. But the Bishop Himself has cut you off. "The
weightier matters of the Law . . . These you ought to have done without neglecting the others," says Christ (Matt. 23:23). If a monk lives
in a monastery, to whom is he useful? Whom does he serve? No one.
He neither prays for the church nor is concerned about it. Others, too,
are serving themselves. What if they pray and fast so often, if in the
meantime no one is providing any service? The anchorites, therefore,
are quite a troublesome crowd. But you who mingle with people and
are involved with the common crowd, if you were to restrain yourself
there, you can refrain from adultery and gain others for Christ, that
they may live soberly, etc. Gerson [15] wrote about this. He comforts

[13] Paul of Thebes, a legendary hermit of Upper Egypt, d. 341. He is known
from Jerome's *Vita S. Pauli primi eremitae* (374).

[14] St. Antony, who died c. 356, was considered the founder of Christian
monasticism.

[15] Cf. *Luther's Works,* 17, p. 65, n. 6.

those sects with this statement. Prayer is quite an outstanding instrument, but the ministry of the Word is greater. There is no work more sublime than teaching. One must water and plant and lead the way. Afterwards the increase comes which prayer gives. Hidden saints are in no wise to be compared with the public saints. St. Jerome confesses his weakness and insignificance, because he had crawled into a corner, because he was not teaching publicly, etc. To train oneself in godliness does not consist of fleeing to a corner, into the desert, and preparing heaven for oneself alone. We ought to take Benjamin, the youngest brother, along so that each one may boast, "I have not lived for myself, but I have brought someone along or have made myself bring someone." Paul sees that he is unable to teach apostolic doctrine thoroughly enough because of this corrupted guise of saintliness, etc. Who is not moved by the saintliness of Augustine, Jerome, Bernard? But they practiced Scripture for you, although they did it coldly. Who can say anything against these examples and this good appearance? *Godliness.* This they interpret as generosity. You are acquainted with this in the common books, in the *Glossa ordinaria.*[16] Even if one should suffer a weakness of the flesh to the end of his life, yet his generosity will set him free. Hence the testaments were established. That is, give your gifts of charity, and everything is all right. But godliness goes toward the advancement of the Word and the Christian religion. If there is still some godliness left over, then tire your body or work with your hands. *In every way.* We cannot take this to refer simply to utility. Understand it in relation to your neighbor. Godliness makes you honorable and sets an example for others, if there is great benefit. But through this there follows no teaching of the weaker members. On the other hand, the practice of godliness teaches comfort. It is of value to all in body and soul. A pious bishop is of value to bodies and souls. Next, among other things, it accomplishes this, that it has a promise, that it will bring a sufficient blessing both now and hereafter. "I have not seen the righteous man forsaken" (Ps. 37:25). Also, Matt. 6:33: "Seek first, etc." Elsewhere we read in Hebrews 13:5: "Be content with what you have, for He has said, etc." There I shall know; He has promised that godly men most surely will be given food and clothing. In time of famine, and even when others die of hunger, he has the promise. He is sure that God feeds him. You see why he precedes this statement with "bodily training," because he wants us

---

[16] Cf. *Luther's Works,* 25, p. xi.

to understand this as the work of our hands. See to it that you work with your hands in such a way that you do not place it before godliness, because godliness can accomplish what the hands cannot. He will give you food and clothing not only in this life but in that which is to come. Therefore do not hinder the practice of godliness. Here he wants to moderate other passages where he speaks of work, as "Those who do not work," in Thessalonians (2 Thess. 3:10). You see, the lay people quickly corrupt these passages, and later they blame us. Here he seems to temper labor, which he everywhere encourages. Peter says in Acts 6:4 that whoever does not have the ministry of the Word should work with his hands. It is not proper that a teacher of the Word should, etc. The work of his hands he should omit where his office requires it, because godliness is above everything else. But when shall I eat? Let God worry about that. After all, godliness has the promise, etc., that God will supply food. See also Matthew 6. This evidently happens: the man who works faithfully has enough, even if he does not have it in abundance. When a man is hungry, it is a sign that he does not care about godliness. You see, you cannot change this passage. That is, let the minister of the Word be more intent on godliness than on the work of his hands. The lay people should not think that it is a simple matter to teach the Word. The man who meditates always has something to learn. I learn the Our Father every day. Therefore, it is not our function to boast of our own wisdom.

9. *The saying is sure and worthy of full acceptance.* I feel that this passage refers to what goes before rather than to what follows. However, I do not fight over it. Whether it relates to the preceding or to the following, its sum is that Paul is speaking out of his own certainty whatever matters are necessary to all of us. So he adds this, "The saying is sure," because we are confident before God. If we teach what up to now, etc. When you can be called faithful, a person should certainly be confident and proud if there is such a promise. He knows that he is pleasing to God, that he is doing a favor to people, and that he is gaining many. I have enough in this life, but when I die, I shall have an eternal sufficiency. O foolish teachers of demons who have uncertain myths and nothing certain of this sort. So they do not say with certainty: "This saying is sure." They are concerned about their stomach.

I have said [17] that this passage seemed to me to pertain to what

---

[17] The lecture of March 2 begins at this point.

he had said before — that Christians ought to have the certain persuasion that Paul has a promise of life. This promise is our confidence,
security, and comfort in all our hardships and afflictions. I have often
said that the sum of our religion is this: that a man be certain and
secure in his own conscience.

10. *To this end.* With his Hebraisms Paul causes what he writes
to appear obscure, etc. It sounds as if hope in God, etc., is the reason
why we are disturbed in difficulties, as if he presses and blames the
foes who afflict us. But these are words of compassion in this wise,
that we have a promise for the present. This firm hope which we have
makes us quick to work and to bear reproach. This statement is sure
because we have this Man who will yet come. So we work, exercise
godliness, do our tasks, observe all things, that the glory of God may
grow and the kingdom of God may be spread. As to our hardships:
then we not only work but also suffer. In both areas we practice the
Word, actively and passively. Why this? Because our hope rests on
a living God. We do not place our hope in the world. We do not work
or suffer reproach so that we experience the favor, wealth, and high
positions of the world. We do not hope in an imaginary god. Such
are the gods of hypocrites, who make up gods for themselves with their
false religion. They work and suffer in vain, because their hopes lie
in an imaginary god. Our hope truly is in a real God. Whoever hopes
in God knows for certain that his works and suffering please God.
He most certainly experiences mercy and grace from God. The man,
then, who has this confidence acts the more freely and endures everything, because he always has this confidence that he pleases God.
"Whether we are at home or away, we make it our business to please
Him" (2 Cor. 5:9). If we are at home, that is, if we are working in the
world and train ourselves in godliness; or if we are away, that is, in
faith; nonetheless, whatever a person has done in work or suffering,
it pleases Him. Those men are Christian teachers who make this clear:
"You are doing this because you are fastened with a clear conscience
to the certainty that we please God. *We toil.* We do all things in the
Word. *Who is the Savior.* I treated this point earlier: "Who desires
all men to be saved" (ch. 2:4). That is the same statement as we have
here. It is necessary, then, that this "to be saved" be taken as corporal
and spiritual salvation. "Man and beast Thou savest" (Ps. 36:6). "Your
kindness is very great, because You save not only men but also beasts."
He preserves all things from death — even beasts. Were God not pres-

ent with His goodness, Satan would not allow a man to pick a single nut. He often brings a plague on animals. He punishes each according to his sin. Otherwise, he is the Savior of all beasts. He takes care of everything. These passages we must mark against those idolaters who say that He is called in Scripture the God of all beasts. We assign to each saint his animals, and everyone has his god for his cows. But we must ask for and receive these animals from God the Preserver, who has created and preserves all things. You see, Satan hates those things which God has created for our general preservation. If an emperor rules well, if a prince or magistrate manages his city well, if the father of a family is safe, this is also a gift of God. After all, He is the Savior of all men. He gives food to everyone, and everyone receives it from that Savior. Therefore we must not call even upon the greatest of the faithful, because they are looking most of all for those things not only in the general welfare but also their own.

Those, then, who practice godliness have enough now and for the future. He also saves those who do not believe. How much the more, then, does He save the faithful. This is real beauty.

11. *Command and teach these things.* He uses two verbs: "Declare these things and teach them." *These things.* "Make these things known to men. Then also teach them." To announce and to teach are two things. To announce is to make known. That is, one should simply be involved and zealous in declaring these matters, lest he keep silent and pass unknown among the people. Then he must treat these matters in such a way that he not only declares them but that he is careful that the people learn them, that those who hear can grasp what he tells them. He is speaking against those, then, who read and teach in such a way that they appear to be learned men who grasp at wonderful and special passages, like the fickle factious spirits, who hold ordinary matters in contempt and are caught up above themselves in miraculous matters from which common people learn nothing. This is not teaching but showing off the ingenuity which they themselves can display. There the good pastor will be concerned that he declare those things which are connected with doctrine, which have to do with teaching. This he should relate to the serious listener so that he watches more the progress of his listeners than his own image. Whenever such men are to seek souls, they seek a good thing — gain.

12. *Let no one despise.* This passage simply explains "not a recent convert." Paul did not want a novice to be established. I have men-

tioned that this refers to newness to doctrine or vocation. Although by itself that age is unsuitable, yet here it is a matter of finding a young man who is better suited to teaching. Therefore we must not consider age as much as newness to doctrine. You see, such novices cannot keep from self-inflation, self-love — an evil plague; for even the best of them suffer from κενοδοξία ("vanity"). He offers a simile in the lives of the fathers: A vain people; others say about it: "an onion with a tunic on." [18] In this way, that very bad fault develops: once one has fallen down in riches, popularity, public office, he grows in knowledge. If so, he grows because of the gifts given him; and if so, then it is from that blow. That fault, then, is like a terrible pestilence that occurs in the bishop as in every other station of life. You see, the admiration and esteem of the common people, his reputation, fame, and glory follow him. He is caught up, then, as if by some attack, by vainglory. *Your youth.* In this age one can be tormented to be so. The youthful teacher, however, has an aura of popularity. Fame agrees with him. One gets the idea from this passage that Timothy was a young preacher. Thus Paul is not simply forbidding a person to be a young man but is encouraging him to be the sort of young man Timothy was. *Your.* Good words! How can I prevent it? Tell others not to despise me. Paul wants to say: "See to it that you conduct yourself so that no one despises you because of your own fault." It is not our job to forbid them to despise us. It is our job not to give others an opportunity to despise. It is as if he were saying: "You are a young man. You are in greater danger of being despised than an older man. You have been installed in this sublime ministry in your youth. See to it that people admire your youth. Convince the detractor not only with your office but also with your youth. See to it that you accomplish more in your youth than another preacher, because his lust and glory are suspect, etc." A heathen is reared for the spirit and accomplishment of glory. This person, on the other hand, is reared to despise the glory of the world. "See to it that you preach and work with double care, harder than the rest, so that you survive the false charges of others, so that people may say, 'If he were sixty, he still would be a good administrator, etc.'" *But set the believers an example.* Show others the example of Titus. They should look at you as into a mirror. *In speech.* That is, in the ministry of the Word. This should be an example not only insofar as the kind of ministry is concerned, but also in respect to con-

---

[18] Persius, *Satires,* 4, 30.

cern for doctrine, that the rest may learn from you the measure of the
doctrine of the Word. You should be the wellspring, the oracle which
abounds with the Word, so that others wonder at you, and as you
handle it — teach love, faith, the cross, and keep away from myths, etc.,
so should they. Let them follow you to the extent that they are like
you in purity, then in zeal. When they see that you do not neglect the
Word, they will be quick to follow. A bishop should be the sort of
man who has the best knowledge of the Word. *And conduct.* Here
he includes behavior and clothing, association with the people, that
he can show that he is modest among people, a man of respect, so that
he does not walk about in a tunic as a prophet under wraps. Rather
he should wear decent clothes, hat, and shoes. In respect to his food,
he should have a reputation not for a splendid table. Rather he should
have moderate and clean foods. He should not have wandering eyes
nor a slippery tongue. *In love.* They should hold him as an example.
"Let the others learn from you. Therefore practice love. Show love
to your brothers, to the weak, to sinners, to the foolish." You see, you
must practice love especially toward the suffering and wretched,
where you have no hope of being paid back. Christian love has as its
object the hateful, while the world has the lovable as its object, because it loves the rich, the renowned, the beautiful. The Christian
loves the mean, the hateful. *In the Spirit.*[19] Are we to hear what he
wanted to say in Corinthians (1 Cor. 2:12)? Against the flesh he sets
down this: "Do not despise people. Don't conduct some office according to the judgment and affection of the flesh. Don't allow pride to
develop. Pray that vainglory does not allure you." *In faith.* "Be an
example of faith for them. They must not see in you the affections or
vengeance of the flesh. Rather let them see you as a man filled with
faith and diligently hearing about faith." *In chastity,* in purity. "You
ought to walk in purity." This is directly opposed to lust; he should
be chaste in word, deed, gestures, eyes, and feet, lest he have what
we have in 2 Peter.[20] He should not have a slippery tongue in his conversation with the other sex.

13. *Till I come.* This is a beautiful text worth noting. *Attend to the
public reading of Scripture.* He considers not just private but also
public reading, as we read. If someone takes this to mean private

---

[19] Some Greek manuscripts add the words ἐν πνεύματι.

[20] The Weimar editor suggests that the reference is to 2 Peter 1:5, but perhaps it is meant to be more general, including especially chapter 2.

reading, that is good too. What follows, however, concerns public matters, because preaching, etc., are public. The factious spirits greatly despise the Word. We must make this passage well known. You see, Paul is commanding his finest disciple in the Spirit to read the Scripture. To the Corinthians he writes, "Don't speak in tongues" (cf. 1 Cor. 14:1 ff.). There is to be reading. To read is nothing else than to proclaim from books. We should recommend and preserve this reading so that we stand firm in our use and understanding of Holy Scripture. Paul does not consider such Scripture useless, even if it is read, and not translated, so that he does not forbid reading it in foreign languages. But greater is he who prophesies. Thus bishops and deacons have been doing this; they have read a chapter from the Gospel, what has so been done the bishop explained with examples, so that our people, etc. But afterwards also the rest. The custom endured. But reading should not be done without translation. Better that one word be understood than not understood. If they understand one line in the Bible, this edifies the church more than a hundred secular lines. *Lectio* ("reading") and *lingua* ("language") are understood from *legere* ("to read"). First, attend to the public reading. Do not omit it. It seems to me that there is a miraculous spirit in those fanatics. Thomas [Müntzer] began it. So they hold the Word in contempt. "The testimony in my inner being is enough for me." [21]

I have here external testimony that I teach others. They say, "That is useless. Why do you want to teach others?" If they have the Spirit without the Scripture, why do they teach? Why don't they say, "You must ask for the Spirit as we do"? They say that they must not teach Scripture; yet they teach others. That spirit is widespread. There are signs. Therefore it has a place. In the church Paul simply wants reading and language to continue, which still is not understood by the church. He even commands the bishop himself to do this, even though he has the least need of this. Yet he ought to attend to reading. You should not think that this is said about the hearers, that is, "attend to reading; see to it that you keep on reading." Therefore the oral reading of Scripture is useful in the church. The Enthusiasts, then, abuse this. Paul establishes reading in the church. It is useful then in this respect, that the Holy Spirit and salvation can come thereby. Otherwise he would not have established it. From this passage, then, we prove the

---

[21] Carlstadt had written in his *Dialogus: Ich will meyn zeugniiss vom geyst in meyner inwendigkeyt haben, das Christus verheyssen hat.* Cf. W, XVIII, 136, n. 2.

institution of public reading, so it is salutary and necessary. So also: *Attend to preaching.* There are two kinds of preaching. Reading ought not to be so cold and obscure. Rather, teaching ought to be added to it when I explain a reading and draw in a passage because I am teaching faith and Christ. *Teaching,* that is, something you don't know. See to the reading. Therefore reading is useful and necessary. Whatever you teach, present it, impress it, foster it, follow it up, lest it grow cold. Use proof texts and examples with which you admonish the conscience of your hearers. Then this conscience has learned and understood.

14. *Do not neglect.* Earlier he said this about prophecies, and then about yourself. So also here. *The gift.* This is a free gift. What kind of gift this was he does not say, but I think it is a power in doctrine and exhortation. We say that it is a singular gift to interpret Scripture soundly. What another person cannot interpret in Scripture he must do. "The Lord has bestowed on you an outstanding gift which another person cannot have. See to it that you attend to, etc., that you do not let this gift lie idle. After all, it was not given you to waste but to train and enrich the brethren. *Which was given you by prophetic utterance.* Here he is treating some ritual which I have already discussed earlier. He has this gift because of the laying on of hands. At that time the Holy Spirit used to be given also visibly when they would lay on hands, as in the primitive church, according to Acts. That laying on of hands was nothing else but the receiving and assigning of those things for which some duty was being committed, as in Acts 13. The same thing was applied to Timothy. What this prophetic utterance is, that they prayed something over them, I mentioned earlier; also that they spoke some prayers from Holy Scripture. This does not lead astray. "Everyone to whom much is given, of him will much be required" (Luke 12:48).

16. *Take heed to yourself.* "Keep on; take care of yourself; have regard for yourself. Don't do this because it is most ennobling for your body, but see what sort of office you have and what sort of man you are. You have the gift. As a bishop, you are a public figure. Everybody will depend on you. See to it that you conduct yourself as you have been established, lest you be a source of scandal. Rather be a cause for salvation, that you may edify, lead all men, harm no one." This is noble for him, etc. You see, if there is anyone in office and he works only for his own advantage, as I said earlier, he is not fit for the

office. Public offices change one's habits, but rarely for the better. Before a young lady is married, she ought to have habits different from those when she is married and at the side of her husband, 1 Cor. 7:34.[22] "When you were still a private citizen, you had other habits. Now watch yourself. Do the things which befit your calling and station. Also carefully consider which is your chief responsibility. Teach the things that befit doctrine, so that you may not be misled. Satan will keep his eye on you."

15. *Devote yourself to them,* to those duties which I have already mentioned. *Be concerned for these things.* Show concern. These are exclusively teachings, purely exhortations from the text. *Teach these things* (v. 11). *Devote yourself to them.* "Don't let other things bother you: tomorrow, the things of the world, food, farming, etc. Let it be that if you carry out your duties, you will then see that you are making progress. All will be forced to say in consequence: 'He will always become more learned.'"

16. *Hold to that.* Stay with it. *By so doing,* accomplish this: You will be a useful minister, not a nonproductive one. Rather, may you receive a crown of glory in addition.

[22] The Weimar text has "1 Cor. 13."

CHAPTER FIVE

1. *Do not rebuke an older man.*

UP to now [1] Paul has established for Timothy how he ought to conduct himself in his associations and in his person. Now he explains how Timothy ought to behave toward various persons, stating for the sake of example, etc. Before this he was to have a sharp tongue, and he was to reprove. Now Paul wants Timothy to have particular regard for his elder. There is no agreement as to whether with this word he means an older man or one who holds an office. I lean more toward the idea that he is speaking in general terms about older men. He spoke in this general way earlier concerning old women, although I did not exclude other possibilities. I presume that the sense will be this, that all old men ought to have our respect. "You shall rise up before the hoary head," we read in Exodus.[2] Moses demands reverence toward old men. We must respect their age and, as the text says, their gray hair. That discipline is necessary not only in the church but in every political unit. It is a disgraceful situation when the young lack such respect. In the papacy younger brothers raise their hats before the elders and monks. This is necessary for discipline; otherwise those who have no manners will increase in number. Civil manners one must learn, even if these have not been established as law. Civil injustice is better than barbaric and mutilated injustice, because it at the same time binds together, etc. Beasts do remain beasts; yet they are more pleasant when they become tame. Civil manners are necessary and quite proper, all the more in the church. Therefore a teacher of the church ought to respect older men, etc. "You should not snap at old people the way you do at younger people and those similar to you in age." You see that Paul established the congregation with very gentle conversation. The monks ask questions. A young prior dealt with an old father in such a way as to make him grieve in his heart, etc. "He must respect you." This is contrary to Christian polity and not correct. We should note this passage. When our preachers felt that they had the gift of speech and of eloquence, they assailed the older men and

[1] The lecture of March 3 begins at this point.
[2] The reference is obviously to Lev. 19:32.

the magistrates and bit at them and stung them in public. Paul speaks
against this. "You should not attack the older men, as the ingrate generally does. If you must rebuke someone, do it in such a way that is
proper for your office and his age." Why? *Exhort him,* admonish him.
You should exhort a pious man if you have seen that he is not doing
what he ought. You should direct the exhortation to those who know
they should be doing the things of faith, love, and Christ. Don't be sarcastic. Don't assail them publicly. Rather, admonish them. Yet one
ought not grow old in his responsibility. He should go forward, sparing no one. Look at Christ. His disciples often slipped. He bore it.
He corrected them both gently and sweetly. Don't you know His
spirit? It was sweet in rebuke, etc., even when you struck Him.
Exhort him. Here Paul makes a grammatical distinction. It sounds as
if we must connect everything with the word for reproving. Paul
here is using his Hebrew grammar. We understand this as follows —
that the sense is absolute. "Exhort him by considering him as your
father, and exhort others according to their own station." You see,
you must not rebuke your father nor get sarcastic with him. If you
hold a person on the level of your father, you will not snap at him
but will exhort him with sweet language. Nature teaches this — that
you not rebuke. All the less is this bearable in the church. *Treat
younger men like brothers.* The point of this is that you rebuke.
They will be like brothers to you. A brother can correct a brother,
exhort him, reproach him.

2. *Older women like mothers.* "You will consider older women
as your mothers." It is a beautiful thing for a young man to call an
older person "father" or "mother." This encourages affection, nourishes peace, harmony, and love. This should set a good example for
a disciple. Even if some are scoundrels, as we call them, yet that outward training is useful. In civilian life, it is all the more useful. Also,
one must not rebuke those older women, but one should say: "Dear
mother, you really ought to do thus and so," and not scold them.
We should not say: "You old hag, witch." This is to bite at them.
Younger women like sisters. Obviously this means that you should see
to it that you just rebuke and exhort them. Because they are the other
sex, there is the danger of lust. This should be done with all chastity.
That sex is the dangerous one. It is dangerous for young women to
be with the other sex. These women to whom he refers have husbands.
What does he say about widows?

3. *Honor widows who are real widows.* This is to be done not only with the respect with which you greet them or with bare head, but this denotes concern, food, provisions. The interpretation is clear from the Gospel of Christ (cf. Matt. 15:4 ff.). "You do not permit his parents to have their due" is to provide for them in a limited way. Later (1 Tim. 5:17) Paul says, "Let the elders . . . be considered worthy of double honor, etc." Therefore he is here saying: "See to it that you take care of widows, because they have been commended in general." The "old women" are different from these. They have husbands. These are others; they are widows. They lack wealth and honor. To provide for them means to see that they are fed and taken care of, yet in such a way that they are truly widows. You see that the same thing happened to Paul as happens to us. There is a splendid arrangement to provide for widows, but many have abused this arrangement. Just as today there is the good arrangement that we have the freedom to eat meat, yet abuse has developed. Who is against this? You will find in accordance with that practice that there are some widows who want to be taken care of although they are not in need. They follow their own flesh, they seek leisure. "I wanted you to take care of widows, but genuine widows." There are three kinds of widows in Paul (1) true widows; (2) not true widows — who have homes to take care of; (3) the worst kind, young widows. Paul speaks first of those who have homes.

4. *If a widow has children,* as some have grandchildren or parents. Even if they should not have grandchildren or children, they still do have parents. These ought not be counted in the number of widows, etc. Don't count those which have sons, daughters, or parents. After all, we should not preach evangelical doctrine against divine commands. They should not desert their parents or children. I don't want them to become pious like the monks — St. Jerome, for instance. With trampling feet and pompous words he has, etc. If your father and mother wanted to compel you to deny Christ, you could run away. But you should not despise them. That's when young people become angry and say, "Father, I will not listen to you." "I have come to separate, etc." (cf. Matt. 10:35). We must take this to mean the spiritual separation which happens through the Word. This is not a physical separation but a separation of affection. We are in the same place, but we have different hearts. Paul simply does not want us to include widows who serve God day and night, even if they are like

Hannah (cf. 1 Sam. 2). Let the prayer go. Rather let her take care
of that for which she was ordained. She has children and grandchildren. *Let them first learn.* That widow, along with her children
and grandchildren, ought to take care first that hers be a religious
home. This is better than hiding in a corner. Even if she were to
have no children and yet should have dependents from her sister or
brother and should know how to manage them, she should do this and
let the worship go. She ought to be concerned that she educate their
souls in piety and feed their bodies. This is better service to God.
This passage says much against the pope and the monks ever since
the time of Jerome, who boasted about their life in the desert and
belittled the authority of parents and the religious training of children. Paul is saying that it is a good thing to make a home religious.
If a widow does not have children, she might have a parent and say:
"I ought to serve my mother, aunt, or uncle." This is a very strong
passage against the monastic life and its plan. He adds the strong
precaution: "If you want to do something good and pleasing to God,
He has put into your hand an abundance of works and of an appreciation for being saved — an abundance given only to His own." This
is the first type of widow.

5. *She who is a real widow and is left all alone.* This is the second type. He is distinguishing this one from the widow who is not
alone because she has parents and children. This widow has no kin
for whom she can care. She is simply by herself. She is also the sort
who *has set her hope on God and continues, etc.* She has placed her
hope in God. This is a great statement. She must take a risk, because
she has no one for whom to care. Such women have been so abandoned that they have nothing left except to hope in God. They should
be called into this company and nurtured there. Such a widow asks
for nothing. She is left alone. Therefore nothing remains for her
except to trust in God and pray to Him. *In supplications and prayers.*
What may this be? She cannot pray *day and night* in such a way
that she never stops. Christ says that the repetitions of the fool and
his many words accomplish nothing.[3] Rather, she should look up
with brief prayers day and night. In private we pray many prayers
frequently, but not long ones. If she offers some particle of prayer as

---

[3] This is a reference to Matt. 6:7. Luther quotes βαττολογία from the Greek
and gives its Vulgate equivalent, *multiloquium.* βαττολογία is sometimes derived
from the name of Battus, who is described either as a stammerer or as the writer
of tedious, repetitious verse, but the word is probably onomatopoetic.

she goes out, comes in, eats, goes to sleep, wakes up — that's what it means to pray day and night.

6. *She who is self-indulgent.* This is the third type — the young widows. Here you will see another kind of widow — the worst. The other kinds are good: the first, because she cares for her own family; the second, because others care for her. This third kind cares for nothing but looks for the idle life. She lives in her self-indulgences, seeks her own pleasures. This is the worst kind. She is even "dead" — dead not in this life but in the sight of God.

7. *Command this.* "Command this especially to those two kinds of widows that they conduct themselves without offending and that they offer their adversaries no cause for slander. These are the three kinds of widows. Now he will rebuke two kinds: the first and the third. The first he rebukes as follows:

8. *If anyone does not provide for his relatives.* This stands in general and in common. "If anyone," or "whoever," therefore it can be applied from the particular to the general. About the first kind of widow he says: "If, under the pretext of religious scruples, she wants to become an eremite nun, she not only is not serving Christ, but she is denying her faith. She is *worse than an unbeliever.* This is a terrible statement. He is speaking about faith in Christ, because he says *worse than an unbeliever.* You see, we have found tribes who care for their children and feed their parents, and they are not Christians, etc. Therefore such a person has denied her faith. This statement also condemns the cloisters of those who, under the pretext of religious scruples, wish to serve God and save their souls. Therefore they abandon their brothers, etc. Such a one has his own reward. Christ will say at the Last Day, "You have renounced your faith. You are worse than an unbeliever. You have neglected your own people whom I entrusted to your care that they might learn to know Me and might learn to live righteously. You have made My command an empty one and have made a new one." All these texts, however, have been abused. No one has thought that it was such an important thing to take care of parents or children. This is the rebuke for the first type of widow. Now, draw out and do the special teaching here in general. Just as widows sin by neglecting their children and parents — for to take care of them is God-pleasing — so every Christian who does not care for his own people as far as body and soul are concerned is an unbeliever. It is a good and acceptable work before God to train

one's own family. But anyone whom this text does not move, he is worse than an unbeliever. Concerning the second type, Paul gives advice as to what sort of widow ought to be chosen. He describes the person to be chosen. Paul burned his fingers. He first took in young widows. He learned by experience certain things which the Holy Spirit did not teach him. Now, having become wise through experience, Paul draws a limit on age. It is a great age — the kind we do not cultivate because it excepts young widows and those who are under sixty. Yet she has a husband, so that she can support herself, do her own work, tend the cradle, take care of children, supervise in the kitchen. She performs many functions. An old woman of fifty years can feed herself by her own effort. If she is sixty, we should take her in. The church ought to take in and feed poor women. This is a special text against monks.

You have heard[4] that passage in which Paul puts the works of one's own calling ahead of all other works, however great the latter may be. Thus, then, upon a widow who has either parents or children he imposes those domestic tasks, even though they are not as glamorous as those spiritual and religious duties. He nevertheless says: "Whoever holds in contempt those lowly domestic duties under the pretext of doing those greater works has done nothing and has renounced [the faith.]" This is a serious statement, well worth noting. Nothing that we invent pleases God. Rather, "to obey is better than sacrifice" (1 Sam. 15:22). That is what God wants, without giving any assessment of works, whether they be great or costly. In fact, it happens more frequently that God commands nothing except the most despised and disgraceful activities in the eyes of the flesh — circumcision, for instance. God does this to teach simple obedience — simply that we should obey His voice and have respect for His Word. Here we do not have the command, "Widow, pray day and night, etc." but "Let no one be enrolled as a widow" (v. 9). That Paul is speaking about the widow whom the church must feed appears clearly from what follows (v. 16): "If any believing woman has relatives who are widows . . . let the church not be burdened." It is obvious, then, that the church had provided for widows. This is the reason for the goods of bishops, the colleges, and the monks. They first began to give their goods to feed the poor. They were set up as providers for such people. We find a very old illustration in Exodus: "For the hope of

---

4 The lecture of March 5 begins at this point.

women, etc." [5] There is another in Kings (1 Sam. 2:22) about the sons of Eli. Finally, there still remains the example of Hannah (1 Sam. 1:9). It was a very old custom for widows to be fed and clothed within the temple, as happens now in the case of nuns and Franciscans. So Paul found this example, and thus he left it. But because certain widows were abusing those benefits of the church, because they were self-indulgent and concerned with their own pleasure, Paul tempers that freedom and checks the abuse. He calls them back to the original use and prescribes that no one should be enrolled as a widow except only one kind. Because she is alone, however, there can be a use for this woman. If she is capable, she ought not live off the public gift of the church but from the results of her own work, to cut off the opportunity for young widows, lest they become wanton and deny their faith. The second qualification is *having been the wife of one husband.* This is an ambiguous statement, just as he spoke earlier (ch. 3:2) about the bishop as being "the husband of one wife." Chrysostom says that he should not have several wives at one and the same time or that he should have only one wife. The Eastern Church preserves the idea that, if his wife dies, he should not take another, but with this proviso, that, if he absolutely wants to marry, he should resign his office. He should marry one virgin and then be content. If he wants another, etc. The Picards [6] totally deny marriage to their priests. Should one of them want to marry, he must resign from his duties and from the ministry of the Word. The pope says that he has an indelible character with his priests, and that they can-

---

[5] The 1545 version of Luther's German translation of Ex. 38:8 has the phrase *gegen den Weibern,* to which Luther added the marginal explanation: "These women were the devout widows and women who served God with fasting and praying at the entrance to the tabernacle, as 1 Sam. 2 shows and as Paul describes in 1 Tim. 5. So Luke, too, describes the holy prophetess Anna in Luke 2." In his translation of 1523 Luther had *auff dem platz der Heere* for this phrase, and his marginal note adds: "The armies *(Heere)* were the devout widows and women. . . . But here the Jews and many others speak of women's mirrors that were supposed to have been attached to the laver. We let them have their way. But spiritually this refers to the stories of the Old Testament which are being preached in the Gospel, for these struggle valiantly to demonstrate faith in Christ over against those who rely on works, etc." Cf. W, *Deutsche Bibel,* VIII, pp. 320—321.

[6] Picards is a variation of the more common name Beghards. They were a semimonastic community of the high Middle Ages characterized especially by their care of the sick and needy. The community demanded celibacy so long as one remained in it, but adherents were free to leave and to marry. See also *Luther's Works,* 25, p. 287, n. 2.

not approach marriage, etc. That is the Antichrist. I believe that all three are in error. The pope does not allow monogamy and makes his men be priests forever. The tradition of the Greek Church is tolerable. A priest should resign, become a layman, and earn his living in a different kind of life. I believe that the Waldensian statement is also wrong, that he have one wife, etc. But all three err. If in the Greek Church there were a good minister of the Word, if he took a wife and she die, and then if he married another to live chastely, then he is frustrated in his vow, because he has sought a remedy in marriage. Paul speaks against this very thing: "It is better to marry, etc." (1 Cor. 7:9). If he were to retire because he took another wife, does he not thereby destroy those very good gifts which he has given to the use of the church because of his own personal marriage relationship? This is contrary to the Holy Spirit. When a man has the gifts to be a bishop, why should two marriages hinder him? We must not take this passage to relate to the laity, but to widows and widowers in general, if they do not marry. The widower says that he has the right, so he marries a second time. This pleases neither the Greeks nor the Waldensians. This is scandalous because they say, "It seems better to Paul that one marry." *Having been the wife of one husband.* For a time, contrary to their usual practice, where they were forced into plural marriages, a divorced wife was still a wife. Thereby scandal in the church of the Gentiles could be avoided. They had the freedom, the decree of divorce, etc.[7] This was a source of offense among the heathen. Paul established that a bishop be the husband of one wife, etc. Otherwise he would be speaking contrary to what he says in 1 Cor. 7. This passage about widows who were married only once they want to connect with the prior statement which speaks about bishops. A widow cannot be the wife of many men; therefore we should make the same application to men. I do not place a limit on the passage. I do, however, state my own sense: Paul wanted this decency to reign in the church, that it should be understood regarding a widow that she is not a divorced woman or one married to another brother upon being divorced who had gone off to marry some other man. She cannot return. She has two living husbands — the one who divorced her and the one whom she has taken. This text can so be understood. But that passage from Corinthians (1 Cor. 7:9) is stronger than this one and takes priority: "It is better to marry than to burn."

[7] Cf. Deut. 24:1 f.

Individual statements in Scripture ought not militate against the general sense of Scripure. The statement in Corinthians is a general one, as is also that of Christ: "He who is able to receive this, let him receive it" (Matt. 19:12). Therefore, we must reduce Paul's statement here to the rank of the particular, not of the general. We can draw no conclusion from that ambiguous passage. We cannot bind consciences, etc. He finds a few others, etc.

10. *She must be well attested for her good deeds.* She should not have been a prostitute or notorious for other criminal acts. What are these "good deeds"? That she earn praise, that she have cared for her sons, daughters, and household, that she be concerned with her children's growth of both body and soul. If she has been an abominable wretch and has raised her children for her own pride — that is to destroy them. *One who has shown hospitality.* This means she should have a spirit of service in return in that she has been a guest herself, etc. This is especially true in the practice of having as guests visiting brethren, washing their feet, serving them food. She should not be a greedy woman who profits no one but accumulates for herself. *Washed the feet of the saints.* This is a ceremonial act. What if she hadn't done this? Those ceremonies have disappeared among us. I despair of bringing them back. It would be a splendid custom to welcome their brothers with a hug and a kiss as did Christ and Paul. The monks have preserved the washing. These customs, nevertheless, are signs of a good heart. If a Judas and Pilate hide beneath them, we must condemn the abuse, not the custom. Those men were trained for excellence in politeness. I don't know whether I would want to live with crude barbarians. In any kind of people I find Satan and the seven deadly sins.[8] Demosthenes and Cicero were men of exceptional talents. Yet, if they were jealous, etc. Among the country bumpkins one can also see pride, etc., except that they exercise such faults crassly. They are venomous, vain, and conceited. Yet, we must behave in such a way as to preserve a well-mannered training rather than a boorish one. I would more easily bear it if I were to choose, etc. To be sure, the people were most civil but very prone to violence. The people have had a very fine training for ceremonial rituals, for encouraging friendship and hospitality. The monks have kept the washing of feet, but not the feet of men of their own order. Christ did it for him who betrayed him. I apply this not

[8] Pride, covetousness, lust, anger, gluttony, envy, sloth. Cf. *Luther's Works,* 25, p. 319, n. 19.

only to washing the feet but to whatever is a ritual of kindness, when people have been cordial and show friendly speech, answer, and mien. Thus in a particular ceremony they show a universal gesture, even kissing, kneeling, shaking hands, and all gestures of kindness. *Relieved the afflicted*. Paul is speaking about the food or substance of this world. Wherever the sick, the needy, the naked, the poor, and the hungry are, Matthew 25, there are the afflicted, those who suffer anguish. That is where one must extend and distribute his own bounty to those in need. That's what it means to relieve the afflicted. "If such a one has been found." We might find a few today as also then who have been married once and are sixty. I, too, would cherish such women. Paul wanted to avoid scandal in the church. Young widows who did not behave well and were not well attested for their good deeds — in such we have little confidence, and Paul has no confidence in them.

11. *Refuse to enroll younger widows.* This is another passage we should note well. Augustine pushes this text strongly. So does Jerome. If this had been someone else, I would say that he is the worst heretic who had ever come into the world and that he had no wisdom or judgment. We explain this passage as follows. Nuns who have taken their vows may not marry. To want to marry is damnable. Augustine believes this, too. First, they ought not take up younger widows into charitable support of the church, although one can limit this by reason of times or individuals. For example, earlier (ch. 2:9) he taught that women should not wear pearls. We must not understand this to mean never, as the Enthusiasts say. Rather we understand that a Christian woman ought not be eager for such jewelry. She ought to behave every day as a bride, as a noble lady. She should not concern herself with the entire household but restrict herself to the kitchen and living quarters. Thus he condemns ostentation in daily life, but he does not condemn it for weddings, provided it is customary. Another example: we must enforce and regulate the ceremonial laws in Scripture according to faith and charity. We read in Acts (Acts 15:29): "Abstain from what has been strangled." These things are matters of love. When there was an opportunity for such ceremonial law, Paul preserves it. Otherwise he doesn't. Did he circumcise Titus, etc.?[9] Such regulations always ought to provide for an exception. Why should we not enroll such widows? In the first place, because they grow

9 Cf. Gal. 2:3.

wanton. Here the text is ambiguous. Jerome lashes out: "Because they committed fornication to the hurt of their former husband." [10] Christians say that he is not speaking here about fornication. The Greeks have an expression: to rage because of food, as when we say "rank," "too well fed," "their food pricks them." First, she grows wild. She breaks the restraints and becomes wanton. But even more, Paul points to her intractability. *They grow wanton against Christ.* That is, those young widows are free. They have no worries about their next meal. They are not subject to a husband; they have no anxieties to bother them. They have free time and freedom to move around. To feed a young widow, then, is to nourish a serpent in your bosom. They begin to grow wanton and to seek out men with their wanton ways. Paul explains himself. They are trifling, nosy gossips, because their bellies are full. They are rebellious, disobedient, intractable. They have no care for faith. They become wanton; that is, they are ungovernable, wild and dissolute. Then follows wantonness. Earlier (5:8) he said: "She has disowned the faith." So also here. She has broken her restraints and is carried about by her own wilfullness. She disowns faith and becomes exactly like the heathen. The text is ambiguous here: *When they grow wanton against Christ, they want to marry.* There are two parts to this: they want to marry, and they grow wanton. Then there follows:

12. *And so they incur condemnation.* One ambiguity lies in whether this has to lead to the latter part. If we connect it to the prior statement, "they grow wanton against Christ, etc." and they disown faith because of this wantonness, they are not keeping discipline in the church. They become coarse and wild and thus *they have violated their first pledge* and have become like heathen, etc. The other ambiguity lies in *they grow wanton . . . and want to marry.* Almost all theologians have followed this sense, that this forbids second marriages. The church has accepted and often used this latter sense. I am inclined toward the first meaning. My first reason is that Paul does not want them to remain husbandless, because he says (ch. 5:14), "I want them to marry." This agrees with "It is better to marry than to burn" (1 Cor. 7:9). Paul therefore does not forbid second marriages to young widows and to those who burn. My second reason is the text itself: "they grow wanton against Christ." He does not say, "They want to marry against Christ." The sense, then, is this:

[10] Jerome, Letter No. 123, *To Ageruchia.*

first they throw off the yoke of Christ and consider faith in Christ a myth. They run around. Then they want to have some honorable pretext that they are very friendly little women to get a husband. They are not looking for marriage, but for a pretext. They are looking only for their mischief. He reproaches this fault because they want to cover up an undisciplined life under the pretext of marriage. The third reason is that they are nosy triflers (v. 13). Here he indicates clearly how they act against Christ in word and deed and have no concern for faith. Let it be that both senses are true. If the fathers say that it is damnable to marry, etc., as above, the text (5:14) is clearly contrary: "I would have younger widows marry." Paul therefore concedes, etc. This means, then, using marriage as a pretext. Our priests prefer prostitutes to marriage, because they are wicked. In this way those younger widows operate with the pretext "I want to have a husband some time." The fourth reason is:

15. *Some have already strayed after Satan.* This does not mean simply to marry but to deny Christ. Whatever it may be, the text does not make a demand, because Paul later established that they not be enrolled unless they were 60, and he allowed them to marry. In addition, this text says nothing about monks but speaks about a widow. This has nothing to do with monastic life. Therefore it means nothing that Augustine and Jerome used this text; it is against monks, etc. The difference between those widows and this text and their rules is the difference between heaven and earth. Here they have not only abused eleemosynary activity; they also want to earn righteousness and heaven. The first abuses, nevertheless, involved the payment of the stipend. So the first meaning seems to approximate closely Paul's sense: they have preferred pursuit of their appetite to pursuit of faith. They want to use marriage as a pretext. Next, even if the sense of Augustine and Jerome were true, we have not established that sort of widow today. For there they seek not only their belly but also righteousness and holiness. This is obviously against Christ.

We had left unresolved [11] that anxiety over the expression "their first pledge" (5:12). Had he simply said, "They violated the faith," it would be a very clear statement without any difficulty, as he earlier said, "She has disowned the faith." Here, however, he adds "first," which raises a question. I take it to mean that those widows grow wanton against Christ and, using marriage as a pretext, want to later

[11] The lecture of March 9 begins at this point.

bedeck themselves. Understand "their first pledge" as faith in Christ. This is the meaning I get. The whole Roman Church takes the "first pledge" to mean a vow of preserving widowhood. Augustine says that it is damnable to want to marry. I have already spoken to the point as to whether a vow can be called a "first pledge." I myself have said that I have no example in all of Scripture, therefore I cannot follow, etc. Even if their idea were to stand up, that "pledge" be taken for a vow of widowhood and chastity, yet today this vow does not stand, because he "would have younger widows marry." This passage would stand especially in our favor if we accept "first pledge" as a vow. After all, he does say that we should not allow younger widows to take that vow but to marry and become mistresses of their households. So, no matter how they may have twisted this passage, it will be opposed to them and in our favor. But the first meaning pleases me, because a vow of widowhood is not a "first pledge," since the baptismal faith precedes it. The first pledge is made before the church. Our first pledge is the one we promised in Baptism, that we want to receive and accept the grace of Christ. Those things which they earlier took up and now reject as they take up a new faith certainly apply to Judaism and heathenism. He is speaking, then, about heretical widows who have abandoned their first pledge, which they promised in Baptism, etc., for Judaism. They are nourished and rage not against the church but against Christ. You see, because of their lack of restraint they become unstable and grasp at new doctrines. They desert their first pledge to Christ and are snatched up into a different pledge, from which they become heretics because of the wantonness of their own flesh. Then they become "idlers" (5:13). There is another argument. This is a fault of the false prophet which Paul generally condemns in no uncertain terms: They misled entire households. Also Timothy is among people who gad about and take others captive, etc. That gadding about from house to house means that they accept new doctrines and useless teachers. It is the gadding about of the heretical mind, just as false prophets also hurry and run. *Not only idlers but gossips and busybodies.* He says that they not only listen to and follow a new faith but are also quick to teach this new faith. There are two sins involved here: picking up new doctrines and teaching and planting that poison. That bad lesson which they learn from false prophets they spread among others — a very bad thing. Therefore we must take this passage to refer to heresy in doctrine and not to widowhood. They have taken a very fine pledge. This they forsake and take up another. Do we not correctly say that Zwingli deserts the one true faith and takes and follows another? Whether they take this for a vow or against a vow, this meaning will stand for us. Augustine's sense is not true when he says that to want to marry is damnable.

Saying what they should not. Paul is against this. That is, they tell those Judaic myths and heathen ideas. When learned women know how to speak more than ten preachers, they have small and crude minds. They have seen no art, just as the ploughboy is oppressed rather than respected because of his labors. In this way, if knowledge comes to the small and crude head, it thinks nothing else except that it is very learned. The ploughboy learns his ABCs, and he thinks he is brilliant. So, when women hear that Baptism is a bath for dogs, no theologian can convince them otherwise. Women are talkative by nature. When they learn something, they become more talkative, and none can be quiet. What they say they should not say. Those are damnable things. He is not speaking about common evil-speaking, but about doctrine. They prattle on about things which they should teach people to unlearn: "The Law must by all means be kept. Moses must stand for something here." [12] Like the false prophets, so also their female helpers mislead their households. Satan tempted Eve. *The first* (v. 12). Now they pursue new doctrines. Deserted is the first pledge as soon as they have taken it. John exhorts us to abide in that which we have received (cf. 1 John 2:24). The "first pledge" is faith in Christ. This is the meaning I get.

14. *I would have younger widows marry.* This is the revocation. This text is very strong. Even if he had spoken earlier about vows, he here revokes it. They should marry, lest they become examples of very bad widows and they gad about. Rather they should have a responsibility, so that they do not become idlers, gossips, and busybodies. Where there is leisure, there is nosiness. If they have husbands, they don't have enough time to sleep or to think. One cannot do better by a young woman than to let her have a child. This is sensible talk. After all, that sex is frivolous, unstable. It is upset by worry and concern for its offspring. Then it can sleep barely two hours, so closely is it involved and ready to serve. What will they do? *They should bear children.* Then they will suffer the trials of the

---

[12] Cf. Luther's summary of what needs to be taught, in *Against the Heavenly Prophets,* Part I, *Luther's Works,* 40, pp. 82—84.

flesh and will mortify their flesh, so that they rule their own homes, are concerned about looking after the home so their household is honorable. Then they will not be able to return to their fault of gossiping. *And give the enemy no occasion.* Paul looks at this sin that he may exalt his teaching, lest our life should offend anyone. The faithless are offended if they see such lazy widows gossiping and bringing new doctrines from their homes. They then say, "I shall remain firm in my faith. Our wives are more honorable than those who live in lazy security." Peter says, "See to it that you care for and serve your children, that you cling to your husband, that one may finally say, etc." (1 Peter 3:1). *To revile.* This is to raise an uproar.

15. *For some have already strayed after Satan.* For example, young widows generally grow wanton against Christ and afterwards want, etc. This is what I said is the rule. I have already proved this with an example. This passage again proves that Paul is speaking about doctrine. "They have strayed after Satan" — after the ideas which Satan propagates through his false prophets. Therefore, "let my doctrine move you to teach younger widows to do some work." Up to this point he has been speaking about widows.

16. *If any believer has relatives who are widows.* He does not want to "burden the church" with unnecessary people. We must carefully note this example. Although we Christians should be prepared for rapine at the hands of everyone, this should still serve some necessary function. Otherwise it serves no purpose. After all, we ought not be the opportunity or the "reed shaken in the wind" (Matt. 11:7), that others might have pleasure at our expense. Otherwise, I would become an accomplice to their wantonness. When I see a brother in need, then I must be generous. If he cannot feed himself, etc. No one ought to be found doing nothing etc. *Let him assist them.* Let him satisfy them, offer them enough. That is, let him provide for them. He is speaking here especially about physical supply. Earlier he spoke about providing for one's own family. That is a different word. He ought not exclude her from his house if he himself can feed her. We would want to lay all our burdens upon the church, if we have a sick servant. While our servants are healthy, we employ their labors. When they are sick, we impose them on others. We should teach that this not be done. If a thief steals my shirt, I should endure this, but I should neither teach nor agree to such theft. In this way the church suffers a burden, but the bishop ought to rebuke such

action and ought not agree to it, so that honorable doctrine and words remain — the doctrine and words with which we close the mouths of our adversaries. If you have healthy servants who serve you, keep them also when you can be of service to them. We can set up this passage against those who say, "Why do we have a common fund, if it is not ready to feed them? — if you want to be Christian?" I want to be Christian. Read that passage. If you are unwilling to be faithful, we take care of them. If someone has driven them out, we must deny him access to the common funds, because he has not taken care of his own people. *Let the church not be burdened.* Here Paul appears to speak as if he despaired of the promises of Christ, whereas he said earlier (ch. 4:8): "It has promise for the present life." This is a statement of Paul's lack of faith, as if Christ could not accomplish this. Why should we say this? When we must feed widows out of the common funds of the church, the Lord will give and supply enough. But were I willing to pour out those funds in worthless and unnecessary uses and believe that God would supply enough — well, that's what Paul is speaking against. It is not a statement of faithlessness but of seeing to the care of people. After all, if I were to deprive the poor and give to people who need it less than they and would say, "God will provide," I would be tempting God. When, however, we provide for those who have need, then there is the promise of enough. On the other hand, if I wanted to take away from those who do not have the necessities and give to those who do have them, that is wrong. After all, the public funds for the needy are established for the needy, not for those not in need. We see from this passage that Paul had to deal with many ordinances of the church about which he has not written much.

17. *Let the elders who rule well be considered worthy of double honor.* He does not say, "They will be or are considered worthy." Rather he uses an imperative, an optative. Without specification nothing will come of it. They ought to be respected with double honor. This does not mean that you should bow twice to them, etc. Rather he is speaking about the honor of support, as "Honor your parents," and Christ, too, speaks about food (Luke 10:7). We say it this way in German: "He treats me with contempt,[13] lest he give me a crumb of bread." To honor, to hold in respect and regard, is to see to it that one may eat, be nourished well, and be watched over. This

---

[13] Luther's German expression is *helt mich in unehren.*

is said as a great favor for those who preach and on behalf of the security of consciences, that worldly goods can be used doubly when for others it can scarcely be used once, etc. But this does not happen. "Double honor" — those are ruling well who visit the sick, who practice other works for the church and for the weak, especially those who are trained in the Word, who meditate on it day and night, who read it. This is the most important work found in this office. These are the people who watch over the church. You have heard what a great treasure an elder is who is a sincere teacher of the church. If the Lord should give such a one, He would give a great treasure, nothing with crowns and pomp of empire. You see, he is taking care of souls and the organ of eternal life through which flow salvation and life. At the other extreme, we have no more harmful an enemy than a false teacher. Now see how difficult it is to find a sincere teacher. Satan corrupts the finest men. Where one is sincere, 10 on the other hand are destructive. How many do we have who teach the sincere Word? If only we had 10 more! To be sure, some are diligent, but those who labor in the Word are rare. Our ingratitude is such that we deserve to have teachers who lead us to destruction. Titus and Timothy were sincere. When we have this blessing, it is well and good. If not, people rebel. But they ought to have triple disgrace before the world.

18. *For the Scripture says: You shall not muzzle the ox when it is treading out the grain, and: The laborer deserves his wages.* Someone might say to this argument, "Why does he say this for elders ahead of those who labor in the Word?" You are speaking about an elder, a preacher. He is speaking about an ox. This is pure allegory. In Corinthians (1 Cor. 9:9) he explains this more beautifully: "Is it for oxen that God is concerned?" There is a reason why Paul makes an allegory from this point. Yet it is a fact that an ox eats with open mouth what it gathers from the threshing floor. Certainly God did not want to write for the sake of oxen, because He is not concerned for them, etc. Yet He is concerned for all things. "Man and beast Thou savest, O Lord" (Ps. 36:6). But He did not give Scripture to oxen, and they cannot preach Scripture. They cannot quote Moses and what he wrote for them. A preacher, however, can do such quoting. The allegory is this: the threshing ox [14] is the worker in the Word. In this way the preacher threshes the people of the world — the chaff. He beats out the grains — the saints, the elect. They lie among the

[14] By metonymy *os* ("mouth") stands for *bos* ("ox").

chaff. Just as such a person allows himself to be established by an ox, so the righteous do not deny the things of the flesh to preachers. The ox does not hoard, but he eats. That is, the bishop should be content with what he has for the present. He should have no greed for gathering a treasure store. Yet we must tell the foolish not to gag our mouths. That is, they should not deny us. It is a beautiful allegory. *The laborer deserves his wages.* These are Christ's words (Luke 10:7). I believe that the Jews had the proverb "A servant has wages coming." Christ quotes this proverb and applies it to the Gospel that preachers may know that they are in good conscience receiving sustenance from their churches. Against the Enthusiasts I say, "I work in the country." The Waldensian preachers are compelled to be workmen and provide for themselves. "If anyone will not work, let him not eat," we read in Thessalonians (2 Thess. 3:10). I interpret "work" as understanding, as working in the Word, as I mentioned earlier. We work, and we work in the Word. To minister the Word is also work. Paul does not order Timothy to become a farmer. "If anyone will not work," that is, the man who gads about like a busybody from house to house and seeks to feed his own belly. But those who labor in the Word ought not only eat, but should be considered worthy of "double honor." This is essential knowledge to have against those spirits which create new sects and new articles not necessary to faith. Paul writes in 1 Cor. 9:13: "Those who are employed." These are the people who work in the Gospel. The evangelist labors in his double task and considers his work thankless. Isn't this the way the wicked act because they are not farmers? This is how foolish those spirits are which trouble consciences so. From a universal axiom they create a particular one. The preacher labors; therefore, let him eat. The pope sins in the opposite direction when he uses this as an outstanding passage about tithing. There he breaks the bones of the poor. That is, everything the poor have must go for tithes and belongs to the papists. "You shall not muzzle the mouth." They want the privilege of having ministers of the Word fed. They want to not muzzle the mouth, but they do not want to do the threshing. They gobble up, but they do no work. Therefore this means here that ministers should not be given an abundance but that they should still have the necessary food and clothing. I would not have thought that this teaching was necessary now if experience now did not teach me that where there used to be 200 florins there now are scarcely 20. The Holy

Spirit saw what would happen — that they would forsake their ministers. Also Christ found this necessary to say when He commanded that those whom the minister serves feed him with deserved dignity. 1 Cor. 9:14.

19. *Never admit any charge against an elder except on the evidence of two or three witnesses.* This is a new idea, very outstanding — the most difficult of all. The text is easy, but the matter itself has been much debated. If a bishop has been diligent, he treats the Word more easily than what, etc.[15] When we are in the preaching office, I address no one separately. Then I can preach that he is safe against evil people, that he is frightened but comforted. But if the preacher is a judge and makes a special charge, then he is beginning to, etc.[16] Paul foresaw it well (ch. 5:21): "I charge you to keep these rules." It is a perilous matter and responsibility because of one work. I would gladly deal with the Word, but to deal with sins is an odious thing. There is danger that we go beyond our bounds, that we teach the contrary. Therefore we must use great prudence there, because cases are so different that a person could lose his mind over them. *Against an elder.* Earlier I mentioned that "elder" is ambiguous in the Greek.[17] Does it mean one who is older or an official? I take it to mean one who is generally an older person, even though one may take it as a minister of the Word. I continue, however, to take it in its general sense. Why does Paul do this? Why is he pressing this idea? It is a natural sin that, where there is a congregation, where there is a church, one is prone to attach oneself to anything lofty to strive for honor, whether that be a person honorable because of his age, etc. In this situation the bishop must be very prudent, not a respecter of persons. Yet he ought to have respect for persons. Whoever has something of a reputation is exposed to the tongues of everyone. Satan cannot endure anything good. For example, a beautiful girl can hardly arrive at the point of getting a husband before becoming a whore, so is she exposed to all who lie in wait for her. Thus if there is some

[15] The thought is left incomplete by the writer, but perhaps Luther's completion of the sentence was something like "than he solves what afflicts a particular individual."

[16] Another incomplete thought. Perhaps Luther dictated even more rapidly on this day than he was accustomed to. Some rather obvious conclusion — one Röhrer felt sure he could remember and supply later — must be supplied, perhaps "exceed his commission" or "get into difficulties."

[17] Cf. p. 332 above.

venerable old man who should be buried with honor, it is his gray
hair, not I, that brings it. "Rise up before the hoary head" (Lev.
19:32). We are in reverence, etc. The kingdom of Satan lets nothing
be good on earth. The learned man has so many jealousies. In this
way all good things are obnoxious to detractors. Paul, then, wants to
instruct the bishop to have good judgment, so that he may not easily
believe wagging tongues but know how things are done in the world.
If he knows the terms and the kingdom of the devil, he can adjust
himself. He is not rash. Rather, he acts with good reasoning, because
he knows this is happening this way. Therefore this is a dangerous
passage. It gives a general rule: "except on the evidence of two or
three witnesses." If someone says something about an old man, don't
believe it, especially if this is about an old and venerable person. You
see, Satan is trying to bring shame on him. Here you note that he is
speaking about public accusation and public charge: that no one be
accused before the church unless two or three declare in public that
he has done this. If this does not occur, you should consider accusers
as detractors. Thus one should not be rash in words or speaking, etc.,
when he passes judgment or makes an accusation on some personal
charge, unless he has two witnesses who know for certain. This is
the way he can protect himself. I would not deprive us of that golden
rule for the comfort of our consciences. If I know that he is sinning
in secret, I act according to Matthew 18. On the other hand, if I want
to pass judgment before others without witnesses, I burden myself
with the sins of others. If two people say, "He does this and that,
which offends others," they may make this accusation before the
church. Paul is speaking about those who are counted among Christians. Others are not included. One should not attack with a personal
accusation. In general, I say that these are heathen. Here he makes a
distinction between the church — those who go to the Sacrament with
us — and the heathen. In the church, you will not accept a charge
unless two people, etc. In the church you ought to behave in this
way: in the first place, one argues all things in general simply by keeping away from personalities. I teach by teaching; I argue by arguing.
There is a second function: if charges are brought to me, I ought not
attack personally, unless these people have been convicted publicly
before the church. If he lies and escapes his witnesses, I am not both-
ered. I can not prove it by witnesses. I leave the judgment to God.
Then the lie will not endure, but it will allow him to fall so that God's

will is done. Yet in the meantime I am safe because I have done my
duty. This rule is a very necessary one for preachers because they
have to deal with sins. This is the proper place for their work — in
the public assembly with their sermonizing. Paul states that in the
case of younger widows he was not able to achieve the ideal. Although this is said about an old man, yet we must take it to refer to
all respected persons. After all, God wants us to have respect for all
His gifts. In the church — that is, outside of the civic administration —
we ought to make a distinction among those gifts, but not before God.
In general, one should attack not with personal reproof, unless this is
proved by two and by such as want to know. If we were to follow
this rule, we would not be quick to accuse, etc. The remaining cau-
tions concern what the result of restraining relationships is. Those
who are very spiritual fail; as long as we stay on the general level,
everything turns out well, but not when we come down to individuals.
In general, it is quickly said how he is cured of the fever, but there
is no judgment or knowledge about particulars. You see, all things
are healers. That's why one cannot determine it so precisely. There
should be "two witnesses" because God wants the honors spared, the
defects covered. If the faults cannot be covered up, they proceed
further. Meanwhile, they apply all the cures they can before making
any public charge. If this does not help, he should be charged by
two witnesses, what we have said earlier to the contrary notwithstand-
ing. Paul wanted this. We must act this way. Because rebuking an
old man is a matter of such great danger, I want to leave his sins
completely unpunished. I don't want you to do this, but you should
rebuke him after his own fashion. When they have thus become sinners — that is, when you have proved this — you ought to charge them
before all.

20. *Rebuke those who persist in sin.* Do this without respect for
person. You ought to rebuke men publicly and generally. You should
not censure them with partiality and with personal intent. Such general reproof should stir them to fear, etc. Then no person, etc. I do
not believe that he treats this sense here, but it does include the person. He says, "Those who persist in sin." You should not allow them
to go unpunished. Rather, treat them in such a way that witnesses
come up and bring proof against them. You should bring the accusation on the basis of two witnesses. Make no charge if it is a private

and uncertain sin according to Christ's word.[18] If he can excuse himself, let him go. If not, bring the witnesses, etc. Afterwards make the reproof. Don't hold up on it, so that *the rest may stand in fear.* Do not give a license to sin by letting his sin go unpunished. You should be patient with the sinners who come to their senses, but you should censure sins which lead to license.

21. *In the presence of God and of Christ Jesus and of the elect angels I charge you.* Look what Paul is doing here. Although we can relate this to every command, yet it applies most nearly to these, because Timothy has quickly forgotten that point about treating sins. Therefore Paul treats and discusses the point with very great earnestness. We must be sparing of the sins, but we must not make a path for sins nor open a door for them, as in the papacy. "I charge you before God, etc." *To keep these rules without favor.* Jurists know what "favor" means: when we anticipate a situation rashly, with temerity; "not with inconsiderate haste." Here Paul clearly means the danger of the bishop in his office. One cannot be deceived more easily than if he trusts rashly and easily. Our nature is of such a kind that we believe and listen to the bad more easily than the good. It is a natural fault to believe the worst about everyone, because we try to do this. Our experience agrees with this. Such credulity is natural. Be careful of yourself that you keep these commands, that you are not rash, that you are cautious, that you think before you act, that you do not believe with rash judgment what is said about old men and public officials. Take your time, do not judge prematurely. Proceed according to the highest judgment. If not, you will make your judgment prematurely. A perverse tongue is prompting you. Even if this doesn't happen, even if it is true, don't go on to the censuring. Be witnesses to me; that is, that you may not be carried along rashly. You will do all this more easily if you know that this is the nature of the kingdom of Satan, who creates discord. If I charge someone who has been accused by witnesses, I know this. And I say that I am not censuring but God is. He has made this law. Thus my conscience is clear.

πρόσκλισις ("favor," "prejudice," "partiality") is a word with double meaning. Our text has *inclinando* ("without inclining"), "that you incline to one side or the other." This is a good idea — one I do not condemn: "that you should not be caught up by affection, love, favor, or profit in the other direction." The other text is also a good one:

18 Cf. Matt. 18:15.

"according to provocation" — according to your own passions; "that you do nothing according to the way you are stirred." One passion takes priority — that you are provoked and stirred before the judgment. Incline in this direction. Both ideas are true. "Restrain yourself from that work and be careful." There are two dangers here. First there is prejudgment, which proceeds to judge on the basis of slander or authority or merits. It judges before the evidence. Evil men promote it. It is extrinsically evil. The other is intrinsically evil: that we easily believe the evil and disbelieve the good. We are easily stirred to believe things just as they are reported. Cast this out of yourself and others. "Let the witnesses take the stand before the church. You do not trust those who flatter you nor your own affection. In the meantime your conscience is clear. Stand firm in public censuring or practice personal censuring in private. The public charge you should not undertake on any account. Let the witnesses do that."

22. *Do not be hasty in the laying on of hands, nor participate in another man's sins; keep yourself pure.* Here again we have a fine description of a pastor's peril — first on the left hand, then on the right. The first pastor's peril is in sharing sins, in perjuring a report, and then in exalting oneself. Here I must not immediately pass judgment because the man is worthless; there not because he is good. Surely, this is a dangerous situation. That is, you do not easily entrust a duty to anyone. At that time ministers were ordained in this way: there was a confirmation of ministers publicly before the church. Thus Paul had the same experience: "I established the younger ones as widows, and they became whores on account of it." "Do not be hasty in the laying on of hands." He does not say: "Lay hands on no one." That we have to do. The pope enjoys doing this. He who has a conscience does not lay on hands hastily. Trust no man easily in regard to his knowledge, learning, or piety. There, too, insist on witnesses who consistently speak about his integrity and circumstances. Then you can say, "I do not believe myself but the two witnesses. I have done this because You have sent it, O God." If this does not happen thus, you should not be rash. *Do not participate.* This is a general statement applying to both parts. If this has been a rash action, I condemn it and bring shame on the man. And so it is when I ordain a preacher. What he does applies to me, and I have to help bear his sins. Therefore beware of another man's sins. If I rebuke him too much and unreasonably, I incur a sin; if I neglect to do it, I sin again. If I help a person who is not

suitable, he falls into sin. On the other hand, if I don't help and he is suitable, [the same thing is true]. Therefore take the keys and set them before the feet of the Lord and take the two witnesses. Then you are free of the sins of others.

We have heard [19] this point on treating the sins of others; that is, how we must correct this situation and yet in such a way that we not harm a person with public censure unless he be proved guilty. In this way the bishop's conscience is clear, if he himself does not reprove but declares that it is the church which reproves. Then follows: *Keep yourself pure*. Whoever must rebuke others about manifest sins should be innocent and blameless. That is, "Keep yourself chaste, pure." Although we could relate this to other faults, we relate it to unrestrained lust, because it is the most common fault. Paul, therefore, gives a rule that one should keep himself pure as a good example. After all, it is shameful for a theologian. A person is not permitted to enjoy censuring others before an assembly. He adds a quite prudent caution: "I want you to be pure, but the preservation of purity requires the chastising of the flesh so that it is free of drinking, laziness, sex, etc." Work is good for this. Love is nothing else but the passion of an empty mind. Chrysostom says that it is the sign of a lazy mind. The busy mind, loaded with its concerns and worries, easily drops the sensual appetite. There are the other guards of purity, too: use life and waking hours carefully. The Greeks held their dialogs in the midst of wine and choice foods. Wine is a natural kindler of the passion. When one has guzzled wine, he follows it with food and then with love. With this precept, then, Paul means that one should live purely, that he should fast and keep watch that he does not give his passion an opportunity through an unrestrained life. On the other hand, you will chastise yourself in such a way that you use your body carefully. Treat your body in such a way that it does not waste away. Both are sins — to go to excess in drinking and in fasting. Gerson says it well.[20] Whenever a body has taken precautions for its lust, as when it eats bread, much strength and power come into the innermost parts of the body. It is different when it drinks wine. We cannot, therefore, establish a rule for so great a diversity of bodies. Here we have to consider the diversity of both the makeup of bodies and bodies themselves. This is what Paul means with this rule. He wants Timothy to train himself,

[19] The lecture of March 12 begins at this point.

[20] Cf., for example, *Regulae morales,* "De gula," XCIII, *Opera,* ed. Dupin, III, ps. I, p. 94.

but no farther than to preserve the health and welfare of his body. Gerson says this well. "Which one is to be thought of as pure, excess in eating or in fasting? Here we ought to compliment no one." It is hardly better, he says, to be excessive in spending than to sin in need. Why? When one's strength is exhausted and has nothing to prepare for food, it drains itself. This is quite dangerous — a situation to be feared. Saints Jerome and Bernard acted this way. They wore themselves out by drinking water, until their clothing and entire bodies stank so much that they were forced to avoid their brethren. They certainly condemned themselves, for they were unable to carry out their ministry of the Word. A certain father kept exhausting himself so that his innards contracted and in his old age were unable to accept food. In the *Lives of the Fathers* there are many such chaste men.[21] There many became so weak that they became insane. This is what happens to the Carthusians. It also occurs in the hospitality convents. They ought to be serving others, but others must serve them. So, if one must sin, it is safer to sin in excess than in need. In the case of the former, there is a restoration, but not in the latter. Everyone should test his own strength like a brave man. The man who burns much has much strength. He ought to wear himself out in a way different from that of a weak man. The man who eats rough bread is assailed differently from the way another is who eats eggs and meat. Therefore we must not behave like the monks. Augustine [22] says that because you are not all equal, you should not eat the same foods but rather do your eating as a superintendent distributes work. This requires prudence; the other is a willful act. Here you have an example that Paul is setting down as a type for all who are abstaining. One must control his body by watching so that it does not become wanton. If the body is weak, one ought to give it meat and drink. He allows wine to Timothy. Nevertheless, we ought not allow wine to the abstainers but forbid it. Yet Paul commands him to drink modestly. If a body is useless to the ministry, one should cease his abstinence, because the body is not altogether his; but in order that it may be of service, let it endure hunger. If anyone feeds his flesh too luxuriantly, he is feeding a domestic enemy. If a body is killed, a friend is killed. Would it be better to kill a friend than to feed an enemy? I shall gladly give a friend a bit too much. Augustine is dealing with the advice of a doctor. Let us thus consult our bishops as our doctors. An old man sleeps for scarcely

21 E. g., *Vitae patrum,* I, *De sancto Helia.*
22 The reference is to the rules of the Augustinian order.

an hour. To summarize this teaching: we must discipline the body, but we must do it wisely, not equally for all, because all men are not equal. We must relax it for the young man who cannot sleep so that a place and time for the healing of his body may be given. On the other hand, the man who has a good head might want to take an example from this. That would be very unfair. Although Timothy was a young man, yet he was a frail person. He had the great work of the Word and a great concern for the church. Even then he would abstain. He would drink water. Paul tells him, "I want you to be pure, to abstain — but to the extent that the health of your body bears this. I want you to feed your body for health's — not for passion's — sake. That is as necessary a matter as any other." The flesh is happy to hear that license is given. It leads a smug life. One must resist this. Again the liar Satan comes and wants to make it completely holy. The doctors of the monks used to say, "How does it happen that all monks work with their head? Equality of food and ceremonies brings this about." There is no wisdom there except for extreme old age. They are murderers, especially the Carthusians. To kill the body because of that training is contrary to Paul. "Is not the body more than food?" (cf. Matt. 6:25). When a body suffers hardship, it should take food.

23. *No longer drink only water.* Jerome boasts: "You see that monks and bishops ought to drink water. Paul permits this to a weak person, but just a little. Paul does this because of the license of the flesh which wants free time when it has a bride. Therefore one should rule his flesh, lest license go too far and lest there be excessive scarcity and restriction." "Timothy, if you need it, use, etc." The body is more than food, and food exists for the sake of the body. The body exists for the ministry of the Word. The man who deprives his body of health deprives the church of his ministry of the Word. Thus the one who should serve others, etc. This is the advice of a prudent man: "No longer." This is the way the housefather or a teacher ought to speak: "Cease drinking water." A doctor can advise best. *A little wine,* to restrain the lustful license of the flesh. If I say, "Use wine," the Enthusiasts abuse it. But Paul wants a person to maintain discipline, so that he drinks wine in such a way that he sees to it satisfactorily that the body is curbed and restored for its work. You, too, should do this if you sense that your body is hungry, etc. If you have a headache because of a din or ringing in your ears and sleep scarcely an hour, sleep either during the day or whenever sleep comes in order to pre-

serve the keenness of your mind. If both stomach and head are weak, nothing is healthy. *For the sake of your stomach.* You see what sort of a man Timothy was. He must have been a lean, miserable person, and it is apparent that he ruined himself, because he speaks about a weakness of the stomach, as if it did not keep his head in order, although this succeeds well where the stomach is in good shape. A cheerful stomach well supports a cheerful mind.[23] Stomach trouble must have been his sickness. One must control his body to preserve his health and bridle his passions. When health is to be safeguarded, one must not save on meat, eggs, wine, but not so when the opposite is true. But if there were some who labor in vain in their abstinence, they can abstain from water. Take a wife. "It is better to marry." This is a beautiful point for those who ought to be ruling. This text relates to the earlier one, because I said that he ought to treat the sins of others. Therefore he ought to be rid of his own sins, and this in such a way that one avoids evil destruction.

24. *The sins of some men are conspicuous.* The key to understanding this lies in the word "judgment." The Vulgate has this as an exposition: Paul is here speaking about the judgment of God and the Last Judgment. The meaning would be this: These sins are conspicuous and well known to man. That is, when Christ comes to judge, He will not have to explain the sins. You see, the sins of Judas, Pilate, and Herod are conspicuous. Likewise, sins of usury, etc., too. *They point to judgment.* Before a person comes to be judged, he is already being indicted. This is one sense. *Of some men.* There are some sins which lie hidden and are not revealed at this time. A person goes to trial primarily because of these. In 1 Cor. 4:5 Paul speaks of "things hidden in darkness." Many sins cannot be judged here. The church cannot pass judgment about secret sins. This we must reserve for God. Also, many take this to refer to the saints, but they do so because the heart of those people was hidden, especially those of the hypocrites and specious saints. They even crown these before they come up before, etc. They are like Paul, who stood before Caesar, etc. (cf. Acts 25:10). These are the conspicuous works, which the world cannot condemn. Rather, the world is forced to say, "They are right." Christ does not have the job of stating that these are good works. After all, it is obvious that they are good. Some works are secretly good but condemned be-

---

[23] *Auff eim frohlichen bauch sthet ein frohlich heubt,* probably a popular German version of *Mens sana in corpore sano.*

fore the world, as in the case of a miracle. Before the world the person who does them is a sorcerer, a thief, an evildoer. Many such things happen and are good. Yet the world condemns them, as happens with us. There is another meaning — that of the judgment of the church or of the bishop. You see, Timothy, as a judge of others, receives this comforting rule about treating the sins of others. "See to it that you do not correct or promote someone too quickly" (cf. v. 22). What shall I do? If I promote him, I do evil. If I do not correct him, I become a participant in his sins. Paul gives a rule: You cannot err in those sins which are conspicuous before you pass judgment. Jurists call this the indictment of the deed. This is what happens to a man who is an adulterer by the public witness of his whole neighborhood. He is found out in the midst of his adultery, when gossip rages in the streets, when children born of that illicit union play in the streets. That is what we call an indictment of the deed. The bishop's judgment follows. It becomes an indictment of the law which declares, etc. There is no need to run about for a trial; there is no need to run about gathering witnesses. Rather the sin is conspicuous ahead of time. The whole city and neighborhood, etc. In this way you may find some good works if you want to select a priest who is learned. You have seen him teach and explain a chapter in the Bible. They have seen that he is chaste. The entire neighborhood cries out, "These are obvious good works." There your judgment is unnecessary. Just see to it that you make an indictment of the deed of the law.

The rule of the pope is good for scoundrels. We have this understanding about the judgment of a bishop, that in promoting or in laying on of hands sinners have the testimony of their neighbors on their behalf, that there may be a loud cry that he is good. It works the other way in the case of a bad man. Your judgment comes later and is added. Then the indictment of the law and of the deed occur together. When this does not happen at first, *the sins of others appear later.* If you find two or three witnesses, evil works then appear later. If you cannot accuse a person, and if his work is not known to you nor shouted through the streets, then witnesses come. Through them come his activities. In this way works follow that person to his judgments.

This is the other sense Paul speaks of in regard to the judgment of the church. Which is better I leave to you. I prefer the latter, because we must always understand Scripture according to its subject nature. The sophist says that he must know the matter which is being debated.

Whoever notes this understands the book more easily. Once he understands the goal, he easily understands what does not agree with the goal. The man who plans to speak about a beer mug does not speak about an egg or chastity and later about the Turks, etc. Therefore, when we are involved in the area where Paul is treating the judging of the sins of others, it is fitting that the same place relate to the same nature. Then there is another reason. You see, it is not clear what advantage there might be in writing about the Last Judgment. Nothing here speaks to that point, nor is there anything like it at issue. What has this to do with the bishop and the rule of the church? After all, Paul sets up this entire epistle that Timothy may know how to conduct himself in the church. This is the goal of the epistle. Therefore we must treat the passage in such a way that it relates to giving a bishop information. This is the twofold reason that this passage speaks about the external judgment in the church of God. The passage is necessary and useful. If we take it as a reference to the Last Judgment, it is not. In the case of conspicuous sins, pass judgment, condemn, take care of them. In the case of other sins, don't condemn a person ahead of his works. The works follow the person, etc. Otherwise see to it that they remain hidden. Let God be the judge.

CHAPTER SIX

1. *Let all who are under the yoke of slavery regard their masters as worthy of all honor.*

You have just heard [1] that all ranks in the church have been established and how bishops and preachers teach. This is the last order — that of servants. There were some servants who had believing masters, some who had unbelieving ones. He teaches that both must learn to be content with their lot, "not only to the kind and gentle but also to the overbearing" (1 Peter 2:18). The first kind are those who have unbelieving masters. He uses this periphrasis, *who are under the yoke.* You see, he is making a concession, as if to say: "I admit that it is quite a harsh situation to be a slave or serf of others." This is what he calls "the yoke." But he adds the comfort: "This is not demeaning but salutary if you wear your yoke properly. Nonetheless, consider them worthy." It is a great thing to owe honor to heathen and overbearing masters. It is a great thing not merely to serve them but also to honor them. *Honor* means not simply to genuflect, bow the head, but to respect them, to be prepared to do their every wish. The very majesty which belongs to God we must see in our corporal master. Therefore God wants them revered in His majesty. Thus this is a worthy person, etc. We must have regard for the majesty, not the person. I owe respect to Julius Caesar because he has majesty. Although David had the right to rule, yet he stayed away from the throne and continued to respect Saul. *Every honor.* They should omit nothing that relates to the respect for and obedience to their masters. In other words, they should be eager to be well pleasing and obedient to their masters. Why? They must avoid every reason for scandal. You see, if a slave were to use the pretext that Christ had freed him and thus abandon his due service, etc., he would set up Christ as a seditious teacher, who made all things free. This is not what Christ wants.[2] This is the way some — the Anabaptists, for instance — explain Christ. You see, they say that no one can be saved unless he leaves his spouse. They upset the established religion of God. God does not want a man to leave

[1] The lecture of March 16 begins at this point.
[2] For instance, in Matt. 19:29.

his wife, a child to leave his parent. He wants them to hold to each other physically but abandon them spiritually. If a situation arises in which the two majesties run into each other, then one must abandon the human majesty. If the two do not clash, he must serve the majesty of men. Whoever teaches otherwise causes sedition. All Anabaptists therefore are seditious, because they abandon wives and families. This is an offense to peace. Our saints conduct themselves in such a way that they do not mislead the heathen. There has been no nation which did not respect majesty and that. But we must live in such a way that even the unbelievers say: "I see nothing in these men. They do everything. They are obedient, except that they do not want to worship our gods. Otherwise, they do nothing for which we can accuse them."

2. *Those who have believing masters must not be disrespectful on the ground that they are brethren.* This is an ambiguous text. We can relate it either to servants or to masters. Those who have believing masters should not become proud and despise their masters. Why does he say it this way? Should he not rather say this in the first verse? Because he is believing, he seems not to despise. The believing slave who has a believing master has the greater chance to despise, etc. You see, the unbelieving master is not submissive. The believing one is humble, a brother, given to love. Therefore the servant has a greater opportunity for license toward a believing master than to an unbelieving one who comes out against the servant with the sword and the law. This, then, is the greater opportunity for the flesh. You see, it thinks, "He is a Christian. Therefore he must be forbearing." This is to despise a master. The first meaning, then, is this: they use as an excuse that they are brothers of their masters. The second meaning is that servants are indeed brothers [of their masters]. I don't know which is better. It is very ambiguous. The Anabaptist relates this to slaves. I am inclined to relate it to masters because of the preceding verse. After all, if slaves must honor unbelieving masters who are not their brothers, they must honor even more those who are believers and brothers. That is what I think. This seems to me a more harmonious and suitable meaning — that Paul says this about masters. There is no great danger in this ambiguity, because both are brothers. Servants of unbelieving masters ought all the more not despise them. After all, they are brothers of the Lord. They should not give an alien uprightness as an excuse but *must serve all the better,* because they are believing brothers. *And beloved,* obviously [so named] after the One loved. *Those who*

benefit by their service. If Paul is saying this about servants, the exhortation is this: Servants should be content in this under their yoke
and glory in God because they are brothers of their masters. As such
they think this way: "I shall serve God gladly. Before the Lord this
man is my brother. What does it matter that he is my master as far
as the world is concerned?" Then he thinks: "God loves me, and I believe that my master, too, shares in all the blessings of God that I enjoy." Therefore you should consider in what a favorable position you
are. To be sure, you are in a slavery of the body, but you are equals
in spirit. When a servant thinks this way, he serves gladly and thinks:
"God could compel me to serve an unbelieving master and to receive
beatings. Why shouldn't I serve a believing master happily?" Here
Paul is at the same time interpreting the Hebrew word חֶסֶד. He is not
speaking of a slave's blessing but of Christ's blessing, that is, of mercy
or grace. We read in Matt. 12:7: "I desire mercy," that is, "I desire
blessing." The blessing is mercy or work paid to a brother. The Greeks
translated "mercy" with the Greek word ἐλεημοσύνη. In German it is
wolthat. Greedy priests rendered alms. חָסִיד is to have been made
generous, a person who gladly does good. Having received the blessing, he is justified by God. We see this at the same time in Paul. This
is a worthwhile passage which is treated and conceived against the
seditious. No one has the right to disturb the peace — not even the
chosen people of God, as God Himself speaks against the wicked servants: "If they should keep the faith for unbelieving masters, all the
more should they do this for believing ones." All the more ought each
one be obedient to his own ruler; all the more ought a wife be obedient
to her husband and a husband not desert his wife. If they say, "Go
and deny Christ," then one must resign his office. But he has no right
to run away, as the Anabaptists do. Rather he should say, "I want to
serve you the way I serve my Lord," and not act against God. If they
then don't want to keep you, they will get rid of you. To be sure,
Christ speaks about leaving children. He is speaking in a spiritual
sense, that one make them angry rather than God. These passages
are worth noting and are necessary at this time. *Teach and exhort
these duties.* That is, teach those who do not know them. Impress
those who do know them and indoctrinate them with them.

3. *If anyone teaches otherwise.* This is an exhortation, an admonition like that of Christ in Matt. 7:15. After He taught, he added the
caution, "Beware. I have taught you correctly. But there will rise up

among you false teachers. Keep that which I have taught you. They
will come as wolves, etc. Keep watch." You, too, teach and preach.
There will come those who will teach otherwise. They will have fine
credentials. So be careful. I think that Paul is making a prophecy
here. I think he has thought of the papacy, as he also did at the beginning of chapter 4. He means the same people here. *The teaching
which accords with godliness.* This is to believe in Christ. This teaching instructs husbands, elders, bishops, servants. *Whoever teaches
otherwise* than this is not a genuine teacher. Who does teach otherwise? Look at the pope and his followers. They all do battle against
grace and the righteousness of faith. Christ is to all "a sign that is
spoken against" (Luke 2:34). On the opposite side are the Anabaptists,
who say that those who baptize are an insult to grace because they
make the first baptism useless. The pope has taught that slaves should
not be obedient. In fact, he has deposed kings. "We depose you,
Philip of France." [3] On the other hand, you should obey the pope, etc.
He would command the powerful to curse their kings and not obey
them, as in the case of the king of Bohemia.[4] "Whoever teaches other
than this, etc.," is the devil, as Jerome tell us, who used to teach departure and flight from the world, parents, and bishops, and who kept
finding new rituals and fasts. Meanwhile the Word of God and administration were neglected. Arsenius [5] was in the court. Naaman the
Syrian [6] was elsewhere. They carried her [7] out of the court that they
might fast. They teach that marriage is a dangerous state. Paul therefore meant the papists here. *If anyone does not agree,* that is, does not
assent. The words which have already been taught do not please them,

[3] The reference is to the long controversy between Pope Boniface VIII (1294
to 1303) and King Philip IV, the Fair, of France (1285—1314). In his bull
Unam sanctam (1302) Boniface announced: *Subesse Romano pontifici . . . omnino
esse de necessitate salutis.* The same bull also laid claim to all spiritual and
temporal supremacy for the papacy on the basis of the two swords of Luke 22:38.
Boniface became a prisoner of Philip's Italian aids but was set free shortly
before his death.

[4] The reference is to the struggles of Pope Boniface VIII against King Albert
of Austria. "King of Bohemia" may refer to Henry VI, king of Bohemia and
Poland (1307—1310).

[5] Arsenius was the name of a legate of Pope Nicholas I (858—867) who
was sent to the court of Lothar II to deal with him in the matter of his unjust
divorce of his wife Thietberga.

[6] Cf. 2 Kings 5:1.

[7] In the case of Lothar II this was his mistress Waldrade, whom Arsenius
took along to remove her from the court. But she escaped and managed to rejoin
Lothar.

as usual. Who would not know this? *With the sound words.* This means to teach each person to serve God in his own calling that each may become rich in his own position. This is to believe in the Lord Jesus, because we are not saved by the duty of our various works and callings but by Him. *Godliness.* This is to worship God.

4. *He is puffed up with conceit.* Who is this? Here one sees the heretics. These words are very obscure. Those who are so puffed up and teach otherwise have an appearance of humility. They treat humility with immeasurable bombast, as do the monks. There they wear humble clothing and have the foolish ritual of shaving their heads. So great, however, is the swelling of their hearts that, etc. Therefore, when Paul says "puffed up," it is a mysterious word which no one but the Spirit judges (cf. 1 Cor. 2:15). They cover up with holy appearance. Paul treated this beautifully in Colossians (2:18): "puffed up . . . by his sensuous mind." A different way begins. His life has a beginning, its name is "willing." He does not walk according to God's command but according to his own will. There there is a certain humility, a gray coat, so that each thinks he has an angelic humility. Yet he is "puffed up by his sensuous mind." Why does Paul make this judgment? Because it is impossible that there be humility where someone walks according to his own will. He does not live in the word of Scripture but behaves according to his own choice. Were he humble, he would subject himself to the Word of God and would stand firm in the condition which God has given him. If a slave suffers all the things which servitude involves, he will find a condition of humility. Whatever follows is a voluntary religious feeling. It puts away the "I should." He has a satanic pride. He is puffed up and wants to accomplish something special. This is the fine appearance of the monks. After complaining among themselves, they call it uniqueness and bigheadedness. All uniqueness is suspect. It is true that whoever walks by a way of his own willing is proud. Therefore the factious spirit is proud. Yet it covers itself so well that it deceives the whole common crowd. The spiritual person says: "I shall see whether you walk according to the manifest Word of God." If you do, he passes no judgment. If you do not, he does not deceive your judgment. The Holy Spirit has passed this judgment: Let him fast to death, he is proud. The will is so perverse. Also it knows nothing. *He knows nothing.* Yet there is very great knowledge in them, as in Zwingli and Oecolampadius. They are very holy men. Thus there is the note: they

are very learned men. Make a careful distinction between the two fruits: those of the Gospel and those of our own will. There appears to be a great lack of fruit in Christians. This happens because Satan is quiet and hides. Thus the Christian is considered a complete angel. There is need for a great judgment. For example: A servant has his condition from God, even though it happens that he is disobedient. So long, however, as he remains in his servitude, etc. Where they are outside the Word, there there is a distribution among the poor of an excellent meal. Satan can put on this appearance, that such a person gives a dollar where the Christian barely gives a penny. Thus their wisdom is much more apparent. Yet they know nothing; and, nevertheless, they preach well. That is, even if they were to speak what is true, they do not understand it. Thus I say: If Zwingli and Oecolampadius understand what they are saying about Christ, I will wager my neck, which no one does willingly. In conclusion, the very wise are called by St. Paul the foolish who know nothing, the ignorant, like the Sacramentarians, our foes in this day. You see, while others — the heathen, for instance — understand something about Scripture, they corrupt Scripture. *But he has a morbid craving.* Here he treats it carefully. This "morbid craving" in Latin is *insaniens* ("unreasoning"). In German we say: *Er ist ein Nar.* He is sick. He is mad and foolish, because he has abandoned the Word of God in its true sense. It is impossible for him not to fall into controversy. As soon as the truth of Christ has been lost, countless controversies arise. When once the pope abandoned the simplicity of faith, one decree gave birth to a hundred more. Later the decrees produced glosses. Then one gloss gave birth to another, and sect produced sect without end. At first Zwingli denied the sacrament of bread and wine. Then he argued about what a sacrament was and about enlightenment. There there was no limit, no end. If a person once errs, there is no end of falling and erring. He has suffered shipwreck of his faith (cf. 1 Tim. 1:19). *For controversy.* This is a significant word, pregnant with meaning. One doctrine is not a controversial issue of opinion and doubt but of fullness. What is the University of Paris? A collection of opinions. Everyone has opinions. This is the way it is at every university. When one has abandoned the certain knowledge of Christ, he must follow opinions. We read in Ps. 5:9: "There is no truth in their mouth." After this there immediately follow λογομαχίαι ("disputes about words"). He has described the pope and the factious spirits beautifully. When I have lost

the righteousness of Christ and make an attack, there follows a dispute
over words. What is righteousness? Discalced friars, gray caps,
"Blessed art thou," etc. Then there develops a dispute in the word
"righteousness." It is the same with "wisdom." "Wisdom" is to know
that Christ, who suffered for us, justifies no man unless you have escaped from the moral law. With Aristotle, Augustine, the Anabaptists
there are many opinions. Then the disputes begin. Here is wisdom:
if you are married or hold office, there there is no righteousness. Opinions cause wisdom to lose the matter at hand. Once that matter has
been lost, wisdom is a frigid thing. Only the words remain. Then the
dispute follows. Once the matter has been lost, the word remains; and
while the word remains, the dispute remains. We read in Ecclus.
34:13: "I am endangered to the point of death . . . but I am freed."
Unless a person remains in simplicity of doctrine, he falls into disputes
over words. *Which produce.* This is not that they themselves feel this
way. Paul is speaking in terms of a mystery. Everyone does not sense
this to be controversy, but he thinks of it as truth. He himself does not
judge his own doctrine but is himself judged. He stands stubbornly
in his own sense and calls it truth. This is not a "dispute over words"
but the very simple sense, as the words indicate. It is impossible for
the eye to overcome the color of the glass, through which, etc.[8] So,
as long as they are held captive, they disregard those who look at them
askance. There is love among them. They emulate the way we do.
Sincere theologians rebuke without fear. They do the same thing.
They operate with *envy*, like Paul and a pious zealot. Paul teaches to
endure it, but in love. This they also do, but they tolerate sins. Paul,
therefore, is wrong. This is not envy then, but simple love. They are
written down for us who are suffering hardship because of envy. These
are not *dissensions* but declarations that they mean to insist on their
thing. *Slander.* When Paul says, "O foolish Galatians" (Gal. 3:1), and
when we read, "O foolish men," in Luke 24:25, this is not slander. They
also say the same things. Paul, however, says, You have been bewitched by Satan (cf. Gal. 3:1). This, then is a genuine rebuke. But
what they say is slander. Christ's "white teeth" (cf. Gen. 49:12) are
brighter than the lead of theirs. The Christian bites, but he operates
with a heart of milk — a heart of mothers' milk. They, on the other hand,
boast that they have Scripture, the Holy Spirit, a "milky" rebuke and

---

[8] Luther carries this comparison out in greater detail in his treatise *That
These Words of Christ . . . Still Stand Firm* (1527). Cf. *Luther's Works*, 37, p. 20.

that we have Satan. Love is not boastful and blasphemous. Likewise it is not suspicious. In fact, they believe the best about our brothers and, on the other hand, the worst about us. Thus we ought to become suspicious when someone teaches the truth badly. If this is not done with envy, etc., when one truly attacks, there there is no suspicion. But Paul's judgment is infallible. "They desire to have you circumcised that they may glory in your flesh" (Gal. 6:13). Paul speaks with correct judgment, because he does not make mistakes. Thus when I speak about Zwingli's followers, I declare with true judgment that they are wicked blasphemers because their doctrine is false. But if this were a brother who was not in opposition, there there would be love without suspicion. Therefore love can never be suspect, because, if they are brothers, it bears their habits as well as their lack of faith. If they are not brothers, it passes certain judgment. But enemies are suspicious. What is the reason? They judge otherwise than the situation directs. As a consequence they err. Whatever evil is spoken against us, etc.[9]

5. *And wrangling.* This is uncommonly well written. This is hostile meeting, παρατριβή ("constant wrangling"), planned session. So also in the Greek I set it first. There is an argument between them, and they are argumentative. They are constantly given to debates. Satan does not rest. These are not debates but futile, harmful debates which have nothing to do with the matter at hand. They cover themselves with a multitude of words.[10] When one word is spoken against them, they bring back ten. If one page is written against them, they write back ten. Because they are men they are *depraved in mind.* They have lost the matter at hand. They are caught up by opinions and are more talkative than others. Also this appears in some who are "bewitched by Satan": some are mute, some are positively garrulous. These are the same ones Paul means here. They talk constantly and endlessly. Not only do they muffle good preachers, they also deafen their listeners. Paul advises: "After admonishing a factious man once or twice, avoid him" (Titus 3:10). Once he has begun to become talkative, he insists on having the last word. "Do not [argue] with a chatterer" (cf. Ecclus. 8:3). He hears no one except a talkative person, both "March!" and then again "Halt!" [11] If they were sound and genuine in their doctrine, they

9 Cf. *Luther's Works,* 37, pp. 21 f.

10 Cf. p. 291, n. 12, above.

11 For *mortatio* we have read *moratio.*

would not, etc. I have learned from experience: I cannot urge them to respond to one passage. I have discussed this with them orally and in writing.[12] *Bereft of the truth.* They have lost the truth. *Imagining that godliness is a means of gain.* This is also suspicious. Why does he say that they are seeking gain? You see, Paul is suspicious but he surely knows and considers it as a point that they love gain. After all, the Holy Spirit does not deceive. Throughout Scripture He calls them "appetite servers" in Rom. 16:18 and Phil. 3:19, and says (Rom. 3:13): "Their throat is an open grave." He calls them "dogs" (Phil. 3:2) who do not know salvation. He assigns them to a slavery to the belly and says (Phil. 2:21): "They all look after their own interests, not those of Christ." What is the reason? Whoever has once fallen from the truth and from faith and errs in wicked works cannot seek the interests of Christ. Therefore the Holy Spirit must drive him. It is Satan who is driving one to seek his own interests. Therefore Paul passes the true judgment that they are seekers of gain. We read in Gal. 6:13: "They seek glory that they may boast," that they may enjoy life here. But these things ought to be impressed on us. They seek the glory of God and of Christ! They are faithful ministers! We seek our own glory and honor! Were you to consider outward appearance only, everything Paul says would be pure lies. Here I again say: the wicked theologian cannot keep from being a greedy seeker of gain. You see, he has a sense of falseness because his is a spirit of falseness. *Imagining.* They think godliness is a matter of seeking gain. They lay hold of godliness, but only in appearance. Earlier I said that the worship of God lies especially in preaching the Word, because by teaching the Gospel one worships God, gives thanks, fulfills all the Old Testament sacrifices and all reverence for the Old Testament. With such worship one serves his neighbor. The image of God also is formed in men so that they do not kill each other but live in such a way that they resemble God. This is godliness. We turn to godliness to the glory of God and men. They glory in and grasp at godliness to get rich. They say that they indeed are seeking the glory of God, but actually they are seeking their own glory and gain, not their neighbor's good. They do not believe. To seek the interests of God and one's neighbor, that is godliness. "To divide." The Spirit is needed, who can discern.

6. *There is great gain in godliness with contentment.*[13] Above,

---

[12] Cf. *Luther's Works*, 37, pp. 18 f.

[13] A marginal note in the Weimar text refers to the following statement in a sermon of Luther's held June 27, 1529: "Thorns is what Christ calls riches in

speaking about widows, he used the expression "Let her assist them" as well as this word "contentment." [14] When a person is content, let him be satisfied. The man who practices godliness and cuts off his greed is content with what he has. Cf. Heb. 13:5. There is a promptitude of the heart which is content. He is a rich man who is content. The man who is not content is unfortunate. That reminds one of the proverb which says: "Do you want to have something to boast about? Practice godliness with contentment." This is true, but it is not believed. There is nothing worse than a greedy man who is in need of a dollar — or, in fact, who needs a dime. He has no expense. Whatever he has is useless. Earlier (ch. 4:8) Paul said: "Godliness is valuable in every way, etc. "Seek first" (Matt. 6:33). "I will fill your bellies, even if heaven and earth are at stake." But it doesn't help. If you have been godly and content, that is great gain. Godliness is to worship God with the Word, that men may be made similar to God. The least and the reason.

7. *For we brought nothing into this world.* "Naked came I from my mother's womb," says Job (ch. 1:21). Consider where you come from. Before our eyes we see examples, but we are blindness itself. One gathers up treasure and doesn't know for whom. He is intent on his gathering. If he is seeking gain, for whom? He doesn't know. "And the things you have prepared, whose will they be?" (Luke 12:20). The title "fool" stands written above all treasures. Many parents have gathered for their children, but who got it? After all, the saying does not deceive: "Even a parent must take a chance; whether his child will receive it, no one can tell. It very frequently happens that someone else gets it." Why, then, do we heap up?

8. *Having food and clothing.* Here comes the contentment. He uses the same expression. Round and round and away we go, abundance and plenty, farewell and good night, this is real food, etc. These are pure maxims against greed. The Greek does not have this.[15] This is a constant exhortation from excellent passages. Then he follows with a condemnation. He condemns an eagerness for wealth,

the Gospel (Matt. 13:22). Paul interprets these thorns by saying in 1 Tim. 6:9-10: 'Those who desire to be rich fall,' yes, they fall into many harmful desires, for 'the love of money' is what Paul is interpreting there, I tell you." Cf. W, XXIX, 438, 7 f.

[14] In chapter 5:16 the verb *sufficiat* ("that the church may assist"), related to the noun *sufficientia* ("contentment") in the present verse, is used.

[15] This may refer to the Vulgate's *haud dubium* (v. 7) or *diaboli* (v. 9).

not their possession. Abraham was not eager for wealth. A man who
is concerned about his household and children does well. But if a person watches for and seeks opportunities to become wealthy, etc., such
a person does not want to be content with what he has. "Do not be
anxious, saying, 'What shall we eat?'" (Matt. 6:31). "Do not exalt
yourselves" (Luke 12:29), as things are done in the world. I want to
have as much as my neighbor. If I want this, more than I have, then
I am exalting myself.[16] Abraham did not do this; he was not eager
to be rich.

9. *Fall into temptation.* It cannot fail. Blessed is the man who is
content with his own lot. Why is this? The man who is not content
but seeks wealth suffers various temptations. As he is tempted, he is
exposed to every peril. He is caught in a snare. If anyone has possessions, he is caught in a snare. If he is free, if the magistrate becomes angry, he goes away. If the magistrate does not do it, an evil
neighbor does it. He must be prepared to bear temptations. He becomes especially bound when eagerness for wealth develops. If he
is a righteous man, he says: "Begone." He laughs at temptations. He
is not *in a snare.* Although he is in the middle of things, still he is not
in a snare. Others are inflamed to take revenge. This is what *temptations* and the *snare* mean. *Into many senseless and hurtful desires.*
He becomes wrapped up in his desires, etc., because he has an interest in money. This interest develops vegeance, anger, envy, various
tricks to devise ways of keeping what he has. Because of his desires
he has no rest. Because of them he sinks into destruction. Paul is
making a severe exhortation against the pursuit of wealth. The man
who is rich and intent on wealth is exposed to the sword and fiery
coals. On the other hand, if their heart does not stand in the way,
they escape the temptation and snares. Those who have free hearts
seek no vengeance. They have no anxieties for preserving or increasing their wealth. There is no concern for thinking about godliness.
This the thorns choke (cf. Matt. 13:7). That is what Paul means with
ruin.

10. *For the love of money is the root of all evils.* The eagerness,
or desire, for money extends more widely than greed. It extends to all
other things, to the desire for power, pleasure, gold, or silver. These

---

[16] Luther's German translation of the last phrase of Luke 12:29 is *fahret
nicht hoch her.* This is based on the Vulgate's *nolite in sublime tolli* ("Do not
exalt yourselves").

are maxims, or ἐπιφωνήματα ("pithy sayings"). The man who is involved with greed has the source of every evil. One evil after another wells up for him. The greedy man is wrapped up in many evils, as already enumerated. Those who are immersed in the pursuits of money cannot pray, give thanks, or hear the Word of God if so much as a penny is taken from them. These desires are *senseless* (v. 9), because they bring no benefit. They are *hurtful,* because they bring great harm. Therefore he says it well, *of all evils.* On the other hand, "there is great gain in godliness with contentment" (v. 6). Also, an enthusiasm for generosity is the source of all good things.

We have heard [17] Paul's admonition against greed, which he describes as the "root of all evils." He means of this life, so that we say nothing about the life which is to come. You see, the greedy man deprives himself of eternal life, because his heart is swollen with many concerns. Because he has all these worries, he is forced to fear the dangers of fire and of water. As many worries threaten him as there are grains of sand on the seashore. Thus he destroys this life as well as that which is to come, just as "godliness has the promise" (cf. 1 Tim. 4:8). Greed is the worship of idols. You see, greed worships money, but godliness worships God. The greedy man is uncertain and is deprived both of this life and that which is to come.

11. *But as for you, man of God, shun all this.* Shun all those useless and harmful desires which deeply prick the greedy. *Aim at righteousness, godliness, faith, love, steadfastness, gentleness.* This is the alphabet, or catalog, of Christian virtues. I think that *righteousness* here is righteousness in general rather than the righteousness of faith. Righteousness means to render to each his due and be godly. Otherwise, if he meant the righteousness of faith, he would not add *faith.* That is, here he means that one be righteous, without accusation, and blameless before God and man. *Godliness* is certainly the worship of God, the exercise of the ministry of the Word, by which one makes a sacrifice to God. Acts of love and kindness are shown to men. To summarize, it means to meditate, speak, pray, visit. *Faith* also might be able to be taken to mean generally faith toward God and men. I, however, take it to mean faith toward Christ. See to it that you do not lack faith as you practice love for all men. Pure *love* does not seek its own good but the good of others. Therefore lust and love are different. The love which has to do with lust seeks its own advantages

[17] The lecture of March 30 begins at this point.

in all things. Christian love seeks the advantages of others in itself. That which the father has he shares in turn with his children. Lust is to want good done to oneself. *Steadfastness* means that you bear the ingratitude in which you lose love and blessing and must accept evil instead of good. If you have done good, there are those who make false accusations against you and persecute you because of your faith and the Word. He includes not only steadfastness but also *gentleness,* that you may not be eager for revenge but "pray" (Matt. 5:44). These are teachings we believe we have grasped for a long time. He gives this singular mandate for this purpose:

12. *Fight the good fight of faith.* You know what the fight of faith is. After all, those who are in Christ and who have the ministry of the Word are attacked not only by impatience and wrath. Satan also attacks us especially in our greatest good, which is faith and the Word. Those who are involved in the fight of faith bear the attacks of the fear of death, hell, and despair. They ought to be exposed to others in their work. They should be patient and gentle. They should not be self-seekers. For them there remains the final battle with the demons, which Paul describes in Eph. 6:12, etc. It is easy to fight against tyrants, because we can understand their insidious strategy. Their object here is understandable. But then Satan comes and transforms himself into the appearance of majesty or of an angel. This he does by various means. He can disguise himself as propitious God, as he does with the heretics. There we cannot comprehend him. He crawls and hisses like a serpent. In this situation the smug person does not recognize him. Here Paul is not speaking about this. Rather he speaks to a Timothy who is secure in the Word, to a Timothy whom Satan assaults with mental dejection, the weakness and temptation under which Job labored, so that he may [mislead] him, etc. Whatever God says Satan turns into something worthless. Thus he can convert the greatest goodness into evil, mercy into poison, so that nothing except wrath appears in God. The contrary takes place in destructive doctrines, so that nothing except goodness, etc., appears in God. In this way Satan can make himself appear as if he were God Himself. The Antichrist did this in the church solely with his external appearance. Yet he brought it about that he sat in God's seat (cf. 2 Thess. 2:4). What would the god of this world not do? This is what he means with the "fight of faith." That struggle is much worse than death, prison, or any disease or persecution, because it

involves faith. Therefore it appears that Timothy was an outstanding disciple. After all, all disciples do not experience that temptation. But as Paul says (2 Cor. 12:7): "To keep me from being too elated . . . a thorn was given me in the flesh, a messenger of Satan, etc." The holy Saint Paul was possessed and oppressed by Satan. He could not get rid of this. Therefore he says to Timothy: "Take hold." Jacob also learned this when he wrestled until dawn (Gen. 32:24). That battle no one understands unless he experiences it. We hear about it from the words and statements of others, but we do not understand its mood and sense. The gross temptations of anger assault us, or, at best, the anger allows us to be burned up. But this we overcome more easily than we win the fight of faith. If the fight of faith — that is, the battle which Timothy was having with heretics and all his adversaries, that is, on behalf of faith or in the cause of faith — had been overcome, it would be the smallest temptation. *Take hold of the eternal life.* These words are easy to say, but it is something else for the mind to be trained in such a way that it seeks life and arms itself for life, as if it were reaching out for it. This is not because it can now live eternally, but exert yourself to this end, that is, train yourself here in all your efforts that you may press forward into the life to come with a very certain hope. So put off and tear away an affection for this life. This is the "suffering" of Rom. 5:3. One must get there through one or two temptations. All must be tempted, troubled, tested. One is tempted by lust, another by other temptations. *To which you were called.* Paul speaks this against faintheartedness, to lift Timothy up into hope because of the recollection of his earlier confession. Whoever has doubts about eternal life never confesses it. We confess: "I believe in life everlasting." Be very sure to convince yourself that God does forgive sins and does give eternal life. Whoever does not believe this has death. Paul realizes that Timothy is struggling in temptation. He therefore comforts him with a twofold comfort: "Take hold of eternal life. After all, you have been called. You have a firm testimony and seal, that you are reaching for eternal life, that God has given you faith and the fruit of the Gospel. You are in the ministry of the Word. Everything is in order for you to seek after eternal life. If you seem to be too insignificant for eternal life, consider the calling which you have, by which follows that we read in Rom. 8:28. To be certain that you have the Word of God is the most important thing." Only let a man not then begin to doubt because he is afflicted and feels that he must argue against contrary teachings. He has the calling because God calls him through the Word. Others hold it in contempt. Therefore teach the Word that you may be afflicted. This is a divine call to which you are called. If the Lord adds that He is establishing you in His ministry, then your calling is increased and confirmed. Therefore know that you have been called to eternal life. Those good things which you have are not given to you on behalf of this life. "Set out by their calling" is what He especially calls those whom He brings to an understanding of the Word — those who feel that they please Him and are stirred by Him. There the calling is genuine, holy, and divine, because the knowledge of God does not grow in our hearts. But He does not grasp me in you. We read in John 6:45:[18] "All who hear . . . from the Father come to Me." Those are the "God-taught." Then also, you should learn this past good, that your calling has been effective and fruitful because *you made the good confession.* Perhaps he was a prisoner and in chains. He was probably with Paul when he was in danger, and Timothy confessed that he was Paul's disciple. Paul uses this to strengthen Timothy: "Since, then, your calling and the effectiveness thereof are such that you advance it with fruit, as you did in the presence of many witnesses, etc., so you ought now bravely depend on it and have no doubts about your calling. Greater is He who called you than every temptation by which Satan attacks you." If Paul had not seen that it was necessary to give Timothy this reminder, he would not have spoken thus. This is the way Christ speaks in Luke (12:32): "Fear not." The apostles could not grasp how to hope for the Kingdom, that there was sin, etc. He had to console them in this way: "Not by your merit, but the Father will do it. You have been called; confess Me and follow Me." It is a *good confession.* He calls it "fine." Here he commends the confession. "That confession was not good in itself, but you have made an outstanding confession. You have had a firm and outstanding manner with confidence." Similarly, we now have the confession of Leonhard Kaiser.[19] "You have not been ashamed that I am your teacher and other things, etc. That confession will not be

---

[18] The Weimar text has "John 8."

[19] Kaiser was burned at the stake at Schärding in Bavaria Aug. 16, 1527, for his adherence to the evangelical doctrine. Luther had written him a letter May 20 to console him during his imprisonment. A biography of the martyr, together with Luther's letter of consolation, was published soon after Kaiser's execution. Cf. W, XXIII, 452—476.

frustrated. Just hold fast. Don't despair. Don't become fainthearted. That comfort is necessary even for us. 'Take hold.' The flesh wants annoyance to weary it. You have much protection and a good start. The end will come too. You have a calling and an excellent confession. This is the right article of faith — a great thing when one does battle with Satan and his angels. In it, the body does not suffer. Faith itself, rather, and hope suffer. In all other temptations, faith stands like a wall, and faith laughs. The bones are the things which suffer. But when the bones tremble, faith marches on with joy, as Agatha [20] laughs and rejoices. Because her faith was in control, she did not suffer. But when our courage becomes weak, there is an immediate battle with demons. This encouragement to strengthen faith and hope is necessary to those who are in the Word.

13. *I charge you.*[21] Paul always keeps one eye on the false apostles. Thus he is always accustomed to teach the point of redemption thoroughly. In the same way it is always his practice to repeat a point of confutation. He wants to preserve the pure Word in the church. Therefore he so often pleads and warns. You see, one cannot teach the doctrine of faith and love too thoroughly. One cannot preach it as diligently as Satan goes about. One must watch, then, what is taught and how one lives, because "he goes about" (1 Peter 5:8). He approaches Timothy with a great oath, because he knows this. *In the presence of God . . . and Jesus.* These are one God, because otherwise he would not swear by both. His had been a "good" confession. Why? It had been His own Word which He had taught. He had been crucified because of His Gospel. They could not bear the Gospel with which He kept attacking their righteousness. That is, He firmly confessed the Word which He taught. "I have spoken openly" (John 18:20), and: "I have come . . . to bear witness of the truth" (John 18:37). Note this: As far as Christ was concerned, He suffered because of us; but as far as the Jews were concerned, He died because of His Word. Because of that confession He paid His own life that we might have the pure Word. Therefore, Paul says, because of Him I charge you. How could he speak more emphatically?

14. *That you keep the commandment.* Namely, keep it unstained. Either you, "free from reproach," keep it. Or you keep the command-

---

[20] A Sicilian Christian martyr of the third century who endured excruciating physical torture with great fortitude.

[21] In the English translation this verb stands at the head of v. 14.

ment "free from reproach." [22] I believe I relate the "free from reproach" to the commandment. After all, Paul intends to give an admonition about preserving the purity of the Word. His interest is for the Word, therefore I relate it to the Word rather than to Timothy, who is a public person who ought not only be "free from reproach" himself but his commandment ought to be also. This should happen not only before men — which could never be done — but especially before God. This is blasphemed before men and is called a doctrine of demons. But if we keep it so that it is without spot before God, it is being taught correctly. This also happens when one teaches that confessing Christ is good. It becomes spotted when we make our own additions. *Until the approaching of our Lord Jesus Christ.* This is a plea that the Word of God remain unpolluted until Christ comes. Is Timothy to live that long? Paul does not seem to be teaching only Timothy. He also understood that what he was teaching would last until the end of the world and that it relates to all ministers of the Word, as we have received from those that went before us and leave it to those who follow us this command, that this Word may remain pure.

15. *And this will be made manifest at the proper time.* Here Paul is moving from the conditions of praise and thanks to the goodness of God, the "appearance." *Sovereign.* He is the Prince of power, not merely a powerful Prince. He wants to say: "No one is a good lord except the one Lord," just as there is one *King of kings and Lord of lords.* He wants to say: "He who will be made manifest is that very God." What is He? He is *blessed.* Other people are not, except as they share in Him. He alone rules. Every throne and power do not have this of themselves but from God, as Christ said to Pilate (cf. John 19:11). Princes are not sovereigns. The statement *King of kings* is in Rev. 17:14. The pope quotes this text, too, and the papists ascribe to him that he is lord of lords. He is happy to fulfill that statement of Paul, "He takes his seat in the temple of God, etc." (2 Thess. 2:4). Paul says it is Christ *alone.* The pope says, "Not only Christ, but I, too."

16. *Who alone has immortality and dwells in unapproachable light.* God does not live physically in that light. Beyond the creatures of

---

[22] The reading is either a nominative form, *irreprehensibilis* modifying the subject you, or an accusative neuter, *irreprehensibile* modifying *mandatum.* Luther outlines this by merely putting down the two endings, *"lis* or *le."*

this world, we consider, is utter darkness. Paul, however, says: "Where we set up darkness, there is an unapproachable light." That takes faith. There you must let speculation go. Believe and you will be saved. The very opposite. *To Him be honor and eternal dominion.* Man cannot see God, nor can he ever see God. Man does not see God. Therefore he does not know God; he cannot speak about Him. What are men trying to do when they speak their own wisdom and clothe it with the title "God's wisdom"? One, then, is not safe in speaking about God except with those words which God has prescribed. If one uses other words, he has doubts. He does not see, therefore he cannot speak. We see, then, what they are pretending when they speak out of their own heads.

17. *As for the rich.* Here you do not see Paul condemning the rich or wealth. After all, these are God's gifts which He distributes. Those who have these gifts he calls Christians. He is making a distinction between the riches "of this world" and spiritual riches. If the wealthy will have used their riches well, they also will be saved, says Paul, lest we condemn well-managed wealth, as David was a king and wealthy. *Charge them not to be haughty.* He attacks those who are inclined this way. They say, "Possessions inspire confidence." [23] Wealth is a natural inflater. This sin, natural as it is for the rich, he censures as follows: "They should not be haughty." In German we have the expressions *Hoffart* ("arrogance"), *Hochmut* ("haughtiness"), and *der hoch her feret* ("he who rides on a high horse"). Their pride is outwardly pompous, as they are ambitious. They should not think too highly of themselves, to the point of contempt for the poor, but they should lower themselves and use those gifts of theirs for the glory of God and use of their neighbor. *Nor to set their hopes on uncertain riches.* Another sin of the wealthy is that they put their trust in their riches. Paul calls the greedy man an idolater (Eph. 5:5). In Baruch 3:18 [24] we read: ". . . in which men trust," and in Job 31:24: "If I have called gold my trust." Every man says in his heart, "Gold is my god, my trust." Where there is Christian faith, gold is not one's god. Gold is the god of the world. Scripture and experience both tell us this. Now again we have a case of misuse. Rather they behave as if they don't have it. In the psalm we read: "Set not your heart on riches" (Ps. 62:10). Riches, Paul says, are uncertain. People who

[23] The German saying is *Gut macht Mut.*
[24] The Weimar text has "Baruch 6."

have riches don't know whether they will keep them for an hour, because a thief may come. Teach them to set their hopes on God, who
is better than all the fortunes in the world. You see, *He richly furnishes
us with everything to enjoy.* Let us set our hopes on Him "who furnishes us with everything to enjoy." Gold cannot do this. It is a mortal
and uncertain thing. God is certain, because He lives and "richly
furnishes." Plutus [25] is uncertain; God abounds in riches. Look at
the facts, whether or not this is true. God gives more than all can
devour. Enjoyment is out of the picture. We make heaping it up the
goal. Who can in this daylight and air accumulate so much water and
land, clothing, wool, milk, cheese, wine, oil as ever he can use up —
barns and chests full of mountains of gold, pure abundance? God
supplies it so abundantly that we cannot use it up. We see Him place
these things into our hands, and we are surrounded by an abundance
of all good things. Yet we keep on scraping. For that reason it happens that many poor and even another rich man do not eat, etc. He
has not given us this abundance to take things away from others or
to be stingy but to enjoy. When it is put to use, it is there in abundance. Although a person may accumulate it, yet more remains. If
some are in want, the fault is that people are not using it correctly. Thus
the rich act like dogs that lie in the manger and on the oats. They
don't eat, nor do they allow others to eat. God furnishes richly for
enjoyment, but we, etc. If God would let a hundred ears grow on one
stalk, it would still not help. You see, the greedy would always be
with us. If God would give a hundred bottles for wine, and if the
whole world would be adorned with gold, the griffins would be there
to plunder it. So God cannot give enough to people whose interest
is in accumulating and scraping together. He does, however, give
enough for enjoyment. If we do enjoy this, we have as great an
abundance of all things as we have of air. This very praiseworthy
text opens our eyes to see the mercy and kindness of God.

You have heard [26] the point how God provides richly for us, but
for our enjoyment. Even the wicked lack nothing, as Christ says (Matt.
5:45): "He makes His sun rise on the evil and on the good and sends
rain on the just, etc." There remains that sole defect, or rather wickedness, that people do not enjoy this abundance but accumulate things

[25] Πλοῦτος, the god of wealth. Luther puns on this name when in the
second part of the sentence he describes God as πλούσιος ("abounding in riches").

[26] The lecture of March 31 begins at this point.

according to the word: "They lay up treasure." *Charge them.* "Who furnishes" is parenthetical.

18. *To become rich in good deeds.* He hits the bullseye of the faults of the wealthy. First, they have proud thoughts of themselves. "Possessions inspire confidence." [27] God must humble the wealthy. David became very proud. God therefore used extraordinary means to humble him. He allowed David to fall into adultery. Paul had a great thorn in his flesh. Thus all of us, the more we are gifted with wealth, the more necessary is some fault by which we are to become humbled. Second, the wealthy set their hopes on riches. Now he wants them to make others rich. Their riches are shadows and signs of true riches. If they want salvation, they should be eager "to become rich in good deeds." *To do good.* He not only says that they should do good but that they should do it richly. After all, they have in their hands the wherewithal to be able to clothe the poor and to give drink to the thirsty. You see, "to whom much is given, of him will much be required" (Luke 12:48). Not only should they do good, but they should do it more abundantly than the rest, that they may be rich not in gold and silver but in good works. *To give easily.* This is specific. Above he spoke in general: "Charge them to do good." They should find it easy to give. *And to be generous.* They should share with those who are in need. They should show a willingness to share as people who have been set forth for the purpose of sharing, so that people may benefit from them. As the common treasury is open for the use of all the brethren, so it is with a rich man. It is difficult to share, to exist for the common good. A canonic [28] a person might well want to become.

19. *To lay up for themselves a good foundation for the future.* This explains the setting "their hopes on uncertain riches" (v. 17), which is what wealthy people do. Here, however, they are seeking a trustworthy "foundation for the future." Christ says the same thing (Luke 16:9): "Make friends for yourselves by means of unrighteous mammon," and (Luke 11:41): "But give for alms those things which are within; and behold, everything is clean for you." Here the wealthy ought to be looking out for the rest who are troubled by want. "O death, how bitter you are to one whose peace lies in his own sub-

27 Cf. n. 23 above.

28 Luther is punning on the words *canonicus* ("canonic," "clergyman") and *koinonicos* ("generous," "communicating").

stance." Ecclus. 41:1. They have abundance, they have progeny, leisure, and all things in great supply, and now they want to rest.

20. *O Timothy, guard what has been entrusted to you.* Paul bitterly hates those false teachers. Therefore he teaches against them everywhere. He cannot forget them. I believe what I have learned from experience. He himself learned from experience, and that is why he always teaches against them. In 2 Tim. 1:15-16 we read that because of false teachers all Asia turned away from the great apostle. The loss was horrendous except for a single household. They came into homes where the Gospel had been sown. He has to say good-bye to it. Satan neither sleeps nor rests. These are genuine, very vital, fiery words which have much power today, especially for preachers. *What has been entrusted* is the Word committed to him — "what He entrusted to your care." It is a divine trust — the mystery which he must preach to the heathen. Paul wants to use this expression to stir up Timothy's diligence. To this trust belong also great confidence and diligence, that that trust be preserved as belonging to Another, etc. Earlier (1 Tim. 1:12) Paul had written: "He judged me faithful." He honors us in this way with what He has entrusted to us that we may guard and keep His precious treasure, which He has purchased with His blood. Why? Because there lie in ambush for you and your church not a single Satan but many who have many false teachers who plot against the Word. Satan can endure all righteousness and holiness except the Word of faith, that is, that which has been entrusted. Therefore one must exercise great care to guard what has been entrusted, etc. How ought I preserve it? In this way: *Avoid the godless chatter and contradictions of what is falsely called knowledge.* "Vanities" (κενοφωνίας) he has changed to "chatter" (*novitates*). "You should avoid the vanities of voices which are godless." He adds a modifier which explains what the nature of these empty voices is. He wants to say: "You will have many teachers who do nothing else except express their empty chatter." This he also says in Titus 1:10 and earlier in 1 Tim. 1:6-7, as well as in this chapter (v. 4): "He has a morbid craving for controversy." "He is puffed up with conceit, he knows nothing." We have treated this point sufficiently above.[29] You see, this is the fault of all false teachers, that they speak empty words which they do not understand. They have their own empty thoughts and speculations, to which they fit and adjust Scripture. This is what

[29] Cf. p. 365 above.

Zwingli and Oecolampadius are doing now. They take a word of
Holy Scripture and give to that word their own speculative ideas.
That is, this "signifies" or "is an image for the body." [30] They pile up
a heap of proof passages of Scripture for themselves, but they treat
them in such a way that they serve their own thoughts. This is uselessness. After all, once the basic matter is lost, they establish their
own idea in place of the basic matter. This is what the Jews do. It is
righteousness if you have kept the law of Moses. Then righteousness
becomes an empty word. The basic concern is changed, although
they have kept the same word. They draw Scripture away from its
legitimate meaning into their own meaning so that we are saved, even
though the basic matter has been lost — that is, by an empty word,
the husks. They come filled with empty words. Watch out for them,
because those deceivers of minds come with an extremely fine appearance. They bring in many outstanding proof passages of Scripture.
"You always have the poor with you." Therefore Christ's body is not
in the Supper, because He said: "Me you will not always have" (cf.
Matt. 26:11). If "we regard Christ not according to the flesh" (2 Cor.
5:16), we therefore do not regard Him as being in the Sacrament.[31]
If you look carefully, you see that this is empty chatter. Yet they
have taken it from Holy Writ. You have the Word which has been
entrusted to you. You have the certain knowledge of faith. It will
be easy for you to make a judgment when they set up another basic
idea. In place of righteousness and faith they put works. In place of
works of love they put their own interests, etc. They are simply empty
chatterers, although their fine appearance seems to make them theologians. Therefore they are "godless," because they offer a great show
of holiness and of the Spirit. So, the holier they make themselves, the
unholier they become.

The contradictions of what is falsely called knowledge. This he
could describe very well because of his own experience. The teachings of these people are "antitheses." What sort of antitheses? Certainly, they are antitheses of knowledge. Great skill is involved, but
they are falsely boasted of and celebrated. Just as empty chatter is
useless, so this knowledge is falsely boasted of. "The Spirit provides

[30] The former was Zwingli's interpretation, the latter that of Oecolampadius.
Cf. *Luther's Works*, 37, p. 30.

[31] These passages are introduced by Luther merely to illustrate the absurdity
of the interpretation of Scripture as practiced by his opponents. These passages
were not used in the controversy concerning the Sacrament. For similar examples,
see *Luther's Works*, 37, pp. 30—31, 37.

it in my heart, etc." [32] This is the knowledge that is praised. It is renowned and has a great name, and it is advertised in glowing terms: "This is something you have never heard before. Listen carefully." They bring a sort of wisdom wonderfully advertised, a glorious wisdom. But it is "falsely called knowledge." They praise it to deceive the people. This is a very fine description. In that wisdom are "contradictions." It is a recalcitrant doctrine. This is the nature of false prophets. So they rise up to teach something different. In chapter 1 he spoke about those "who teach any different doctrine," who were not teaching what they had been taught. These seemed to be disciples or equals, but they had to lay hold of something different to become the authors of something new. This, however, does not happen unless they set themselves up in contradiction. In this way Satan sees God setting Himself up against him, and so he himself does the same. The Enthusiasts act this way to be able to contradict. Whatever the others do, always be ready to speak against them.[33] They affect and seek a new way of teaching which they can set up in opposition. Then there develops this vaunted, false knowledge. Paul has experienced this. In their false teaching they teach nothing other than what they can use to contradict sound and true doctrine. Thus their teaching becomes a contradiction which crucifies sound doctrine. They have the truth and advance into glory. We, on the other hand, have foolish wisdom. It is not strange that today the Enthusiasts tear into things so. It has to be this way. That which is of God, whether it be deed or word, must be crucified. Today the Sacrament and Baptism have not suffered damage as yet. A strange thing happens: Satan crucifies and destroys the Sacrament. In the meantime those false teachers become the restorers of Holy Scripture. Paul says, "Watch out for this, but guard what has been entrusted to you. Do not be moved by those who teach contradictory things."

21. *For by professing it, some have missed the mark as regards the faith.* They have jabbed into thin air. I have experienced what I am saying. I have known many people who have promised this "wisdom." They wanted to make people intelligent and learned. But what have they done? When they thought they were hitting it, they went wide of the mark. In Gal. 4:24 f. he addresses all those who have walked according to the Law. The "Mount Sinai" is to walk in good

[32] Cf. p. 329 above and n. 21.
[33] The source of this Latin hexameter has not been identified.

order. Here he is speaking about those. They have wandered from that path. They tread new paths which they have discovered and disregard faith altogether. It is impossible for faith to endure when the Word has been taken away. But when the Word has been taken away from the sacraments, then Satan can allow one to say: "Christ has redeemed us without His blood, etc." Under the pope Satan has been quite content to have the Sacrament remain. If the net is torn, if there is just one hole, the fish do not remain in it. God also has knowledge and contradiction. This we must use in opposition to wickedness and lack of faith. But they, etc. O, how Paul everywhere blasts away against those false teachers! It is the other part of his own persecution that he must have truck with them. This also happens to us today. It is not a gentle persecution for us to see this where we have built up earlier. You have in this epistle the establishment of the bishop and what he should do to take special care of the Word so that it remains pure.

Index

By JOHN H. JOHN

A particulari ad univer-sale 95
Abela, wise woman of 276
Abiron 254
Abraham 49, 98, 195, 271, 280
  alive in God's sight 120
  not eager for wealth 371
Abstinence
  from foods 313, 315, 317, 355, 356
  from women 10, 11, 317
Absumit ebrius sitientem 66
Abundance 379, 381
Accusation 351, 352, 359
Adam 50, 97, 98, 176
  broke his neck over hidden will of God 263
  and Christ 195, 196
  and Eve 163, 194, 196, 277, 278, 279, 291, 345
  first created for natural life 192, 194
  first terrestrial man 195, 196
  flesh and blood from 168, 194, 197
  mastery of, over woman 278
  origin of death in world 113, 115, 116, 118, 120, 204
  spiritual 192
  type of Christ 113, 114

Adornment 273, 274, 275, 284, 285
Adultery
  cause for divorce 34
  greatest thievery 13
Adversus Iovinianum, by Jerome 11, 13, 14, 284
Aeneid, by Vergil 292
Agatha 376
Ageruchia, Letter to, by Jerome 342
Aim 223, 224, 225
Albert, king of Austria 364
Allegories 175, 176, 348
ἀλλοίωσις 265, 266
Ambrose 317
Ambrosiaster 14
Amsdorf 3
Anabaptists 199, 233, 361, 362, 363, 364, 367
Analogy of faith 320
Angels 113, 172, 178, 179, 187, 196, 306
Anger
  hindrance to prayer 272, 273
  momentary 38, 374
  one cause of divorce 32, 33
Anima 189
Animale corpus 189
Animalis homo 191
Animals 183, 186, 191
  God Savior of 325, 326, 348
  killing of, forbidden by Manichaeans 313

  which are not used for food 313
Anna 306, 338
Antichrist 237, 339, 373
Antony, Saint 292, 322
Apocrypha 74
Apodoses 315
Apostacy 308, 309, 314
Apostles 22, 23, 24, 25, 60, 75, 76
  faithful witnesses 102
  and letters of recom-mendation 298
  Paul and 90, 91
  in suffering and peril 152, 153
Appearance
  of being theologians 382
  consolation against 107
  of humility 365
  hypocrisy 310, 311, 314, 316
  and teachers of the Law 228
Aquileia 150
Aquinas, Thomas 85
Arguments 94, 95, 96, 260, 261, 368
  a breviori 288
Arians 229, 303
Aristarchus of Samo-thrace 294, 295
Aristotle 261, 367
Arius 253
Arsenius 364
Article of faith 59, 60, 62, 63, 80
  chief, and epitome of

Gospel 69, 82, 94, 96
indifference to 100
linked together like a chain 94, 97, 150
proved from Scripture and experience 75, 80
reason cannot cope with 69, 70, 169, 201
Asia 90, 381
Athanasian Creed 265
Augustine 235, 261, 285, 309, 317, 323, 341, 343, 344, 345, 356, 367
Augustus, by Suetonius 300
Aureole 48
Austria 131
Authority 127, 128
belongs to husband 51, 276, 277, 278

Babylon 191
Babylonian Captivity of the Church, by Luther 24, 33
Baptism 59, 60, 62, 68, 84
Anabaptists see only water 199, 233
for the dead 149, 150
into death 132, 133
first pledge 344
over graves 150, 151
preaching about 66
incorporated in Christ through 114
not only of soul but also of body 193
and resurrection 147
and speculation of reason 70, 269
stretching Scripture with regard to 78
teaching after 101
testimony of redemption in 267, 268, 269
Barabbas 130
Barbara 247
Barnabas 90

Battle of faith 73, 74, 157
against death 155
against sadness and fear 104, 105
against Satan 373, 374
against six enemies 136, 137
Battus 335
Begging the question 94
Beghards 338
Believers, use all things in holy way 34, 35
Bellum Jugurthinum, by Sallust 152
Benjamin 323
Bernard, Saint 210, 323, 356
Bible
German 21, 149, 164, 204, 338, 371
older Latin 267, 275
RSV vii, 164
versions vii
Bigamist 23, 24
Birds 183, 290
Bishop(s) 12, 13
blameless before world, not God 284, 295
call of 281
children of 288
good soldier 251, 252
marriage of 22, 23
means watchman 283
responsibility of 281, 286
should be tested 290
trials of 219
Blasphemy 99, 241, 242, 243, 368
Boasting 86, 87, 88, 91, 133
of certainty 239, 240, 269, 270
of Enthusiasts 221, 222
of God's grace 89, 90
of Gospel 66, 75
of life in death 155
of pursuing doctrine commanded 217, 218, 238, 239

Body
Baptism of, and blood as well as of soul 193
chastising of 15, 17, 321, 322, 355
decomposition of 185, 186, 187
destroyed by devil 111
exercise of 321, 322
follows the head 110, 123
in heaven 143, 144, 171
kind of 170, 171, 172, 173, 180, 181
in life to come 184, 197
male and female 171, 172, 173
members of 184, 185
natural and spiritual 189, 190, 191, 192, 193, 194, 196, 198
new clarity of 123, 151, 181, 183, 200
not same as flesh and blood 198; see also Flesh
own peculiar clarity for each 183
and religious orders 18, 20, 21
and resurrection 59, 100, 168
rule over 13, 14, 46
and soul reunited 69, 135, 150, 190
sown in dishonor 187
sown in weakness 187
troubles of 51
wants of 142, 143, 170, 171
Boniface VIII, pope, 364
Book of Wisdom 250
Books, no end to writing of 84, 85
Bread
cannot help Christian 107
and life 142, 143
not object of hearing Gospel 108

Brides of Christ 48
Briefe, by Luther 253
Bugenhagen, Johann xi
Burning with passion 27, 28, 29, 30

Caiaphas 198
Call
of bishop 281
never exists without doctrine 217, 218
Calling 46, 47, 337, 374
Candace, queen 276
Canon law
bigamy under 23, 24
divorced persons 37
Carlstadt, Andreas Bodenstein von 229, 244, 267, 283, 329
Carthusian 116, 225, 281, 356, 357
Cato 221
Celestial bodies 184, 190, 194, 195, 197
Celibacy ix, x, 3, 47, 48
condemned by Moses 9
gift of 10, 11, 12, 16, 17, 26, 27, 52
and Jews 21, 22
placing righteousness in 231, 312
Ceremonies 150, 319
lifting up hands in prayer 271, 272
washing feet of the saints 340, 341
Certainty 238, 239, 240, 246, 269, 270, 324, 325, 374, 375
Certamen forte dedit ei 74
Change
through agency of death 201
movement from one place to another 200, 201
qualitatis, of the form 200, 201
Charles V 243
Chastising, of body 15, 17, 321, 322, 355

Chastity 3
of clergy 5, 313, 328, 355, 356
desire and love for 9, 10, 11
elevated view of 12
gift of 10, 11, 12, 16, 26, 27, 28, 52
as looked upon by pope 312, 313
reserved for the few 17, 27, 28, 313
secret suffering of 11
temporal advantage of 49, 50
three states of 15
true state of 21
Childbearing 279, 280
Children
of bishop 288
to conform lives to words of parents 164
conversant with doctrine 66
of deacons 299
and marrying from own whim 54, 55
of mixed marriages 35
training of 279, 280, 335
of widows 334, 335
Christ
Beginner of life 121, 122
brides of 48
calls Himself a Sinner 211
consumed devil and death 108, 109
depicted as Enemy of death 132, 134, 135
enemies of 128, 129, 131, 135, 136, 137
eternal rule with 60
exalted article of 69, 94
first celestial Man 195
Firstfruits 100, 109, 110, 111, 122, 123
God and Man, one Person 265, 266
greatest Treasure 115

Head 100, 110, 113, 120, 122, 123
incorporated in, through Baptism 114
initiated resurrection 111, 114
and laws of Moses 42
Lord over death and grave 72, 74, 105, 109, 113, 211
low regard for 60, 61
not sent to condemn 247, 248
our only Hope 218
Poison and Pestilence to death and hell 204, 205
purchase price of freedom 44, 45, 264
second Adam 113, 114
sermon on resurrection of 75, 76
spiritual rule of 128
spouse of soul 34
sweet in rebuke 333
transported into spiritual life 192, 193
two natures of 253
victory gained by 202, 203, 210, 211, 212
Christian
commended by outsiders 294
especially wretched person 104, 105
external and internal suffering of 103, 104
feels death and misery he has from Adam 118
illustrations for 175, 176, 178, 179
lord over enemies 138
sermon for 114, 117
servant of all men 236
thrown to lions 156
thrust into death in Baptism 132, 133
Christian life
of bishop 294
distinguished in faith and love 236

found in all estates 39
of misery, sadness, and
distress 103, 104,
105, 107
not helped by bread
107
Chrysostom 299, 338,
355
Church
laying burdens upon
346, 347
no compulsion in 220
orders in 281
provided for widows
337
set in order 217
where the Word is
present and is active
302, 303
Cicero 340
Circumcision
and commanding the
disgraceful 337
and converted Jew 40,
41, 42
Clarity, new, of body
123, 151, 181, 183,
200
Clergy
canonic, generous 380
chastity of 5, 313, 328,
355, 356
Commandment
and advice 31, 33, 47
bond of matrimony 79
of faith and love 42
Communication of attri-
butes 265, 266
Concession 15, 16
Confession 375, 376
Conscience
attacks Christian with
Scripture 104
and devil's poisonous
darts 111
and holding to Word
of grace 69, 70, 71
placed in vise by
teaching of men 44
and question of mar-
rying 41
restless 312
seared 310, 311

secure in Christ 252
and sinful suffering 11,
30
terrors of 208, 209
Consolation 105, 114
of Christ's spiritual
rule 128, 129, 133
against death's sting
and sin's power 210
against enemies 136
against external ap-
pearances 107
through sighing 118
of yonder life 121,
146, 191
Contentment 370, 371
*Contra negantem prima
principia non est
disputandum* 96
Controversy 366, 367
Convents 3; *see also*
Nunneries
Conversion
of Paul 83, 88, 240,
241, 245, 248
of unbelieving spouse
38, 39
Corpus Reformatorum x
Council of Constance
242
Council of Jerusalem 309
Creation
not changed in resur-
rection 171, 172
illustrates what God
intends to do with
us 179, 180, 181
of "living soul" 191
outstandingly good
318
of various kinds of
flesh 183
Creed
Athanasian 265
"I believe in life ever-
lasting" 374
"I believe in the res-
urrection of this
flesh" 150, 168, 196,
197
preaching on 66
Cruciger, Caspar x
Curiosity 66, 67

Danger 153, 154, 155
Daniel 119, 131, 156
David 195, 378
allowed to fall into
adultery 380
and article of resur-
rection 98
clings to mercy of God
226
comforting example
246, 247
prayed with good con-
science 272
respected Saul 361
Deacons 295
children of 299
and rivalry with
bishop 300, 301
should be tested 297
Dead 72, 73
Baptism for 149, 150
fallen asleep 109, 110
Masses for 315
Death
Baptism into 132, 133
battle of faith against
155
in bed or by fire,
water, rope, or
sword 110, 111
boasting of life in 155
to cease entirely one
day 123, 126
change through
agency of 201
Christ, Lord over 72,
74, 105, 109, 113,
211
Christian view of x,
71, 72
comes over us through
one man, Adam 113,
115, 116, 120, 204
"Death, I will be your
death" 98
devoured by Christ's
death 108, 109
"The greater one's
piety, the earlier
one's death" 106
has already almost de-
voured world 119

last enemy 132, 133, 135, 136
for multitude, not unlike that of cow 104, 116
penalty for sin 116
peril of 157
seems repugnant to flesh 120
serves purpose of transformation 182, 200, 201
song of defiance against 207, 213
swallowed up in victory 203, 204, 206
transmitted by Adam 113, 115, 116, 118, 120, 204
treated with levity 158, 159
two facts concerning 71
using heavenly language in speaking of 178, 179, 190
as viewed by reason 69, 70, 80
Deborah 276
Decency 273, 274
Decomposition 185, 186
Demons 310, 311, 314, 373
Demosthenes 300, 340
"Der Tod ist mein Schlaf worden" 110
Despair 208, 209, 246
Deutsche Bibel, by Luther 21, 149, 164, 204, 338, 371
Devil
attacks with Scripture 104
battle with 157
body destroyed by 111
butcher by trade 111
gives Christian no rest 106, 108
God's worst and chief enemy 135
and his tricks 14
leads to murder through lies 62, 135

lord over world 71
lures us away from Word 74
martyrs of 311
passes through the two gates of satiety and curiosity 66
poison of 204, 205
and temptation to disbelieve 61, 70, 71
Dialogus, by Carlstadt 329
Diet of Nürnberg 56
Dietrich, Veit 21
Differences, in yonder life 173, 183, 184
Diligence 381
Disputations 63, 68, 69, 72; *see also* Arguments
Divorce 31, 32, 33
adultery cause for 34
anger one cause of 32
and fault of nonreconciliation 32
of non-Christian partner 33, 34
and unbelieving partner 36, 37
Divorced persons
and freedom to marry another 36, 37
not to change status 32, 33
Doctrine
boasting of 217, 218, 238, 239
children conversant with 66
daily involved with 217
different 221, 383
figurative portrayal of 175, 176
future development of 308, 314, 364
of Gospel 82, 93
judging of 67, 81, 82
not for regulating this body and this life 101, 107, 108
part of call 217, 218
principia of 96, 98

progress in 66
right way to defend 97
sound 238, 260, 308, 320
Dr. Martin Luthers Sämmtliche Schriften 309
Dog in manger 379
Double-tongued 296, 297, 300, 301
Doubt
of after life caused by evil talk 163
of Enthusiasts 223, 240
sin of 99
Dress 273, 274, 275, 284

Eck, Johann 242
Edict of Worms 257
Edifying 223, 224, 254, 260
Egypt 191
Elbe 146, 316
Elders 332, 347, 348, 350, 351
Elijah 122
Eloquence 289, 290
Emser, Jerome 244
End 123, 124, 126, 129
Enemies 128, 129, 131, 141
battle of faith against six 136, 137
of Christ 128, 129, 131, 135, 136, 137
Law, sin, and death 135, 136, 137, 139
prayer for 257, 258
world, flesh, and devil 135, 136, 137, 138
Enemy 128, 129, 131
death 131, 132, 134, 135, 136
Enjoyment 379
Enoch 122
Enthusiasts 79
add own interpretation 228
boasting of 221, 222
full of good works 252
look for glory 281, 282

not apt teachers 285
preach a little of the
Gospel 218
and sacraments as
symbols 304, 305
uncertainty of 223,
240
Envy 300, 301, 367, 371
Epithalamium 3
Erasmus, Desiderius ix,
22, 244, 264, 285,
290, 295
Erlangen edition 5
Error 61, 62, 63, 67, 93,
309
hypocrisy, power of
310
proceeding with hu-
mility against 88
sliding from one, into
another 223, 255,
315, 366
Esau 237
Esther 274
Eternal life 5, 99, 126,
145, 146, 172
consolation of 121,
146, 191
distinction in, on basis
of works 173, 183,
184, 185
empty delusion if dead
do not rise 101, 102
by faith 74
greatness of gift of
247, 249
and greedy man 372
through one Man 120
reaching out for 374
Eustochium, Letter to,
by Jerome 28
Eve 163, 194, 196, 277,
278, 279, 291, 345
*Eversio Lutherani epi-
thalamii*, by Conrad
Kollin x
Evil talk 161, 162, 163,
164, 165
Example
of apostolic solicitude
220
comforting, of David
246, 247

of God's grace in
Paul's conversion
240, 241, 245, 248
of saints 317
in speech and conduct
327, 328
Excommunication 254,
286
Exercise 321, 322
Exile, Babylonian 160
Experience 71, 97
articles of faith proved
from Scripture and
75, 80
Holy Spirit and 289,
296, 297, 299, 337
Paul instructed by 107
Scripture and 75, 76,
77, 80, 81
teaches mastery of
Adam over woman
278
Extreme unction 62

Faber, Johann ix, 5, 6
Factious spirits 59, 61,
62, 63, 66, 72, 76,
77, 79, 80, 81, 93,
94, 146, 148, 197,
366
accomplish much 252
do not have call 217
hold ordinary doc-
trines in contempt
326
Paul contemned by 84
Paul worked more
than 90, 91
say resurrection is past
122
spread unbelief 100
want to abolish gov-
ernment 128
Factum est 203, 204
Faith
aim of charge 223,
225, 226
analogous to 320
article of; *see* Article
of faith
battle of; *see* Battle of
faith
changed into sight 141

departure from 308
empty dream if dead
do not rise 101, 102
and feeling 69, 70, 71,
72, 190
toward God and men
372
and good conscience
252, 254, 297
growing in 224
kingdom of 124, 125,
126, 141
makes all men equal
before God 44
and marriage 16, 17,
18, 19, 20, 33, 34,
35, 41
measure of 297, 320
mystery of 296, 297,
304
not to be forced on
spouse 38, 39
queen over every law
236
and reason 69, 107
in resurrection and
death of Christ 82,
202
shipwreck of 253, 254,
366
small spark of 73
struggle of 104, 105
a valiant hero who
holds to Word 73
False doctrine 63, 64,
136
neglects godly edify-
ing 223
refuted by two kinds
of proof 76
False teachers 64, 75,
100
all Asia lost to 381
avoiding of 220, 221
boast about their pur-
ity 227
crucify sound doctrine
383, 384
gad about 344
and necessity of call
281
warning against 364,
365, 376

Fasting
and controlling of body 321, 322, 355
and prayer 14, 15, 323
of St. Jerome 28
Favor 353, 354
Fear 104, 105, 106, 119
battle of faith against sadness and 104
of God 311
Feeling
of death and misery 118
faith and 69, 70, 71, 72, 190
judging contrary to 99, 177
of Law and sin 208, 209, 210
Word greater validity than 70, 106
Feet washing 340, 341
Female 171, 172, 173
Ferdinand I of Bohemia 243, 257
First Commandment 242
First John xi
First pledge 342, 343, 344
First Timothy ix, xi
Fish 183, 384
Flesh 183, 184
applied to body and soul, reason and senses 192
of Christ 305, 306
Christ's and our enemy 135, 136
creation of various kinds of 183
necessitates marriage 26, 27
resurrection of 150, 168, 196, 197
weakness of 14
Flesh and blood 197
from Adam 168, 194, 197
Christ's body of 193
as physical life 189
will rise in new spiritual essence 198

Food 313, 315, 316, 317, 355, 356
Fool
in fearing death loses own life 104
one who judges God's affairs according to reason 174
story of 29, 30
Forgiveness of sins
in Baptism 268
no use to me if not preached 230, 267
Fornication 3, 5, 6, 24
how to avoid 9, 12, 13
inclined to 9, 10, 12
against law of love 13
France
hair style of women in 275
prayer for king of 257
Francis I, king of France 257
Francis, Saint 274
Franciscans 338
Freedom 44, 45, 46, 47, 52, 264, 314
Frustra niti 151, 152
Function and act 230, 231, 304, 305

Garment, smeared, in Isaiah 226
Gems 184
Genealogies 222, 223, 230, 270
Generalization 95
Generosity 323, 372, 380
Gentiles
apostle to 83, 88, 90, 91, 270
Christ preached among 306
torment Christians 131
George, Duke of Saxony 6, 258
Gerhardt, Paul 109
Germans 183, 189, 191
Germano 218
Germany 131, 257
hair style in 275
Gerson 322, 355, 356

Gift 10, 11, 12, 16, 17, 26, 27, 28, 52
of chastity or marriage 16, 17
of eternal life 247, 249
of food 316, 317
of God in Christ 137
of good government 258, 259
to interpret Scripture soundly 330
Glory 201
Christ taken up in 306
differences with regard to 183, 184, 185
of God alone 238
Glossa Ordinaria 323
Goal
faith and good conscience 252, 254
never achieved by wicked doctrines 222, 223
of Scripture passage 360
God
abounds in riches 379
all outward things optional with 45, 46
bestows great gifts 256, 258
denial of 96, 97, 98
Father 124, 125, 139, 140, 141
hidden will of 262
as Husbandman 176, 177, 182
instituted marriage 6
long memory of 160
not of dead but of living 120
only Savior 261, 262, 325, 326, 348
undivided devotion to 53
wants to make a fool of world 117
will be everything to everyone 141, 142, 143, 144, 146, 172
Godliness 321, 322, 323, 324, 347, 364, 365, 369, 370, 372

Good works 114, 252, 310, 380
Gospel
  boasting of 66, 75
  chief article and epitome of 82, 94, 96
  doctrine of 82, 93
  fruit of 65, 66, 67
  ingratitude toward 131
  not for learning how to obtain bread 108
  opposed to sin 238
  oral presentation of 67
  poison and pestilence of death 206
  preached to whole man 193
  principle point of 308
  remission of sins in 268
  rule of 129, 130
  standing in and saved by 74, 75, 82
  suppressing of 64
Goths 130
Government 78, 92
  in the home 128
  not object of hearing Gospel 108
  persecution by 129, 130
  prayer for 256, 257
  to terminate in next life 124, 126, 127, 143
Grace of God
  boasting of 89, 90, 91
  Christian's boast 89
  definition of 245
  Paul and 84, 85, 86, 88, 89, 90, 240, 241, 245
  that we shall have life again 113, 120, 121
Grammar 265, 267, 315
Gratitude 258
Grave
  Baptism performed over 150, 151
  Christ, Lord over 72, 74, 105, 109, 113, 211

dishonor connected with 186, 187, 188
escorting dead to 151
halfway out of 110, 119, 132, 133
new speech when referring to 178, 179
sleep in 200
Greed 287, 288, 296, 369, 370, 372, 378
Greeks 130, 149, 162, 183, 339
  adornment of women 275
  assumed soul lived after death of body 150
  treatment of women 277
Gregory 309
Growing 224

Hannah 335, 338
Happiness
  of first year of marriage 12
  in God's kingdom 141, 142, 144
  identical in life to come 173, 185
  in marriage 28
  renouncing of 106
  of unmarried state 11
Health 356, 357
Heathen
  believe that all ends with death 103, 104, 185
  concerned about evil company of youth 161
  not convinced by Paul's arguments, 94, 95
Heaven 143, 144, 171
Hebrew 189, 191, 204
Hell 100, 102, 105, 116, 144, 145, 204, 205
Henry VI, king of Bohemia and Poland 364
Henry VIII 257

Heretics 69, 70, 193, 198, 344
  fight of faith against 374
  have appearance of humility 365
  and use of Scripture 230, 231
  weary of general doctrine of faith, love, and cross 254
  young widows 344
Herod 358
Heroides, by Ovid 321
Holiness
  in mixed marriages 35
  under Law 83, 84
Holy, all things holy to 34, 35, 36
Holy Spirit
  different language of 178, 179
  enables faith to cling to Word 69, 197
  and experience 289, 296, 297, 299, 337
  justifies 306
  received through external Word 67, 77
  received through Gospel 66
  sin against 244, 292, 312
Homer 85
Hope, 60, 61, 114, 218, 242, 325, 335
Horace 292, 293, 300
Hospitality 285, 340
Huldah 276, 280
Human nature 12
Humility 88, 365
Hungary 131
Hus, Jan 242, 243
Husband
  authority of 51, 276, 277, 278
  of one wife 284, 299, 338, 339
Husbandman 176, 177, 182
Hypocrisy 310, 311, 314, 316

Hypocrite
and conscience 311
double unchastity of
10

Ignorance 243, 244
"Ihm ein Haar krüm-
men" 109
Illustration
from nature 184
used to inculcate ar-
ticle already proved
175, 176, 178, 179,
183
of various kinds of
seed 173, 174, 175,
181, 183
Immortalitas 203
Immortality 203, 249
Imperial order, regard-
ing published ma-
terial 56
Indictment of the deed
359
Indifference, to article of
faith 100
Indulgences 312
Ingratitude 62, 63, 131,
244, 258, 348
Intercession 257, 258
Isaac 280
Isaiah 158, 174
Italy 61, 90

Jack Ketch 126, 127, 147
Jacob 14, 74, 191, 374
James 76
Jerome x, 11, 13, 14, 28,
49, 284, 309, 322,
323, 334, 335, 341,
342, 343, 356, 357,
364
Jerusalem 90
Jews
and burning of chil-
dren 29
chastity among 21, 22
commanded to marry
9
converted, and Jewish
law 40, 41
divorce permitted to
31

forbid pork and clov-
en-hooved animals
313
immature fruit without
Christ the sun 83
incorporating with 222
rejected Paul's preach-
ing 164
repelled in Garden of
Gethsemane 109
separate men and
women 271
and treatment of
women 277, 299
used secular power
against Christ 130
Job 373
John Frederick I x
John the Steadfast, elec-
tor of Saxony x
Jonas, Justus ix 3, 6
Judaizers 253
Judas 198, 340, 358
Judgment 67, 81, 82,
115, 116, 144, 353,
358, 359, 360
Junker Hans 59
Junker Scharrhans 158
Jurists 107
Justification
through Christ 232,
234, 235
exercise of 230
by Word 269

Kaiser, Leonhard 375
Kingdom
of clarity 125, 126
difference between
God's and Christ's
141
exists to help us
against enemies 139
flesh and blood does
not belong into 198
ruled by Word 124,
125
spiritual and secular
127
Knowledge of God 168,
169
Kollin, Conrad x
Korah 244, 254, 284, 308

κόσμος 273, 284, 285
Krönlein 48

Labor
and godliness 324
of married life 5, 6,
11, 15, 16, 18, 27,
49
in the Word 349
Last Day 60, 69, 108,
111, 122, 123, 141,
151, 160, 176, 190,
193, 358, 360
end to all enemies of
Christ 129
how things will be on
197, 199, 206
no comfort for non-
Christian 114, 115,
117
those still living on
119, 120, 199, 200
Law
disagreement over use
231
double function of
233, 234, 236
leads to acknowledg-
ment of sin 227
misuse of 232, 233
our enemy 135, 136
the sharpness or power
of sin 207, 208, 209
teachers of 228
understanding of 229,
230, 231
Lawless 237
Laws
divorce 31, 32
for the wicked 318
Laying on of hands 250,
354, 359
Lazarus 99, 148
Leah 14
Leipzig Debate 242
Leisure 335, 336, 345,
381
Letters, by Pliny 294
Letters of recommenda-
tion 298
Liars 102, 310

Life
and Adam 192, 194,
195, 196
Beginner of 121, 122
and bread 142, 143
death 132, 133
despising of 52
full of misery and suf-
fering 30, 103, 104,
105, 106, 123 ⁻
long 106, 107
in midst of death 155,
156, 157
natural, physical 189,
192, 193, 194, 196
nothing more precious
on earth than 146
present distress 48, 49
spiritual 190, 192, 193,
196
after this one 5, 107,
108, 114, 115, 124,
127, 145, 172, 184,
197; *see also* Eter-
nal life
two kinds of 192
Listening, to other doc-
trine 66, 67, 68
Lives, by Plutarch 300
Lives of the Fathers 291,
356
Lives of the Saints 29
Lombard, Peter 85, 223
Lord's Prayer
meditating on 324
prayed over food 319
preaching on 66
in public prayer 271
Lord's Supper
modesty of woman's
dress at 274, 275
Real Presence in 244,
382
remission of sins in
230, 268, 269, 304,
305
Löser, Hans von x, 3
Lothar II 364
Love 16, 42, 47
aim of charge 225, 226
first fruit of 256, 257
of hateful 328

and lust 372, 373
is without suspicion
368
Lucifer 291
Luther, Martin 21, 24
*Against the Heavenly
Prophets* 231, 268,
345
*Against the Perverters
and Falsifiers of the
Imperial Mandate*
56
*Avoiding the Doctrines
of Men* 309
*Bondage of the Will,
The* 244
*Confession Concerning
Christ's Supper* 265,
267
Ein feste Burg 88
*Estate of Marriage,
The* 33
experience as monk
81, 114, 241, 290
*Freedom of a Chris-
tian, The* 42
*Herr, nun lässest du
deinen Diener* 110
and imperial order on
publishing 56
Kirchenpostille 55
Lectures on Galatians
42
Lectures on Romans
29
"To the Leipzig Goat"
244
in poor health x
Psalm 118. *Confite-
mini* 175
*Sermon on the Estate
of Marriage, A* 55
*Sermon on Keeping
Children in School*
256
*Sermons on the Cate-
chism* 165
*That These Words of
Christ . . . Still
Stand Firm* 367
95 Theses 293
Luther, Paul 3

Luther's works
on Biblical books viii
*Dr. Martin Luthers
Sämmtliche Schrif-
ten* 309
editions vii
in English vii
Reformation writings
viii
Luther's Works xi, 3, 24,
29, 33, 42, 55, 81,
85, 87, 110, 153,
158, 165, 175, 228,
231, 239, 242, 243,
244, 247, 256, 257,
258, 261, 265, 267,
268, 284, 290, 292,
294, 295, 309, 312,
313, 322, 323, 338,
340, 345, 367, 368,
369, 382
Lying 238
Lyra 295

Male and female 171,
172, 173
Malvasier 142
Man
from clod of dirt 194
creature and work of
God 25
not created that he
should sin and die
203
Manichaeans 313
Manners 332, 333, 340
Marriage ix, x, 3, 5
better than burning
27, 28, 29, 30
of bishops 22, 23
commanded 9, 16
compared to virginity
16
condemned by Tatians
312
conscience and ques-
tion of 41
entered into from curi-
osity 52
evil days of 12, 15, 50
an exercise of faith in
God 18, 19, 20
faith and 16, 17, 18,

19, 20, 33, 34, 35, 41
forbidden 312, 315
giving daughters in 54
good conscience in 11
instituted by God 6, 19, 24, 79
laws concerning 31, 32, 37
as medicine 26, 27
mixed, children of 35
obligations of 13, 14
an outward physical thing 33
reasons for 27
second 342
used as pretext 343
will no longer exist in life to come 124, 172
Martha 53
Mass 241, 243, 312, 315
Master 92
Matrimony 31
to avoid fornication 9
book against 6
conjugal rights of 13, 14, 16
and divided interests 52, 53
labor and trouble of 5, 6, 11, 16, 18, 20, 27, 49
most religious state of all 17, 18
and priesthood 24, 25
Scripture stretched against 78, 79
two views of 5
Means 231, 269
Mediator 263, 264, 266
Meister Hans 126
Melanchthon, Philipp x, 3, 294
Members 184, 185
Menander 161
Mercy
bishop in need of 219
experienced by Paul 243, 244, 248
pure heart clings to 225, 226

understood as blessing 363
Metamorphoses, by Ovid 292
Metaphor 176
Miriam 277
Mockers, 157, 158, 159, 160, 161, 163, 164, 195
Moderation 13, 14, 15
Modesty 280
Monasteries 3, 10, 28, 29, 49, 315, 322
Money 107, 111, 133, 134, 137, 143, 145, 370, 371
Monk 40, 41, 53, 113, 114, 116, 197, 357
angelic humility of 365
false conscience of 311
impure heart of 227
serve only themselves 322
and vice of singularity 221
Moses
believed article of resurrection 98
and commandment to marry 9
and draft of newly married man 12
permitted divorce 31
refused ministry six times 282
Müntzer, Thomas 229, 309, 329
Mystery 296, 297, 303, 304, 305
Myths
of Enthusiasts 221, 222, 270
Judaic 345
womanish 321

Naaman the Syrian 364
Natural body 189, 191, 192, 193, 194
Nature
not comprehended by reason 201

perishable and mortal 201, 202
Necessity, of marriage 26, 27, 28, 52
Net 130, 131
New earth 143, 144
New Testament
German 149, 164
Greek 22
Nicholas I, pope 364
Ninety-five Theses 293
Non-Christian
and article of resurrection 114, 115
consecrated through partner 34, 35
in marriage 33, 34, 35, 38, 39, 40
and sighing 119
Novice 289, 290, 320, 326, 327
Novum Instrumentum, by Erasmus 22
Nun 16, 17, 40, 41, 336, 338, 341
Nunneries 10, 28, 49, 336

Oath
"by my pride" 154
Obedience 337, 338, 361
Odes, by Horace 292
Oecolampadius, Johannes 244, 365, 366, 382
Og and King Sihon 235
Old
men 232, 333, 350
women 333
Old Adam 52
Old maid 54
Opinions 367, 368
Opus adversus nova quaedam et a christiana religione prorsus aliena dogmata Martini Lutheri, by Johann Schmid ix, 5
Orders 17, 18, 19, 20, 21, 40, 281
Ordination 250, 251, 354
Ovid 292, 321
Ox 348, 349

Papists
  prayer for 259
  stuck in works 236
  teach otherwise 364
Parents
  children to comform
    lives to words of
    164
  consent of 55
  father 92
  and rearing of children
    161, 162
Paris, University of 366
Partekenhengst 256
Passion, burning with
    27, 28, 29, 30
Pastor 91, 92
  by the grace of God
    89
  office of, despised by
    people 84
Patrologia, Series Latina
    11, 13, 14, 28, 29,
    284
Pattern of teaching 221
Paul
  and apostles 90, 91
  commissioned directly
    by Christ 82, 83, 88
  conversion of 83, 88
  exceptional example of
    God's grace 240,
    241, 242, 245
  excursus on his office
    84, 85, 86, 87, 88,
    89, 93
  fond of emphasizing
    article of resurrec-
    tion 107, 118
  foremost of all sinners
    247, 248
  "I die every day" 154
  in peril every hour
    152, 153
  reproached for small
    figure, voice, and
    pronunciation 85,
    89, 94
  thorn in flesh 380
  thrown to wild beasts
    156, 157
  widower 21, 22, 23, 24
  and wife 21, 22

Paul of Thebes 322
Peace
  between spouses 38,
    39, 40
  of the Crucified 220
  granted by devil 106
  in the world 257, 259
Peasant
  revolt 259
  story of, and extreme
    unction 62
Pelagians 253, 309
Penelopé 85
Peril
  of death 157
  salvation from 261
  and suffering of apos-
    tles 152, 153
Persecution 49
  of church by Paul 83,
    84, 85, 86, 88
  for faith 101
  by government 129
  in Rome 156
  by world 153
Persius 327
Peter 76, 173, 309
Petere principium 94
Pharisees 164
Philemon xi
Philip, evangelist 277
Philip IV, the Fair, king
    of France 364
Philosopher 195
Picards 338
Pilate 210, 340, 358, 377
Pliny 294
Plutus 379
Poison and pestilence
    203, 204
Poor 295, 341
Pope
  collect for 259
  decrees of 223, 366
  false doctrine of,
    prophesied 308, 364
  forbids food 315, 316
  forbids marriage 312
Possessions 133, 134,
    135, 136, 142, 143,
    145, 146
Potestates 127

Power, 127, 128, 202,
    371
Plutarch 300
Prattlers 228
Prayer
  for all men 262, 263,
    270, 271
  day and night 335
  fasting and 14, 15,
    323
  for government 256,
    257, 258
  hindrance to 272, 273,
    372
  lifting up hands in
    271, 272
  for pastors who adhere
    to Word 62, 63
  and the unmarried 53
Preachers 62
  can lead a multitude
    to destruction 67
  seditious 286, 287
  suffer peril at hands of
    world 153
  worthy of double hon-
    or 348, 349
Preaching 100, 101
  always the same mes-
    sage 66
  about Baptism 66
  on Creed 66
  in a human form, in
    accord with reason
    68, 69
  not introduced to gov-
    ern people 101
  two kinds of 330
  of Word with cer-
    tainty 269, 270
Pregnancy 14
Pride 21, 87
  in Christ 154
  of country people 340
  of novice 291
  of the rich 378
Priest
  marriage of 22, 23, 24,
    25, 231, 312, 313,
    339
  unholy lives of 237
Primitiae 109, 123
Prince 257, 259, 300

Principatum 127
Prior Analytics, by Aristotle 261
Privata resurrectio 122
Probare negatum per negatum 94
Profane 237, 321
Progress, in doctrine 66
Promise, of godliness 323, 324, 347
Proof, of resurrection 94, 95, 96
Prophecies 250, 251, 330
Proverbs 29
concerning married state 5, 11, 12
ψυχικός 191
Public office 256, 257, 330, 331
Pulpit 62, 63, 101, 103, 105
Punishment 159, 160, 255
Pure doctrine 62, 255
to become sated with 64
warning regarding 86
Pure heart 225, 226, 227
Purgatio 206

Questions, endless 223
Qui mortem metuit, quod vivit, perdit id ipsum 104

Rachel 173
Ratisbon meetings 257
Reading 328, 329
Reason 59, 63, 69, 70, 76, 79, 100 174
Baptism and speculation of 70
cannot cope with article of faith 69, 70, 169, 201
death viewed by 69, 70, 80
judges by what it sees and feels 69, 70, 107
matrimony viewed by 78, 79
preaching in accord with 68, 69

resurrection viewed by 69, 70, 169, 172, 184, 185
and Scripture 77
Rebuke 332, 333, 336, 352, 367
Reconciliation, of spouses 31, 32, 33, 38
Redemption 264
principal theme 270, 308, 309, 319, 376
and testimony 267, 268, 269
Reducere ad absurdum 95
Reducere per deductionem ad impossibile 95, 100
Refutation of the Lutheran Wedding Song, by Conrad Kollin x
Regulae morales, by Gerson 355
Religion
mystery of 303, 304, 308
principle of 308
Religious 17, 18, 19, 20
Reminder 64, 67, 72, 175, 176
Resurrection 59, 60, 69, 71, 72, 93
appears preposterous 116, 117
Baptism and 147, 148
basis for article on 75, 94
believed by Adam and fathers 163
body and 59, 100, 168
of Christ, sermon on 75, 76
creation not changed in 171, 172
of damned 198
denial of 94, 95, 96, 98, 99, 253
does not bring joy to the world 114, 115
of flesh 150, 168, 196
as having already

taken place 167, 168, 193
initiated by Christ 111, 114
as pertaining only to soul 168, 169, 198
as putting on new garment 202, 203
ridicule of 170, 171
of several saints 121, 122, 123, 133
viewed as having already begun in Christ 110, 119, 132, 133
and village mayor 102
witnesses of 76
Revelation 75
Reverence
toward the old 332
of slave toward master 361
Ridicule
of article of faith 59, 60, 99, 134, 150, 157, 158, 170
of Paul's past life 88, 94
of Paul's person 85, 94
of Word of God 145
Righteousness
in Law 83
placed in celibacy 231, 312
virtue of 372
Romans 130, 183, 299
Rome 156
Rörer, George x, xi
Roth, Stephen xi
Rule 127, 128, 141, 143
over body 13, 14, 46
eternal, with Christ 60
spiritual, of Christ 128, 129, 133
RSV vii, 164

Sacrament 60, 62, 81, 124, 125
disdained by blind spirits 67
of marriage 24, 25

and speculation of reason 70, 167
stretching Scripture with regard to 78
Word taken away from 384
Sadducees 59, 100
Sadness, battle of faith against fear and 104, 105
Saints 121, 122, 123, 133, 317, 322, 323, 358
Sallust 152
Salvation
corporal and spiritual 325, 326
general 261, 262
temporal and eternal 263, 264
Samuel 173, 284
Sarah 49, 173
Satan
battle of faith against 373, 374
cannot endure anything good 350, 351, 381
cleverness of 220, 373
corrupts statements of Scripture 219, 250
deliverance to 254
and devil 291
fall of 291
wants to add to religion 303
Satiety 64, 66, 165, 167
Satires, by Persius
Saxony 3, 6
Saying 5, 11, 12, 13
"The greater one's piety, the earlier one's death" 106
"Out of the abundance of the heart" 202
Schmid, Johann, of Constance 5, 6
Scotus, Duns, fundamentals of 223
Scriptum est 203
Scripture
articles of faith proved from 75, 80

battle over correct use of 230
and experience 75, 76, 77, 80, 81
forgiveness of sin credited to 268
is more than the thinking, feeling, experiencing of men 72
language of 189, 208
misinterpretation of 79, 167, 198, 382
newcomer in 290
public reading of 329
resurrection revealed in 96, 97
speaks of spiritual resurrection 168
stretching of, with regard to Baptism 78
testimony of, extolled by Paul 76, 77
unrestricted printing and sale of 56
Secret 197, 199, 201
Secular 17, 31, 92, 123, 124, 125
Security 61, 62, 105, 165, 200, 325
Sedition 308, 309, 362
Seduction
away from Gospel 67
of false apostles 75
Seed 173, 174, 175, 176, 177, 178, 186, 188, 195
Self-control 26, 27
Senses 98, 99, 107, 111, 125, 174, 189, 191, 196
Sentences, by Peter Lombard 85, 223
put works in place of grace 236
Separation
of bride and bridegroom 14
of sexes 10, 271
of spouses 31, 32, 33
Septembertestament 149
Sermones, by Horace 293, 300

Servants 236, 361, 362, 363
Seven deadly sins 340
Shipwreck 253, 254, 366
Sighing 118
Siloam 159, 260
Simeon 305
Simeon atop a pillar 29
Sin
Christian comes into life through and from 118
of doubt 99
holding to Word in face of 69, 70, 71
and Law our enemies 135, 136
no remission of, if Christ did not rise 102, 103
of one man 115, 116, 117, 120
public censure of 351, 352, 355
secret 358
state of 46, 47
the sting or spear of death 206, 207, 210
Singularity, vice of 221
Slanderer 291, 292, 293, 294, 295, 298
Slave 42, 43, 44, 45, 55, 191, 361, 362, 363
Slavery 46
of body 363
of Christian 236
kidnappers 237
Sleep 110, 200
Sodom 246, 271
Soldier 251, 252
Solomon 84
Sophists, glosses of 241
Soul
already in heaven with Christ 110, 133
body not to be distinguished from 192
Christ, spouse of 34
German's use of word 189, 191
resurrection of 168, 193, 198
united with body in

resurrection 69, 135, 150, 990

Sowing 185, 186, 187, 188

Spalatin 294

Speculation
empty thoughts and 381, 382
of Enthusiasts 223, 224, 252, 254, 304
of newcomers in Scripture 290
of reason, and Baptism 70, 269

Spirit 192

Spirits, deceitful 309, 314

Spiritism 67

Spiritual body 189, 190, 192, 193, 194, 196, 198, 199

Spiritual consequences 227

Spirituality 19, 94
excessive 15

Stapulensis 295

Stars 184, 185, 190

Stephen 242, 258, 295

Strengthening 239, 240

Suetonius 300

Suffering 11, 29, 30, 50, 51, 103, 104, 105, 106, 123, 325, 374
from hand of devil 108
and peril of apostles 152, 153
secret, of chastity 11, 30

Sun 184, 185, 190, 195
illumines all men 262, 263, 379

Supplication 257, 335

Sword 318

Synagog 83

Tatians 312

Teacher(s) 60
bishop as 285, 286, 327, 328
bold at another's risk 229
of the Law 228
no end to criticism of 84, 85

recent converts as 289, 290, 320

Teachings
with appearance of piety 228
after Baptism 101
concern of, how we may get from this to yonder life 101
devotion to 331
of men 44, 45

Temptation 10, 12, 13, 135, 373, 374,
to disbelieve article of faith 61, 70, 71
a snare 371
to take counsel with reason 77

Ten Commandments, preaching on 66

Terrestrial bodies 184, 190, 195, 196

Terrors of conscience 208, 209

Testimony 267, 268, 269

Testing 290, 297, 298

Thais, by Menander 161

Thanksgiving 316, 317

Thietberga 364

Thievery 13, 237, 238

Thoughts
of death and God's judgment 104, 105
mixed with Scripture 78
of resurrection 177, 191, 196, 202
of shameless things 10

Tischreden, by Luther 21, 29

Titus xi, 281

Titus, lectures on 228, 240, 284

Tobias 14

Training 321, 322, 336, 337
of children 279, 280, 335

Trajan 294

Transformation 182, 200, 201

Treasure

our glory in Christ 137, 191
greatest, Christ 115
hidden 125
like a mystery 297

Treasury, common 285, 295, 337, 347, 380

Trials 219

Tribulation 248
of childbearing 279

Trojan War 321

Troubles, of body 51

Trumpet 200, 201

Truth, of doctrine and life 302, 303

Turk, 97, 117, 130, 154, 257, 258

Twelve disciples, witnesses of entire life of Christ 76

Two natures of Christ 253

Typhoeus 292

Unam sanctam 364

Unbeliever
arguing with 94, 95
and eternal torment 201
and resurrection 102
as spouse 33, 34, 36

Uncertainty 223, 240

Understanding 228, 229
young in 290

Ungodly 237
Universal proposition 261

Unmarried 47, 48, 49, 50, 52, 53
shame of 54

Ursula von Portzig 3

Use 34, 35, 230, 231, 232, 267, 268, 304, 305, 316

Usury 315, 358

Vandals 130

Vanity 327

Vergil 292

Victory
already present 206
gained by Christ 202, through our Lord

Jesus Christ 202, 203, 210, 211, 212
Vigilance 165, 166, 167
  against own brethren 168, 169
Virgin 48, 49
  crown of 48, 54
  happiness of 11
  in monastery 312
Virgin Mary 247
Virginity 15, 16, 48, 49
Virtues, catalog of 372
Virtutes 127
Vita S. Pauli primi eremitae, by Jerome 322
Vitae patrum 28, 356
Vocation 92
Vow 43
  of chastity 9, 10, 17
  of preserving widowhood 344
Vulgate 66, 164, 218, 220, 239, 267, 273, 288, 292, 298, 303, 335, 358, 370, 371

Waldensians 339, 349
Waldrade 364
Wants, bodily 142, 143, 170, 171
Warfare 251
Warning 61, 63, 131
  to differentiate among pastors 91
  by example 159, 160
  to keep doctrine pure 86
  not to feel smug 220
  not to listen to what reason has to say 79, 197
  of punishment already initiated 145
  to retain Word preached 67, 68
Watchman 283
Water, and Anabaptists 199
Weakness
  of anger and hatred 32
  body sown in 187, 188
  of flesh 14

Wealth 371, 378, 379
Wedding
  adornment for spouse 274, 275, 276, 341
  of Hans Löser 3
Wedding song 3
Weimar
  edition 5, 7
  editor 17, 19, 20, 39, 44, 227, 328
  text 5, 19, 20, 75, 277, 331, 369, 375, 378
Whole man 189, 190
  Gospel preached to 193
Whore 5
Whoremonger 6, 23, 315
Widow(s)
  children of 334, 335
  three kinds of 334, 336
  who have homes 334, 335, 336
  without kin 335, 336
  young 336, 337, 341, 342, 345, 346
Widower 21, 22, 339
  advice to stay single 31
Widowhood 15, 21
  and apostle's advice 31
Wife 5, 11, 12
  of apostle Paul 21, 22
  being possessed by 52
  conjugal rights of 13
  of deacon 298, 299
  of one husband 338
  in the resurrection 59
  should not teach in public 276, 277
  troublesome 50, 51
Wine 286, 296, 299, 313, 316, 355, 356, 357
Wisdom
  belongs to old age 294
  of flesh and blood 197
  of God 249, 250
  and knowledge 317, 367
  ours and God's 117
  of pagan reason 190
  taken to school by its children 84

Witnesses
  apostles, faithful 102
  false 102
  two or three 350, 351, 352, 354, 359
Wittenberg x, xi, 84
Wolfenbüttel manuscript 237
Woman
  abstinence from 10, 11, 317
  created specifically for marriage 5, 6, 7, 79
  equal to man before God 44
  instigators of Trojan War 321
  man nobler than 16, 278
  must be serious 298
  proper dress of 274, 275, 276, 298
  public office and authority taken from 276, 277
  and public prayer 271, 272, 273, 274
  from rib of Adam 194
  saved by bearing children 279, 280
  subject to man 51, 276
  talkative 298, 299, 345
  touching of 10, 11, 12, 49
  weak vessel and fragile 51, 298
Woman's Seed 98
Word of God
  being awake in 166
  clinging to 163, 164
  correctly divided 246
  like a mother's lap 74
  nothing higher or more inward than 19
  only source of knowledge of God 169
  only weapon against devil 217
  physical, written, poured into letters 76, 77
  power and might of God in 72, 73, 74

preaching, hearing, and reading of 166
preserving purity of 376, 377, 384
and reason 69, 70, 76, 79, 100
redemption enclosed in 269
on side of marriage 6, 79
unadulterated 61, 62
and unmarried man 53
world despises 144, 145, 146
Work
in marriage 20
of our hands 324
of Paul 89, 90
in the Word 349
for young widows 346
Works 81, 82, 113, 115, 119, 173
again reestablished 309
do not justify 234
of one's own calling 337

World
believes in merit 117
can take nothing with it 135, 136, 137
dealings with 52
full of broken marriages 38
has accepted Gospel 306
loath to relinquish this life 114
our enemy, to be destroyed by fire 135
puts money above Gospel 106
relies on money and goods 111, 145
troubles of 51
and view of marriage 5, 11, 12, 50
wisdom of 71, 97
Worry 103, 104, 105, 372
Worship 369, 372
Wrath 70, 103, 104, 107, 135, 136, 140
examples of 245, 246

and God's Law 209
no joke 264
when God no longer grants desire for Word 144
Wycliffe, John 242, 267

Yellow, about the beak 290
Yoke 361, 363
Yokefellow 22, 218
Youth 3
and bad company 160
how to rebuke 333
outward chastity forced on 10, 11
and respect for elders 333
of Timothy 327, 357

Zwingli, Ulrich 228, 229, 244, 252, 258, 264, 290, 345, 365, 366, 368, 382

INDEX TO SCRIPTURE PASSAGES

Genesis
1 — 317
1—3 — 55
1:12 — 313
1:28 — 25, 26
2:7 — 191, 194
3:7 — 291
3:15 — 98, 203
3:16 — 26, 51, 279
3:19 — 20, 194
3:19, 17 — 50
14:22 — 271
19:33 — 286
32:24 — 374
46:25-27 — 191
49:12 — 367

Exodus
3—4 — 282
4:14 — 282
25:25 — 48
38:8 — 338

Leviticus
19:32 — 332, 351
27:9 ff. — 17
27:14 ff. — 17
27:17 ff. — 17

Numbers
12 — 277
16 — 308
16:1 — 254
16:15 — 284
21:33 — 235
30:13 — 17

Deuteronomy
6:4 — 238
6:6 ff. — 166
8:3 — 143
13:6-10 — 34
18:22 — 309
24:1 f. — 339
24:1 ff. — 31

24:3-4 — 37
24:5 — 12
29:19 — 66

Judges
4:14, 17 — 276

1 Samuel
1:9 — 338
2 — 335, 338
2:22 — 338
12:3 — 284
15:22 — 337

2 Samuel
20:14-21 — 276

2 Kings
5:1 — 364
22:14 — 276

Job
1:21 — 370

4:20 — 103
31:24 — 378

Psalms
5:9 — 366
8:6 — 139
18:20, 24 — 273
18:26-27 — 35
25:1 — 271
36:6 — 325, 348
37:25 — 323
41:4 — 211
51 — 306
53:5 — 311
58:8 — 83
62:10 — 378
69:9 — 211
73:5-6 — 20
86:4 — 271
90:10 — 240
104:27-28 — 19
107 — 261, 262
110:1 — 128, 132,
    136, 137
116:10 — 306
118 — 175
143:2 — 233
143:8 — 271
145:15-16 — 19
147 — 3

Proverbs
11:22 — 273
26:5 — 29

Ecclesiastes
12:12 — 84

Isaiah
1:15 — 272
6 — 251
22:13 — 157

Jeremiah
16:2 — 17
23:21 — 218, 281
32:35 — 29

Ezekiel
3 — 251

Daniel
6:16 — 156
7 — 119
11:37 — 5, 24

Hosea
13:14 — 98, 203

Zechariah
2:8 — 138

Matthew
2:1-12 — 55
4:4 — 143
4:6, 10 — 219
5:8 — 225
5:24 — 272
5:44 — 257, 258, 373
5:45 — 379
6 — 271, 324
6:7 — 335
6:25 — 357
6:31 — 371
6:33 — 323, 370
7:15 — 363
9:38 — 62
10:35 — 334
10:37 — 33
11:7 — 346
11:19 — 84
12:7 — 363
12:34 — 202
13:7 — 371
13:22 — 370
13:33 — 206
13:45-46 — 149
15 — 311
15:4 ff. — 334
15:8 — 311
15:9 — 311
15:14 — 164
16 — 229
16:17 — 198
16:18 — 270
18 — 254, 272, 351
18:15 — 353
18:15-18 — 286
19:8-9 — 31
19:11 — 313
19:12 — 340
19:29 — 78, 79, 361
22:30 — 172
22:32 — 120
22:37 — 78
23:23 — 322
23:27 — 246
23:37 — 244
24:24 — 302
25 — 341

25:3 ff. — 50
25:21 — 282
26:11 — 382
27:42 — 108
28:19 — 263

Mark
10:29 — 79
11:25 — 272
16 — 306
16:16 — 199
16:19 — 230

Luke
2 — 338
2:29-32 — 110
2:30 — 305
2:34 — 364
2:38 — 306
4:23 — 282
7:29 — 306
8 — 302
10:7 — 347, 349
10:16 — 96
10:18 — 291
10:42 — 314
11:41 — 380
12:20 — 370
12:29 — 371
12:32 — 375
12:48 — 330, 380
13:5 — 159
16:9 — 380
16:19 — 147
17:10 — 233
18:1 — 15
19:20 — 321
21:35 — 200
22:38 — 364
23:43 — 305
24:21 — 72
24:25 — 367
24:47 — 230

John
1:1 — 229
1:7 — 261
1:29 — 305
3 — 236
3:3 ff. — 198
3:6 — 192
3:11 — 80
6:45 — 375
6:63 — 221, 230, 265

9:7 — 260
9:26-37 — 266
10:1 — 281
11:52 — 129
12:24 — 181
13:18 — 261
15:2 — 321
16:8 — 238
16:33 — 220
18:5 — 109
18:20 — 376
18:37 — 376
19:11 — 377
20:24-29 — 283

Acts
2:24 — 130
2:38 — 149
6:1-6 — 295
6:4 — 324
7:56-60 — 258
8:27 — 276
10:15 — 318
13 — 330
13:1-4 — 251
13:2 — 90
13:46 — 164
15:1 — 232
15:5 — 232
15:10 — 235
15:29 — 341
21:9 — 277
25:10 — 358
26:20 — 83

Romans
1 — 234
1:4 — 303
1:19 f. — 304
1:21 — 272
1:22 — 249
2 — 234
2:24 — 294
3:4 — 238
3:13 — 369
3:21 — 232
3:27 — 232
3:29 — 262
4:3 — 240
4:15 — 135, 136
5:3 — 374
5:14 — 113
5:20 — 245
6:4 — 132

7:2 ff. — 55
7:6 — 209
7:8 — 136
7:16 — 235
7:18 — 302
7:23 — 136
7:24 f. — 118
8:3 — 238, 265
8:7 — 135
8:18 — 154
8:28 — 34, 279, 374
8:32 — 211, 247
9 — 290
9:3 — 16
13 — 236, 318
13:8 — 46
13:10 — 233, 235
14:14 — 319
15:4 — 241
15:19 — 90
15:33 — 38
16:18 — 369
16:26 — 267

1 Corinthians
1:5 — 217
1:21 — 249
1:25 — 250
2:9 — 297
2:12 — 138, 328
2:15 — 365
3:10 — 224
4:3 — 244
4:4 — 233, 284
4:5 — 358
4:9 — 153, 282
4:13 — 306
5:3 — 286
6:13 — 135
7 — ix, 3, 7, 14, 56, 339
7:1 — 49
7:9 — 339, 342
7:22 — 47
7:34 — 331
8:1 — 294, 317
8:4 — 310
8:9 — 317
9 — 22
9:5-6 — 21
9:9 — 348
9:13 — 349
9:14 — 350

9:17 — 238
9:21 — 83
9:26 — 239
10:12 — 61
11:3 — 277
11:16 — 261
13:6 — 244
14 — 277
14:1 ff. — 329
14:16 ff. — 87
14:33 — 38
15 — ix, x, 82
15:11 — 82
15:19 — 61
15:27 — 113
15:32 — 105
15:50 — 168, 193
15:56 — 135

2 Corinthians
2:7 — 246
3:7 — 209
5:4 — 193
5:9 — 325
5:16 — 383
11 — 156
11:20 — 294
11:23 ff. — 153
11:25 ff. — 155
12:7 — 374
12:11 — 83
12:18 — 219

Galatians
1:1 — 83
1:11, 12 — 75
1:14 — 83
1:17 — 75
2:2 — 239
2:3 — 341
2:7 — 238
2:11-21 — 309
2:17 — 232
2:20 — 266
3:1 — 367
3:28 — 44
4:24 f. — 383
5:1 — 45
5:26 — 301
6:8 — 312
6:13 — 368, 369

Ephesians
2:20 — 224

3:5 — 267
3:20 — 72
5:5 — 378
5:32 — 296, 297
6:10-17 — 217
6:12 — 373

Philippians
2:7 — 264
2:20 — 218
2:21 — 282, 283, 369
3:2 — 369
3:6 — 83
3:19 — 369
4:3 — 22, 218
4:5 — 287

Colossians
2:14 — 135
2:18 — 80, 365
3:5 — 288

1 Thessalonians
2:18 — 291
3:8, 5 — 220
4:5 — 280
4:13 ff. — x
4:15-17 — 200
4:16 — 201

2 Thessalonians
2:3, 8 — 237
2:4 — 373, 377
2:10 — 310
3:10 — 324, 349

1 Timothy
1 — 383
1:1 — 238
1:5 — 223, 297
1:6-7 — 381
1:7 — 169
1:8 — 235
1:11 — 238
1:12 — 381
1:13 — 243
1:15 — 243
1:16 — 241
1:19 —366
2:4 — 261, 325
2:9 — 341
2:12 — 276
3:2 — 273, 338

3:6 — 320
4 — 262, 364
4:1-7 — 309
4:4 — 270
4:6 — 321
4:8 — 347, 370, 372
4:10 — 261, 262
4:11 — 331
4:13 — 53
4:14 — 250
4:16 — 252
5 — 279, 338
5:8 — 342
5:9 — 337
5:12 — 343, 345
5:13 — 343, 344
5:14 — 342, 343
5:16 — 337, 370
5:17 — 334
5:21 — 350
5:22 — 359
6:4 — 381
6:6 — 372
6:8 — 288
6:9 — 372
6:9-10 — 370
6:17 — 380

2 Timothy
1:15-16 — 381
3:7 — 67, 222, 270
3:10 ff. — 218
4:2 — 321
4:3-4 — 309

Titus
1 — 267
1:2 — 267
1:3 — 238
1:7 — 287
1:9 — 286
1:10 — 228, 381
1:11 — 271
1:14 — 223
1:15 — 34, 225, 270, 279, 317
2:3-5 — 299
2:8 — 294
3:8 — 239, 260
3:10 — 368

Philemon
2 — 271

Hebrews
5:4 — 281
11:1 — 18, 297
13:5 — 323, 370

James
2:1-9 — 302
4:3 — 272

1 Peter
2:18 — 361
3:1 — 346
3:1 f. — 39
3:7 — 51, 272
4 — 290
5:8 — 74, 217, 376

2 Peter
1:5 — 328
2 — 328
3:10 — 135
3:13 — 143

1 John
1:1-3 — 80
2:24 — 345
3:3, 6 — 198

3 John
4 — 249
10 — 285

Jude
3 — 221

Revelation
17:14 — 277
18:11-13 — 191

APOCRYPHA

Tobit
8:4 — 14

Wisdom of Solomon
10:12 — 74
17:11 — 227

Ecclesiasticus
8:3 — 368
28:3 — 272
31:12 ff. — 189
34:13 — 367
41:1 — 381

Baruch
3:18 — 378